Imperial Mecca

COLUMBIA STUDIES IN INTERNATIONAL AND GLOBAL HISTORY

COLUMBIA STUDIES IN INTERNATIONAL AND GLOBAL HISTORY

Cemil Aydin, Timothy Nunan, and Dominic Sachsenmaier, Series Editors

This series presents some of the finest and most innovative work coming out of the current landscapes of international and global historical scholarship. Grounded in empirical research, these titles transcend the usual area boundaries and address how history can help us understand contemporary problems, including poverty, inequality, power, political violence, and accountability beyond the nation-state. The series covers processes of flows, exchanges, and entanglements—and moments of blockage, friction, and fracture—not only between "the West" and "the Rest" but also among parts of what has variously been dubbed the "Third World" or the "Global South." Scholarship in international and global history remains indispensable for a better sense of current complex regional and global economic transformations. Such approaches are vital in understanding the making of our present world.

IMPERIAL MECCA

Ottoman Arabia and the Indian Ocean Hajj

MICHAEL CHRISTOPHER LOW

COLUMBIA UNIVERSITY PRESS *NEW YORK*

Columbia University Press
Publishers Since 1893
New York   Chichester, West Sussex
cup.columbia.edu
Copyright © 2020 Columbia University Press

Library of Congress Cataloging-in-Publication Data

Names: Low, Michael Christopher, author.
Title: Imperial Mecca : Ottoman Arabia and the Indian Ocean hajj / Michael Christopher Low.
Description: New York : Columbia University Press, 2020. | Series: Columbia studies in international
and global history | Includes bibliographical references and index.
Identifiers: LCCN 2020001931 (print) | LCCN 2020001932 (ebook) | ISBN 9780231190763 (cloth) |
ISBN 9780231190770 (paperback) | ISBN 9780231549097 (ebook)
Subjects: LCSH: Muslim pilgrims and pilgrimages—Saudi Arabia—Mecca. |
Muslim pilgrims and pilgrimages—Indian Ocean Region. | Hejaz (Saudi Arabia)—History. |
Great Britain—Relations—Saudi Arabia. | Saudi Arabia—Relations—Great Britain. |
Great Britain—Foreign relations—Turkey. | Turkey—Foreign relations—Great Britain.
Classification: LCC BP187.3 .L69 2020 (print) | LCC BP187.3 (ebook) | DDC 297.3/524—dc23
LC record available at https://lccn.loc.gov/2020001931
LC ebook record available at https://lccn.loc.gov/2020001932

Columbia University Press books are printed on permanent
and durable acid-free paper.
Printed in the United States of America

Cover image: Panoramic View of the City of Mecca, by Shawkat/Şevket. Turkey,
dated 1341 A.H. (1922–1923). Khalili Family Trust, the Khalili Collections,
Hajj and the Arts of Pilgrimage (700–2000), MSS 1163.

Cover design: Chang Jae Lee

For Cari, Annabelle, and Josie

Contents

CONTENTS

Illustrations

A Note on Sources, Transliteration, and Dates

AT ITS CORE, this book is a transregional, connective, and comparative study. It situates the Hijaz and Arabian Red Sea littoral between two rival imperial powers, the Ottomans and the British. From a spatial perspective, the Hijaz appears as a liminal borderland between the Ottoman Empire's Arab frontiers and a British-dominated Indian Ocean. In order to represent some facsimile of the transregional, multiethnic, and multilinguistic texture of this time and place, the pages of this book are populated by a dizzying mélange of Ottoman officials, Arabs, Europeans, Indians, Jawis, and diasporic Hadramis. To strike a balance between these overlapping worlds, I conducted the bulk of my research at the Başbakanlık Osmanlı Arşivi (now the Türkiye Cumhuriyeti Cumhurbaşkanlığı Devlet Arşivleri) in Istanbul and the National Archives of the United Kingdom (formerly the Public Record Office) at Kew. In addition to these two main collections, I also used the British Library's Asia, Pacific, and Africa Collections (India Office Records) and the Thomas Cook Group Archives (now part of the Record Office for Leicestershire, Leicester and Rutland). I was also fortunate to be invited to examine a private collection of letters, photographs, and ephemera held by the Khalili Family Trust's Hajj and the Arts of Pilgrimage Collection. In Istanbul I also made use of the Beyazıt Devlet Kütüphanesi and the İslam Araştırmaları Merkezi (İSAM).

This book draws on archival and published primary and secondary sources in Ottoman Turkish, modern Turkish, and Arabic. In translating and transliterating these materials, in general I have been faithful to the *International Journal of Middle East Studies* transliteration guidelines. Where feasible, I have tried to make terms from these languages as accessible as possible to nonspecialist readers. Thus when Turkish or Arabic words have been adopted widely in English, I have opted for the commonly understood English version—for example, hajj, not *ḥajj* or *hacc*; sharif, not *sharīf* or *şerif*; pasha, not *paşa*; and jihad, not *jihād* or *cihad*.

Because Ottoman and modern Turkish are the primary research languages featured throughout this study, I have opted for Turkish rather than Arabic spellings of technical terms, legal concepts, and governmental jargon. However, in some cases I have also deployed Arabic terminologies and spellings.

For place names I have generally opted for spellings most commonly adopted in English. Likewise, place names follow their primary linguistic affiliation. Thus for Arabic-speaking places I have opted for Jeddah, not Cidde, and Hijaz instead of Hicaz.

For individual names and titles, however, things get a bit trickier. I have tried to transliterate titles and proper names in a way that reflects each individual's primary official or linguistic affiliation. All Ottoman officials' names are rendered with Ottoman-Turkish spellings. For example, we find Mehmed Ali Pasha, not Muḥammad ʿAlī. By contrast, for the Arabic-speaking cultural milieu of the Hijaz, I refer to ʿAwn al-Rafīq, the sharif of Mecca, not Avnürrefik Pasha, the Şerif of Mekke.

Finally, this study includes the names of a great many colonial subjects either working for or receiving protection from the British consulate in Jeddah. For these names I have retained the Latin transliterations used in British documents. Thus for the Indian Muslim vice-consul, I use Dr. Abdur Razzack instead of Dr. ʿAbd al-Razzāq. Likewise, for the British translator at Jeddah, I refer to Yusuf Kudzi and not Yūsuf Qudsī. At least part of the logic behind retaining these idiosyncratic nineteenth-century spellings is to ensure that readers with an interest in the British Empire will be able to locate and match these names with other archival and secondary materials. However, for diasporic figures such as Sayyid ʿUmar al-Saqqāf or Omar al-Sagoff, who is known in Hadrami-Hijazi circles but is equally well known in the historiography of Singapore and Southeast Asia, I have provided both spellings.

Common Era (Gregorian) dates are used throughout the text. In citing Ottoman-Turkish and Arabic documents and secondary sources, I give the full *hijrī* date followed by the Common Era date. The vast majority of the Ottoman documents and other sources cited throughout the text follow the *hijrī* Islamic lunar calendar. However, a handful of Ottoman sources refer to the solar-based Ottoman Rumi calendar (also known as the Maliye or fiscal calendar).

Hijrī Calendar Months in Ottoman Turkish/Arabic

M: Muharrem/Muḥarram
S: Safer/Ṣafar
Ra: Rebiülevvel/Rabīʿ al-Awwal
R: Rebiülahir/Rabīʿ al-Ākhir
Ca: Cemaziyelevvel/Jumādā al-Ūlā
C: Cemaziyelahir/Jumādā al-Ākhira
B: Receb/Rajab
Ş: Şaban/Shaʿbān
N: Ramazan/Ramaḍān
L: Şevval/Shawwāl
Za: Zilkade/Dhū al-Qaʿda
Z: Zilhicce/Dhū al-Ḥijja

Acknowledgments

BY THE time these lines pass beneath the eyes of readers, this book will have been a part of my life for nearly a decade and a half. The research trips, language study, and other explorations that made this book possible have taken me from Atlanta to India and Yemen, from London to Cairo, from New York to Istanbul, and from Iowa to Singapore. At every stage it has been an unlikely global odyssey, one that I never would have been able to make without the support and sacrifice of family members, mentors, friends, and fellow travelers. Likewise, it is a testament to the kindness and generosity of countless archivists, acquaintances, and strangers scattered across multiple continents, many of whom opened their homes, shared their tables, and lent their time, energy, curiosity, and patience to help me through the many journeys that crafted this story.

The research contained in this book would not have been possible without the kind assistance and meticulous professionalism of the archival staffs at the Başbakanlık Osmanlı Arşivi in Istanbul, the National Archives of the United Kingdom at Kew, the British Library, and the Thomas Cook Group Archives. In addition, the travel, research, and writing of this work were made possible by grants from the American Institute for Yemeni Studies; the David L. Boren National Security Education Program; the Department of History at Columbia University; the Foreign Language and Area Studies fellowship program; the Institute of Turkish Studies; the Columbia-London School of Economics exchange fellowship; Columbia University's Institute for Religion, Culture, and Public Life Research; Koç University's Research Center for Anatolian Civilizations; and Iowa State University's Center for Excellence in the Arts and Humanities. Partial support for the publication of this work also was contributed by the Iowa State University Publication Endowment.

Earlier iterations of parts of this book appeared in the pages of the *International Journal of Middle East Studies*; the *Journal of the Ottoman and Turkish Studies Association*; *Comparative Studies in Society and History*; and Umar Ryad, ed., *The Hajj and Europe in the Age of Empire* (2017). I am grateful to Cambridge University Press, Indiana University Press, and Brill, respectively, for their permission in allowing me to reprint, adapt, and revise parts of these essays for inclusion in this book. I would also like to recognize Qasira Khan and Nahla Nassar for their timely assistance in providing access to and permission to reproduce images and illustrations from the Khalili Family Trust's Hajj and the Arts of Pilgrimage collection.

Ultimately none of this work would have been possible without the kindness of my undergraduate mentor at the University of West Georgia, Ronald S. Love. Ron was that one teacher who envisioned a career and future that I could not have imagined for myself. He showed me a world of possibilities and set me on the path to becoming a historian. I am eternally grateful for his mentorship and, later, his friendship. I am still deeply saddened by his passing but hope that this book would have made him proud. From my time at West Georgia, I also would like to recognize Aran MacKinnon.

The project that ultimately gave rise to this book began its life at Georgia State University in a series of seminar papers and directed readings with Ian Fletcher, John Iskander, and Donald M. Reid. Without Don Reid's intervention, I doubt very seriously that I would have had the courage to take up Persian and Arabic. I also thank Stephen Rapp, then director of Georgia State University's World History program, for his friendship, mentorship, and our shared adventures from Harar to Moscow. From my time in Atlanta, I'd also recognize Khalil Abdur-Rashid, Isa Blumi, Hossein Samei, Christine Skwiot, and Dona Stewart for their mentorship and warm intellectual camaraderie.

At Columbia University, I would like to thank my dissertation committee: Richard Bulliet, Rashid Khalidi, Alan Mikhail, Timothy Mitchell, and Christine Philliou. Each played a part in shaping the dissertation and ultimately the book that grew out of it. But more important, they all contributed to my overall development as a scholar and helped guide me through the maze of professionalization, publishing, and the academic job market. I am especially indebted to my dissertation sponsor, Richard Bulliet. His imprint as a mentor and influence over this book are obvious, and I am equally thankful for his constant presence as a friend and intellectual companion during my time in New York. I also extend a similar word of special thanks to Rashid Khalidi, who patiently calmed my nerves through every stop along the seven-year journey. I feel incredibly fortunate to have had two truly engaged advisers to rely on at every turn. In the latter stages of my time at Columbia and during my tenure at Iowa State, I have come to rely heavily on Alan Mikhail. Alan has been both a mentor and a friend, providing sound advice, nurturing the environmental side of my work, and cheerfully supporting my career at virtually every turn.

I also would like to take this opportunity to remember the late Adam McKeown. His encouragement, especially during my first few years at Columbia, was instrumental in shaping the transregional and global contours of this study. I hope that he would have been pleased to see this book published in the series that he cofounded. I also am thankful for the opportunity to receive training and advice from Matt Connelly, Marwa Elshakry, Mark Mazower, Anupama Rao, and Nader Sohrabi.

I owe a similar debt of thanks to my language teachers. I could not even have attempted this project without the patient and truly remarkable teaching of Züleyha Çolak and Ihsan Çolak, whose one-on-one mentoring nurtured and transformed my modern and Ottoman Turkish proficiencies. Sevim Yılmaz Önder and Abdullah Uğur at Yıldız Teknik University's summer Ottoman program offered critical guidance as I approached the maze of Ottoman paleography.

I would like to thank a number of colleagues, friends, students, and fellow travelers who shared the ups and downs of my professional life and influenced its progress while I worked in the archive, at conferences and workshops, and through both in-person and digital conversations: Patrick Adamiak, Faiz Ahmed, David Akin, Seth Anziska, Zeinab Azarbadegan, Roy Bar Sadeh, On Barak, Nora Barakat, Hannah Barker, Beth Baron, Michael Belding, Jeb Boone, Neilesh Bose, Isa Blumi, Isacar Bolaños, Guy Burak, John Chen, Omar Cheta, Hannah-Louise Clark, Julia Phillips Cohen, Camille Cole, Jennifer Derr, Andre Deckrow, Ashley Dimmig, Sam Dolbee, Jeffery Dyer, Stacy Fahrenthold, Amal Ghazal, Chris Gratien, Nile Green, Zoe Griffith, David Gutman, Mustafa Emre Günaydı, Timur Hammond, Will Hanley, Engseng Ho,

Faisal Husain, Toby Jones, Mehmet Kentel, Thomas Kuehn, Mandana Limbert, Jared Manasek, Patrick Manning, Victor McFarland, Owen Miller, Keith Orejel, Michael O'Sullivan, Umut Özsu, Graham Pitts, Casey Primel, Umar Ryad, Kent Schull, Jack Seitz, Nir Shafir, Andrew Shryock, John Slight, Will Smiley, Dale Stahl, Justin Stearns, Lindsey Stephenson, Trey Straussberger, Nathan Stroupe, Eric Tagliacozzo, Katherine Warming, Margaret Weber, Joshua White, Sam White, John M. Willis, Nurfadzilah Yahaya, Murat Yıldız, and Seçil Yılmaz.

From among this long list of wonderful colleagues, I reserve a special place of honor for William Ochsenwald. I first met Professor Ochsenwald at the Middle East Studies Association's annual conference in Boston in 2006. In the years since, he has read embryonic versions of dissertation chapters and articles, giving private advice and speaking to me through anonymous peer reviews. His classic books and articles on the Ottoman Hijaz were constant companions throughout this journey. Having spent many years with his writings at my side, I can say it has been an honor and a privilege to receive his kind encouragement.

I would like to underscore the outsized contributions of Lâle Can and Aimee Genell. Since my time at Columbia, Aimee has been a constant companion and coconspirator. Aimee's encyclopedic knowledge of late Ottoman diplomacy and international law have continuously reshaped my thinking over the course of nearly a decade. In a similar fashion, I've happily passed countless hours debating the minutiae of the late Ottoman hajj with Lâle. Indeed, in many respects our books were written in conversation with each other. I hope that our readers will read them together in that same spirit. Collectively the three of us have collaborated on an edited volume, workshops, and countless conference panels. In the process this book has benefited from their boundless expertise, but more important, it has been nurtured by their friendship.

In the final stages of transforming this project from dissertation to monograph, I have had the good fortune to work alongside a remarkable cast of colleagues in the Department of History at Iowa State University. In particular, I would like to recognize my faculty mentor, Tim Wolters, for his friendship and encouragement over the past five years. I am also grateful to the chair of my department, Simon Cordery. Simon has been absolutely instrumental in supporting my research and helping to advance plans for Iowa State University's partnership grant with McGill University's Indian

Ocean World Centre. Here I also express my gratitude to William Gutowski, Wolfgang Kliemann, Surya Mallapragada, Sarah Nusser, Beate Schmittmann, and the staffs of both the Office of the Vice President for Research and the College of Liberal Arts and Sciences for their tremendous support in launching this partnership. Their investment in my work proved vital in the final stages of this book's revisions.

I owe a special debt of gratitude to Zozan Pehlivan. Zozan has been a tremendous friend, travel companion, and intellectual comrade over the last few years. She was kind enough to introduce me to her wonderful colleagues at McGill, who hosted several talks related to this book. Ultimately Zozan's efforts led to my inclusion in Gwyn Campbell's successful grant project, "Appraising Risk, Past and Present: Interrogating Historical Data to Enhance Understanding of Environmental Crises in the Indian Ocean World." I extend the warmest thanks to Gwyn, Peter Hynd, and Jon Unruh for their support. Here I also wish to acknowledge the ongoing support for the partnership provided by the Social Sciences and Humanities Research Council of Canada.

I am extremely pleased that this book found its way into Columbia University Press's International and Global History series. First and foremost, I am grateful to series editors Cemil Aydın, Timothy Nunan, and Dominic Sachsenmaier for believing in this project. In particular, Cemil's support and encouragement throughout all phases of the publication process, from book proposal to finished product, gave me the confidence to keep moving forward. I feel extremely fortunate to have had Caelyn Cobb as my acquisitions editor. I could not have hoped for a smoother, more efficient pathway to publication. Similarly, Monique Briones, Kathryn Jorge, and Ben Kolstad have handled each of my questions with precision, care, and good cheer. I would also like to thank the press and the series editors for identifying a perfect mix of anonymous peer reviewers. The feedback that I received was insightful and constructive. I have tried to incorporate their astute suggestions. In the end, however, any faults that remain are entirely my own.

Now for the contributions that can't be easily measured or described. During my years at Columbia, Keith Orejel was a constant source of deep friendship and intellectual stimulation. He shared my successes and failures, endured endless rehearsals of my schemes and dreams, and bore all of my shortcomings and idiosyncrasies as only family can. He listened— genuinely listened—to the stories that made this book and many more that did not. For that and much more, you and Laura will always be a part of my family.

Finally, my deepest debts are owed to family. My parents, Michael and Wina Low, have listened to my triumphs and woes and cheered on my exploits with the unconditional love that only parents can provide. To my wife, Cari: Simply put, I would not have made it here without you. You've always been and will continue to be my best friend and center of gravity. You've supported my passions and followed me across the world. You've endured with saintly patience the stresses of academia and the long absences caused by language training and foreign travel. Time and again, you've picked me up and carried me throughout this long journey. Nothing that I could write here could adequately express my gratitude for the sacrifices that you've made for me. I am truly fortunate to have you and our wonderful daughters. Annabelle and Josie, I hope that when you hold this book many years from now, you will remember our adventures together and how much your father loves you. This book is dedicated to you.

Imperial Mecca

Between Two Worlds

An Ottoman Island Adrift on a Colonial Ocean

[I]n Egypt, Arabia, and even in the Hijaz the English have taken some villainous measures and conspired to foment a plot to sever the Ottoman Sultanate from the Holy Islamic Caliphate. . . . The English are attempting to plant the seeds of all manner of disunion and strife within Islam . . . Piece by piece, I have submitted this information by telegraph . . . I have taken the necessary measures to uncover who is involved in this plot and get to the bottom of these diabolical enterprises.

—SALİH MÜNİR PASHA, OTTOMAN AMBASSADOR TO PARIS, 1899

IN THIS and many similar intelligence reports, Salih Münir Pasha, the Ottoman ambassador to Paris, repeatedly warned his superiors in Istanbul that the British Empire was engaged in a sweeping strategy to transfer the Ottoman Caliphate to the sharif of Mecca and bring that most sacred Islamic office under the sway of Britain's Indian empire. By doing so he believed that the British planned to bring the Hijaz, Najd, and Iraq under British protection and eventually turn them into colonies such as Aden or any other British possession.[1] Despite his dramatic tone, what is perhaps most notable about the ambassador's breathless claims of "diabolical" plots is their utter ordinariness. Although the timing, detail, and plausibility of these files differ slightly from case to case, from the 1880s on this genre of intelligence reportage emerges as a ubiquitous feature of the Ottoman archival collections from the reign of Sultan Abdülhamid II (r. 1876–1909) and the empire's final years leading up to World War I.

Reports of British efforts to transfer the caliphate from Istanbul to Egypt or Mecca and wider British strategies to colonize Ottoman possessions in the Persian Gulf and Red Sea come in many forms. There are lengthy briefs from Ottoman diplomatic personnel stationed in Europe, Egypt, and even

[1]

the empire's fledgling network of consulates across the Indian Ocean. There was an almost endless supply of translations and press clippings from European, Egyptian, and Indian newspapers dedicated to this subject. There are also colorful reports from spies and informants (*jurnalciler*) recounting their efforts to shadow anti-Ottoman propagandists.

In one such *jurnalci* report from 1910, an Ottoman informant warns of the rapidly multiplying Indian population in Mecca. As the author cautions, the Indian population numbered in the tens of thousands and had doubled several times over in recent years.[2] A cursory glance at these numbers gives some credence to our informant's concerns. In the 1860s, British consular reports estimated that there were at least 10,000 Indians living in Arabia.[3] By 1880, the British consulate estimated that in Mecca alone, the Indian colony had reached as many as 15,000.[4] By the close of the century, British subjects in the Hijaz, the bulk of whom were Indian Muslims, accounted for at least one seventh of the province's total urban population. In Jeddah alone there were more than 300 Indian families. And as a result, over half of all Hijazi trade flowed through Indian hands.[5] In short, Indians constituted both the single largest diasporic community in the Hijaz and the largest contingent of hajj pilgrims each year. In many ways Mecca was as much an Indian or Indian Ocean space as it was an Arab, Ottoman, or Middle Eastern one.

As the anonymous Ottoman informant hypothesizes, the British had undertaken a project to encourage Indians to take up residence in the Hijaz with the intention of using them to lay the groundwork for the ultimate goal of transferring the caliphate to the sharif of Mecca. As proof of this scheme, the author cites a recently published article in the pro-British Egyptian newspaper, *al-Muqaṭṭam*, which apparently had been translated and circulated in the European press. The piece, supporting British designs on moving the caliphate to Mecca, was signed anonymously "an Indian in Mecca" (*Mekke-i Mükerreme'de bir Hintli*). Here our Ottoman informant paints a scene worthy of a Hollywood spy thriller. He claims to have set out to uncover the identity of this Indian author. In the course of his inquiries, he discovers that the author had arrived in Cairo recently. The informant goes on to detail the whereabouts of what he believes to be an Indian spy in the service of the English Crown (*İngiliz casusluğunda*). Our Ottoman informant's sources reported multiple sightings of this suspected Indian spy, tracing his movements from the offices of *al-Muqaṭṭam* through the labyrinthine alleys, shops, and coffee houses of the Khan el-Khalili bazaar. In the end, however, the Ottoman informant claims that his suspect escaped back to Mecca, melting into the steamer traffic headed to Jeddah.

What is most striking about this evocative fragment from Cairo—regardless of the veracity of this kind of intelligence chatter—is that although it warns of precisely the kind of vague plot to transfer the caliphate as those "uncovered" by the Ottoman ambassador in Paris and countless others, the *jurnalci*'s version hints at something more specific. It suggests a deeper cluster of anxieties about the Ottoman state's inability to fully control the Hijaz's heterogeneous, mobile populations, whether Bedouin or transient foreign pilgrims, and strengthen its territorial sovereignty over this traditionally autonomous province. Due to its sacred status, the Hijaz was never an ideal—or even realistic—candidate for occupation, annexation, or formal colonial rule. Likewise, both British imaginings and Ottoman fears of a colonial plot to transfer or otherwise manipulate the caliphate—at least until the cataclysmic events of World War I and the Arab Revolt—remained entirely in the realm of fantasy. However, as this report suggests, in the final decades of the nineteenth century, Britain's creeping involvement with the day-to-day affairs of the hajj and its diasporic colonial subjects had forced Ottoman officials to acknowledge the Hijaz's vulnerable position as a contested frontier and interimperial borderland nestled in the extraterritorial shadows of the Raj's Indian Ocean empire.

The vexing questions raised by these anxieties form the core subjects of *Imperial Mecca*. This book asks how European imperialism, the advent of steamship transport, and the increasingly interconnected nature of the Muslim world changed the traditional complexion of Ottoman pilgrimage administration. And in turn, the book addresses how the rise of colonial rule in the Muslim world altered the Ottoman Empire's relationship with non-Ottoman Muslims. Did the diaspora of Indian Muslims sojourning or settled in the Hijaz represent the cat's paw of British extraterritorial legal and political influence? Did the Ottoman state really consider ordinary pilgrims and diasporic subjects of Britain, France, the Netherlands, and Russia living in Jeddah, Mecca, or Medina as potential fifth columns?[6]

To be clear, there is no evidence to suggest that Ottoman officials believed that Indian and other foreign Muslims ever actually constituted a seditious threat to the Ottoman state. However, by virtue of foreign pilgrims'

FIGURE 0.1 Indian pilgrim, 1888. Photograph by Christiaan Snouck Hurgronje/al-Sayyid ʿAbd al-Ghaffār. *Source*: BL: IOR, 1781.b.6/48, in Qatar Digital Library.

acquisition of colonial nationalities and the extraterritorial legal claims this entailed, they provided a powerful pretext through which European states could interfere in the affairs of the Muslim holy places. As a result, Yıldız Palace officials were forced to impose previously unthinkable—even exclusionary—policies to shield the territorial sovereignty of the Hijaz from the potential threats posed by ordinary pilgrims and migrants whose colonial passports and nationalities had come to mark them unfairly as potential pawns of hostile European powers.

In turn this conceptual transformation of ordinary pilgrims into potentially dangerous foreign subjects opens a paradox. On one hand, how should we square these anxieties with the Hamidian regime's promotion and even weaponization of supranational Pan-Islamic solidarity and spiritual authority as tools of geopolitical strategy? On the other hand, how could a non-Muslim colonial empire realistically hope to pose a credible challenge to the Ottoman sultan-caliph's claims to Islamic legitimacy and sovereign authority over Islam's most sacred sites? How did the introduction of this new colonial element alter the shape of Ottoman governance in the Hijaz and even threaten to unravel the region's traditional system of layered sovereignty and power sharing between the central government and the Sharifate of Mecca? Finally, how did the late Ottoman state seek to defend itself and mitigate the symbiotic internal and external risks posed by this combustible mix of weak autonomous rule and aggressive colonial extraterritoriality?

Taking this heightened Ottoman sense of vulnerability as its point of departure, *Imperial Mecca* seeks to understand how European colonialism arrived in the Ottoman Hijaz as a steamship stowaway. It tells how the Hijaz and the hajj simultaneously were reshaped by the competing dynamics forged between the ever-expanding reach of Britain's informal empire in the Indian Ocean and Arabia and the nascent projects of frontier modernization that the Ottoman Empire deployed to shield this most sacred, most *exceptional* territory. The book excavates the curiously understudied case of a far-away frontier province at the very heart of Islam and imperial legitimacy. It attempts to locate an enigmatic place caught between two imperial worlds, an Ottoman island adrift on a colonial ocean, lost in the gaping chasm between the area-studies regions that we now artificially divide into the Middle East and South Asia.[7]

The Steamship Hajj: Colonial Crises of Cholera and Muslim Mobility

To begin this journey, we must start with the intertwined colonial crises of cholera and Muslim mobility that focused Britain's and the rest of Europe's attention on the Indian Ocean hajj for nearly a century. It is here that we find the deepest roots that fed and sustained this most brazen and unlikely of colonial challenges to Muslim rule and sovereignty in the age of imperialism. From the mid-nineteenth century on, the Ottoman Empire was no longer free to act as the sole custodian of the hajj. The affairs of foreign Muslim subjects making the pilgrimage to Mecca gradually came under the scrutiny and surveillance of European colonial regimes. For the first time in its history, the pilgrimage to Mecca, Islam's most sacred rite, became an object of international regulation and non-Muslim intervention.

Although European interest in the hajj was a global phenomenon affecting multiple empires, the most decisive, most threatening driver of this dramatic shift in the administration of the hajj was the expansion of the British Empire in India and the rest of the Islamic world. As Britain's power in the Indian subcontinent grew, so did its maritime supremacy throughout the Indian Ocean basin. Looking to secure its access to India, ward off its European competitors, and expand its commercial, political, and security interests in Arabia, the Red Sea, and the Persian Gulf, Britain intensified its role in the region by the transit opportunities that emerged with the development of regular steamship routes between the Mediterranean and India from the 1830s to the 1860s and the eventual opening of the Suez Canal in 1869.

Although the impetus for the British Empire and Europe's sustained diplomatic and security interests in the Hijaz and the Red Sea stemmed most directly from the international sanitary and trade concerns generated by repeated pilgrimage-related cholera outbreaks from the 1860s on, such interests cannot easily be separated from more directly political considerations. In the decades following India's Great Revolt of 1857–58 (variously known as the Great Rebellion or by its now antiquated colonial moniker, the Sepoy Mutiny), British officials also became obsessed with the Hijaz and the hajj as potential threats to the Raj's security. In the wake of the uprising in India, British officials became convinced that a diasporic network of Indian dissidents, exiles, and outlaws domiciled in the Hijaz were complicit in violence against Christians in Jeddah. They also came to believe that these Indian exiles might be exercising a radicalizing influence on returning pilgrims or forging anticolonial ties with the Ottoman state itself. By the late 1870s and early 1880s, this conception of the Hijaz was incorporated into new concerns that the region was becoming an outlet for Sultan Abdülhamid II's Pan-Islamic outreach and propaganda to Muslims living under colonial rule. Despite their highly tenuous basis in reality, these deeply Islamophobic British fantasies of the Hijaz as a haven of criminals and fanatics or a den of Pan-Islamic and anticolonial radicalization constituted durable scripts that would partly define the empire's expansionist interests in the region from the 1850s through World War I and its aftermath.

Although British administrators' panicked suspicions of the hajj as a conduit for anticolonial subversion largely belonged to the realm of fantasy, the interimperial administrative challenges facing the rapidly industrializing hajj were all too real. With the dawn of the steamship era and the opening of the Suez Canal in 1869, the volume of oceangoing traffic between India and the Red Sea increased exponentially. In the span of less than a generation, the spread of new networks of rail and steam linking the Mediterranean and the Middle East with the Indian Ocean and the rest of Asia revolutionized Muslim mobility and redefined the modern hajj. The contraction of space and time through faster and cheaper rail and steam connections enabled an explosion in travel opportunities for nearly all classes of Muslims. In short order the railheads and port cities of the Mediterranean, Indian Ocean, and Asia were bringing the disparate peoples of the global *umma* into closer and more sustained contact than ever before. In the midst of this industrial transportation revolution, the hajj, Islam's quintessential journey, swelled many times beyond its previous size. And in the process, the most basic experiences, rites of passage, laws, infrastructures, and material conditions of pilgrimage were transformed forever.[8]

With the hajj freed from the rhythms of sailing in accordance with the monsoon cycle, the costs of transport and the length of passage for Indian Ocean pilgrims were reduced drastically. Although previous generations of pilgrims were confined mainly to elite officials, wealthy merchants, and the *ulema*, the modernizing hajj also became accessible to Muslims of more modest means. As steamship services expanded, the numbers of ordinary pilgrims arriving in Mecca multiplied exponentially. With the opening of the Suez Canal, new steamship services also brought increased traffic from North Africa, the Balkans, and the Ottoman Mediterranean;

FIGURE 0.2 Turkish (Ottoman) pilgrims praying on a steamship en route to Jeddah. *L'Illustration*, March 16, 1901. *Source*: Khalili Family Trust, Hajj and the Arts of Pilgrimage Collection, ARC.PT 553.

in addition, Russian subjects were making their way via the Black Sea. Although a still sizable proportion of pilgrims would continue to journey to Mecca aboard smaller sailing ships such as dhows and *sambūqs*, or by camel caravan, by the latter half of the nineteenth century, the traditional hajj of camel and sail gradually had succumbed to the modern pilgrimage of rail and steam.[9]

The vanguard of this steam-powered pilgrimage revolution was composed of growing numbers of Indian and Southeast Asian pilgrims. Around the mid-nineteenth century, the annual flow of oceangoing pilgrims from the subcontinent is estimated to have hovered between 5,000 and 7,000.[10] By the 1880s, average numbers of Indian pilgrims rose to around 10,000.[11] Doubling again during the pilgrimage season of 1893, the number of Indian pilgrims was reported to have exceeded 20,000.[12] By the 1890s, Indian pilgrims accounted for roughly a quarter of all pilgrims arriving by sea. Combined with Jawis hailing from both British and Dutch jurisdictions in Southeast Asia, Indian Ocean pilgrims accounted for nearly half of oceangoing arrivals.[13] By comparison, Ottoman pilgrims arriving in Jeddah accounted for less than 15 percent.[14]

Although Indians and Jawis sent the largest contingents of pilgrims each year, the growth of the steamship-era hajj was not confined to these groups. Around 1850, the total number of pilgrims was roughly 50,000. Two decades later the 1870s witnessed hajj seasons with estimates running as high as 200,000. By 1910, the number of pilgrims had crested over 300,000. And after World War I, the golden age of the steamship hajj would stretch on until air traffic finally outstripped maritime arrivals in the late 1960s.[15]

The Indian Ocean's steamship hajj burst onto the international stage in 1865. That year a particularly virulent cholera outbreak spread from India and struck the Hijaz. It was a *Hacc-ı ekber* year, when the standing at Mount Arafat falls on a Friday. Because such years are considered particularly auspicious, the number of pilgrims ballooned to four times the previous year's attendance, leading to overcrowding and food and water shortages.[16] Between March and April casualties ranged from 15,000 to 30,000 out of a total attendance of roughly 150,000. To make matters worse, when ships of returning pilgrims arrived at Suez in May that year, it was falsely reported that no instances of disease had been detected despite the fact that more than a hundred corpses had been tossed overboard during the voyage.

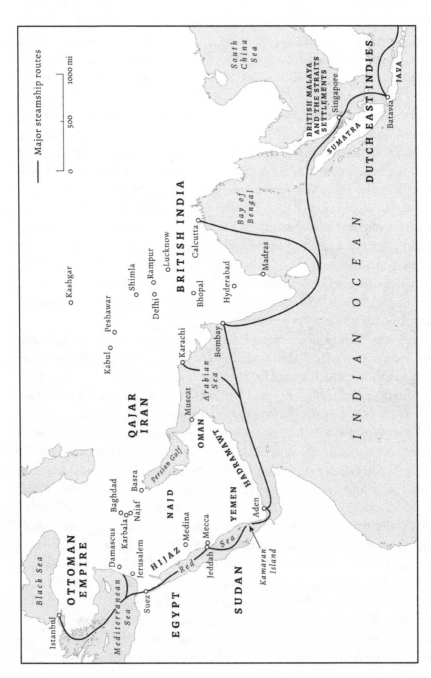

FIGURE 0.3 Map of Indian Ocean steamship hajj routes. Map created by Erin Greb.

Prior to the opening of the Suez Canal, pilgrims moved by train to Alexandria. By the first days of June, cholera had arrived in Alexandria by rail. The epidemic in Egypt would rage for months, killing 60,000. From there, cholera set sail across the Mediterranean to ports from Beirut and Istanbul to Marseilles and Algiers, setting off a chain reaction that eventually would ravage Anatolia, Europe, and Russia. By November 1865, cholera had spread as far as New York City and would smolder until 1874 in some locations. By the epidemic's end more than 200,000 European and North American lives had been lost in major cities alone.[17]

In the wake of the global carnage of 1865, for the remainder of the nineteenth century, the Ottoman Empire and Europe, acting on the conclusions of the 1866 international sanitary conference held in Istanbul, embarked on an ambitious and often highly contentious program of sanitary reform, surveillance, and quarantine.[18] Given the severity of the 1865 epidemic, international attention immediately focused on India's role as the cradle of epidemic cholera and the hajj as its most visible means of conveyance to the Middle East, Europe, and the rest of the globe. The relative affordability and democratization of the steamship-era hajj also made the journey possible for what came to be identified as a "dangerous class" of so-called pauper pilgrims (*fukara-ı hüccac* or *miskīn*) by both Ottoman and European officials.[19] As the numbers of indigent, destitute, and stranded pilgrims rose, so did the incidence of death and disease in the Hijaz. Much to the dismay of Ottoman, Egyptian, and European officials, and to the great embarrassment of the British, who vehemently denied that British India and its pilgrims were the source of epidemic cholera, by the 1860s, international consensus was converging on the special connections among the hajj, India's pilgrim masses, and the dissemination of epidemic disease.

From 1865–66 on, the Indian Ocean's pauper pilgrims were repeatedly blamed for being the primary conduit for the globalization of cholera. In an attempt to discourage the poor, European colonial regimes marshaled Islamic legal arguments against making the hajj without the necessary physical and financial means. They advocated for the imposition of passport fees, financial means tests, and mandatory roundtrip tickets, and they even attempted to manipulate steamship markets to raise ticket prices. For its part, the Ottoman Empire found itself in an awkward position, trapped between a desire to protect its own territories from the ravages of cholera and the ecological fallout emanating from British India through more stringent quarantine and mobility regulations and the need to protect the pilgrimage, Muslim religious liberty, and even the holy cities themselves from colonial intrusion.

The struggle to combat the scourge of cholera and manage the steamship hajj has been understood largely as a "European crusade" for nothing less than "global epidemiological survival."[20] Yet if it was a crusade, it was a deeply ambivalent one. For British officials in India, this combined crisis of cholera and Muslim mobility was complicated by the looming anxieties of Muslim-inspired political subversion that haunted colonial authorities in the wake of India's Great Rebellion. Although colonial officials often were concerned that the hajj was a possible source of political subversion, they also feared that direct interference with this fundamental Islamic practice carried even greater potential to incite a backlash in India.

Despite the Raj's ambivalence, fear of direct interference in the hajj should not be mistaken for disengagement or a lack of aggression. During the height of the cholera era, from the 1860s to the 1890s, these considerations placed Britain in direct conflict with the reform-minded public health policies being advocated by the Ottoman Empire and other European statesmen. Britain's concerns were threefold. First and foremost, the Raj worried that restricting access to the hajj would agitate its Muslim subjects. Second, Britain feared that strict quarantine measures would threaten the free flow of trade between India and Europe. As a result, British officials obstinately denied a mounting body of scientific evidence and international consensus that cholera was a contagious disease. Thus for three decades Britain obstructed and undermined Ottoman and international efforts to impose more stringent quarantine restrictions and documentary practices designed to limit the number of infected and indigent pilgrims and strengthen Ottoman sovereignty in the Hijaz and the Red Sea.[21]

Bearing Britain's reticence in mind, we should be careful not to get too carried away with Foucauldian visions of colonial sanitary surveillance and security controls.[22] An overemphasis on this framing tempts us to imagine stronger, more coherent public health and security apparatuses than the tense, often ad hoc interimperial practices that existed at the time. This approach also runs the risk of conjuring a decisive European colonial response while willfully ignoring or failing to account fully for the agency and centrality of the Ottoman state's role in the day-to-day reorganization and administration of the Hijaz and many of the international sanitary measures, which often have been misleadingly ascribed solely to European colonial actors. As this study shows, the reality on the ground was a decidedly more muddled and complex patchwork of competing Ottoman, local, and European interests.

What is clear, however, is that from 1866 on, questions surrounding the hajj's—and with it, the Hijaz's—proper administration were no longer completely in Ottoman hands. Thereafter, stewardship over the hajj, although still primarily under Ottoman control, emerged as an internationalized issue that was subject increasingly to the extraterritorial and capitulatory demands of the European powers. Although the Ottoman Empire's Board of Health (*Meclis-i Umur-ı Sıhhiye* or the Conseil Supérieur de Santé de Constantinople) ostensibly was responsible for administration of the international quarantine system and policing of the hajj, in reality this organization was itself a mixed body of Ottoman and European representatives, an almost perfect symbol of the Capitulations and European legal manipulation.

The situation in the Hijaz and the Red Sea was no better.[23] By the 1880s, European consular agents in Jeddah were spending much of their time charging their Ottoman counterparts with fleecing pilgrims and gross medical and administrative incompetence. By contrast, Ottoman officials posted to the Hijaz rightly suspected that European attempts to extend consular protection to their colonial subjects merely provided a pretense for espionage and intelligence gathering.

However, as Ottoman officials well knew, the sultan-caliph and his administration could no longer govern the steamship hajj independently. By the conclusion of the nineteenth century, the conduct of the hajj had morphed into an interdependent system requiring coordination and cooperation among the Ottoman Empire, British India, the Dutch East Indies, French Algeria, Russian Central Asia, and the rest of the European colonial world. Pilgrimage had become entangled in an interimperial web of overlapping—often conflicting—regulations governing passports, quarantines, shipping firms, pilgrimage guides, and camel brokers. The result was a weak and fractured regime of mobility controls, which produced decades of diplomatic gridlock and horrific levels of mortality and human suffering.

Owing to these competing interests, the steamship-era hajj produced the first global crisis of Muslim mass mobility. Muslims were racialized, pathologized, and singled out as the carriers of both dangerous microbes and subversive, even uniquely violent, ideas. In many respects the plight of steamship-going Muslims invites loose comparisons with the present. Today the Islamophobia of the post-9/11 era has branded Muslims worldwide—even the most vulnerable refugee populations—as potential terrorists, giving rise to additional border security, more stringent passport and visa controls, racial profiling, and even outright travel bans. Although today's Islamophobia revolves around air traffic, immigration policies, and the assumed threat of al-Qaeda or ISIS terrorists, such fears are neither new nor novel. Recent Western attempts to restrict Muslim travel, mobility, and migration share an intellectual lineage forged in the age of steam.[24]

Although their fears were not always grounded in reality, European colonial empires had the power to rewrite the terms of pilgrimage and Muslim travel. This power affected the lives of millions of ordinary Muslim pilgrims and migrants. And, as this book shows, it also dramatically reshaped the task of governing the Hijaz and the hajj for the world's only remaining Muslim power. In this sense the first global controversies over Muslim mobility also help us to better understand the impossible dilemmas of Muslim imperial sovereignty in the age of European colonialism. In order to refocus our attention on how the Ottoman Empire dealt with this crisis, this book advocates a change in perspective, one that builds on and engages with the colonial archive and historiography of the hajj but recenters the story on the Ottoman Empire and the Hijaz.

The Caliph's Double Burden: The Ottoman Pilgrimage State in a World of "Muslim" Colonial Empires

In his seminal 1982 article, "Sanitation and Security: The Imperial Powers and the Nineteenth Century Hajj," William Roff describes how the hajj came to be understood by British colonial administrators as a "twin infection" of sanitary and security risks.[25] Following in Roff's footsteps, conventionally, the steamship-era hajj has been treated, first and foremost, as a potential security threat to European colonial regimes, including British India, Dutch Indonesia, French Algeria, and Russian Central Asia. In this equation, colonial states are presumed to have feared Mecca as a meeting place of anticolonial exiles and outlaws or as an outlet for pro-Ottoman Pan-Islamic propaganda. More recently, however, John Slight and Eileen Kane have complicated the

British and Russian empires' respective relationships to the hajj. As they both point out, whereas Britain and Russia certainly pursued programs of surveillance, over time they also developed more sophisticated strategies aimed at currying favor with their Muslim colonial subjects and normalizing rule by a non-Muslim power by presenting themselves as facilitators, patrons, and even protectors of the hajj. This critical revision reframes the hajj less as a threat and more as an opportunity for colonial empires.[26]

The British Empire's long engagement with the hajj shows that although a mixture of medical and political security risks might have provided some the initial prompts for the Raj's deepening involvement with the hajj, over time British officials, both non-Muslim and Muslim, gradually familiarized themselves with the medical, legal, and financial needs of Indian and other British Muslim subjects traveling to or living in the Hijaz. This sharpened ethnographic and practical interest in the quotidian details of pilgrimage gradually reshaped British policy. Islamophobic fantasies of anticolonial subversion were replaced, or at least tempered, by more realistic and pressing concerns over cholera prevention, steamship regulation, and consular representation. Thus instead of focusing solely on rooting out potential security threats, officials from Bombay to the British consulate in Jeddah began to refocus their attention on administering and regulating the steamship hajj. Through this multidecade process of immersion, Britain's erection of an empire-wide pilgrimage bureaucracy would pose an increasingly credible challenge to the Ottoman sultan-caliph's legitimacy as the sole custodian of the Muslim holy places and the hajj.

In the process, the Hijaz and the hajj became ensnared in an asymmetrical clash of competing claims pitting the Ottoman Caliphate's sovereignty over the *haremeyn* (Mecca and Medina) and spiritual authority over non-Ottoman Muslims living under colonial rule against the technological, military, diplomatic, and legal might of the British Empire, a non-Muslim state, asserting its quizzical status as the world's most populous and powerful "Muslim" empire. As Slight acknowledges, Britain was never the "benevolent" protector of the pilgrimage that it claimed to be. Its "concern to sustain imperial rule" and "desire to uphold prestige in the Muslim world" always guided its calculations.[27] Despite the bald hypocrisy and ultimate futility of this effort, it did succeed on a certain level. It forced the Ottoman state to defend itself on previously unimaginable ideological, legal, and technological terrain and fundamentally to reconsider the Hijaz and the hajj as potentially vulnerable, even quasi-colonial spaces rather than as uncontested symbols of Islamic sovereignty and legitimacy.

Imperial Mecca takes this dramatic role reversal as its central problem. As a result, this book takes up a line of inquiry very different from those previously pursued by historians of the colonial-era hajj. Rather than focusing solely on the sanitary and security risks, both real and imagined, that the hajj presented to colonial empires, this book explores how the extraterritorial evolution of Britain's Indian Ocean pilgrimage bureaucracy presented an even broader challenge to the Ottoman Empire's traditional role as protector of the Hijaz and the hajj. It details how the advent of the steam-based colonial hajj radically altered the traditional duties and responsibilities of the Ottoman sultan-caliph in his capacity as the Servant of the Two Holy Places (Arabic: *Khādim al-Ḥaramayn al-Sharīfayn*; Ottoman Turkish: *Hadim ül-Haremeyn eş-Şerifeyn*).

With the notable exception of Lâle Can's groundbreaking work on the fraught legal statuses of Central Asian pilgrims, the Ottoman Empire's central role as the pilgrimage's primary patron and administrator has been curiously absent from the now lively literature on the colonial-era hajj. As a result, the previous dominance of these colonial archival approaches to religious patronage and legitimacy has produced a kind of warped vision of the global hajj. To suggest that the experiences and expectations of European powers such as Britain or Russia—strategically branding themselves as patrons and sponsors of the hajj or "Muslim powers"—are somehow comparable with or equivalent to the religious duties and political, fiscal, and administrative burdens expected of the Ottoman sultan-caliph flirts with a kind of unintended "conceptual flattening," which threatens to drain away all meaningful distinctions between the constraints facing Muslim and non-Muslim states. It somehow mutes the stark differences between how Muslims themselves actually judged and responded to these claims.[28]

Just as European powers long had claimed to protect the Ottoman Empire's Christian subjects from despotism and violence, in the concluding decades of the nineteenth century, Ottoman statesmen were confronted with the mind-boggling prospect of European powers claiming the right to protect their Muslim colonial subjects and even Islam's most sacred rites from Ottoman corruption, ineptitude, and mismanagement. As issues such as cholera, quarantine, steamship regulation, passport controls, and consular representation emerged as matters of global significance and interimperial interest, as early as the 1880s, the Ottoman Empire found itself in an unprecedented bind. The sultan-caliph remained the legitimate sovereign responsible for the administration and protection of the land-based hajj. Yet custodianship of the steamship hajj represented an almost entirely novel field of governance. Ottoman custodianship was no longer a matter of merely providing subsidies to the Bedouin, patronage to the denizens of the holy cities, and seasonal security for the camel caravans from Egypt and Syria. The advent of the steamship and mass pilgrimage had altered the scope, scale, and global import of the hajj by several orders of magnitude. As a result, the sultan-caliph was forced to shoulder a double burden: the Ottoman state had to continue its traditional duties and early modern practices of custodianship and simultaneously to coordinate its administration of the Hijaz and the steamship hajj with rival colonial empires that often were intent on undermining Ottoman legitimacy.

Here it is also important to note that although the hajj was the undeniable centerpiece of the Ottoman Empire's pilgrimage bureaucracy, the hajj to Mecca was itself part of a much wider set of Ottoman practices of patronage, endowment, and custodial supervision of sites of pious visitation (*ziyaret*), including Sufi lodges, mosques and madrasas, mausoleums, and tomb complexes dating from the reign of Süleyman I (r. 1520–66). These architectural and charitable commitments included some of the world's most iconic Muslim, Christian, and Jewish sacred sites in Jerusalem, ranging from Süleyman's refurbishment of the Dome of the Rock to the humbler, but no less critical, operations of the city's soup kitchens.[29] However, the map of pilgrimage destinations stretched far beyond the Hijaz and Palestine. Ottoman sponsorship also included sometimes overshadowed sites from the tomb and shrine complex of Mevlana Celaleddin Rumi (Jalāl al-Dīn al-Rumī, d. 1273) in Konya to major pilgrimage stations and service hubs like the Süleymaniye Külliyesi complex in Damascus.[30]

Similarly, in Iraq there were Süleyman's efforts to rebuild the Baghdad mosque-tomb complex honoring Abū Ḥanīfa (d. 767), the eponymous founder of the Hanafi legal school, which had been destroyed by Safavid forces during the reign of Shah Ismail I (r. 1501–24).[31] Süleyman also commissioned a shrine honoring ʿAbd al-Qādir al-Gīlānī (d. 1166), nominal founder of the Qadiriyya Sufi order. Collectively these sites were positioned as alternative Sunni pilgrimage destinations, envisioned to counterprogram against the Safavid-sponsored shrine cities of Najaf, Karbala, al-Kazimayn, and Sammara, home to the the ʿatabāt, the holiest sites of Shiʿi ziyaret.[32]

Ottoman patronage did not always neatly adhere to the state's Sunni-Hanafi preferences. For example, during the reign of Abdülhamid II, a mixed bag of Pan-Islamic notions of Sunni-Shiʿi unity and efforts to thwart the projection of Qajar influence over Iraq led Istanbul to undertake major repairs to tombs and shrines in Najaf and Karbala. Nor was Hamidian support for Shiʿi sites limited to Iraq. It also would include major repairs to tombs and shrines in Medina and the cemeteries of Bāb al-Ṣaghīr in Damascus.[33]

In Istanbul itself, Ottoman-sponsored Sufi lodges served as major diasporic hubs for itinerant Indians, Afghans, Uzbeks, and other Central Asians. Pilgrims passing through Istanbul also helped to define the imperial capital's own sacred geography. They incorporated the shrine and mosque of Abū Ayyūb al-Anṣārī (Hazret-i Eyüp)—a companion of the Prophet Muḥammad (ṣaḥāba) who died during the failed first siege of Constantinople in 674—into their hajj and ziyaret itineraries.[34] Whether seeking to settle permanently, looking for work or educational opportunities, or just pausing on their way to Jerusalem, Mecca, or Medina, even with the advent of more direct routes created by the hajj of steam and rail, these smaller stations of pious visitation and tourism continued to constitute the spine of Islamic travel infrastructures. These complexes sheltered the ethnic and fraternal networks on which pilgrims depended to sustain themselves. Thus Ottoman ziyaret sites from North Africa and Egypt to Anatolia, Syria, and Iraq, though significant in their own right, also fleshed out the subitineraries that conveyed pilgrims toward the empire's signature pilgrimage destinations in the Hijaz, Palestine, and Iraq.[35]

Although a more rigorous comparison of the hajj with these and many other examples of Ottoman pilgrimage administration is a task for another study, it is worth noting that the late Ottoman Hijaz, despite its conventional treatment as an extreme exception to the broader trends of Ottoman governance, was not so different from other pilgrimage destinations administered elsewhere in the empire. In the latter half of the nineteenth century, the Hijaz, Jerusalem, and the Shiʿi shrine cities of Iraq all came under intense pressure from outside imperial forces. Each of these destinations featured large diasporic and itinerant populations hailing from territories ruled by hostile European powers. And each of these sites provoked claims of extraterritorial protection from one or more colonial powers.

For example, in Jerusalem multiple European powers set out to reinforce their influence over the Ottoman Empire's non-Muslim subjects by asserting extraterritorial protection over religious authorities and institutions in Palestine and greater Syria. France supported Catholics, Russia championed Orthodox causes, and Britain acted as the protector of Protestant and Jewish interests.[36] From the 1840s on, Russia was especially aggressive in its support of Orthodox pilgrimage to Jerusalem and Palestine. In turn, tsarist support for Orthodox pilgrimage and patronage for local churches revealed a wider imperial strategy to extend Russia's landholdings and consular influence throughout Palestine and greater Syria. Most famously, the escalation of Russian and French demands for new privileges over the holy sites of Jerusalem set in motion the events that ultimately led to the Crimean War (1853–56). In Russia's case, however, a secondary outcome of its growing familiarity with Christian pilgrims and Jewish settlers in Palestine also helped to stoke Russia's subsequent interest in the facilitation of its Muslim subjects' pilgrimages to Jerusalem and the Hijaz.[37]

In Iraq the story was much the same. From the middle of the nineteenth century on, the Ottoman state found itself combating the extension of Shiʿi patronage networks, foreign land acquisitions, and capitulatory legal claims by both Qajar Iran and British India (a subject to which I will return in chapter 2).

Whereas Ottoman-administered pilgrimage destinations in the Hijaz, Iraq, and Palestine suffered from varying degrees of European intrusion, unlike the Hijaz and Iraq, one striking difference among these three sites stems from the fact that Jerusalem was not subjected to the same level of sanitary scrutiny that was reserved for the empire's Muslim pilgrimage destinations. In part the Hijaz and Iraq's more intimate maritime and diasporic ties to the Indian cradle of cholera made such precautions understandable. However, as the complaints of Ottoman public health officers make clear, the lack of quarantine and other international public health controls surrounding Christian pilgrimage and Jewish migration to Palestine only served to further underscore the Islamophobic double standards and hypocrisy inherent in the entire interimperial project of regulating pilgrimage and other forms of Muslim mobility.[38]

The thankless task of harmonizing long-established Ottoman practices of Muslim and non-Muslim pilgrimage patronage with newer international and European colonial expectations for pilgrimage regulation and protection produced a raft of irreconcilable dilemmas for the Ottoman sultan-caliph. And although it is true that many of the challenges of pilgrimage administration were indeed shared with the British, Dutch, French, and Russian empires, as this study argues, it is also critical for us to take stock of the Ottoman Empire's unique position as the only *real* Muslim empire among them. Moreover, the Ottoman Empire was the only pilgrimage bureaucracy tasked simultaneously with balancing all of these overlapping commitments, old and new, to both Muslim and non-Muslim sites and governments. Thus whereas a great deal has been written about European imperial attempts to manage and even instrumentalize the hajj as tool of colonial rule, we know comparatively few details about how the Ottoman Empire—the Muslim state at the very heart of this story—responded to these brazen non-Muslim challenges to its legitimate dominion over the Hijaz and the hajj.

Pan-Islamic Pillar or Unfinished Project?

Arguably the most critical underpinnings of the Ottoman state's titular claims to the caliphate and Pan-Islamic legitimacy were its sovereignty over the Hijaz and the hajj and its ability to defend those claims effectively against European intervention. Just as the colonial hajj has been consistently framed as a threat to colonial order, conventionally, custodianship over the Muslim holy places has been treated as a relatively uncontested pillar of late Ottoman legitimacy. The Hijaz and the hajj often have been portrayed as ideal venues to burnish the Ottoman Caliphate's benevolent image among non-Ottoman Muslims living under colonial rule. Thus at least in theory, Mecca was supposed to provide a firm base from which the Ottoman sultan-caliph could promote his supranational spiritual authority, instilling a sense of "dual loyalty" among Muslim colonial subjects aimed at making European colonial powers think twice about military and diplomatic aggression against the Ottoman state.[39] And yet in the empire's final decades, Ottoman rule in the Hijaz was not the stable foundation of tradition and Islamic legitimacy that many Ottoman officials and subsequent historians have liked to imagine.

In the concluding decades of the nineteenth century, the very globalizing technologies of steam, rail, print, and telegraphy that had made the dissemination and management of the sultan-caliph's carefully curated image possible were only just beginning to make conceivable the erection of more meaningful structures of Ottoman territorial sovereignty and pilgrimage modernization.[40] As a result, the construction of the kind of Hijaz and hajj envisaged and promised by the Hamidian regime remained an immature, incomplete project. And although modern technologies of imperial rule lay at the heart of the Hamidian impulse to reform, develop, and more fully integrate the empire's vulnerable semiautonomous and tribal frontiers, those innovations simultaneously risked arousing local resistance and provided new pathways for European colonial regimes to extend their extraterritorial influence into the region. Indeed, by the time that the Hamidian state began to deploy a new repertoire of governing practices and technologies to the region in the decades between 1880 and 1909, both the Hijaz and the steamship hajj already had emerged as deeply contested transimperial spaces.

In practice the Hamidian-era mobilization of Islamic symbols such as the caliphate or the hajj depended on much more than mere rhetoric and symbolism. In order to achieve its goals, Hamidian Pan-Islamism had to be translated into tangible actions and demonstrations of the state's power, sovereignty, and competence. Rhetoric had to be made materially manifest at the level of everyday procedure and administration on the ground at the absolute outer limits of the state's logistical reach. To better understand these dynamics, *Imperial Mecca* moves beyond grand strategic questions surrounding the caliphate and other forms of Pan-Islamic legitimation to identify the previously overlooked assemblages of legal, diplomatic, documentary, technological, scientific, infrastructural, and environmental questions—the minute, quotidian mechanics of imperial rule—that were quietly and consistently escalating and intensifying Anglo-Ottoman and wider international struggles over the status of the Hijaz and the administration of Muslim pious mobility. By focusing on the granular technocratic details of hajj logistics and the challenges of rationalizing Hijazi governance, I argue that we are likely to find that the everyday application of imperial policy might not always conform to our previous historiographical models and predictions.

To be sure, the goals and aspirations of Hamidian Pan-Islamism cannot (and should not) be dismissed easily. These big ideas figured prominently in both the cold calculations and misguided anxieties of both Ottoman and

British statesmen. At the same time, this study does not shy away from the messy reality that Pan-Islam was not always a coherent project. Pan-Islam often has supplied a kind of casual shorthand for arguing that Ottoman policies were inspired or driven by the politicization of religious legitimacy, generally without supplying a cogent explanation of how and why seemingly all notions of Islamic authority could be forced to fit into this rubric.[41] A reckoning with the assumptions that this shorthand entails challenges us to consider more seriously how and why particular government policies and practices were or were not manifestations of Pan-Islam. It also frees us to admit that Pan-Islamism was not the only strategy of imperial rule available to late Ottoman statesmen. Sometimes examples of Islamic patronage were simply continuations of long-standing Ottoman governmental priorities, albeit updated and modernized. Thus despite its seemingly omnipresent association with the Hijaz and the hajj, this study also tries to consider the limitations and risks entailed in Pan-Islam's application to their administration. It seeks to acknowledge that Pan-Islamic ideals frequently were subordinated, retooled, or even contradicted by the competing logics of modernization, centralization, public health, territorial sovereignty, citizenship and nationality, international law, and the raw realpolitik of interimperial rivalry.

The Shifting Shape of Hijazi Autonomy

Understanding the changing shape of Ottoman rule in the Hijaz is critical to rethinking the challenges posed by British India's encroachment on the Arabian Peninsula and the hajj. On the one hand, the hajj provides a panoramic window into the Hijaz's inner workings. On the other hand, the Ottoman Hijaz constitutes the missing piece at the heart of the historiographic jigsaw puzzle of the interimperial hajj.

An unfortunate by-product of our previous dependence on colonial archival sources—which focused primarily on the regulation of Muslim colonial subjects in transit to Jeddah—has been the conspicuous absence (or murky portrayal) of the Hijaz itself from the burgeoning historiography of the colonial hajj. In response, this study attempts to bring a more Ottoman sense of space, place, population, environment, and territory back to the forefront of our understanding of the transimperial hajj. Here Jeddah,

Mecca, Medina, and the Hijaz province more broadly figure as critical elements rather than merely being relegated to the pale background on which the drama of the colonial hajj plays out. By relying on Ottoman sources to look beyond the more limited view of Jeddah's consular authorities, I seek to present a broader, more diverse vision of Hijazi society, one composed of overlapping layers of urban locals, Bedouins, diasporic populations, pilgrims, multiple levels of Ottoman officialdom, and colonial actors.

Unlike the case with its European rivals, the Ottoman task of governing the hajj also overlapped with the much broader demands of the Hijaz's provincial administration and its interface with the semiautonomous Sharifate of Mecca. To shelter the hajj from the extraterritorial influence of the British Raj and other European colonial powers, Istanbul had to build up and modernize the state's administrative, technical, and infrastructural capacities and impose new notions of governmentality, centralization, and territorial sovereignty. All of these actions constituted alien threats to the traditionally privileged constitutional and religious statuses of Hijaz, the Sharifate of Mecca, and their Bedouin inhabitants. Often this delicate process of rebalancing and retrofitting early modern and Islamic traditions of governance to suit the altered circumstances of colonial encroachment raised insoluble dilemmas, many of which proved difficult—if not impossible—for the late Ottoman state to fully resolve.

Here again, the historiography of Pan-Islam poses another stumbling block. Iconic works on Pan-Islamic mobilization by Selim Deringil and Kemal Karpat have offered rich descriptions of how Sultan Abdülhamid II sought to promote the caliphate both to shore up his domestic legitimacy among Ottoman Muslims and to wield greater influence over the foreign Muslim subjects of his imperial rivals. These foundational works tell us a great deal about how Ottoman statesmen imagined the symbolic power of the caliphate, but they offer fewer sustained examples detailing how this rhetorical power was translated into day-to-day governmental practices in the Hijaz.[42] When scholarly attention has turned to how the symbolic power of Pan-Islam was manifested on the ground, it has overwhelmingly focused on the Hijaz Railway.[43] Although this project was undeniably the most ambitious expression of Hamidian Pan-Islamism, its partial completion and brief period of operation between 1908 and World War I mean that it offers only a very narrow slice of the wider story of the interimperial competition over the Hijaz and the hajj. This project also must be contextualized as part of a much broader set of responses to European encroachment on the hajj and the central state's attempts to integrate more fully the autonomous sharifate and Bedouin tribal frontier. As *Imperial Mecca* shows, these questions had been unfolding in less ostentatious but no less significant ways for at least a half century prior to the Hijaz Railway's partial completion in 1908.

Aside from the disproportionate attention lavished on Pan-Islamic symbolism and the Hijaz Railway, curiously, both the regular administration of the Hijaz province and the hajj have remained understudied.[44] Filling the historiographic gaps between the advent of the steamship hajj and the turn of the twentieth century, *Imperial Mecca* offers a first attempt to reconstruct how early modern Ottoman practices of autonomous rule and seasonal projections of pilgrimage administration evolved into an ambitious reimagination and modernization of frontier governance aimed at adapting to the new challenges posed by the interimperial system of mass pilgrimage that emerged from the 1850s on.

Following the conquest of Mamluk Egypt and Syria by Selim I (r. 1512–20) in 1516–17, the Ottomans claimed suzerainty over the Hijaz. During this period the Ottoman dynasty had taken up the title of Servant of the Two Holy Places, making its custodianship over the holy cities and the hajj the bedrock of its later claims to the caliphate. Traditionally this title entailed two principal responsibilities: the continued provisioning of grain and foodstuffs from Egypt and the maintenance of security along the caravan routes to the Hijaz. However, the Hijaz in general, and Mecca and Medina in particular, were only nominally under Ottoman rule. Ottoman control would remain loose, often little more than a titular and symbolic display. The Hijaz's effective ruler remained the Hashemite sharif of Mecca. The Ottoman state continued to allow the sharif many of the trappings of an independent prince. Owing to their Hashemite lineage and religious legitimacy as descendants of the Prophet, the Ottomans granted them the titles of amir and sharif. And even down to the final years of Ottoman rule, the province would retain its traditional exemptions from taxation and conscription. Likewise, the Ottoman state entrusted virtually all functions of government, taxation, and public security to the sharif of Mecca.[45]

Because the Ottoman state did not derive its legitimacy through descent from the Prophet, its claims to the title of Servant of the Two Holy Places and caliph had to be demonstrated continually through material expressions of generosity toward the pilgrims, the sharifate, the inhabitants of the holy places, and the region's Bedouin tribes. In the sixteenth and seventeenth centuries, this largely amounted to a continuation of earlier Mamluk practices of provisioning and protection. For the year-round inhabitants of the holy cities, the regular delivery of the *sürre* purse and grain transfers extended the sultan's patronage and bound the local population to the state. Similarly, the continued distribution of cash and food subsidies to the Bedouin along the caravan routes was meant to secure their cooperation and discourage raiding.[46]

For much of the sixteenth and seventeenth centuries, the provincial governments and treasuries of Egypt and Syria were largely responsible for overseeing the Hijaz and the administration of the hajj. In the eighteenth century, Jeddah became the seat of the *Habeş eyaleti* (province of Ethiopia) encompassing Massawa, Suakin, and other Ottoman possessions in East Africa. However, the governor's authority within the Hijaz itself essentially was limited to Jeddah. Even there, half of the port's customs revenues were given over to the sharif.[47] Indeed, prior to the Hamidian-era attempts to build a stronger Ottoman presence in the Hijaz, there was little to no direct Ottoman administration outside Jeddah. And even throughout the Tanzimat and into the Hamidian period, the deployment of Ottoman troops and provision of resources remained a more or less seasonal affair tied to the rhythms of the caravan pilgrimage.

However, the trajectory of this traditional pattern of autonomy was partly disrupted at the start of the nineteenth century. During the Wahhabi occupation of the Hijaz (1803–18), the Ottoman center lost complete control of the region. The Wahhabi seizure of Mecca was an utter humiliation that threatened to completely undermine both the Ottoman dynasty's internal political legitimacy as well as the sultanate's leadership of the global Islamic community. During the first decades of the nineteenth century, Istanbul was beset by more immediate challenges as the state struggled unsuccessfully to impose modernizing reforms and simultaneously bring to heel the Janissaries and the provincial notables of Rumelia and Anatolia. Under these circumstances Mahmud II (r. 1808–39) was forced to delegate the mission to recapture Mecca and Medina to the governor of Egypt, Mehmed Ali Pasha.

Emboldened by his successes in the Hijaz and his decisive interventions on behalf of the Ottoman state during the Greek rebellion in 1820s, Mehmed Ali and his sons had carved out, by the end of the 1830s, a small empire at the expense of the sultan's domains. They extended their control to the Hijaz,

Sudan, Yemen, eastern Arabia, Crete, Syria, and Adana. By 1832, İbrahim Pasha had marched into Anatolia, threatening to advance on Istanbul and ultimately to take over the sultanate itself. Throughout the 1830s, Mehmed Ali's Egyptian empire seemed increasingly poised to swallow up the remaining core of the Ottoman state. Ultimately, however, Europe intervened on behalf of Istanbul to protect the territorial integrity of the state. Under the terms of the 1840 London Convention, Mehmed Ali was forced to withdraw from Syria, Adana, Crete, and Arabia. In exchange, the sultan was forced to issue a *ferman* (edict) naming Mehmed Ali governor of Egypt for life and granting his male descendants hereditary rights to the governorship.[48]

The legacy of the Wahhabi occupation of the Hijaz and the legal precedents set by the province's subsequent absorption into Mehmed Ali's Egyptian subempire would have long-lasting consequences. On the one hand, the Ottoman center lost complete control of the Hijaz for nearly four decades. Ottoman rule in the Hijaz was restored only through European intervention and the internationalization of the sultanate's conflict with its rogue governor. Mehmed Ali's administration and troops finally were forced to withdraw in 1841, in accordance with the London Convention. On the other hand, Mehmed Ali had achieved a level of centralization previously unthinkable under Istanbul's control. Most strikingly, in 1836, the amir of Mecca was detained and held in Egypt. Thereafter, secular Egyptian administrators governed the Hijaz until 1840.[49]

From the 1840s on, the sharifs and amirs of Mecca would be appointed and deposed at the pleasure of the sultan. From the 1850s, they were gradually absorbed into the administrative structures of the Ottoman bureaucracy. With the advent of the Tanzimat's centralizing reforms, the sharifs of Mecca were elevated to the level of ministers (viziers) and granted the honorary title of pasha. Thenceforth potential candidates for elevation to this post also would have to prove their loyalty to the sultan. They were brought to Istanbul, where they often served on the Council of State (Şura-yı Devlet). Ideally this experience served as both administrative training and political indoctrination, inculcating a sense of loyalty to the central state.[50]

In addition to the bureaucratization of the sharifate, Tanzimat reforms reconfigured the Hijaz's administrative structure and its jurisdictional boundaries. Between 1868 and 1873, the 1864 Provincial Reform Law and the 1867 Law of Vilayets were applied partially to the region. As a result, the old governorship of Jeddah was replaced with a new-style *vilayet*. For the first time, the province was referred to as the *Hicaz vilayeti*, and its jurisdiction swelled to encompass the entirety of the geographical Hijaz. Even the center of the new province was Mecca. Whereas previous incarnations of Ottoman provincial rule had maintained an administrative and geographical distinction between Jeddah and the Sharifate of Mecca, the new Hijaz province overlapped the sharif's jurisdiction, circumscribing the traditional character of the autonomy enjoyed by the sharifate. At the same time, the governors of this restructured province were put in the awkward position of sharing and negotiating their jurisdiction and power with the sharif of Mecca. In many respects this reformulated Hijaz lingered in a kind of purgatory between its customary autonomous status and the halting, incomplete advance of the late Ottoman state's aspirational projects of centralization and frontier modernization.[51]

One of the biggest impediments to the integration of the Hijaz into the wider landscape of Ottoman history has been the assumption that its sacred and semiautonomous status made it completely exceptional. To be sure, the Ottoman state did attach special significance to Mecca and Medina. However, this did not mean that it set the entire Hijaz and its Bedouin inhabitants apart from wider trends in Ottoman provincial governance and frontier policies. As Suraiya Faroqhi warns with regard to the Ottoman administration of the Hijaz and the hajj, "slow change" should not be mistaken for "no change at all."[52] At first glance there are seemingly sound reasons for assuming that Mecca's exceptional status and incomparability continued unchanged until the empire's end. However, even though the Hijaz province and the Sharifate of Mecca always had featured a system of semiautonomous power sharing and layered sovereignty, the meanings, usages, and risks of autonomy changed dramatically over the course of the nineteenth century. With the rise of positivist international law, autonomy transformed from an accepted tool in the management of a large multiethnic empire into a characteristic of weak or compromised sovereignty.[53] Despite the Hijaz's singularity as the linchpin of the caliphate and a pillar of Hamidian Pan-Islamic image-making, it was not as unique as we often imagine. In reality, the Hijaz shared core similarities with a host of other vulnerable provinces throughout the Ottoman Empire.

One of the most overlooked aspects of Mehmed Ali's subempire was its deep impact on the rapidly evolving definitions of autonomy and sovereignty in nineteenth-century international law. In 1840, the Ottoman state was forced to formally recognize Mehmed Ali's hereditary dynasty and Egypt's status as an autonomous or "privileged" province, one of the so-called *eyalat-ı mümtaze*.[54] Over the nineteenth century this list of special territories grew to include Serbia, Montenegro, Bulgaria, eastern Rumelia, Moldavia and Wallachia, Samos, Crete, Cyprus, Mount Lebanon, Egypt, Tunisia, Algeria, and the Sharifate of Mecca.[55] In most cases their special statuses were by-products of conflicts that had precipitated some form of European military intervention, occupation, partition, or annexation. Indeed, this list reads like a map of the hotspots of Europe's gradual dismemberment of the empire via the Eastern Question and the absorption of its Arab peripheries as protectorates or colonial possessions of one kind or another. The real problem with autonomous provinces was that "local political tendencies" produced a "centrifugal force" pulling territories away from the concerns of the central state and raising the likelihood of "international pressure and intervention." Thus no matter how well the Ottomans administered these territories, autonomy continued to leave the door open for European intervention. Indeed, their special status only further underscored their vulnerability in European eyes.[56]

Engineering a Solution: Istanbul's Technocratic Gaze on the Tribal and Colonial Frontiers

Between the 1870s and World War I, the Ottoman state displayed renewed vigor in the Red Sea. Following the opening of the Suez Canal in 1869 and the reconquest of Yemen by 1872, Ottoman efforts to consolidate control over the Hijaz and defend the Muslim holy places from European encroachments gained a new sense of urgency.[57] During the reign of Abdülhamid II, stewardship over Mecca and Medina also took on a new significance for the sultan-caliph's Pan-Islamic image. At the outset of his reign, however, control of this semiautonomous province remained tenuous. The first half of the nineteenth century had been an unmitigated disaster for the empire. In addition to having lost control of the region for nearly four decades, during the 1850s, the province had been rocked by an anti-Ottoman insurrection stemming from the prohibition of the slave trade in 1855 and the massacre of Jeddah's Christian population in 1858.[58] It was not until the early 1880s that Istanbul began to exert a stronger influence over the province.

In the aftermath of the devastating defeats of the Russo-Ottoman War of 1877–78, most of the empire's European provinces were lost (see figure 0.4). Abdülhamid inherited an empire that was more Muslim than ever. This demographic shift has been cited as one of principal reasons for the sultan's promotion of supranational Islamism as an alternative to the secular

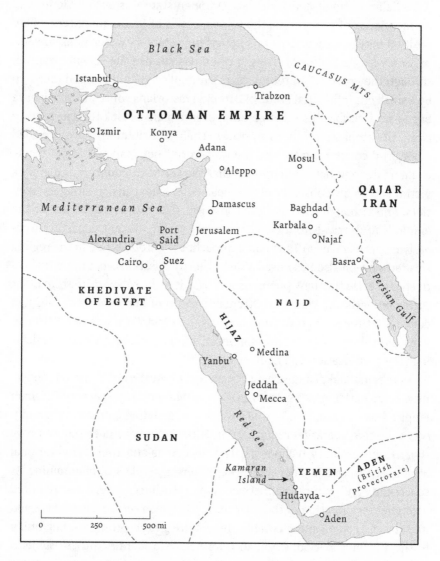

FIGURE 0.4 Map of Ottoman Empire and Arabian Peninsula, c. 1877. Map created by Erin Greb.

ideology of the Tanzimat. Another outcome of this changing demography was the increased value placed on shoring up the empire's sovereignty over its remaining territories and bringing its Arab and tribal frontier provinces under more direct control in order to tap into their neglected manpower and economic potential.

As Selim Deringil notes, the late Ottoman state was both a victim and a practitioner of imperial methods. As a result of its unique intermediate position between subalterns and imperial masters, however weak in comparison with its European rivals, it often has felt like the "empire that fell through the cracks."[59] In recent years Deringil's lament has been taken up by a small but influential group of Ottoman historians who collectively have begun to describe this reinvigorated, even expansionist Ottoman posture along the empire's southern frontiers. Their contributions have provided a powerful counternarrative to the well-worn "Sick Man of Europe" trope, challenging long-held assumptions that the Ottoman Empire was merely a victim and passive observer of European colonial expansion along its frontiers. And although there is clear consensus that this new approach to the empire's Arab tribal frontiers represents some significant departure from early modern and even Tanzimat approaches to Ottoman rule in the region, this recognition also has raised a set of thorny questions about exactly how to characterize this new phenomenon. Was it a clear departure from older Ottoman methods? Was it an Ottoman version of European colonialism, a colonial attitude, or an Ottoman civilizing mission? Or was late Ottoman expansion along its southern frontiers an exceptional, hybridized case defying easy classification and nomenclature?[60]

As Ussama Makdisi observes: "In an age of Western-dominated modernity, every nation creates its own Orient. The nineteenth-century Ottoman Empire was no exception." As he explains, articulating Ottoman modernity was a delicate operation requiring the Turkish core of the empire to prove that its state, military, technological advancement, and level of civilizational attainment were equivalent to those of Europe while still maintaining its sovereignty and cultural distinctiveness as a Muslim empire. It also required a parallel recalibration of the relationship between the Turkish center and its subject peoples, most notably the empire's Arab provinces. Beginning in the Tanzimat period, Ottoman reformers had identified these subjects as "potential" citizens. At the same time, they came to see these subjects "as backward and as not-yet-Ottoman, as hindrances as well as objects of imperial reform."[61]

As the state worked to consolidate and homogenize its core territories in Anatolia and eastern Thrace, by contrast, its Arab provinces increasingly were imagined as a quasi-colonial space characterized by "nomadism and savagery." Thus as Deringil argues, at some point "in the nineteenth century the Ottoman elite adopted the mindset of their enemies, arch-imperialists, and came to conceive of its peripheries as a colonial setting." Within its remaining frontier territories, the Ottoman state began to adopt its own "civilizing motif," imitating and borrowing a variety of practices from European colonial empires.[62]

As Tahsin Pasha, head of Abdülhamid's royal secretariat from 1894 to 1908, confirmed in his memoirs, the problems posed by the empire's autonomous and tribal frontier provinces were never far from the sultan's mind. As he explained, the empire's evolving posture toward "far away" provinces was sometimes understood as something akin to a "colonial policy" (müstemleke siyaseti). From the sultan's perspective, "the people living there are not like those living in other regions of the [Ottoman] domains and the same laws and forms of administration would not have been possible." Thus the sultan thought it prudent to tailor "a system of administration in accordance with the local inhabitant's capacities." But how are we to read this notion of an Ottoman "colonial policy"? Did Tahsin Pasha mean that the Ottoman state needed to practice European-style colonial methods along the empire's frontiers, or was he trying to articulate something subtler? In other words, was this colonial policy simply a realization that the empire's autonomous provinces would require firmer conceptions of territorial sovereignty to insulate them from various forms of colonial meddling? As he put it, "The affairs of the Hijaz, Yemen, Baghdad, Syria, Beirut, Mount Lebanon, and Tripolitania were among the internal problems that caused Sultan Hamid the greatest anxiety." In most cases these territories shared two overlapping problems. All of these regions were subject to "foreign influence" and various forms of "intrigue" and "trickery." And, perhaps even more ominously, the most troublesome among these semiautonomous territories harbored would-be "independent" rulers, such as the khedives in Egypt, the imams in Yemen, the Sanusiyya in Libya, and the sharifs of Mecca in the Hijaz.[63]

From the perspective of the British Empire, the presence of these alternative sovereigns offered proof of the Ottoman state's compromised and incomplete sovereignty over its frontiers. Yet while Istanbul puzzled over how to centralize and better integrate these autonomous "princely states" into its own domains, the British Empire had no trouble imagining how it might incorporate these vulnerable appendages of the Ottoman state into its own imperial system. In various ways both the British Raj and its Arabian offshoots were already a patchwork of princely or "native" states featuring various forms of layered, fragmented, or "minor sovereignties." Whether Arab tribal shaykhs and chieftains in Yemen and the Persian Gulf or the khedive of Egypt or the sharif of Mecca, these were precisely the kinds of native rulers that the Raj's system of protectorates, occupations, and indirect rule sought to collect and reproduce in Arabia.[64]

In part, Tahsin Pasha's commentary on the empire's interconnected tribal, autonomous, and colonial threats also represented a critique of the failed one-size-fits-all approaches of Tanzimat centralization. Hamidian-era administrators claimed that the "customs and dispositions" of the local inhabitants in provinces such as the Hijaz, Trablusgarb (Libya), Yemen, and parts of Iraq rendered them unfit for full incorporation into the imperial system imagined by the universalizing ideology of the Tanzimat. The lack of censuses, regular taxation procedures, cadastral surveys, land registration, conscription, and the *nizamiye* court system indicated that local inhabitants remained outside the realm of civilized Ottoman subjects. In response the state sought to articulate new forms of provincial governance designed to narrow this presumed civilizational gulf. At the same time, however, the Hamidian state's efforts to extend its administrative reach farther into frontier provinces than ever before would necessitate a greater reliance on local tribal and religious leaders and the continued management of various degrees of autonomy. Here Thomas Kuehn argues that Ottoman readings of indirect rule in places such as British Aden, Sudan, and India also inspired new debates on how best to "repackage and rehabilitate" older pre-Tanzimat Ottoman practices, which had tolerated various measures of decentralization and local autonomy.[65]

Arguably the most difficult problem in describing Ottoman adaptations of and to colonial practices has been the need to distinguish them clearly from European colonialism itself. In an attempt to navigate this question, Kuehn admirably tries to thread the needle and articulate a hybrid brand of provincial administration, which he dubs "colonial Ottomanism." While

clearly arguing that there were some colonial characteristics to late Ottoman rule in Yemen, he is also careful to tease out their ambivalent and
contradictory nature. He describes the gap between Tanzimat-era ideals
and Yemeni particularities as the "politics of difference." As he cautions,
however, colonial Ottomanism was distinct from European colonialism in
that it never produced dual structures of governance and separate codes of
law. Nor did it mobilize discourses of race or sexual segregation in order to
uphold a stark dichotomy between colonizing citizens of the metropole and
colonized subjects of the periphery. Rather, for Kuehn, colonial Ottomanism implied a "hierarchy of subjects" that marked Yemenis as "Ottomans
of a lesser kind."[66] As Mostafa Minawi clarifies, this new brand of Ottoman
frontier governance "posited cultural, not racial or ethnic characteristics,
as a way of differentiating Ottoman rulers from the local population." As
a result, unlike European colonialism, in the Ottoman case "the difference
between colonizers and colonized was traversable over time and not an
essential condition of Ottoman imperial rule."[67]

I have taken tremendous inspiration from these debates. In their own
ways, each of these authors points to the late Ottoman state's increasingly
nimble adaptations to the overlapping internal/local and external/trans-
imperial challenges posed by the European colonial environment in which
the empire's southern frontiers had become embedded by end of the nineteenth century. And although this study repeatedly shows Ottoman officials
in direct dialogue with European methods and technologies, I also believe
that it is important to make a clear distinction between Ottoman learning
from or responses to European colonial methods and European colonialism
itself. Thus rather than reading the rapid evolution of late Ottoman frontier
strategies as processes of colonial Ottomanism or "borrowed colonialism,"
this book reframes these changes more as questions of modern governmentality, bureaucratic rationality, and territorial sovereignty.[68]

From the 1880s on, Ottoman administrators increasingly understood that
the juridical, geographical, and physical environments of its autonomous
frontiers produced an unevenness and ambiguity that threatened imperial
sovereignty. These unstable frontier zones, though endowed with traditional elements of a "fragmented" or "lumpy" form of imperial sovereignty,
were, in the heightened context of high imperialism, "launching points for
competing assertions of legal authority and territorial control," whether
local, colonial, or both.[69]

In order to address these new concerns, Istanbul began to envision an ambitious respatialization of the empire's Arab tribal frontiers. Modern engineering, technology, and ethnographic approaches to the particularities of local populations were taken up as the keys to solving the frontier's bio-political and juridical weaknesses. Armed with this emergent "technocratic gaze," they set out to manage human life and the resources needed to sustain it, improve Arabia's defective nature, transform Bedouins into proper subjects, and gradually replace autonomous forms of political life with more rigorous territorial power. By taking this broader assemblage of concerns as a whole, this book traces the making of a different brand of pilgrimage and provincial administration, a nascent—never fully articulated—frontier technostate.[70] Thus in contrast to the Hijaz's conventional associations with Abdülhamid II's Pan-Islamic legitimacy structures or more recent attempts to identify a Hamidian "colonial policy," this study outlines an alternative narrative of maturing technocratic expertise, state building, and development practices tailored to address the unique challenges facing the empire's overlapping autonomous, tribal, and interimperial frontiers.

Having learned from the limitations of previous iterations of Tanzimat centralization and homogenization, Hamidian state officials pragmatically understood that they could not simply rebuild the empire's autonomous frontiers from scratch. Instead, they would have to build up and deploy new forms of expertise and governance alongside the existing ones. Although the Hamidian state considered a variety of strategies to more directly subordinate the Hijaz, the Sharifate of Mecca, and the region's Bedouin tribal inhabitants to Istanbul's authority, time and again suggestions of direct constitutional changes to the Hijaz's exceptional status were deemed too risky.

Abdülhamid and his closest advisers believed that this strategy would require a full-scale military campaign and occupation of the region. In the end, this idea was discarded as too likely to provoke violent resistance and increase the chances of European intervention. At the same time, this did not mean that the state simply abandoned the idea of centralizing and modernizing the Hijaz. Instead, Istanbul opted for a more gradualist approach of technocratic development. Rather than abolish or directly confront the Sharifate of Mecca, Istanbul pursued a slower, more stealthy policy of building new infrastructures, including quarantines, hospitals, telegraph lines, and railways. If Hijazi autonomy was too difficult to dismantle, the Hamidian state would opt simply to build up new facts on the ground around it.

These development projects were designed to gradually narrow the parameters of Meccan and Bedouin autonomy and accelerate the frontier's integration with the empire's more centralized core.

As it turned out, the much maligned Sick Man of Europe was capable of competing with its European rivals and executing dizzyingly ambitious development projects. However, the Hamidian state's engineered solutions and technical fixes could never completely overcome the deeper underlying weaknesses inherent in the Hijaz's early modern system of semiautonomous rule. In the end, no combination of Pan-Islamic legitimacy and modernizing expertise could overcome the mutually reinforcing threats posed by frontier autonomy and colonial extraterritoriality. There was simply not enough time. By World War I the clock had struck midnight. The late Ottoman dream of taming its southern frontier and defending its imperial borders and territorial sovereignty remained an unfinished project. And yet this story of global ambition and determined reinvention in the face of insurmountable odds is no less worthy of our attention. It remains foundational to our understanding of the Ottoman encounter with Europe and the colonial Muslim world and their symbiotic roles in the making of the modern hajj and Arabia.

Structure of the Book

This book is organized in three parts. In part 1, "Extraterritorial Frontiers," I introduce the intimate relationship between European extraterritoriality and the Ottoman Hijaz's exceptional autonomous legal status. Chapter 1 explores British India's first commercial and diplomatic encounters with the Hijaz and the hajj. It details how, between the 1850s and early 1880s, colonial and consular officials imagined the Hijaz as a haven for violent anticolonial fanatics and Wahhabi enthusiasts and, later, an outlet for Hamidian-era Pan-Islamic propaganda. By the mid-1880s, however, the urgency of the logistical challenges facing the rapidly industrializing steamship-era pilgrimage—most notably, the near-constant threat of epidemic cholera and the associated question of indigent pilgrims—already had begun to force European colonial administrators to engage more thoughtfully with the affairs of the hajj. Thus as British India became more deeply entangled in the details of the pilgrimage, the colonial state's efforts to better understand the hajj and provide for its subjects' safety and security rebalanced British attitudes toward the Hijaz.

Chapter 2 traces how British consular officials, both Muslim and Christian, in Jeddah began to poke holes in the Hijaz's exceptional religious and legal statuses. By the conclusion of the nineteenth century, the vast majority of the Muslim world found itself living under European colonial rule. As a result of this unprecedented situation, the traditional legal fabric of the Capitulations was stretched beyond recognition. Although the Capitulations were never meant to apply to Muslim foreign subjects, and the Hijaz always explicitly had been exempted from these agreements, from the early 1880s on, British consular officials waged an aggressive campaign to extend the privileges of consular protection to Indian and other colonial subjects traveling to or residing in the Hijaz. In turn, British India's extraterritorial protection of its pilgrim subjects came to present an increasingly vexing challenge to Ottoman sovereignty and the empire's legitimacy as the rightful protector of the Hijaz and the hajj.

In part 2, "Ecologies of Empire," I move from legal entanglements to epidemiological and environmental ones. Although the book's midsection is partly a history of the hajj's emergence as global public health and diplomatic crises, these chapters also trace the transimperial environmental history of cholera itself. Typically the Ottoman Empire's role in questions of quarantine and international sanitary regulation has been overshadowed by the concerns of Europe. Often in this literature, the erection of the sanitary state reads as an almost exclusively European project and the Ottoman Empire is positioned as a semicivilized buffer, the last line of defense between Europe and the teeming hordes of cholera-carrying pilgrims in the Indian Ocean basin. Thus the challenges facing the Ottomans and their interests generally have been relegated to a secondary status.

In chapter 3, instead of asking how the global crises of cholera and pilgrimage regulation affected Europe, free trade, or its colonial possessions, I recenter this story on Istanbul, the Hijaz, and the Red Sea. By doing so I show the Ottoman state fighting a war on two fronts. Once again, the Hijaz was caught in the long shadow of British India. As pilgrimage-related cholera outbreaks attracted ever more international attention, consular and colonial officials sought to exert greater extraterritorial authority over their colonial subjects during their time in the Hijaz. However, even in the face of a mounting body of scientific evidence to the contrary, Britain repeatedly denied that India and its pilgrim masses were in any way responsible for the spread of cholera to the Hijaz and the rest of the Ottoman Empire. Thus rather than supporting Ottoman and international quarantine initiatives, between the 1860s and 1890s, British India emerged as the chief obstacle to the imposition of stricter international quarantine regulations.

Yet even in the face of this campaign of British denial and obstruction, the Ottoman state took an active, even enthusiastic, role in the erection of international quarantine systems during the late nineteenth century, raising several difficult questions. What exactly did the Ottoman state hope to achieve through its participation in international quarantine regulations directed against the Red Sea and the hajj? Was this merely a defensive policy directed at British India, or did cholera and the erection of the Red Sea quarantine systems play more of a constructive role in the late Ottoman resurgence in the Arabian Peninsula?

Quarantines were only one piece of a larger puzzle. In chapter 4 I consider the question of hajj-related water infrastructures. Here I trace how the Ottoman state deliberately sought to deploy new forms of technoscientific discipline to simultaneously meet its international sanitary commitments, re-engineer the region's defective environments, and tame its resistant urban and Bedouin populations. In chapters 3 and 4 I ask how the implementation of European-inspired medical practices, infrastructures, and technologies were understood and received by foreign pilgrims, urban Hijazis, the Bedouin, and the Sharifate of Mecca. And most critically, what were the limitations of Ottoman sanitary and environmental discipline in a religiously conservative, tribal, and traditionally autonomous frontier province? As all of these questions suggest, although the colonial archive fixates on international maritime controversies, the Ottoman archive reorients us toward a more complicated collision betweeen interimperial rivalry and expertise and more localized stories of cholera's role in the dynamics of reform and resistance as Istanbul sought to adapt its own modernizing visions to the realities of the empire's tribal frontier.

In part 3, "Managing Mobility," I examine the regulation and restructuring of pilgrimage transportation systems from steamships and passports to camels and railroads. Chapter 5 explores how the Ottoman state's inability to curtail the Sharifate of Mecca's autonomy would have consequences reaching well beyond more traditional concerns around Bedouin disorder along the Hijaz's caravan routes. Instead of thinking of the sharifate and the Bedouin as essentially land-based interests, existing apart from the transoceanic industrialization of the steamship hajj, this chapter demonstrates how both local and transimperial Hijazi pilgrimage service providers moved with the times, reimagining and reasserting their authority over the Indian Ocean hajj. This chapter also examines how the lack of coordination among Ottoman, British, and international approaches to major questions surrounding indigent pilgrims, passports, and steamship regulations allowed for the growth of an increasingly coercive and corrupt monopoly system governing nearly every aspect of the pilgrimage experience, from steamship tickets and water supplies to pilgrimage guides and camel hires. I show how weak mechanisms of interimperial regulation were consistently conditioned, evaded, and subverted through the collaboration of a constellation of Ottoman governors, European consular officials, and Indian Ocean business interests, all working in concert with the sharif of Mecca.

In chapter 6, I decelerate from the industrialized world of the steamship to the supposedly preindustrial domain of camel transport. Here again we find that even the Bedouin world of the camel caravan had been assimilated into the Indian Ocean pilgrimage services monopoly. Thus instead of the figure of the atavistic Bedouin blindly defending a so-called timeless or traditional Hijaz against the forces of modernization, we find Bedouin camel guides, the sharifate, and an Ottoman governor acting as innovators and defenders of a new synthesis of steam and camel labor. In turn, we find each of these actors presented with a stark choice between protecting their own entrenched commercial interests in the Indian Ocean's steamship and caravan economies and serving the advancement of Ottoman centralization being conveyed along the Hijaz's telegraph and railway lines.

In a cruelly ironic twist, the overlapping crises of mobility and sovereignty surrounding the steamship hajj proved instrumental in framing the underlying logic of the Hijaz Railway's utility and marshaling political and financial support for its construction. Yet between the early 1880s and 1908, the durability of the economic and political alliances forged around the local administration of steamship and camel transport—linking Ottoman officials, the sharifate, urban Hijazi elites, and the Bedouin—worked assiduously to undermine Istanbul's rail-based technical solutions. In the end, Abdülhamid II's patient gambit, deploying new infrastructures and technologies to rearrange the Arabian landscape in a bid to gradually narrow the Hijaz's traditional autonomous privileges, collided with his long tolerance for his provincial government's alliance with the sharif of Mecca. In the end, the sovereignty and administrative competence that this ultimate Pan-Islamic symbol sought to project would remain incomplete, stalled in Medina and denied by the Hijaz's stubbornly durable autonomy even before the empire's British rivals struck the final blow to Ottoman rule in the region.

Finally, the epilogue examines the legacies and afterlives of the modern hajj that were forged between the Ottoman and British empires. In these concluding sections, I examine how World War I and the ouster of the Ottoman Empire from Arabia revived Britain's long-latent fantasies of transferring the caliphate to the sharif of Mecca. Ultimately this ill-fated project was met with almost universal anger in India and across the Islamic world. And yet even in failure, Britain's long campaign to place the Hijaz and the hajj under British protection unleashed shockwaves that would reverberate from Istanbul to India. In the years following World War I, the Ottoman Empire-turned-Turkish Republic would abolish the caliphate even as Indian Muslims rallied to its defense. And even though the Hashemite kingdom and puppet caliphate that Britain had tried to foster were rapidly overthrown by Saudi Arabia's Najdi-Wahhabi warriors, the international administration of the hajj would remain in British and European colonial hands until 1956–57. By tracing the slow decolonization of the hajj, we find a modern pilgrimage system shaped by the legacies and scars of decades of interimperial rivalry and the pathologization of pious mobility. And even today we hear echoes of this rivalry in the Saudi monarchy's reanimation of hajj custodianship as a cudgel of counterinsurgency at home and ideological warfare abroad.

PART ONE

Extraterritorial Frontiers

ONE

Blurred Vision

The Hijaz and the Hajj in the Colonial Imagination

AS JOHN M. WILLIS has suggested, "Historians of Arabia should perhaps look beyond the peninsula that carries its name." As he points out, "the legacy of a postwar concept of 'area studies' or nationalist constructs of the 'Arab world' and 'India' have left scholars with a warped view of the British Empire." Using definitions employed by the British government itself, we arrive at "a far more inclusive definition" of its Indian empire.[1] In reality, British India and its "informal sub-empire" extended well beyond the national boundaries that constitute present-day India and South Asia; its western frontiers stretched into the Persian Gulf, Arabia, the Red Sea, and the coasts of East Africa. Far from being a contiguous landmass, British India was a transregional Indian Ocean and Arabian empire, which safeguarded the Raj's regional interests through an archipelago of indirectly ruled dependencies, native and princely states, treaty shaykhdoms, consulates, and agencies.[2]

These various agencies "met India's strategic needs, served commercial interests, dealt with the consequences of the Indian diaspora, facilitated pilgrimage to Arabia, and acted as listening posts across much of the Islamic world."[3] During the eighteenth and early nineteenth centuries, such outposts originally developed around the commercial needs of the East India Company and the large communities of Indian Muslims as well as Armenian and Hindu traders scattered from Egypt to Jeddah, Mocha, and Aden.

Company residents and agents became involved in preexisting pilgrimage networks of shipping, lodging, and financial transactions.[4]

With the arrival of regular steamship traffic in the Red Sea, however, the Hijaz underwent a dramatic respatialization. The steamship drew the Hijaz closer to Britain's Indian Ocean orbit, further revealing its vulnerability and geographic isolation from the rest of the Ottoman Empire. Repositioned along Britain's route to India, the Hijaz and the Red Sea took on new military-strategic importance for both empires. And by the close of the nineteenth century, the Hijaz's spiritual and ideological significance to the Ottoman Empire, India, and the wider Islamic world had fully captured the attention of British colonial administrators and intellectuals. This chapter tells the story of the British Empire's arrival on these sacred shores and the subsequent evolution of the Hijaz and the hajj in the British colonial imagination, setting the stage for the novel challenges to Ottoman rule that constitute the remainder of the book's core subjects.

Colonial Arrivals in the Sea of Suez

The East India Company's earliest ventures in the Red Sea in the seventeenth and eighteenth centuries had not been especially successful. They faced opposition from Indian merchants, Ottoman and Hijazi authorities, and even English pirates operating in the region. In 1724, a mob massacred several British merchants in Jeddah. British traders came under threat again in the late eighteenth century when the East India Company refused to continue the Mughal tradition of sending annual donations from Surat to support the upkeep of Mecca and Medina.[5] By the close of the eighteenth century, however, wider global events pushed Britain to take a more aggressive stance in the Red Sea. In the wake of France's invasion of Egypt in 1798, Napoleon Bonaparte informed the sharif of Mecca that he would continue to send Egypt's customary donations to the Hijaz and would continue to oversee Egyptian responsibilities related to hajj caravans. In response, Bombay's governor dispatched naval forces to the Red Sea, attacking the French-occupied ports of Suez and Qusayr in 1799.[6]

In 1800, Captain Sir Home Popham was sent to the Red Sea to coordinate forces from Britain and India against France. Popham was also charged with securing the support of local rulers, especially Sharif Ghālib (Ghālib ibn

Musāʿid ibn Saʿīd, r. 1788–1803). Popham was tasked with establishing an East India Company trading factory, securing concessions and treaty privileges from the sharif. Given the inherently awkward position of a Christian emissary to the sharif of Mecca, Popham enlisted an Indian notable, Mahdi Ali Khan, to assist in the negotiations with Ghālib. Although Ghālib harbored deep reservations about the prospect of working with Christians, he floated the idea of accepting Popham's proposals, but only if Britain could guarantee the Amirate of Mecca's independence from Ottoman suzerainty. However, British concerns over the Ottoman Empire's overall territorial integrity ultimately tied Popham's hands.[7]

Although Britain's first diplomatic flirtation with the Hijaz and the sharifate ultimately failed, Popham's mission represents the beginning of a long string of efforts to at least partially integrate Jeddah and the Hijaz into its "informal" economic, legal, and security orbit. However, at the same time, as William Roff and John Slight have noted, this episode also underscores the "inherent ambivalence" of British attempts to influence Hijazi affairs. Because Christians were prohibited from traveling beyond Jeddah, throughout the nineteenth century, Popham and other British representatives were largely powerless without Muslim employees like Mahdi Ali Khan to guide and represent their interests.[8]

As early as 1806, George Annesley (Viscount Valentia) reported the presence of an East India Company agent by the name of Hammed Nasser. In 1826, the British appointed Hüseyin Agha, who simultaneously served as Mehmed Ali Pasha's commercial agent. In 1832, he was succeeded by an Armenian Muslim of Baghdadi origin, Maalim Yusof. Later, Yusof demanded and was eventually granted a regular salary and the insignia of vice-consul.[9] By the 1830s and 1840s, Indian Muslim agents and vice-consuls also were being deployed in Mocha.[10]

The growing intensification of the East India Company's consular interests in the region coincided with the voyage of the steamship *Hugh Lindsay* in 1830. Aggressively backed by the Bombay Presidency, even when plans for the ship and its proposed Red Sea route had been discarded by the East India Company's court of directors, the *Hugh Lindsay* quickly proved its worth, reducing the journey from Bombay to Suez to a mere twenty-one days. Seeing the potential benefits of steam technology, the Bombay Presidency looked to the Red Sea with renewed interest.[11] By 1837, a regular monthly steam-powered mail service had been established between Bombay and Suez. In 1841, the Peninsular and Oriental Steamship Navigation Company secured a concession for the rights to regular service between Egypt and Bombay. And by the 1840s and 1850s, European shipping companies began chartering steamships to facilitate pilgrimage traffic. By the end of the century, the majority of goods imported to Jeddah were British, and roughly half of all commerce had fallen into Indian hands.[12] Thus from at least the 1850s on, the increasing interconnectedness of steamship travel had begun to accelerate Jeddah's incorporation into British India's strategic thinking.

The opening of the Red Sea to regular steamship services, however, remained dependent on military support from British India to ensure its success. In order to provide a coaling station for its ships, the Bombay Presidency forcibly seized the island of Socotra, off the Horn of Africa, in 1835. Britain's escapade in Socotra ultimately proved disastrous. Four years later, when the port of Aden was found to offer a better harbor and climate than that of Socotra, Aden's ruler, like Socotra's, was intimidated, bribed, and ultimately overpowered.[13]

For Istanbul, British aggression in the southern Red Sea was a troubling development. Although the Ottoman state had not ruled Yemen directly since 1636, the seizure of Aden was deeply provocative.[14] The arrival of European colonialism on the Arabian Peninsula, particularly in such close proximity to Mecca and Medina, openly challenged Ottoman and Islamic beliefs in the sanctity and inviolability of the Arabian Peninsula by non-Muslims. In response, between 1849 and 1872, the Sublime Porte would launch its own defensive expansion into the Tihama coast and northern Yemen aimed at reestablishing Ottoman claims to territorial sovereignty in the region and to safeguard against further encroachments on Yemen and the Hijaz.[15]

Britain's aggressive stance in the Gulf of Aden also heralded a new era of extraterritorial representation throughout the region. By the 1820s and 1830s, East India Company contacts with southern Red Sea ports such as Jeddah and Mocha began to shift from more informal relations via commercial agents into more institutionalized modes of extraterritorial representation. Roughly coinciding with the 1838 Treaty of Balta Liman, through which Britain forced the Ottoman Empire to liberalize trade, open its ports, and lower tariffs, as well as the seizure of Aden in 1839, the East India Company began to appoint "English" (i.e., non-Muslim or nonnative) agents to

Red Sea posts such as Jeddah, Mocha, Suez, and Qusayr. In 1838, Alexander Ogilvie was recognized by the Foreign Office as Jeddah's first English vice-consul. Emulating the British, the French founded a vice-consulate with a local Armenian representative in 1839, who eventually was replaced by a Frenchman, Fulgence Fresnel, in 1843. The opening of British and French consular posts would serve as a precedent, eventually leading to the opening of new consulates in Jeddah by the Netherlands (1869–72), Sweden and Norway (1876), Austria (1880), and Russia (1891). By the end of the century, Greece and Spain also had opened consulates. In addition to these European states, Qajar Iran's consulate was the only one representing an independent Muslim power.[16]

To underscore the significance of this dramatic shift in the Red Sea's balance of power, only a few decades earlier, in 1778, Sultan Abdülhamid I (r. 1774–89) had considered "the sea of Suez" and the "noble pilgrimage to Meccah" to be wholly Muslim affairs. The sultan had warned his governor in Egypt that "to suffer Frankish ships to navigate therein, or to neglect opposing it, is betraying your Sovereign, your religion, and every Mahometan."[17] As Ottoman authorities eventually came to understand, citing the precedent of India itself, although Europeans might arrive under the guise of commerce or science, the prospect of violence, both physical and epistemological, was never far behind. By the 1850s, the arrival of regular European steamship services had even begun to infect the Ottomans' cartographic imagination of the region, leading to a shift away from the traditional usage of Sea of Suez (*Bahr-ı Süveys*) to the adoption of the Europeanized "Red Sea" (*Bahr-ı Ahmer*).[18]

By the 1870s, visions of Ottoman supremacy in the Red Sea had been consigned to the realm of bitter fantasies. Writing in 1874–75 aboard the first Ottoman frigate to pass through the Suez Canal en route to India, Yeniçeşmeli Hâfız Fâik Efendi, a student at the Ottoman Naval Academy (*Mekteb-i Fünun-ı Bahriye*), could do little more than document the sense of loss and anger that he felt while sailing through the southern Red Sea. Hâfız Fâik's account brims with enthusiasm over his visit to Jeddah and the Hijaz, but as the crew moves farther south, the mood of his text darkens. When the crew approaches Perim Island, Bab al-Mandab, and Aden, the omnipresence of the British flag flying over territories that previously had flown the Ottoman standard stirred a sense of grief and sorrow in him. Perhaps it was only fitting that British authorities imposed an unexpectedly harsh twenty-one-day quarantine on their vessel. On hearing this news, the Ottoman consul could do little more than commiserate with the plight of the frigate and its passengers. Confronted with the material manifestations of British occupation, Hâfız Fâik fumed, "hour by hour our fury and hatred for the English increased." As he complained, although the British might appear to be lovers of justice (*adaleti sever görünürler*), in reality they were little more than an internationally sanctioned "band of thieves" (*gasıb güruhu*) and "pirates" (*deniz hırsızları*). Indeed, he wondered how anyone could possibly distinguish between Aden's supposedly legitimate occupation as a coaling station and outright piracy.[19] Despite the depth of these resentments, throughout the nineteenth century no Muslim power—not even the Ottoman Empire—was in a position to impede Britain's naval expansion into the Red Sea.

Dangerous Exports: Mecca as the Refuge of Indian Fanaticism?

The middle decades of the nineteenth century revealed that Britain's steam-powered imperialism had spawned a number of unintended consequences. By the 1850s, British observers had begun to note the potential dangers and embarrassments presented by the rising tide of Indian Ocean pilgrims and long-term pious settlers residing in the Holy Cities (*mücavir*; plural *mücavirin*). As early as 1814, explorer Johann Ludwig Burckhardt had commented on the wretched state of Indian pilgrims, but little urgency was attached to these observations before the Indian Revolt of 1857–58 and the international cholera crisis of 1865–66.[20] Prior to these events British officials had not yet fully considered the potential link between the hajj and its capacity to fuel epidemics, political subversion, and interimperial legal conflicts. As a consequence, no passports or travel documents were required of pilgrims from British territories despite Ottoman proposals from as early as the 1840s. Likewise, no real effort was made to document the numbers of pilgrims and migrants, nor was there much that British officials thought could be done to curb the proliferation of indigent pilgrims because the government felt strongly that it had "no right to prevent any person who desires to do so, from proceeding on pilgrimage."[21]

In sharp contrast to this laissez-faire attitude, Richard Burton's experiences during his infamous pilgrimage in disguise in 1853 convinced him that the problem of indigent pilgrims and pious refugees eventually would have much wider political implications. In his pilgrimage narrative, Burton relates the tale of a Punjabi who, "finding life unendurable at home," sold his possessions, gathered his family, and set out for Mecca. As with many poor pilgrims of the period, it was highly likely that this family either would fall victim to physical privations or settle in the Hijaz permanently. Using this example, Burton described what he considered a dangerous pattern of Muslim emigration and potential radicalization. He warned, "To an 'Empire of Opinion,' this emigration is fraught with evils. It sends forth a horde of malcontents that ripen into bigots; it teaches foreign nations to despise our rule; and it unveils the present nakedness of once wealthy India. And we have both prevention and cure in our own hands."[22]

Burton's so-called cure prescribed that pilgrims should be made to prove their solvency before being permitted to embark from Indian ports. He further recommended that pilgrims be made to register with the vice-consul on their arrival in Jeddah. Burton also pointed to the need for a stronger British diplomatic presence in the region. In short, Burton accurately predicted that the hajj increasingly would be perceived as an outlet for anti-British sentiment. Moreover, he understood how easily negative opinions about British rule could be spread to other parts of the Muslim world via the hajj and the diaspora of Indian exiles who were beginning to circulate around it. In retrospect, the steps recommended by Burton were at least twenty to thirty years ahead of their time. Only two years after the publication of his pilgrimage account, the Indian Revolt shook British India to its core. For much of the rest of the nineteenth century, but especially prior to the 1880s, the traumas of Indian resistance provided the primary lens—or, perhaps more accurately, the blinders—through which British relations with the Hijaz and the hajj would be viewed.

For the most part, British officials labeled the Indian Revolt as an example of Muslim fanaticism. Despite the oversimplified assumptions behind such views, much of the symbolism of the rebellion was undeniably Islamic. On capturing the Mughal capital of Delhi and collecting their would-be emperor, Indian rebels fashioned the elderly Mughal emperor, Bahadur Shah II (r. 1837–57), as leader of the revolt. Uprisings followed in predominantly Muslim areas, such as the North West Frontier and the recently annexed province of Awadh. Therefore, it is not surprising that contemporary British observers tended to conflate the revolt with previous frontier jihads in the subcontinent.[23]

Such responses are best exemplified by the life and work of Sayyid Ahmad Barelvi (1786–1831). Like many Indian religious leaders dislocated by rapid changes in India's legal and educational systems, he took refuge in Mecca. During the 1820s, he twice performed the hajj and resided in Mecca from 1821 to 1824, where he is purported to have come under the influence of the militant Arabian reform movement of Muḥammad ibn ʿAbd al-Wahhāb (1703–92).[24] In his semiofficial history, *The Indian Musalmans* (1871), W. W. Hunter explicitly blamed Barelvi's religiopolitical activism in North India as the inspiration behind the Indian Revolt. Lacing his analysis with stereotypes and exaggerations, Hunter vividly described "Wahhabi" influence as a "chronic conspiracy" and a "standing rebel camp" threatening India's frontiers and internal security.[25] Although subsequent scholarship has repeatedly proven that Wahhabism and the numerous nineteenth-century renewal and reform movements of India do not share a common ancestry, the terminology used to describe these groups was interchangeable from the perspective of colonial officials and an essential element of British fears concerning Indian contacts with the broader Islamic world.[26] As a consequence Hunter's readership was left to assume that external "Arabian" influences or an inherent Muslim "exceptionalism," rather than heavy-handed British policies, were the primary source of Muslim radicalism in India. As Cemil Aydın argues, it was during this era that colonial officials began to render all Muslims as racially distinct. Muslim resistance was framed as a racial defect, explainable only through reference to their peculiar faith and civilizational identity. As a result of these racialized assumptions, Muslim resistance to unjust colonial rule and demands for more equitable rights within European empires were consistently delegitimized, minoritized, and denied as manifestations of an irreducible Muslim alterity.[27]

As colonial officials struggled to interpret the root causes of the revolt, they consistently chose to frame the rebellion as a racial or "anthropological failure," not "as a political or economic event." There was "an explosion of ethnographic research, collection, and writing in the last decades of the nineteenth century, as the state sought to accumulate the knowledge necessary both to explain the occurrence of the rebellion and to assure that it would never happen again." By acquiring comprehensive ethnographic knowledge of Indian customs, religion, caste, and ethnic character, colonial officials believed that ultimately they could come to "know" the peoples and cultures of India and differentiate between loyal communities and those suspected of harboring fanatical tendencies. It was this transformation in the production of knowledge that marked the ultimate transition from the rule of the East India Company to that of the British Crown. It signaled British India's rebirth as an "ethnographic state."[28]

Despite Queen Victoria's 1858 proclamation of religious tolerance and noninterference declaring the end of aggressive missionary activity in India, the Raj's ethnographic turn ensured that religion would become the primary "site of the colonial encounter."[29] The colonial state's reliance on anthropology not only made it a consumer of ethnographic knowledge pertaining to religion, but increasingly this meant that it would act as the ultimate arbiter of Islamic law and the "protector" of proper Islamic tradition and ritual. In turn, the notion that religion could genuinely be exempt from colonial interference was an unsustainable fiction because colonial officials so thoroughly conflated Islam and Islamic law with the causes of political subversion.[30]

In the immediate aftermath of the Great Rebellion and continued Muslim resistance, the British constructed their narrative of Muslim disloyalty around the notion of so-called Wahhabi conspiracies. The "phantom" threat of Wahhabi plots sparked a wave of persecution and trials throughout the 1860s and early 1870s, which led to the transportation and exile of rebel leaders.[31] In this climate of fear, Muslim leaders accused of harboring jihadist sentiments were harassed and made to prove their loyalty. It became increasingly clear that the newly installed British Raj would take up the tools of Islamic theology and law against its Muslim subjects. As the post-revolt realities of British colonial rule set in, Indian discourse on jihad was reframed accordingly. A flood of fatwas challenged the validity of jihad, arguing that as long as Muslims were allowed to practice their religious duties without interference from the state, India could not be considered *dār al-ḥarb* (abode of war). As direct confrontation with the British government became increasingly impractical, Muslim intellectual discourse largely shifted from jihad to a pragmatic advocacy of principled accommodation to alien rule.[32]

Many of those who refused to temper their dissent found themselves labeled as fanatics, fugitives, and outlaws. Some of these men were swept up in anti-Wahhabi show trials, while others were left to languish without trial in the penal archipelago of the Andaman Islands. The more fortunate were either deported or escaped into exile in Afghanistan, Central Asia, Istanbul, and the Ottoman Empire's Arab provinces. Many of these exiles had sought refuge in the Hijaz and subsequently had settled there. With the exception of Jeddah, the Hijaz was forbidden to non-Muslims because of its sacred status. More important, Indian exiles seeking refuge in Mecca, Medina, or Ta'if also found shelter from British extraterritoriality and extradition because they became symbols of the Ottoman state's defense of its sovereignty in the face of British interference. Istanbul also came to understand the value of these exiles as interimperial middlemen. Labeled convicts and outlaws by the British, in the eyes of Muslims, Indian exiles such as Sayyid Faḍl ibn ʿAlawī, Maulana Rahmatullah Kairanwi, and Haji Imdadullah Makki were men of great religious authority and communal prestige. They offered Ottoman officials in Istanbul ready-made access to political influence over a variety of Indian and Hadrami networks with tentacles stretching from the Hijaz and Yemen to India and Southeast Asia. Thus Istanbul's extension of official patronage to these colonial cosmopolitans allowed the Ottoman state to associate itself with their scholarly or evenly saintly credentials. These exiles also provided a nonmilitary means for the Ottoman state to signal sympathy with Muslim resistance to European colonialism or to disseminate anticolonial propaganda across the Indian Ocean. As a result, even decades after the 1857 revolt, British officials continued to worry over the far-reaching dimensions of the Indian Muslim diaspora in the Hijaz and the wider Ottoman Empire.[33]

If, as W. W. Hunter suggested, Muslim anticolonialism in India was subject to external influences from Arabia and the rest of the Islamic world, colonial officials also found it reasonable to assume that events in India eventually might have a similar impact on public opinion in the Hijaz, the Arabian Peninsula, and the wider Ottoman and Islamic worlds. In an increasingly interconnected world of steam and print, seemingly unrelated anti-European or anti-Christian episodes in one corner of the Islamic world held the potential to kindle outbreaks of violence in other areas, further contributing to widening patterns of Muslim resistance to European expansion. Thus as Richard Burton had predicted, the fallout generated by India's numerous frontier jihads, the First Anglo-Afghan War (1839), and the Great Rebellion of 1857–58 likely had sent tremors of anti-British sentiment throughout the Muslim world.[34]

Violent Precedents: The Death of a Consul and the Birth of the Capitulations in the Hijaz

The first evidence confirming British fears of diasporic radicalism seems to have been the outbreak of anti-Christian violence in Jeddah's infamous 1858 *fitna* (civil unrest, riots). On June 15, 1858, a premeditated slaughter of Christians, Europeans, and European-protected persons took place in Jeddah. That night the British and French consulates were attacked and ransacked and their respective flags pulled down. Among the victims, the British vice-consul was reportedly cut into pieces and thrown from the window of his residence. The French consul and his wife also were murdered. Allegedly their bodies were dragged naked through the streets, urged on by the cheers of local women. The homes and property of Christians and persons closely associated with the European consulates were plundered. In all, twenty-two Europeans and Christians, mostly of Greek origin, were slain. Twenty-six more victims were eventually rescued by *The Cyclops*, a nearby British steam frigate.[35]

This spasm of violence was the culmination of tensions that had been building in the Hijaz since the Crimean War (1853–56) and its immediate aftermath. With the conclusion of the Treaty of Paris in 1856, the Ottoman Empire ostensibly became a member of the European family of nations, guaranteeing the Ottomans the same legitimacy and rights to international existence and territorial integrity as any other member of this club. It is no coincidence that the *Islahat Fermanı* (Reform Edict) of February 1856, formally granting equality to non-Muslims in all aspects of life and paving the way for the complete overhaul of Ottoman state and society, was issued barely a month prior to the conclusion of the postwar settlement. The Treaty of Paris directly tied domestic reforms to international recognition. Indeed, the promises of reform were the price of admission into European international society.[36] However, pressure for their immediate and full implementation opened deep rifts between the imperial center and its Arab provinces. Muslim apprehensions concerning the leveling of legal distinctions between Muslim and non-Muslim subjects (*dhimmīs* or Peoples of the Book) were especially pronounced in the Hijaz. Combined with Istanbul's open alliance with Britain and France during the Crimean War, secularizing reforms opened provincial administrators to charges that the center had taken a radically pro-European/pro-Christian turn.[37]

At the local level, Hijazi opposition to the Tanzimat reforms coincided with growing anxiety over the increasing dominance of European capital and shipping interests in Jeddah and the wider Red Sea. These economic concerns were further compounded by the growing visibility of European consular officials and their local protégés. However, no issue was more controversial than the potential abolition of the slave trade. In 1847, the British had been able to push Istanbul toward major concessions regarding the trafficking of slaves.[38] In April 1855, the sharif of Mecca, ʿAbd al-Muṭṭalib ibn Ghālib (r. 1851–56 and 1880–82), circulated a rumor that Egyptian authorities had been ordered to prohibit the sale of Circassian, Ethiopian, and African slaves. It also claimed that slaves exported from the Hijaz to Egypt would be returned. In addition to voicing their displeasure over the steps that had been taken, the letter echoed rumors that a complete prohibition on the slave trade soon would be imposed.[39]

As the sharif concluded, Ottoman prohibition of the slave trade provided the perfect "pretext" for an open rebellion against Istanbul. On October 30, 1855, on ʿAbd al-Muṭṭalib's instructions, a fatwa was produced proclaiming that any ban on the slave trade was "contrary to Islamic law." The fatwa declared that as a result of this and other anti-Islamic innovations, the Turks had revealed themselves as apostates (mürted). A jihad was proclaimed against the Christians and polytheists (jihād ʿalā al-Naṣārā wa-l-mushrikīn yā muʾminīn), a category that now included the Ottoman state. Throughout Mecca Ottoman garrisons and foreigners were attacked by mobs.[40]

It would take seven months to put down the sharif's revolt. Although ʿAbd al-Muṭṭalib's capture in June 1856 and subsequent exile to Salonica (and later Istanbul) eventually quelled the immediate crisis, the revolt proved a harbinger of things to come.[41] Prohibition of the slave trade was only one manifestation of the widening gulf between Istanbul's Western-facing modernization and the Islamic character of the Hijaz. Again, in 1857, British pressure produced an Ottoman ferman prohibiting the trafficking of African slaves.[42] However, this time the Hijaz was exempted. Despite this concession to Hijazi opposition, local resentments against Istanbul and its European allies continued to fester.

In June 1858, European consular overreach reignited the embers of Hijazi resistance to Western intrusion. The incident that precipitated the massacre of Jeddah's Christian population began with a quarrel between

FIGURE 1.1 Ottoman illustration of Jeddah's harbor. *Source:* BOA, PLK, 46/1.

two members of an Indian Muslim household, both of whom initially were presumed to be British subjects. It was a seemingly banal dispute involving questions of property, inheritance, power of attorney, and the contested registration of a ship docked in the Jeddah harbor (see figure 1.1), the *Irani*. The boat was registered under the English flag and originally part of a company jointly owned by members of the Jawhar family. Originally ownership had been shared between Ibrahim Jawhar and his slave, Salih Jawhar.[43] Following Ibrahim's death, his brother Said was named the administrator of his commercial property. Shortly thereafter Said also died, leaving the administration of the property to his daughter. As a result, Salih Jawhar was elected as the estate's agent. However, when Hasan bin Ibrahim Jawhar, the estate's ultimate beneficiary, reached the age of majority and married his uncle Said's daughter, Salih Jawhar's oversight was no longer required.[44]

At this point Salih and Hasan Jawhar fell into deep dispute over the vessel. When Hasan asked for his share of the business in order to trade on his own, Salih refused to relinquish control. In response, Hasan sought the assistance of Faraj Yusr, an Indian Muslim under British protection, who was the chief merchant of Jeddah and by all accounts its richest person in the 1850s.[45] In addition to his shipping interests, Yusr emerged as the Hijaz's principal banker, lending money to the Ottoman provincial administration at exorbitant interest rates.[46] As Hijazi and Hadrami merchants well understood, access to large-scale credit arrangements offered Europeans and their colonial protégés an undisputed advantage over local capital. Yusr also had cultivated close contacts with the British consulate, periodically serving as the acting vice-consul in Jeddah.[47] In many respects, Yusr was the perfect embodiment of the rifts that consular protection and privilege opened not just between Muslims and Christians but also within the Muslim community itself.

Faraj Yusr, allegedly a personal enemy of Salih's, had called him to account for his financial supervision of Hasan's inheritance. Fearing punitive actions from Yusr, Salih decided to dissolve his partnership with Hasan and seize full ownership of the boat. To do so, Salih Jawhar claimed that he was an Ottoman national. Despite his intimate ties to Jeddah's Indian Muslim community, as the investigations surrounding the 1858 massacre eventually revealed, he was a Muslim born in what had been the Ottoman province of Morea (ceded to Greece in 1829).[48] In his attempt to disentangle the vessel from the partnership, he applied to the *kaymakam* (district governor) of Jeddah, Ibrāhīm Agha, to have the ship's flag changed from British to Ottoman. The *kaymakam* forwarded the application to the governor (*vali*), Mehmed Namık Pasha, and the provincial council. The council decided that the partnership's property could be divided and Salih awarded the *Irani*. According to Ottoman documentation of the affair, at this point Salih declared his wish to conduct his future business concerns under Ottoman legal protection.[49]

Because the company was originally registered under British protection, under the terms of the Capitulations, the attendance of a British consular representative was required. However, Vice-Consul Stephen Page was away in Egypt, and the consulate had been left in the hands of Faraj Yusr, who was the acting vice-consul. Although Yusr argued that they had no jurisdiction, Ottoman authorities ignored him. On his return from Egypt, Page learned of the situation. Within a matter of hours, Salih Jawhar was being held in the British consulate. The register of the ship was produced from the consular files, certifying that Salih and Ibrahim Jawhar were the co-owners of the vessel, that it had been registered in Calcutta, and that it had always flown the British flag. According to British Admiralty law, however, any attempt to change the registration of a British vessel to avoid legal action would render it subject to confiscation.[50]

At this point, Vice-Consul Page reached out to Captain William Pullen of the *Cyclops*, a British warship anchored off the coast surveying telegraph cable routes. As Pullen recounts, Page's advice was clear. The Capitulations gave him full authority to seize the ship:

> The Consul then suggested to me to haul down the Turkish flag, which she, at the moment, was flying illegally, and take possession of the ship for the purpose of sending her to a Vice-Admiralty Court to be adjudicated upon. He called my attention to several Treaties existing with Turkey, giving to the Consular authorities *full jurisdiction* over all British subjects in the Ottoman ports *"in the same and as ample manner as if Her Majesty had acquired such power or jurisdiction by the cession or conquest of territory."*[51]

The implications of this legal logic were far reaching. From 1858 on, British officials began to assert that Indian Muslims residing in Hijaz were subject to the empire's extraterritorial jurisdiction. In essence Page and Pullen were making a de facto declaration of Jeddah's absorption into the legal orbit of British India. And as will be discussed in greater detail in chapter 2, they were also advancing the hitherto unprecedented argument that the Capitulations and consular jurisdiction were fully applicable to the sacred territories of the Hijaz.

Acting on this position, Page and Pullen notified the *kaymakam* that the *Irani* would be seized. The vessel was boarded, the Ottoman flag was lowered, and the British standard was once again raised. According to Aḥmad ibn Zaynī Dahlān's famous chronicle, *Khulāṣat al-Kalām fī Bayān Umarāʾ al-Balad al-Ḥarām* (1887), the violence that ensued was a result of the vice-consul having insulted the Ottoman flag (and, by implication, the sultan, the caliphate, and Islam). As Dahlān explains, "news spread that after he brought down the Ottoman flag, he trampled upon it with his foot, and spoke in an indecent manner."[52] This basic narrative also made its way into Ottoman reporting. In the Ottoman version, after the English soldiers lowered the Ottoman flag, according to the testimony of a number of local witnesses, the flag was then "thrown into the sea."[53] Thus as Ottoman authorities argued, the massacre arose spontaneously from anger over the confiscation of the vessel and desecration of the flag.

However, European observers argued that such a trivial incident could not have precipitated an impromptu slaughter of Jeddah's Christians. Although the Foreign Office believed that the most probable cause for the violence was Muslim bitterness over the increasing presence of Christians in the Islamic holy land, noting that such an uprising had long been expected, British officials also feared that the violence was related to the ongoing rebellion in India. In reality, however, the violence was more the product of simmering anger over the increasingly interventionist role of European consuls in Jeddah's economic affairs. And, as subsequent investigations proved, the disputes that sparked the riots had extremely specific local roots, differing widely from the transregional causes imagined by panicked British officials.

In the aftermath of the violence, the British foreign secretary ordered Captain Pullen to obtain the punishment of the murderers. Pullen threatened that if justice was not meted out hastily, he would attack Jeddah. Although Pullen was told that all of the murderers were known, the governor informed him that he would have to wait for the approval of the sultan before any executions could be performed. As Ottoman records make clear, Istanbul had hoped to avoid European interference in the case. As a result, "symbolic" convictions were needed to restore relations with Britain and France. However, as Mehmed Namık pointed out, the participants numbered in the hundreds. He refused to accept the idea of executing a handful of individuals as a peace offering. In the meantime, Lieutenant General İsmail Hakkı Pasha was dispatched from Istanbul to investigate and carry out the demanded executions. However, he would not arrive until August 2. Assuming that Ottoman hesitation was merely a stalling tactic, on June 23, Captain Pullen issued a thirty-six-hour ultimatum. Two days later, the bombardment of Jeddah commenced. By the end of the crisis, seven (including one family and two female slaves) were dead and much of Jeddah's population had fled either to Mecca or to the desert interior.[54] Despite the governor's pleas, Captain Pullen rashly opted to fire on Jeddah just as pilgrims were returning from Mecca. Although the British ambassador eventually would apologize for shelling Jeddah, blaming Pullen's impetuousness, the message sent by this overwhelming show of force was crystal clear.

In the aftermath of the bombardment, British demands for blood would not go unsatisfied. On August 5, İsmail Hakkı Pasha gave the British the rough justice they sought, approving the public beheading of eleven men.

As Mehmed Namık suggested, these were merely sacrificial peace offerings. The group consisted of a tinsmith, a tobacconist, a coffeehouse keeper, a banker, a shoemaker, a butcher, a blacksmith, a diver, a ship pilot, and two seamen. Whatever their respective roles, they were not the elite architects of the uprising.

Reflecting on the bombardment and the executions, Captain Pullen wrote,

> In carrying out this business, my endeavor was to impress on the people of Jeddah that I had been sent to punish, and that they could not commit such deeds without paying for them. For I cannot banish the idea that they have fancied from their position, and almost in the character of a holy city, from its nearness to Mecca, that they might do many things with impunity. I trust this will be a lesson they will not soon forget . . .
>
> The bombarding happened at a time when no pilgrims were in the town; and they will be able to carry to all parts of the Mahometan world how England and France avenge the murder of their subjects and Representatives, and also how the hostilities ceased as much for their sakes as for other considerations. And taking into account the state of affairs in India it was one great reason why I insisted on the execution taking place in sight of the ships.[55]

As Pullen's comments demonstrate, he viewed the Jeddah uprising almost entirely through the prism of the 1857 revolt and the ongoing security crisis in British India. With this in mind, on the day before the executions, he sent an officer to instruct the Ottoman authorities on the exact spot where the punishments should be meted out. The spot was "a dry spit of coral reef, running out into the inner harbour, and so situated as to be visible from the town and from the merchant-vessels." At the time of execution, Pullen positioned the fully armed crew of the *Cyclops* alongside the beach and ordered all Anglo-Indian ships in the port to do the same. Pullen's motive was to ensure that this gruesome spectacle of collective punishment and "retributive justice should be known in India."[56]

Captain Pullen officially declared that although there were "no doubt many murderers and instigators still unpunished," he considered any "further effusion of blood" to be "unnecessary." However, the matter was not over. Pullen would eventually convince the British ambassador that the principal instigators of the violence remained at large. Citing Article 42 of the Capitulations, British authorities demanded that the case be reopened and tried by a mixed tribunal composed of British, French, and Ottoman representatives, which would operate independently from the Hijaz's provincial government.[57] Under these rules, the British and French commissioners were to "take direct part, on the same footing with the Turkish authorities, in the trial of the accused."[58]

Under enormous pressure, the Ottomans consented to the mixed tribunal and eventually concluded a fresh round of investigations in January 1859. The commissioners' final report revealed that the violence had been plotted with the knowledge and consent of Ottoman officials in the Jeddah customs house. It was discovered that on the day of the massacre, *kaymakam* Ibrāhīm Agha, on hearing of the consul's unilateral decision to remove the Ottoman flag from the *Irani*, had called a meeting in the customs house. ʿAbdullāh Agha, the *muhtesib* (market inspector) of Jeddah, was tasked with gathering the meeting's principals. As a result of this meeting, what ostensibly began as a more limited plot to intimidate the British consul eventually grew into a full-blown mob under his direction.

ʿAbdullāh Agha was implicated in ordering Shaykh Saʿīd al-ʿAmūdī to rouse the Hadrami community. Following evening prayers, the Hadramis were armed and led to the docks to plot the massacre.[59] The *muhtesib* nursed a long-running grudge against the British consulate for its role in the revocation of the Ottoman salt monopoly that he had once controlled. Much like the *muhtesib*, the Hadrami mercantile community saw itself as the victim of European steam power. The primary source of Hadrami anger stemmed from their opposition to Anglo-Ottoman efforts to abolish the slave trade. The Hadrami colony in Jeddah, numbering some 2,000 around 1850, was, like their compatriots in other Red Sea and East African ports, heavily involved in that lucrative trade. More generally, Hadrami ship owners, crew members, and stevedores resented the damage being done to their share of the shipping and pilgrimage trades as a result of the proliferation of Egyptian, Greek, and Indian protégés with superior access to European capital and consular protection.[60]

In January 1859, ʿAbdullāh Agha and Shaykh al-ʿAmūdī were found guilty in the first degree and sentenced to death. The *kaymakam* and the other notables present at the meetings where the plot had been hatched were found guilty in the second degree and sentenced to life imprisonment and exile to Ottoman Europe. Those deemed guilty of abetting the violence indirectly or neglecting their official responsibilities to protect the Christian population were each given five-year prison terms.[61]

Fanatical Fantasies: "Mutiny" and "Massacre" in the Colonial Imagination

Despite the conviction and execution of the *fitna*'s leading figures and the painstaking investigations, which mined the minutiae of the local rivalries that had precipitated the violence in Jeddah, British officials were left with lingering doubts. Both during and after the investigations that followed the massacre, British officials obsessively, yet misguidedly, attempted to draw a direct connection between the violence in Jeddah and the simultaneous rebellion in India. One of the initial theories put forward by Captain Pullen suggested that an itinerant shaykh from Delhi, accompanied by some sixty followers, was somehow responsible for inciting the violence in Jeddah. Fearing that similar attacks might be in store for Europeans stationed in Cairo and Suez, Alfred Walne, the British consul in Cairo, remarked that "from the breaking out of the revolt in India, in which Moslems have taken such a prominent part, there has been reason to suppose that Indian and Persian partisans have done their best to increase, if not excite," anti-British sentiments across the region.[62] Despite the overwhelming evidence that a more localized set of grievances had sparked the violence in Jeddah, over time the British conflation of the Jeddah massacre with the so-called Sepoy Mutiny developed into a kind of colonial legend. British theories concerning the far-reaching anticolonial influence of ex-mutineers and Indian exiles in the Hijaz remained in circulation even decades later. As Sir Bartle Frere, a former governor of the Bombay Presidency, observed, "the Hedja[z] is the natural asylum for fanatical Moslem exiles from India." He added that even though many of the exiles "pass their lives in a congenial atmosphere of fanaticism," their strong influence "cannot be safely disregarded either in Aden or in India."[63]

Initially it was believed that one of these "fanatical" exiles ultimately was responsible for orchestrating the 1858 massacre of Jeddah's Christian population. In the months following the violence in Jeddah, British imaginings of an Indian connection coalesced around one personality, Sayyid Faḍl ibn ʿAlawī (1825–1900).[64] Sayyid Faḍl was born in Malabar to an elite

Hadrami family. He was the son of Sayyid ʿAlawī (1749–1843), who, owing to his leadership in the ʿAlawiyya order, had gained the status of a saint. His shrine at Mambram became a site of pilgrimage memorializing his martyrdom and anticolonial resistance. Following his father's death, Sayyid Faḍl used his family's prestige to mobilize Muslim peasants in violent protests against British land tenure policies and the Hindu landlords they benefited. In 1852, as a result of the so-called Moplah Outrages, on the recommendations of Malabar commissioners H. V. Conolly and Thomas Strange, Faḍl was deported to the Hijaz. Later in 1855, Faḍl also was accused of having orchestrated the murder of Conolly in revenge for his exile.[65]

As soon as Sayyid Faḍl arrived in the Hijaz, however, British authorities in India began to worry that Mecca was becoming an anticolonial haven. During ʿAbd al-Muṭṭalib's 1855–56 revolt, vice-consul Page had raised the alarm in Aden and India that Faḍl had "taken a very forward part in the bloody outbreak at Mecca" in resistance to the suppression of the slave trade. As Page warned prior to his murder in 1858, Faḍl's influence was magnified by his constant contact with Indian pilgrims in Mecca.[66] Page also was extremely concerned by Faḍl's 1853 visit to Istanbul, where he was reported to have been feted and given official recognition and a stipend of 2,500 Ottoman *kuruş* per month.[67]

Owing to these suspicions, during the investigations of the 1858 Jeddah riots, Captain Pullen became obsessed with the idea that Faḍl must have played a leading role in the violence. During his investigations the political agent at Aden, W. M. Coghlan, also raised the issue that in the aftermath of the violence in Jeddah, Sayyid Faḍl had paid frequent visits to Mecca from his residence in Taʾif. Coghlan claimed that Faḍl had openly "expressed his hatred of the British," advocating that all "true believers" should resist their "authority" and work to "expel and destroy the Kafirs." Moreover, he warned that under the influence of Faḍl and his ilk, "Mahometans" who "flock" to Mecca from "every part" of the British Empire's "Eastern Possessions" were likely to return to their homes "imbued with baneful doctrines" and all too "willing to propagate them still further."[68]

At the same time, the events in Jeddah presented an opportunity to pressure Ottoman authorities into either surrendering Faḍl to British authorities or deporting him "to some remote part of the Turkish dominions, where his evil influence will not be felt."[69] Owing to accusations that Sayyid Faḍl had been one of the "chief instigators" of the violence at Jeddah, the Foreign

Office attempted to use the formation of the mixed tribunal at Jeddah to kill two birds with one stone. The Foreign Office instructed consul Walne to demand that Faḍl be extradited, deported to Aden, and dealt with by the Indian government. The Foreign Office also wondered if there might not be sufficient evidence to prove that he had been privy to the conspiracy. If so, they recommended that Article 42 of the Capitulations be invoked. Thus despite having exiled Faḍl and branded him an outlaw, the Foreign Office still considered him a British subject and eligible for extradition. Foreign Office correspondence also makes clear that any proceedings against Faḍl in Jeddah were to be treated as a predetermined kangaroo court. If he was convicted, it was recommended that Faḍl be executed and that special care be taken "that he is tried for the murder of someone whose friends will not accept blood-money [diyya] in lieu of capital punishment." However, failing execution or extradition, it was hoped that Faḍl could be transferred "to some place situated in the Turkish dominions in Europe."[70]

In the end, however, there was simply no evidence incriminating Sayyid Faḍl. Nor was there any treaty of extradition through which he might be given up legally by Ottoman authorities for crimes committed outside Ottoman territory. As Mehmed Namık cautioned, owing to his revered status in the Hijaz, Faḍl's forced expulsion could not possibly be achieved without enormous embarrassment to the Ottoman government. The governor suggested that an "invitation from the Sultan would probably suffice to induce that person to remove to Constantinople, where authorities could make such provision as to his future residence as would be satisfactory to the British Government."[71]

Although no proof of Sayyid Faḍl's connection to the 1858 massacre in Jeddah was ever uncovered, this did nothing to allay British anxieties. Faḍl remained under British surveillance for decades. He was repeatedly denied permission to return to India. And although Faḍl is perhaps most famous for his failed attempts to install himself as the governor of Dhofar under Ottoman suzerainty in the late 1870s, in many respects Mehmed Namık's suggestion that Sayyid Faḍl be placed under Ottoman surveillance in Istanbul ultimately did come to pass. From 1880 on, concerned that he might provoke a dangerous confrontation with British authorities, Sultan Abdülhamid II kept Faḍl in Istanbul as an honored guest and occasional adviser on questions related to the Hijaz, Yemen, Oman, and the Indian Ocean. This, of course, only further stoked British imaginings of his role in Abdülhamid's supposed Pan-Islamic conspiracies.[72] In this way, Sayyid Faḍl, however accidentally, played a critical role in Britain's escalating obsession with the political surveillance of the Hijaz and the hajj between 1858 and the early 1880s. Throughout this period Faḍl became an archetypal symbol of the runaway outlaws and exiles haunting British fantasies of the Hijaz as a den of radicalization. Despite its deep flaws, this theory proved a remarkably durable script, one that would continue to resurface and evolve, particularly during moments when Anglo-Ottoman relations were most strained.

Titles in Transition: Caliph and Servant of the Two Holy Places

Between the late 1850s and early 1880s, the Hijaz also emerged as a focus of Britain's growing awareness of its connection to the Ottoman Caliphate. Following the psychological watershed of the 1857 revolt, Indian Muslims were forced to come to terms with the loss of a Muslim state and the consequences of foreign domination. Even after 1857, there were still those Muslim leaders who called for either jihad or *hijra*, citing Shah Abdul Aziz's (1746–1824) famous fatwa of 1803, which declared British-controlled India to be *dār al-ḥarb*.[73] However, British repression in the wake of the rebellion made it clear to most Indian Muslims that jihad was at best futile and at worst suicidal.[74] Defeated and deprived of Mughal power and prestige, Indian Muslims turned increasingly toward the Ottoman Caliphate "in search for an alternative psychological and spiritual center."[75] The Ottoman sultan was the only remaining independent Sunni power and the Servant of the Two Holy Places. The Ottoman dynasty embodied not only the survival and supremacy of Islamic law but also a living link to the temporal power and glory of the Islamic past.

India's gravitation toward the Ottoman Caliphate was a major change from the Mughal era. Although the Ottomans' and Mughals' diplomatic exchanges continued into the late eighteenth century, during their prime from roughly 1526 to 1707, the Mughals repeatedly refused to concede Ottoman claims to the "universal caliphate." Rather, the Mughals had regarded themselves as "caliphs within their own realms," citing Jalāl al-Dīn al-Dawwānī's (1427–1501) fatwa legitimizing the simultaneous presence of multiple caliphs.[76] However, Indian Muslims rapidly responded to the destruction of Mughal power by engaging in "the invention of tradition," a process of legitimizing change through references to the past, which usually occurs "when a rapid transformation of society weakens or destroys the social patterns for which 'old' traditions had been designed."[77] Indian Muslims were not the only Islamic society to engage in this kind of reevaluation of Ottoman caliphal authority. As the social and political fabric of the Muslim world as a whole came under increasing pressure from the imperial powers of Europe, especially Britain, France, the Netherlands, and Russia, disparate groups of Muslims from Central Asia to Indonesia rallied around the Ottoman Caliphate.

Eventually, the Ottoman state learned to harness and encourage this sentiment, but it was never completely theirs to control. In reality, the emerging global consciousness of Muslim solidarity and unity in the face of European imperialism, what became known to the West as Pan-Islam, was a by-product of the age of steam, print, and telegraphy. Although these technological revolutions emerged from European and American manufacturers and often were disseminated via colonial rule, Muslims worldwide quickly adopted the tools and infrastructures of empire and adapted them for purposes that their inventors had never imagined. Suddenly North Africa, Eurasia, and the Indian Ocean were linked by steamships and trains. From the 1860s on, telegraphy and the rise of a dynamic Muslim press linked intellectuals from disparate corners of the Muslim world like never before. Naturally, Muslims used these newly forged connections to discuss and debate their shared experiences of colonial domination and racism. Between the 1860s and 1880s, Istanbul-based journals such as al-Jawāʾib and Peyk-i İslam and the Paris-based al-ʿUrwat al-Wuthqa advanced the argument that Muslims shared an obligation to defend the newly reimagined Muslim world from colonial rule and work for the revival and reform of Islam.[78] By the 1870s and early 1880s, the diffuse strands of this global Pan-Islamic discourse eventually coalesced under the auspices of loyalty to the Ottoman sultan-caliph.

Especially during the reign of Abdülhamid II, the global revolutions in steam and print technologies enabled the Ottoman state to bolster the sultan-caliph's public image both at home and abroad. On the domestic front, the state was able to articulate official religious and national practices like never before. Partly in response to the shortcomings of the secular Tanzimat ideology of Ottomanism and the dramatic loss of European territories following the Russo-Ottoman War and the 1878 Treaty of Berlin, the Hamidian period was characterized by a growing sense that the Islamic character of the state needed to be reasserted. Internally, this ideological shift was meant to inoculate the empire's Muslim populations against the metastasis of proto-nationalist sentiments. Although theoretically the multinational empire could survive the loss of its Christian peripheries, if nationalism spread among its Muslim populations, representing roughly 73 percent of its remaining post-1878 population, the empire's fate would be sealed.[79]

This simultaneous shift in demography and imperial mood translated into a self-conscious effort among Ottoman intellectuals and bureaucrats to reinvigorate basic institutions, most notably shariʿa law and the caliphate. Within Ottoman lands this effort would manifest itself in revamped mechanisms of imperial education and loyalty production. There were new missionary efforts to convert or reform heterodox Muslims, such as the Yazidi and Shiʿi populations, and to promote an officially sanctioned Hanafi version of Sunni Islam. The state established a monopoly on the printing and inspection of the Qurʾan and supported the printing of thousands of Islamic legal and religious texts. Not coincidently, many of these works explicitly promoted and reinforced the legitimacy of the Ottoman dynasty's claims to the caliphate and its Hijazi appanage.[80]

According to the official myth, the title of caliph had devolved from the last Abbasid caliph, al-Mutawakkil III, to the Ottoman blood line as a result of the conquest of Mamluk Egypt by Selim I in 1517.[81] More important, the conquest of Egypt also brought Ottoman suzerainty over the Hijaz and custody of Mecca and Medina. Like the Mamluks before them, the Ottoman state took responsibility for the security of the hajj, its caravan routes, and the provisioning of economic and food subsidies to the barren Hijaz and its pious denizens. Although the Ottoman dynasty could not feasibly claim the Arab or Qurayshi descent from the Prophet Muḥammad that technically was required of heirs to the caliphate, the title of *Khādim al-Ḥaramayn al-Sharīfayn* and the responsibilities that it entailed proved more than sufficient support for Ottoman claims to global leadership of the Islamic community.[82] By the late nineteenth century, the legitimacy of Ottoman claims had acquired the customary weight of nearly four centuries.

A prime example of this promotion of Hamidian stewardship of Mecca and Medina can be found in the writings of Eyüp Sabri Pasha, an Ottoman naval officer, historian, and ethnographer of the Hijaz and Arabia. He also was an anti-Wahhabi polemicist and wrote extensively on the spiritual and legal underpinnings of the Ottoman Caliphate. His writings provide a vivid example of Hamidian public image-making. Eyüp Sabri explicitly stresses that the Ottoman sultans were the legitimate claimants to the title of caliph. As such, they were to be regarded as God's shadow on Earth (*Zıllullah fi'l Arz*), and obedience to their will was an immensely important sacred obligation (*fariza-i mühimme*) specified by Islamic law.[83]

In *Mirat ül-Haremeyn* (1883–88), an encyclopedic history and ethnography of Mecca, Medina, and the wider Arabian Peninsula, Eyüp Sabri elaborates on the connection between the Ottoman Caliphate and service to the Two Holy Places in Mecca and Medina. As he explains, although much ink had been spilled analyzing this title, in reality most of the supposed services provided by previous Islamic dynasties—such as the Umayyads, Abbasids, and Fatimids—were little more than tall tales and meaningless talk (*laf-ı bi mana*). Here he contrasts Ottoman solicitude for Mecca and Medina with what he regards as a shameful record of "indifference, injustice, and even attacks on the sacred towns" (*ilgisizlikler, haksızlık hatta mübarek beldelere hücumlar*) under previous dynasties. For Eyüp Sabri, the proof of Ottoman service to the *haremeyn* lay in the tangible public works (*asar-ı fiiliye*) provided by the state.[84]

In many respects Eyüp Sabri's modern clarification of the connection between caliphal legitimacy and material service to the Two Holy Places was a perfect expression of the age of modernizing progress in which he lived. His works speak to the dramatic uptick in the intensity of Ottoman state building and development in the Hijaz from the 1880s on. In this sense *Mirat ül-Haremeyn* serves as both a reaction to and an anticipation of the reengineering of the technologies of Ottoman rule and the physical infrastructures of the Hijaz taking place at the time. This Hamidian emphasis on the modernization of the Hijaz and the pilgrimage experience was meant to signal to Muslims and non-Muslims alike that the sultan-caliph was capable of properly organizing the hajj, ensuring the health and safety of the pilgrims, maintaining the Holy Places of Islam, and protecting Arabia from foreign attack. As we shall see, however, it also was an acknowledgment of the degree to which the European modernization of pilgrimage transport and administration was raising new expectations of the Hijaz's Muslim custodians. Indeed, European colonial regimes—most notably Britain—were beginning to explicitly challenge the Ottoman state as the premier sponsor and facilitator of the hajj's steam-powered modernization.

Europe had not always worked to challenge or undermine Ottoman claims to the caliphate. In the eighteenth and nineteenth centuries, the legitimacy of the Ottoman Caliphate paradoxically received validation from two unlikely sources: Russia and the caliphate's incorporation into Eurocentric diplomacy and international law. In 1774, the Treaty of Küçük Kaynarca, concluded after a devastating war with Russia, recognized Catherine the Great as the protector of Orthodox Christians in Ottoman lands. In exchange, the treaty recognized the Ottoman sultan's religious authority over Muslims living in Crimea and Russian lands. Thus the caliphate's ecumenical religious authority was formally extended outside Ottoman territory for the first time. In addition to validating Ottoman claims to the caliphate in an international treaty with a European power, the Treaty of Küçük Kaynarca offers important clues for understanding the Hamidian state's later retooling of the caliphate as an instrument of Ottoman foreign policy, extraterritoriality, and international law in the latter half of the nineteenth century.[85]

Particularly during the reign of Abdülhamid II, Ottoman claims to spiritual leadership over British and Russian Muslims were constructed as a kind of mirror image of European extraterritorial claims of protection on behalf of Christians living under Ottoman rule. By accentuating his roles as caliph and Servant of the Two Holy Places, Abdülhamid hoped to bolster the international standing of the Ottoman Empire as the preeminent protector of the global Muslim community. The international legal and diplomatic deployment of the caliphate was meant to remind Christian monarchs that if they could assert extraterritorial claims over Ottoman Christians, the caliph could hold a reciprocal right to assert his spiritual authority over Muslim subjects of European colonial empires.[86] Thus although the Ottoman Empire was unable to extend the same kinds of formal extraterritorial legal protections that Europeans could, it still approached foreign Muslim populations as potential assets. In this sense, the Pan-Islamic caliphate was articulated as a defensive instrument of diplomacy, foreign policy, and international law.[87] In a Christian-dominated imperial order, ideally the Ottoman Caliphate provided a safeguard (albeit a weak one) against European aggression and extraterritoriality at home. It also provided a platform from which the Ottoman state could advocate on behalf of the dignity and rights of Muslims facing discrimination, repression, and violence at the hands of European colonialism abroad.[88]

Here I second Faiz Ahmed's call for the "demilitarization" of the study of Pan-Islam. Too often, Euro-American scholarship has depicted Pan-Islam, similar to more contemporary transnational Islamist movements, as thoroughly anti-Western, fundamentalist, radical, and violent.[89] In reality Islamism, especially as practiced by the Ottoman state, was as much a search for peaceful accommodation with a belligerent, Islamophobic Europe as it was about civilizational conflict and revolt. Hamidian Pan-Islam actually imagined a more pragmatic vision of world order, positioning Ottoman spiritual sovereignty over the *umma* as a check on British temporal domination of the Islamic world. The sultan's Pan-Islamic foreign policy sought to guarantee Ottoman sovereignty by binding foreign Muslims and their colonial masters—especially the British—in a symbiotic embrace of "dual loyalty" to the caliph and the Crown. In turn, the Hamidian state hoped that colonial Muslims' deepening spiritual attachment to the caliphate would act as an effective deterrent to European military aggression against the Ottoman state.

This strategy generated a host of unintended consequences. Hamidian rhetoric aggravated Islamophobia in the European press and deepened colonial officials' fears of Muslim revolts. Thus even if the sultan's ultimate goal was to discourage European aggression against the Ottoman Empire, Pan-Islamic paranoia among colonial administrators ensured the reclassification of the caliphate as a threat to colonial security. As a result, the legitimacy of the Ottoman Caliphate and its connections to the Hijaz and the hajj increasingly became targets of British propaganda.[90]

This had not always been the case. Prior the 1870s, rather than demonizing it, the British Raj repeatedly had sought to emphasize its friendly diplomatic ties to the Ottoman Caliphate. During the Indian Revolt, the British sought and obtained permission for the safe passage of troops via Egypt. It also secured a proclamation from Sultan Abdülmecid I (r. 1839–61) advising Indian Muslims not to fight their British allies. The proclamation was circulated and read in mosques across India. Grand Vizier Mehmed Emin Ali Pasha even sent a message congratulating the British government on the recapture of Delhi. The Ottoman government donated one thousand pounds in relief funds for orphans, widows, and wounded soldiers. The sultan's indebtedness to British support during the recently concluded Crimean War left him with little choice but to give his caliphal blessing to the brutal suppression of the Indian uprising.[91]

In the two decades between the Crimean War and the Russo-Ottoman War of 1877–78, the British were more concerned with Russian expansion in Central Asia. As a result, Anglo-Ottoman relations remained strongly aligned against Russia. And on multiple occasions, the British encouraged pro-Ottoman sympathies in order to bolster their own legitimacy as allies of the caliphate or to check Russian advances in Central Asia. By the 1870s, however, Austen Henry Layard, the British ambassador at Istanbul, and Lord Lytton (Edward Robert Bulwer-Lytton), the viceroy of India, began to worry that the rising tide of pro-Ottoman sentiment in India eventually might be directed against the British in the event of a future deterioration of relations between London and Istanbul. As Lytton worried, "If either by pressure of public opinion at home, or political difficulty abroad, Your Majesty's Government should be forced into a policy of prominent aggression upon Turkey, I am inclined to think that a Muhammedan rising in India is among the contingencies we may have to face."[92] Lytton's worst fears ultimately would come true during the Eastern Crisis of 1875–78, when William Gladstone spearheaded a public denunciation of the so-called Bulgarian horrors perpetrated by the Ottomans against their Christian subjects in the Balkans. Gladstone's rhetoric sparked an anti-Turkish crusade in the press. As a result, the post-1849 image of liberal Ottoman reformers gave way to one of rapacious Muslim tyrants presiding over the slaughter of innocent Christians. Similarly, Abdülhamid II was caricaturized as the bloodthirsty "red sultan" and derided in European newspapers as nothing short of an irrational, reactionary monster.[93]

Gladstone's assault on the Anglo-Ottoman alliance led to a radical reassessment of British naval strategy and the defense of India. Between the opening of the Suez Canal in 1869 and the British occupation of Cyprus in 1878 and of Egypt in 1882, it had become increasingly clear that British interests in the Near East and India could be maintained even if the Ottoman Empire were allowed to collapse. This strategic shift meant that earlier British assurances to defend Ottoman territorial integrity against Russia were no longer guaranteed.[94] Thus when Russia invaded the Ottoman Balkans in 1877, Britain did nothing. As a result, Britain was no longer able to tout itself as the sultan-caliph's ally and protector. As a result of this anti-Ottoman turn in British foreign policy, even previously loyal Indian Muslims became disillusioned and began to question why British support for the Ottoman Empire, considered sacrosanct in the 1850s, had abruptly ended just two decades later. Undoubtedly this sense of disillusionment led a great number of previously quiescent Indian Muslims back into the political arena, particularly into the embrace of Pan-Islam.[95]

In the wake of the Russo-Ottoman War, it is not surprising that the Sublime Porte was eager to harness the rising Indian enthusiasm for the sultan-caliph. Although the rapid growth in Pan-Islamic sentiment in India often has been narrated as part of the wider transregional influence of Salafi-cum-Pan-Islamic pioneers such as Muḥammad ʿAbduh (1849–1905) and Sayyid Jamal al-Din al-Afghani (1839–97), a parallel but often underemphasized factor in this process was the growth of India's vernacular press in Persian and Urdu. The expansion of the vernacular press created the vehicle and the marketplace though which Muslim reformers and even the Ottoman state itself could market themselves. Whereas in 1835 only six vernacular newspapers were published in India, by 1850 that number rose to twenty-eight. By 1878, northern India alone had nearly a hundred vernacular papers with a total circulation of some 150,000. By 1880, the number of vernacular journals had risen to 330. The explosion of publications around the time of the Russo-Ottoman War provided Indian Muslims with greater access to up-to-the-minute news from around the Islamic world, much of which was translated from Ottoman Turkish and Arabic newspapers such as al-Jawāʾib, Akhbār dār al-Khilāfa, Tercüman-ı Meşrik, and Tercüman-ı Rum. Arguably, the most influential publication of all was Peyk-i İslam, an Istanbul-based journal written in Ottoman Turkish and Urdu and edited by an Indian Muslim. Designed as an official organ of the Porte, it raised the sultan-caliph's profile and promoted closer ties between Indian Muslims and the Ottoman Empire.[96]

As a result of the proliferation of pro-Ottoman newspapers and journals, numerous voluntary organizations sprang to life decrying the empire's plight and urging Indian Muslims to give financial aid to the Ottomans in their time of need. According to Ottoman registers (Defter-i İane-i Hindiye), Indian support for the Ottoman war effort was overwhelming. More than 124,840 Ottoman lira were collected, an amount equal to more than one million (10 lakh) Indian rupees. More important, organizations such as Anjuman-i Islam, Anjuman-i Teyyid-i Turkiye, and Meclis-i Müeyyid-i İslamiye drew this financial support from diverse quarters of the Indian community. As a result, normally divergent Indian Muslim groups such as Sir Sayyid Ahmad Khan's Aligarhi loyalists, Deobandis, and Shiʿi donors—and even Hindus—joined in this massive charitable outpouring.[97]

In recognition of this considerable wave of sentimental and financial support, the Ottomans redoubled their efforts to build up a system of consulates, missions, and emissaries in India and the wider Indian Ocean region. After the termination of the Mughal dynasty in 1857, diplomatic ties between the Ottoman state and Muslim India had been maintained largely through outreach to the semiautonomous rulers of princely states, most notably the Begum of Bhopal and the Nizam of Hyderabad, neither of which state had embassies in Istanbul.[98] In 1870, however, the Ottomans opened their first Indian consulate-general (*başşehbenderlik*) in Bombay. During the Russo-Ottoman War, that first Ottoman consul, Hüseyin Hasib Efendi, worked tirelessly to solicit donations for the war effort and circulate Ottoman-friendly news in the Indian vernacular press. Owing to his efforts, Istanbul saw an opportunity to open more Indian consulates. In 1877, the Porte sought permission to open a new consulate in Peshawar. However, the Foreign Office rejected Istanbul's request on the grounds that the Ottoman Empire had no substantial "commercial interests" in the region. Ottoman attempts to appoint a consul to the princely state of Hyderabad also were denied. Between 1887 and 1891, however, British authorities eventually acquiesced to the appointment of new consuls in Calcutta, Karachi, and Madras.[99]

In many respects Ottoman attempts to build a diplomatic presence in the Indian Ocean mimicked the extraterritorial influence that European consuls had wielded so effectively in Ottoman lands. Ottoman consuls encouraged Indians to invoke the sultan-caliph's name during the Friday sermon. They bestowed honorific titles and medals on elite Indian benefactors. They even urged average Indians to write to the sultan. These letters varied from expressions of spiritual support and demands for more Ottoman consulates in India to protect Muslim rights to complaints about the conditions of the hajj. In turn, many of these letters were used as propaganda in the Turkish press to emphasize the sultan-caliph's ecumenical prestige at home and abroad. Similarly, Ottoman press agencies circulated news and appeals for financial support in India's vernacular press. Ottoman press abstracts, republished in India, included glowing accounts of Abdülhamid's good deeds and the need for strengthening the bonds of religion.

Clearly these journalistic efforts served as an important medium for the transmission of Pan-Islamic thought to distant Muslim communities. However, British officials from Calcutta to London became increasingly suspicious of the Ottoman Empire's Indian Ocean consular network. Ottoman representatives were kept under close surveillance, and their access to the vernacular press was circumscribed. Although intelligence inquiries into the Ottoman consulates consistently failed to yield evidence of any political subversion, the British remained perpetually paranoid about the potential for Ottoman-sponsored insurrections from Bombay to Afghanistan. Thus despite considerable evidence of the growing bureaucratic professionalization of Ottoman diplomatic outreach to the Indian Ocean's colonized Muslim populations, colonial administrators continued to view Ottoman consuls as Pan-Islamic firebrands.

Much of the Hamidian state's Pan-Islamic outreach was not undertaken on colonial soil. The relatively sheltered, uncolonized space provided by Mecca represented the perfect base from which to solidify the bond between non-Ottoman Muslims and their caliph. However, even this sacred bond sometimes involved the profane business of propaganda distribution and fundraising. Great care was taken to draft propaganda materials that would appeal in multiple languages to many nationalities in imperial contexts. Some pamphlets called for Central Asians, Afghans, and Persians to resist and fight Russian expansion, while others called on Indians for moral and financial support. Such materials urged Indian Muslims to send their alms to the Ottomans, reminding them that they too shared the burden of supporting the jihad against Islam's archenemies in Russia. By doing so, one tract declared that "God would reward them, otherwise they would be punished and disgraced both now and in the hereafter." As if God's wrath were not enough, pamphlets even included disclaimers for Indian Muslims loyal to the British Crown, reminding them that Anglo-Ottoman relations were still friendly and that "the British Government would not object to support given by the Indian Muslims."[100]

The Future of Islam: British Fantasies of a Post-Ottoman Caliphate, Hijaz, and Hajj

Despite Istanbul's relatively more cautious approach to India's British subjects, the overt use of propaganda in Mecca during the Russo-Ottoman War reignited British anxieties about the Hijaz's potential as an outlet of Indo-Ottoman intrigue and conspiracy. Such reports also helped to resurrect and revise a familiar script, once again invoking the subversive influence of prominent Meccan exiles such as Sayyid Faḍl and Rahmatullah Kairanwi. As Austen Henry Layard warned, "ex-Mutineer Indians at Mecca were in communication with the Porte and that through them the Ottomans could make an attempt to bring about a rising in India."[101] In a similar reaction to the spike in Pan-Islamic sentiments during the war, English adventurer John F. Keane's 1877–78 pilgrimage account paints an ominous picture of the Hijaz as a tinderbox of anti-Christian fervor, harkening back to Jeddah's violent eruption in 1858.

> Who can know what alarming projects or conspiracies may not at this moment be on foot in Meccah, that center and hotbed of Mohammedan intrigue? For my part, I regard the Christians in Jeddah as sitting on the safety valve of the Hijaz, and sooner or later an explosion is inevitable.[102]

Here Keane's Islamophobic sentiments are almost identical to those expressed by the newly appointed British consul in Jeddah, James Napoleon Zohrab, who wrote the following in 1879:

> The province of the Hedjaz is the centre to which the ideas, opinions, sentiments and aspirations of the Mussulman world are brought for discussion. The annual meeting at a fixed time ostensibly for the purposes of the Pilgrimage of Representatives from every Mussulman Community affords a means without creating suspicion to exchange opinions, to discuss plans, to criticize the actions of the European Governments and form combinations to resist the supremacy of the Christian Powers.[103]

Zohrab hailed from an Armenian family that had fled Persia in the late eighteenth century. Following in the footsteps of his father and brothers, he joined Britain's diplomatic service. At an instinctual level, Zohrab believed that Islam was basically reactionary, plagued by exclusivist conservatism and prejudice, and in desperate need of reform.[104] By contrast, Zohrab and his fellow travelers believed that "England, Christian but benevolent, would be the best protector of Islam."[105] Having concluded that the Hijaz was destined to become a "major power base" from which the Ottoman Caliphate could "incite the Muslims of India to revolt." He argued that Britain should establish a kind of protectorate over the Hijaz and bring the Sharifate of

Mecca under British control in order to allow the British Empire to "guide the whole Mussulman world."[106]

Zohrab was not the first to imagine decoupling the Ottoman Caliphate from the spiritual legitimacy that its bond with the Hijaz and the hajj provided. In the late 1870s, British debates surrounding the Islamic legal legitimacy of the Ottoman Caliphate had begun to gain momentum among ex-Indian civil servants, intelligence officers, and members of parliament, most notably Sir George Campbell, George Percy Badger, and James Redhouse. A series of articles and pamphlets appearing in 1877 questioned whether tracing the Ottoman dynasty's transfer of the title from the last Abbasid caliph in 1517 constituted a legitimate claim. Collectively these writings pointed out that the Ottoman dynasty—whose members were not descendants of the Quraysh tribe and the Prophet Muḥammad—was unfit for the title.[107]

In an article in *The Times* from June 1877, George Birdwood laid out what was to become the central axis of Britain's anti-Ottoman version of Pan-Islam. As he put it, "it is a great pity that we do not get the Muhammedans of India to look up to the Shareef of Mecca as the Caliph of Islam for he lives by the side of our road to India and would be as completely in our power as the Suez Canal."[108] In many respects, Birdwood's desire to bind the caliphate to British naval dominance in the Red Sea was an obvious outcome of the rapid deterioration of relations between London and Istanbul during the late 1870s and early 1880s. In the wake of this sea change in Anglo-Ottoman relations, Birdwood's argument for the transfer of the caliphate to the Hijaz would blossom. In 1881, Wilfrid Scawen Blunt, an eccentric English aristocrat, traveler, and Arab enthusiast, visited Zohrab in Jeddah to gather material for a book. Ultimately Birdwood and Zohrab's ideas would find their fullest expression in a series of essays by Blunt featured in the *Fortnightly Review* in the summer and fall of 1881 and published as a book in 1882.[109]

In *The Future of Islam*, Blunt prophesizes a growing crisis in the Islamic world, predicting the inevitable fall of the Ottoman Empire. He also outlines the benefits that might accrue from disentangling the spiritual authority of the caliphate from its connection to a hopelessly compromised Ottoman territorial sovereignty. With the collapse of the Ottoman state close at hand, Blunt believed that it would be to England that "the various nations of Islam should look mainly for direction in their political difficulties." As a result, the British Empire would have a golden opportunity to position itself as the

Muslims world's principal "adviser and protector" in a post-Ottoman world. Blunt also believed that with the disappearance of the Ottoman Caliphate, there would no longer be "any great Mussulman sovereignty in the world and the Mohammedan population of India, already the wealthiest and most numerous," would naturally "assume its full importance in the counsels of believers." With the rise of India as Islam's new center of gravity, Blunt argued that the "English Crown . . . should then justify its assumption of the old Mohammedan title of the Moguls, by making itself in some sort the political head of Islam." As such, Queen Victoria would "be left" as Islam's "most powerful sovereign."[110]

Supporting his most grandiose claims, Blunt also provided some practical examples of the kinds of services that Britain's protectorate over a post-Ottoman Caliphate, Hijaz, and hajj might provide to the Raj's Indian subjects, many of which eventually would be realized in some shape or form. Here Blunt stressed the absolute necessity of bringing the hajj "under English auspices." Shocked that this critical question had been left entirely to chance, Blunt argued that the safe and efficient regulation of the hajj was a "necessary part" of the British Empire's "duty," central to its "influence in the Mussulman world," and "one we should be grossly in error to neglect." Parroting Zohrab's opinions, Blunt laid out an ambitious plan to atone for the "culpable negligence" that Britain had shown toward its pilgrims. Blunt outlined a plan for the "systematic development" of the British-sponsored hajj. He listed everything from the construction of a railway connecting Jeddah and Mecca to government-chartered ships and the transfer of *waqf* funds to support various projects in Mecca.[111] As we shall see, in the decades between 1882 and World War I, in one form or another, versions of Blunt's proposals ultimately would find their way into competing British and Ottoman plans for the reform of pilgrimage transport and administration. However, perhaps Blunt's most consequential proposal was his and Zohrab's suggestion that a special Muslim agent be appointed to attend to British subjects' health, safety, and legal and financial interests, a subject to which I will return in the next chapter.

By taking a more overtly interventionist role, Blunt argued that "the English Government will gain, not only the good-will of the whole Mohammedan population of India, but they will also inspire the Hajjis with the wholesome feeling that they owe allegiance to, and can claim *protection* from, an empire other than that to which the people of Arabia are subject (the Turkish)." In Blunt's eyes, such measures stood "in very favourable contrast to the sufferings, which the pilgrims undergo from maladministration at Mecca." In his opinion, this kind of active assistance would serve to counteract any Ottoman propaganda designed to "animate" Indian pilgrims "with hostility toward the British supremacy in India."[112]

Conclusion: From Surveillance to Service?

As this chapter has argued, between the 1850s and the early 1880s, the Hijaz, the hajj, and their relationships to the Ottoman Caliphate loomed ever larger in the colonial imagination, giving rise to two competing narratives. On the one hand, Mecca was imagined as a safe haven for Indian rebels and fanatics bent on anti-Christian violence and anticolonial insurrection. For consuls and colonial administrators from Jeddah and Aden to Bombay and Calcutta, Jeddah's anti-Christian or anti-consular riots in 1858 could be understood and explained only through the prism of the 1857 revolt and Muslim fanaticism. This semilegendary brew of fact, fiction, and phantom connections would persist for decades to come. In times of crisis like the Russo-Ottoman War of 1877–78 and even as a late as World War I, colonial officials continued to fear Jeddah and Mecca's potential as centers of anticolonial subversion.

In the wake of the Russo-Ottoman War and the overall cooling of Anglo-Ottoman relations, this narrative evolved again. Older fears of radical Indian exiles influencing ordinary pilgrims blended with new concerns over official Ottoman contact with both Indian exiles and the pilgrim masses. As the Hamidian state sought to promote the sultan-caliph's spiritual sovereignty among non-Ottoman Muslims, his increasingly visible role as the Servant of the Two Holy Places made the hajj a critical outlet for Ottoman image-making, propaganda, and fundraising.

Abdülhamid's Pan-Islamic turn fed the colonial paranoia that Mecca and the Ottoman Hijaz remained untamed sites of colonial disorder, reinforcing the need for greater political surveillance of the hajj. Indeed, Zohrab and others even raised the possibility of deploying Muslim covert agents as spies.[113] At the same time, British attitudes toward the hajj remained deeply conflicted, often outright contradictory. The fever of Pan-Islamic panic that spiked in the late 1870s and early 1880s continued to be tempered by grave concerns that overt interference with the hajj would only provoke Muslim unrest in India. As a result, most of the more dramatic schemes proposed by Blunt and Zohrab were ultimately discarded as either unrealistic or too dangerous.

On the other hand, British avoidance of overt interference in the hajj did not equal disengagement. The same ethnographic impulses that had singled out and racialized Muslims as uniquely predisposed to jihad and anticolonial rebellion eventually led the Indian government to reimagine the hajj as a potent part of a colonial repertoire tailored to manage Muslims in India and elsewhere. By the early 1880s, inaction was no longer a viable option. From the 1860s on, the rise of the mass steamship hajj had set in motion a raft of intractable issues that included cholera, quarantines, steamship regulations, passports, and questions of extraterritorial protections. As a result, political subversion was no longer the only issue on the table. Thus as Blunt suggested, if the British could act to protect the interests of its pilgrim subjects, perhaps they might be able to transform the Hijaz and the hajj from weakness to strength. By repositioning the British Empire as the "protector of the hajj," safe and efficient pilgrimage administration and legal protection might provide the mechanism through which the legitimacy and prestige of the Ottoman Caliphate might be challenged and eroded. With this goal in mind, Britain was never the benevolent "protector of Islam" that Blunt imagined. Even Britain's most genuine attempts to make hajj travel safer and more humane were always partly motivated by a quixotic and, ultimately, futile desire to cultivate its imperial prestige and legitimacy as a so-called Muslim power.[114]

As the renowned Dutch Orientalist Christiaan Snouck Hurgronje pointed out at the time, colonial panic over the hajj was overblown. In reality, the hajj was an eminently manageable ethnographic problem. Throughout his career, he reassured nervous elites in both the Dutch and the British Empires that the supposedly unruly hajj could be policed and disciplined, or even deftly manipulated, as an instrument to further subjugate the Islamic world to the colonial order. Having spent nearly a year in Jeddah and Mecca in 1884–85, Hurgronje became convinced that Europeans had "greatly exaggerated" Mecca's "role as a breeding ground for anti-colonial agitation." To prove his point, he emphasized the inherently conservative nature of the hajj and the mundane business of the pilgrimage industry, arguing that "the vast majority of hajjis returned home exactly as they departed—not as

rebels but as 'sheep.' " Hurgronje also painted native Meccans as more concerned with "fleecing their prey" than fomenting rebellion. In sharp contrast to the "herd of gullible hajjis," Hurgronje acknowledged the presence
of a small minority of "conspirators who turned their piety into fanaticism
and rebellion." He argued that the true danger of the hajjis lay in the "networks of exiles and students who took refuge in Mecca's many expatriate
communities, exploiting the freedom of the hajj to propagandize visitors
from their homelands."[115]

Hurgronje's solution to this paradox was deceptively simple. He argued,
not unlike Blunt, that instead of restricting access to Mecca—a strategy
that he reasoned was needlessly provocative—colonial governments should
increase their diplomatic, intelligence, and sanitary presence in the Hijaz.
He believed that by taking an active role in supporting and protecting the
hajj, whether through consumer protections, technological modernization,
or sanitary reforms, colonial regimes could endear themselves to the majority of their subjects while still keeping a watchful eye on any potentially
subversive elements.

In the closing decades of the nineteenth century, to varying degrees,
British India, the Straits Settlements, and the Dutch East Indies followed
Hurgronje's advice. Colonial governments across the Indian Ocean became
intimately involved in the administration and business of pilgrimage transportation. As we shall see in chapter 2, the British Empire also launched an
aggressive campaign to impose its consular authority and extraterritorial
legal jurisdiction on pilgrims traveling in the Hijaz, even to Mecca itself.
The British gradually inserted themselves into virtually every aspect of the
pilgrimage's conduct, extending the tentacles of colonial regulation and
surveillance to include pilgrimage institutions spanning the entire Indian
Ocean basin. In the process, colonial administrators would become intimately familiar with the legal and material concerns of Indian and other
Muslim subjects traveling and residing in the Hijaz. Over time this increasing ethnographic interest in the day-to-day affairs of the Hijaz and the hajj
shifted and rebalanced British concerns from visions of conspiracy and subversion to the quotidian mechanics of pilgrimage administration.

Through this decades-long process, Britain's extraterritorial reach into
the Hijaz and the hajj via consular representation and the Capitulations
posed an increasingly thorny challenge to Ottoman legitimacy as custodians of the Muslim holy places. By gradually prying sole responsibility

for pilgrimage administration from Ottoman hands, Britain pushed the Ottoman state to try to strengthen and centralize its control of the semi-autonomous Hijaz and Sharifate of Mecca and to improve the safety, security, and health of the hajj. In turn, the Hijaz and the hajj became new ideological and material battlegrounds on which the British and Ottoman empires would engage in a contestation of sacred space. The stakes ranged from suzerainty over the Hijaz and the administration of the hajj to even larger questions of hegemony and prestige throughout the entire Muslim world.

TWO

Legal Imperialism

Foreign Muslims and Muslim Consuls

AS DISCUSSED in the previous chapter, although the British government of India initially imagined the Hijaz as a launching pad for anticolonial radicalism and Ottoman-sponsored Pan-Islam, by the mid-1880s the urgency of the logistical challenges facing the rapidly changing steamship-era pilgrimage—most notably the near-constant threat of epidemic cholera and the associated question of indigent pilgrims—had begun to force European colonial administrators to engage more deeply with the day-to-day affairs of the hajj. As Britain became more deeply entangled in the quotidian details of the pilgrimage, the colonial state's efforts to better understand the hajj and provide for its subjects' safety and security rebalanced its attitudes toward the Hijaz. Over time, calls for covert colonial surveillance morphed into a more robust regime of consular protection based on the principles outlined in the Capitulations. From an Ottoman perspective, the nature and direction of these threats took a series of unexpected "international legal" turns, calling into question who was more afraid of political subversion emanating from the Hijaz: European colonial administrators or the Ottoman state itself? As a result, Istanbul came to view foreign (non-Ottoman) Muslims as potential Trojan horses unwittingly bearing European extraterritoriality and "legal imperialism."[1]

Conventional wisdom suggests that the Hijaz was excluded from the extraterritorial privileges granted by the Capitulations. Although this might have been true in theory, following the tentacles of Britain's Indian

Ocean empire shows that British consular officials were at least partly successful in extending the privileges of protection to Indian and other colonial subjects traveling to or residing in the Hijaz. Concurrent changes in Ottoman legal definitions of nationality, naturalization, and subjecthood— themselves grounded in efforts to defend against the proliferation of European protégés—also exacerbated this problem by subjecting non-Ottoman pilgrims and sojourners to unprecedented levels of suspicion and exclusionary practices.

By examining this Anglo-Ottoman clash over the extension of the Capitulations to the Hijaz and the Sharifate of Mecca, this chapter questions some of our most basic assumptions regarding the region's exceptional status. It traces how Ottoman officials struggled to delicately subvert the logics of international law and colonialism threatening the Hijaz. On the one hand, Ottoman officials pointed to the Hijaz's obvious religious exceptionalism and traditional exemption from the Capitulations. On the other hand, they also found it necessary to deploy the new language and logic of international law. Taking advantage of the Sharifate of Mecca's semiautonomous status, blurry jurisdictional boundaries, and divided sovereignty, both provincial administrators and the empire's highest legal authorities sought to buffer the holy cities from the brunt of European legal imperialism. Although Ottoman officials failed to fully shield the Hijaz from the Capitulations, examining the novelty of their approaches provides new perspective on the fragility of the post-Tanzimat Hijaz's exceptional status. By reframing the Hijaz through international legal lenses, we find that both the increasing pressures of European extraterritoriality and the unintended consequences of the very legal and administrative maneuvers meant to blunt them combined to radically alter and undermine the Hijaz's privileged religious and ideological positions within the empire.

The interconnected problems of autonomy and extraterritoriality were further complicated by the promotion of the Hijaz as a pillar of Sultan Abdül-hamid II's Pan-Islamic public image. Probing beneath the surface of Hamidian legitimacy structures, however, we find a constant tension between the soaring rhetoric of Pan-Islamic outreach to the rest of the Islamic world and the increasingly exclusionary policies adopted to insulate the empire from the extraterritorial threat posed by foreign Muslims and their colonial masters. Although counterintuitive to the dominant historiographic image of the Hamidian state, this friction reveals how the sultan-caliph's

Pan-Islamic universalism was continually recalibrated and often subordinated to suit the new realities of territorial sovereignty and international law.[2]

The Most Privileged Province? Autonomy and the Fragility of Hijazi Exceptionalism

As early as 1889, the sharif of Mecca, ʿAwn al-Rafiq (r. 1882–1905), began to openly express his opinion that the Amirate of Mecca should be made a hereditary office. ʿAwn al-Rafiq reportedly favored abolishing the overlapping jurisdictions of the Ottoman provincial government and the amirate, arguing for a truly "autonomous administration" (idare-i muhtare).[3] In the wake of Mehmed Ali Pasha's successful creation of a hereditary dynasty in Egypt, this ambition was the worst possible trajectory that the central government in Istanbul could imagine for this semiautonomous province.

The most notable critic of the Sharifate of Mecca was Gazi Ahmed Muhtar Pasha, the Ottoman special commissioner (Fevkalade Komiser) in Egypt between 1892 and 1908. Throughout his tenure in Egypt, Ahmed Muhtar repeatedly urged Abdülhamid II to abolish the amirate, transfer the sharif to Istanbul, and place the Hijaz solely under the governor's control. Although the Hijaz fell well beyond his own jurisdiction, Sharif ʿAwn al-Rafiq's corruption and abuses of pilgrims were running scandals in the Indian and Egyptian presses and constant sources of aggravation for the British Embassy. As he warned, the sharifate's oppressive and unjust administration of the hajj was providing Britain, France, and the Netherlands with perfect excuses to intervene more directly in the Hijaz.[4]

From Ahmed Muhtar's perspective, there was nothing to be gained from indirect rule via local notables. Drawing on his experiences from the reconquest of Yemen in the early 1870s, during which a number of sharifs were sent to assist him, he remarked that contrary to the government's opinion, the sharifs' noble ancestry meant little to the Bedouin.[5] Whatever influence they might have over the tribes was a pale reflection of the imperial government's sovereignty. If they were stripped of this connection to the empire, they would have no more "power" or "influence" than an "ordinary Arab shaykh."[6]

Ahmed Muhtar's varied experiences on the overlapping frontiers of the Ottoman and British Empires provided another dimension to his strident calls for the abolition of the sharifate. Presiding over the occupation of Egypt alongside the British had taught him the dangers posed by autonomous rulers such as the khedive and the sharif. It also left him with a keen sense of how the Scramble for Africa had put the Hijaz in a completely indefensible position at the heart of the colonial world, sandwiched as it was between Egypt, the Suez Canal, Sudan, and the road to India. He pleaded that the Hijaz, the very "object of pride" of the caliphate, was in imminent danger. To compensate for the loss of Egypt and British naval dominance in the Red Sea, Ahmed Muhtar urgently advocated the establishment of land-based rail and telegraph links to better connect the Hijaz to Istanbul.[7]

In response to one of Ahmed Muhtar's appeals, the eminent statesman Ahmed Cevdet Pasha (1822–95) was consulted. Cevdet cautioned that transferring the sharif to Istanbul would not be prudent because he might become a focal point for discontent and anti-Ottoman intrigues. Cevdet also worried that the abolition of the sharifate might cause a backlash among Ottoman subjects or enflame global Islamic public opinion. Ahmed Muhtar's opinion was so poorly received that it was even suggested that his ideas might have been the product of foreign influence.[8] In the end, Abdülhamid II viewed his proposal as wholly unrealistic, noting that if the sharifate were to become dysfunctional, "holding sway over the Arab public only with appointed governors would be impossible" without turning the region over to a full military occupation.[9]

To be sure, Ahmed Muhtar's blunt call for centralization was completely out of step with the prevailing Hamidian preference for subtler frontier experiments with indirect rule. However, his argument was no less prescient. As Cevdet Pasha argued, foreign interference in the Hijaz was intolerable. Thus "it is clear that the administration of the holy land of the Hijaz, the cradle of Islam, *could never be comparable* to any of the considerations put forward by foreign powers concerning some [other] imperial provinces."[10] But even Cevdet's firm declaration of the Hijaz's "incomparable" status belies the deepening anxieties over this question. In hindsight, the privileged status of the Hijaz was not as unique as either Cevdet or most present-day scholars imagine. It is too difficult to overlook all of the province's similarities to the other autonomous and irregular provinces on the vulnerable frontlines of European intervention and partition. Indeed, when viewed alongside the lengthy list of privileged provinces (*eyalat-ı mümtaze*) and other non-Tanzimat-compliant frontier regions such as Iraq, Libya, and Yemen, the Hijaz's incomparable status begins to look more ordinary.

Although it is probably unwise to second-guess the wisdom of Cevdet's cautious approach to the sharifate, the threats posed by British support for a rival caliphate or extraterritorial influence over the Hijaz were more than mere figments of the Hamidian imagination.[11] They were also based on more than the wild speculations of figures such as Wilfrid Scawen Blunt. These fears were also by-products of London's long-term shift toward the promotion of autonomy and decentralization for all of the Ottoman Empire's subject peoples. As Ahmed Midhat Efendi framed the problem for Abdülhamid II,

> It is clear that England—God forbid!—is striving to dissolve the Ottoman Empire into statelets (müluk or küçük devletçikler). It amounts not to autonomy (otonomi or muhtariyet) but to anatomy (anatomi), by creating for example, an Albanian Albania, an Armenia in the Armenian inhabited places, an Arab government in all the places inhabited by Arabs, and a Turkey in the Turkish-inhabited areas.
>
> Meanwhile, [England] also wishes to transfer the great Caliphate from Istanbul to the Arabian Peninsula, to Jeddah, or somewhere in Egypt. And by using the Caliphate as a tool in her service, to rule all Muslims as it pleases.[12]

Lurking beneath the general question of autonomy was the British-backed threat of a rival caliphate and Arab separatism. Although we know that British attempts to undermine the legitimacy of the Ottoman Caliphate surged between 1878 and the early 1880s, the intersections among international legal thought, the British Empire's promotion of autonomy, and its long-term adoption of an ethnonationalist view of the sharif of Mecca as the rightful "Arab" caliph have been poorly articulated in the existing literature on Pan-Islam. By contrast, Yıldız Palace saw clear connections among the 1878 Treaty of Berlin, Britain's autonomy policy, and its simultaneous promotion of Arab claims to the caliphate. As a Yıldız memorandum on the subject explains, the "idea of independence" (fikr-i istiklali) and the prospects of "an Arab state stretching from the Nile to the Euphrates and from the Indian Ocean to the Taurus Mountains" had been cause for concern since the conquest of Syria by Mehmed Ali's son, İbrahim Pasha, a half century earlier.[13]

But the international context was considerably different after 1878. Reflecting on the catastrophic territorial losses suffered as a result of the treaty, Yıldız Palace attempted to draw something of a line in the sand, arguing that "comparing Ottoman territories as a whole and Ottoman provinces located in Europe to each other is unacceptable."[14] As the report cautioned, the state's submission to the Treaty of Berlin had set a dangerous precedent for the continued spread of ethnonationalist successions, territorial losses, and the multiplication of autonomous provinces spilling beyond the empire's European territories. In other words, it warned that Europe would apply the same logic to the rest of its Asian and Arab frontier provinces.

This was the web of concerns underpinning Ahmed Muhtar's warning, the same logic that he had learned firsthand from the British occupation of Egypt. In his view, traditional Ottoman conceptions of autonomy, frontier management, and Hijazi exceptionalism carried new risks in the colonial age. Autonomy was now the cracked door through which European extraterritorial influence would inevitably slip. In the long run, the sharifate's privileged status and autonomy would always provide a tempting rationale and opportunity for Britain's intervention on behalf of its subjects in the Hijaz. This was the wider interimperial environment that helped bring the Capitulations to the Hijaz.

Complicated Subjects: The Capitulations, Nationality, and the Problem of Non-Ottoman Muslims in the Hijaz

Scholars of the Ottoman Empire have long been preoccupied with how the Capitulations and Tanzimat reforms placed Christian protégés and protected persons beyond the reach of Ottoman justice, but surprisingly little attention has been paid to the analogous projects of European powers claiming to protect their Muslim colonial subjects from the supposed corruption of Ottoman rule and the arbitrary nature of the shariʿa courts of Mecca. At the most basic level, capitulatory privileges, tax exemptions, and concessions of consular protection were originally meant to provide early modern Europeans—generally Christians—with partial, if not complete, immunity from Ottoman jurisdiction. In the nineteenth century, however, as European consuls sought to encourage commercial relationships and expand their influence in Ottoman territories, they began to grant letters of protection (berat) to thousands of Ottoman Christian protégés and, eventually, to Muslim clients.[15]

In theory, the Capitulations should have been abolished as a result of the 1856 Treaty of Paris. The treaty's signing ostensibly had welcomed the empire into the Concert of Europe, guaranteeing the Ottomans the same legitimacy and rights to international existence and territorial integrity as any other member of the European family of nations. However, far from resulting in their abolition, the Treaty of Paris formalized and further entrenched the Capitulations. Over the course of the nineteenth century, European diplomats increasingly came to understand these previously unilateral grants and revocable privileges as binding obligations, which, through their incorporation into bilateral and multilateral treaties, essentially gave them the full force of international law.[16]

Even so, the Capitulations never included the Hijaz. The first article of the original Capitulations (*ahdnameler*) granted to France in 1535 provided individual freedom of trade, travel, navigation, residence, and worship, but it explicitly exempted the Hijaz.[17] There were also later legal exemptions beyond the Capitulations themselves. The Ottoman state's attempt to construct the Hijaz as an exceptional space deemed unfit for many of the secularizing Tanzimat reforms also provides useful clues. For example, the Hijaz was exempted from the 1857 edict calling for an empire-wide prohibition on the African slave trade.[18] Similarly, when the Ottoman government lifted the ban on foreign real estate (*emlak*) or "immovable property" (*gayrimenkul mülkiyet* or *taşınmaz mal*) ownership throughout the empire in 1867, the Hijaz was exempted.[19]

Given that Christians were forbidden from traveling or residing outside Jeddah or owning real estate in the Hijaz, prior to the advent of regular steamship service, there was little real danger of this situation arising anyway. Prior to the 1850s one could safely argue that the Hijaz *was* truly beyond the reach of the Capitulations. But historians have also taken for granted that the Hijaz's exceptional status remained intact from the Tanzimat era up until the empire's demise.

At first glance, there are a variety of sound reasons for assuming that Mecca's incomparability remained unchanged. Historians have rightly emphasized how the Hijaz theoretically stood outside the framework of most (though not all) Tanzimat-style reforms. And yet, from the 1850s and 1860s on, European consular protections enshrined in a post-1856 reading of the Capitulations, coupled with Tanzimat redefinitions of Ottoman subjecthood and nationality, would have profound impacts on this most exceptional province.

By the conclusion of the nineteenth century, millions of Muslims across Africa and Asia found themselves living under various forms of European colonial rule, protectorates, or spheres of influence. As a result of this previously unimaginable scenario, a paradoxical rift in the traditional fabric of the Capitulations was opened. Up to this point, the Capitulations had been predicated on the idea that the foreign subjects being excused from Ottoman jurisdiction would be non-Muslims. But what if the subjects of states enjoying capitulatory privileges were Muslims hailing from European colonies or protectorates? As Muslims became colonial subjects of European states, Ottoman authorities were suddenly forced to grapple with the hypocritical claim that non-Ottoman Muslims sojourning or residing in Islam's holiest cities needed the protection of their colonial masters to avoid the "uncivilized" dictates of shari'a law.[20] International legal justifications for humanitarian interventions claiming to protect the Ottoman Empire's Christian subjects had long been based on European accusations of Ottoman despotism, corruption, and the arbitrary nature of Islamic jurisprudence. In many respects it was a natural progression for these concepts to be applied gradually to Muslim colonial subjects as well.[21] As in other parts of the Ottoman Empire, where European manipulation of the Capitulations often placed Christian protégés and protected persons beyond the reach of Ottoman justice, this new extension of extraterritoriality raised the troubling prospect of European powers claiming to protect their Muslim colonial subjects—and even Islam itself—from Ottoman despotism.

As Selim Deringil has suggested, by the Hamidian period, the Ottoman state had begun to fear "that the Muslim subjects of foreign powers could act as potential fifth columns and infiltrate the holy land of the Hicaz."[22] Istanbul came to view the Hijaz as a kind of quasi-colonial frontier, both unsuited to Tanzimat centralization and increasingly vulnerable to European expansion. In an attempt to anticipate some of the problems that the colonial element in Mecca might present, significant thought was put into squaring the Hijaz's exceptional status with Tanzimat-style redefinitions of Ottoman subjecthood and nationality.

As a result of the 1856 *Islahat Fermanı*, the traditional Ottoman civil distinctions between Muslims and *dhimmīs* (Peoples of the Book) were theoretically leveled. However, the reconfiguration of these older categories was not fully realized until the 1869 Ottoman Law of Nationality (*Tabiiyet-i Osmaniye Kanunnamesi*). Recent scholarship on Ottoman citizenship has made great use of the 1869 Ottoman nationality law. However, as Will Hanley argues, this literature consistently has drawn a somewhat misleading link between the term *tabiiyet* and citizenship as opposed to subjecthood or nationality. Whatever the longer-term aspirations of the Tanzimat project might have been, the 1869 law's immediate objective was not to define citizenship. Rather, it was mainly designed to clarify the terms of Ottoman nationality and naturalization. As a result of this slippage in terminology, the 1869 law's relationship to the Capitulations has been obscured. In fact, the 1869 legislation was the sequel to an 1863 decree designed to restrict the proliferation of foreign protégés or protected persons. The 1863 legislation sought to force protégés to naturalize as foreign subjects or submit to Ottoman territorial jurisdiction. When these protégés responded by trying to naturalize with foreign states while retaining their Ottoman residency and nationality, Istanbul was once again forced to tighten the terms of Ottoman nationality.[23]

Under the new Ottoman nationality law, the most important differentiating criterion was no longer whether one was Muslim or Christian. The 1869 law changed the practice whereby any non-Muslim converting to (Sunni) Islam on Ottoman soil was to be considered an Ottoman citizen. The bond between confessional and civic identities was radically altered. From 1869 on, the operative question became whether or not one was an Ottoman national. In addition to formalizing the nondenominational legal status of Ottoman nationality, the law also introduced a new category, *ecnebi* (foreigner), which included all foreign nationals regardless of religious affiliation.[24] Because the distinction between Ottoman and foreigner essentially replaced the old divide between Muslim and *dhimmī*, this also necessitated the creation of a more precise descriptor for foreign or non-Ottoman Muslims (*ecanib-i müslimin*). Given that the majority of the nineteenth-century Islamic world had fallen under British, Dutch, French, or Russian rule, this effectively placed non-Ottoman Muslims under a similar cloud of suspicion as non-Muslims claiming the capitulatory protection of foreign states.

As a result, traditional expectations of the Hijaz as a nonterritorial space of refuge, a cosmopolitan magnet for foreign *mücavirin*, where the only meaningful bar to claiming rights as an Ottoman subject in the past had been defined by confessional status (i.e., being a Sunni Muslim), were suddenly overturned.[25] To further compound this paradox, in the absence of standardized passport and visa controls, which began to be haltingly experimented with in the Hijaz only in the early 1880s, there were Muslim migrants from India, Central Asia, and elsewhere who had been born in the Hijaz or had been settled there for decades, sometimes even centuries.[26] These individuals often lived as de facto Ottoman subjects without ever being forced to produce evidence of their nationality.[27] There were Indians carrying British identity and travel documents who nevertheless claimed and maintained Ottoman nationality. There were Ottoman subjects who claimed Ottoman nationality but sailed vessels under British flags and conducted their commercial and financial lives under British consular protection. However, after the passage of the 1869 nationality law, anyone living in Ottoman territory would be considered an Ottoman subject until documentary proof of foreign nationality was produced. The Hijaz's diasporic communities theoretically were forced to choose whether to accept Ottoman nationality or to secure evidence of foreign nationality.[28]

Despite this tightening of Ottoman naturalization processes, the Hijaz province and Sharifate of Mecca's ambiguous semiautonomous statuses and layered sovereignty provided perfect breeding grounds for the proliferation of foreign nationals who were adept at leveraging this extraterritorial system of "negotiated" or "manipulated" identities to maximize rights and privileges. These individuals were "borderlanders par excellence."[29] Often the complicated identities juggled by these expert "identity freelancers" confounded both European and Ottoman authorities.[30] However, as we shall see, the Ottoman state fought hard to prohibit this kind of affiliation switching and forum shopping, which had created a new level of legal uncertainty for non-Ottoman Muslims in the Hijaz.[31] Nevertheless, despite determined resistance from both Hijazi locals and the Ottoman state, attempts to turn back the clock on European consular authority proved impossible. Instead, the Hijaz became a new kind of interimperial battleground for influence and allegiance.

The Union Jack Over Mecca:
The Advent of the Muslim Vice-Consulate

Although the British Raj could control much of the legal and regulatory framework of the industrializing Indian Ocean pilgrimage services industry, its ability to monitor the hajj did not extend past the port city of Jeddah. And although European colonial powers accepted that their Christian consuls were confined to Jeddah, they also sought to extend consular protection for their colonial subjects by appointing Muslim agents or vice-consuls to act on their behalf in Mecca and Medina. The Ottoman government vehemently opposed this scheme and denied Muslim colonial agents the full standing afforded European Christian consuls. It also prevented these officials from residing permanently in Mecca. Nonetheless, between the 1850s and World War I, European consular officials became increasingly enmeshed in the affairs of the Hijaz. This emerging system of consular and commercial representation often involved mundane issues surrounding the protection of pilgrims and protégés in their commercial and real estate dealings, legal proceedings in Ottoman courts, interactions with Ottoman public health authorities, cases of robbery, tribal raids, disputes over ship registration, and the repatriation of remains or property of deceased subjects.

Despite the political and epidemiological threats now associated with it, officials deemed it too risky to overtly discourage Muslims from the hajj. Instead, they opted for a dual strategy of increased extraterritorial protection and surveillance of British subjects. On his arrival in the Hijaz in 1879, Consul James Napoleon Zohrab was stunned by the plight of Indian pilgrims. As he put it, British subjects traveling or residing in the Hijaz simply "ceased to enjoy British protection." As such, they were subject to robbery, abuse, and the whims of the Ottoman legal system. Zohrab was equally appalled by the increasingly commonplace tragedies that befell destitute pilgrims, many of whom were reduced to scavenging for scraps of food and even faced starvation. As Zohrab pointed out, this level of destitution was wholly unique to British subjects. Coupled with the almost annual visitations of cholera to the Hijaz through this period, the consul warned that the question of better protecting Britain's Indian pilgrim subjects was no longer optional. Yet strategies for the execution of such assistance remained elusive. Although the Indian government was well aware of the situation, administrators remained apprehensive that their interventions would be interpreted as interference by India's Muslims. By contrast, Zohrab's Muslim interlocutors in Jeddah wondered why, if Britain saw such an obvious humanitarian need to protect its subjects, it had not provided legal and financial support during their journeys. This dissonance raised the question of why the Raj had failed to fill the void left by the demise of Mughal institutions, which traditionally had supported India's pilgrims. Through his private interviews with elite Indian pilgrims in Jeddah, Zohrab came to believe that Britain should exercise an increasingly active and visible role through the entire hajj process. As he noted, however, whatever their personal feelings, for most Muslims, acknowledging—much less calling for—greater official intervention by a Christian empire was still a deeply uncomfortable subject.[32]

Zohrab believed that in order to reform the hajj, Britain would have to introduce a system of compulsory return tickets to prevent insolvent pilgrims from departing from India in the first place. Zohrab apparently formed this idea through conversations with Hijazi *ulema*, who believed that such regulations were justified by the Qur'anic stipulation that only those who were physically and financially able should perform the hajj. Here Zohrab urged the Raj to follow the example of the Dutch East Indies, which had imposed a system of deposits and compulsory return tickets. The Dutch system also required pilgrims to register with the consulate. Once pilgrims had registered in Jeddah, they would receive the deposit for their return journey and a government certificate as proof of their status as hajjis. As we shall see in chapter 5, Zohrab's call for a compulsory ticket system and other reforms to address the question of indigent pilgrims remained a subject of intense debate, yielding mixed results, for many years to come.[33]

Before Zohrab could hope to effect any of these changes, however, he recognized an even more fundamental flaw in the administration of the Indian Ocean hajj. Despite his and other European consuls' positions as representatives of imperial powers backed by the potential for overwhelming military force, Zohrab and his contemporaries were also keenly aware of their weakness. This was reflected in their jittery rhetoric about the constant threat of conspiracy and anti-European violence emanating from Jeddah and Mecca. At the same time, it also involved more practical matters. European consuls could not travel beyond Jeddah and were essentially isolated from local society, both physically and linguistically. Their inability to better integrate themselves into Hijazi society left them both ill-informed and haunted by a nagging sense of their impotence.[34]

What Zohrab needed were Muslim eyes and ears to guide Britain's rapidly evolving pilgrimage needs. On a practical level, Zohrab understood that the consulate simply could not provide adequate services for its ethnically and linguistically diverse constituencies without Muslim employees. To that end, in 1880, Zohrab requested an Indian who spoke Arabic, English, and Hindustani. He also asked for two clerks with similar language skills plus Malay, and another three multilingual interpreters. He believed that these employees could help pilgrims better navigate Ottoman public health procedures, legal proceedings, and the multilayered networks of pilgrimage transportation and guide services. He also hoped that these assistants might be able to administer his proposed fund for the repatriation of indigent pilgrims. Eventually, in some shape or form, all of these ideas would inform British approaches to hajj administration in the decades that followed.[35]

At the same time, there was always tension between British officials' legitimate calls for the reform of Indian pilgrim services and their initial instincts to view the Hijaz and the hajj as security threats or intelligence blind spots to be solved through covert measures. Following this logic, in 1879, Zohrab recommended that "in order to thoroughly sift the questions of aid and protection to pilgrims," the entire pilgrimage experience must be better understood. Furthermore, "to do this effectively it is in my opinion necessary that a Confidential Agent of the consulate be sent to watch this year's pilgrimage."[36] In June 1880, Austen Henry Layard, the British ambassador in Istanbul, also proposed that the Indian government employ Muslim secret agents to infiltrate the holy cities. Although Layard's plan was rebuffed at the time, British agents in Aden, Istanbul, and Jeddah were charged with monitoring Ottoman propaganda efforts. In the meantime, British intelligence continued to receive reports of Ottoman intrigues from French and Dutch sources as well its own. At this point all of the colonial powers were alive to the possibility of Muslim radicalism transmitted via the hajj. As a result of this common interest, in December 1880, the Dutch foreign minister proposed to Layard a program of intelligence sharing and political surveillance related to pilgrims traveling from India and Southeast Asia to Mecca.[37]

In September 1881, Lord Dufferin (Frederick Hamilton-Temple-Blackwood) once again revived Layard's suggestions, arguing for the appointment of a "secret paid agent residing in Mecca." It is ironic that the ideal man for Dufferin's proposed secret agent was already at work in the region. In 1878, the government of India had attached Dr. Abdur Razzack ('Abd al-Razzāq), assistant surgeon of the Bengal Medical Service, to accompany that year's pilgrimage from India. Apart from the espionage envisioned by Dufferin, Abdur Razzack's appointment was made with more pressing material questions in mind. The growing administrative and diplomatic questions associated with repeated cholera outbreaks in the Hijaz, the general welfare of the pilgrims, overcrowding on vessels carrying pilgrims, and rising number of indigent pilgrims constituted a clearer danger than the Pan-Islamic bogeymen imagined by Zohrab, Layard, and Dufferin.[38] Thus on his maiden voyage to the Hijaz, Abdur Razzack was to report only on the sanitary and logistical conditions of the hajj, a task that he successfully performed in March 1879. Although Abdur Razzack's primary role was to monitor the hajj's sanitation, he was also keenly aware of both the conflicted nature and inherent risk involved in his covert mission:

> If it had become known in Mecca, the sanctuary land of the Muhammadans where a large number of Muhammadan fanatics from India and many a rebel of the time of the mutiny of 1857 are domiciled, that an agent of the British Government had arrived incognito, there is no doubt that some sort of commotion might have ensued. They would have never appreciated the benevolence of the motives with which I was sent, but would, on the contrary, have considered it as an uncalled for intrusion and an unnecessary trespassing and prying into the workings of one of the noblest rites of Islam; and there is small doubt that, under the countenance of the ruling authorities, they would have at least tried to thwart me by not throwing difficulties in my way, but restricting my personal freedom, if not to do away with me altogether in a quiet and secret manner.[39]

Between 1878 and 1882, Abdur Razzack accompanied the hajj each year, acting primarily in his capacity as a physician. In light of the lingering concerns over Indian exiles and Pan-Islamic propagandists, however, Abdur Razzack was pressed repeatedly to perform more overtly political services. In 1882, the doctor was chosen as the best candidate for political surveillance activities in Mecca and the Hijaz. His recommenders described him as "an excellent man" and "altogether separated from the Delhi and Wahhabi schools . . . clever and ambitious." Although Abdur Razzack's primary duties were to assist Britain's Muslim subjects, promote the health and comfort of pilgrims, and protect them in their dealings with Ottoman officialdom, he also was instructed that the consul in Jeddah "may wish to avail himself of your assistance in obtaining trustworthy information regarding the course of affairs, and of public opinion, in Mecca and neighboring places."

In 1888, Abdur Razzack was once again pressed to play a more prominent role in the surveillance of potential Indian security threats. As the doctor pointed out to the consulate in his reply, he would need to visit Mecca frequently to obtain such information, to take a house there to avoid arousing Ottoman suspicions, and to have an allowance that would permit him "to give some small presents to some of the religious heads." Although Abdur Razzack's requests were approved, it remains unclear whether he provided anything like the covert intelligence that his employers envisioned.[40]

Ultimately Abdur Razzack's primary impact on the Hijaz and the hajj would not come as a covert agent. In August 1882, he was appointed as Jeddah's first Indian Muslim vice-consul. Given that Christians were unable to travel beyond Jeddah, Abdur Razzack's status as a Muslim was meant to circumvent Ottoman objections to the extension of British consular representation to Mecca and Medina. This way he could openly attend to public health questions while gathering intelligence and securing greater British influence in the holy cities.[41] To be sure, Abdur Razzack was far from immune to the security-obsessed logic of his British superiors. On a number of occasions, he warned of Meccan exiles, "relics of 1857 and the later Wahhabi movement," who were plotting to influence events in India. The doctor even wondered about the possibility of implementing "some sort of secret surveillance" to keep tabs on these high-risk individuals. Despite his periodic reports on potential Indian subversives, not to mention his receipt of Indian and Egyptian secret service funds, it would appear that he was either unable or unwilling to fully perform this task himself, nor were his employers willing to act on his suggestion of further surveillance activities.[42]

Perhaps in recognition of the Muslim vice-consulate's inability to secure sufficiently actionable intelligence, following Abdur Razzack's murder in 1895 (discussed in chapter 3), in 1896–97, the surveillance question was briefly revisited as part of a wider proposal to establish an "Indian Muhammadan Detective Agency" with branches in Istanbul, Mecca, Jeddah, and Baghdad. In the end, however, the government of India "found it difficult to believe that any respectable Muhammadan would consent to work as a secret agent at Mecca, Jeddah, or Baghdad." Once again, the government conceded that its most dependable source of intelligence would likely continue to come from Abdur Razzack's successor as Jeddah's Muslim vice-consul, Dr. Mohammed Hussein.[43]

Although the degree to which Abdur Razzack and his Muslim colleagues actually served as covert spies is debatable, their influence over pilgrimage affairs is unquestionable. From 1878 until his death in 1895, he served as the British point man for pilgrimage and public health affairs. He became the face of Britain's rapidly evolving pilgrimage administration and the empire's principal interlocutor with Ottoman officials and the Sharifate of Mecca. Abdur Razzack's importance and longevity reflected his ability to more fully engage with the minutiae of the hajj experience and to communicate more freely with both British pilgrim subjects and his Ottoman and Arab counterparts, a marked contrast to the more limited capabilities of European consular employees stationed in the Hijaz. As a result, the doctor's arrival in the Hijaz signaled the institution of more accurate documentation of pilgrim statistics. The suggestions made in his detailed annual reports were read by officials from London and Egypt to India and Malaya. Ultimately his writings would form the practical basis for the government of India's efforts to reform and institutionalize the pilgrimage experience. His reports also proved instrumental in reshaping British policies on everything from cholera, quarantine, and sanitation to the plight of indigent pilgrims, steamship regulations, passports, and pilgrimage guides.[44]

As John Slight cautions, Muslim consular employees such as Abdur Razzack and his successors should not be dismissed or caricatured as venal "collaborators." Whatever the intentions of their colonial masters, the reams of correspondence produced by these men repeatedly make clear that their primary objective was to ameliorate the sufferings of ordinary pilgrims. That they found themselves embedded in a colonial bureaucracy run by Christians should not detract from their dedication or nullify their observations. Their work put them in an unenviable, nearly impossible, position. It required them to serve as advocates on behalf of ordinary pilgrims, translating Muslim voices into a language that the colonial state could understand. It also required them to act as interimperial mediators, a task that consistently required them to question prevailing pieties and stand up to deeply entrenched British, Ottoman, and local Hijazi political and commercial interests.[45]

Abdur Razzack's nearly two decades of service in the Hijaz prompted a multidecade transition in Britain's approach to the hajj. First, the doctor's ability to map out the quotidian minutiae and day-to-day mechanics of the pilgrimage demonstrated that Muslim employees were an indispensable component of Britain's emerging pilgrimage regulatory system. Second, his grasp of the details of the hajj's public health, transport services, financial and charitable systems, and interimperial legal frameworks produced an altogether more realistic picture of the Indian Ocean hajj and Britain's material interests in its reform. As a result, he was able gradually to rebalance his superiors' primary concerns, shifting them away from their myopic visions of seditious exiles and Pan-Islamic conspiracies and refocusing their energies toward more technocratic policies of pilgrimage protection and reform. Officially, the government of India would continue to tout its strict adherence to a policy of nonintervention in religious affairs, underscoring its anxiety about the risk of enflaming Muslim public opinion.

At the same time, Abdur Razzack's detailed intelligence was gradually eroding and chipping away at this position. Rather than framing the hajj only as a potential security threat, the doctor prescribed a more robust and interventionist approach, promoting hajj reform as a golden opportunity simultaneously to undermine Ottoman outreach to the colonial Islamic world and promote Britain's role as the extraterritorial guardians of pilgrimage safety and security. Over time, the British Empire gradually came to see the hajj at least partly through Muslim eyes. Through the agency and advocacy of Abdur Razzack and other Muslim employees, the British Empire learned to assert itself more intelligently as a pilgrimage stakeholder of nearly coequal importance to the Ottoman sultan-caliph.[46]

Ottoman authorities quickly recognized the dynamic threat that Britain's turn to Muslim employees might entail. Apart from their potential as British spies, from an Ottoman perspective, the greatest threat that Abdur Razzack and other Muslim consular employees posed lay in their potential to move freely beyond the Jeddah's city gates. It amounted to nothing short of an extraterritorial declaration of legal warfare on Mecca's exceptional legal and religious status. Around the time of Abdur Razzack's appointment in 1882, British authorities had hoped to secure Ottoman permission for the consulate's translator (tercüman or dragoman), Yusuf Kudzi (Yūsuf Qudsī), to act as a second consular agent in Mecca. In February 1881, Kudzi traveled to Mecca at the request of Consul Zohrab but was expelled and sent back to Jeddah by Sharif ʿAbd al-Muṭṭalib, who accused him of attempting to meddle in "matters involving the internal politics" of the amirate.[47] On learning of the incident, Zohrab pleaded the vital importance of maintaining the consulate's "right to send Mussulman employees" to Mecca. Although he acknowledged that the legal limits of consular authority granted by ferman and berat extended only to Jeddah, he began to sketch in the gray areas of informal precedent through which extraterritorial authority over Mecca gradually might be secured through the consulate's Muslim employees. As he pointed out, until Kudzi's expulsion, although the sharifate had denied the right of consular jurisdiction within the holy cities, it had "*permitted it by courtesy.*" Thus it was a question "of whether precedent has not established the right."[48]

This was the crux of the argument that British and Ottoman authorities would continue to circle around through World War I. Fearing that precedent indeed would become a right, Osman Nuri Pasha, then governor of the Hijaz, heartily supported the sharif's expulsion of Kudzi. He reminded Zohrab that all inquiries related to the interior policy of the sharifate should be addressed only to the Sublime Porte.[49] In an odd twist, Osman Nuri, a strident proponent of Ottoman centralization, fiercely determined to strip the Sharifate of Mecca of as much power as possible, seems to have come to appreciate the utility of defending the "internal" sovereignty of the sharifate as a strategic buffer against the extension of consular protection to Mecca.

Osman Nuri recognized the danger of Muslim consular agents and translators having unfettered access to Mecca. He worried that the prolonged presence of British representatives in Mecca would set the stage for the opening of a full-fledged consulate and an ever-expanding threat of British espionage and political subversion.[50] He also emphasized how Abdur Razzack's appointment had agitated local public opinion. As he reported, the locals had taken to saying that once a Muslim consul is allowed in Mecca, inevitably "the flag will be unfurled" (*bayrak açılacak*).[51] The specter of the Union Jack flying over Mecca might have been hyperbole, but the legal consequences would have been all too real. Once the British established this right, all the other European powers soon would have demanded Muslim consular representation in Mecca as well.[52]

"The Consul of the Christians Cannot Help You"

During the 1880s, a series of court cases involving Indian Muslims accused of crimes in Mecca placed the legal status of the Hijaz under a new level of scrutiny. As these cases unfolded, the British deployed a patient strategy of stealthily enveloping Mecca within the framework of the Capitulations. The Foreign Office repeatedly claimed that under Article 42 of the Capitulations, Indian Muslim subjects making the hajj or residing in Mecca had the right to trial by a mixed tribunal in the presence of a consular officer or translator. From their perspective, Article 42 applied to the entirety of the Ottoman Empire and contained "no provision to except the Hedjaz or the holy cities from their stipulations."[53]

The clearest precedent for the application of Article 42 to Hijaz was set in the wake of the Jeddah riots of 1858. Following the slaughter of Jeddah's Christians and the British and French consuls and the subsequent bombardment of the town, Ottoman authorities were in no position to resist demands for the application of the Capitulations and the assembly of a mixed tribunal to adjudicate the investigation and punishment of the perpetrators. In that case, however, the application of extraterritorial consular authority had affected Jeddah. And when British authorities sought to expand their purview beyond Jeddah by requesting the extradition of Sayyid Faḍl ibn ʿAlawī, Ottoman authorities refused. Nevertheless, it was a demonstration that the Capitulations had arrived at the gates of *haremeyn*.

As early as 1861, Istanbul began to anticipate that this question was likely to be raised with increasing frequency. That year the vexed question of consular protection and the status of foreign *mücavirin* was put before the Special Council of Ministers (*Meclis-i Mahsus-ı Vükela*). As the ministers' response reveals, the highest levels of the Ottoman government understood the intractable nature of the problem. In light of the sacred status of the Two Holy Cities, it was decided that the recognition of "foreign protection" (*himaye-i ecnebiye*) was not "legally permissible." However, because the individuals concerned were Indian and Jawi subjects, "in light of the requirements of *international law* it would not be feasible to not recognize [their] *nationality* at all." It was recommended that every effort should be made to handle such cases as amicably as possible. However, the council also realized that the autonomous status of the holy cities could be used to deflect and circumvent the internationally binding requirements of the Capitulations and prevent the application of foreign protection beyond Jeddah. They argued that because there were no mixed courts in the holy cities, all cases involving non-Ottoman *mücavirin* should be handled in the shariʿa courts of Mecca and Medina.[54]

In 1883–84, this Ottoman attempt to use the sharifate's autonomy and the Hijaz's multilayered sovereignty as a shield against consular interference would be put to the test. In March 1883, a British Indian subject named

Abdul Aziz was arrested and imprisoned in Mecca. When the consulate made inquiries on his behalf, Governor Osman Nuri Pasha argued that the holy cities were excluded from the Capitulations. Therefore, Indian subjects accused of a crime in Mecca could not avail themselves of consular protection or the presence of a translator or be tried by a mixed tribunal. Here Osman Nuri echoed the 1861 decision almost verbatim, noting that "all foreigners who are in Mecca the Holy, whatever may be their nationality, and whether they are permanent residents, or stopping there temporarily, on the occasion of any claim made by or against them," the case would be tried in the shari'a courts.[55]

Eventually Osman Nuri relented, allowing the consulate to send Yusuf Kudzi to Mecca to assist in the proceedings. Although Osman Nuri and his superiors firmly objected to the practice, they attempted to find a modus vivendi through which cases of this nature could be expedited without risking further interference. From the British perspective, however, even this limited form of cooperation constituted a legal precedent establishing its future right to extend consular protection to Mecca.[56]

This was the prelude to an altogether more explosive affair in 1884. Between September and November 1884, a bizarre case involving a complicated struggle over inheritance, real estate, and power of attorney placed members of the Indian diasporic community in Mecca on opposite sides of the Anglo-Ottoman/Jeddah-Mecca jurisdictional divide. Two decades earlier, a wealthy British Indian subject, Hajji Ibrahim Abdus Sattar ('Abd al-Sattār), had died in Mecca, leaving a wife and daughter. Abdul Wahed Yunis, also a British subject, was entrusted with the management of the family's personal and commercial assets. In addition to being a wealthy merchant, Abdul Wahed Yunis was a business associate of Osman Nuri. In 1883, Abdul Wahed Yunis traveled to Calcutta, leaving his son Abdullah in charge of his and, by extension, the Abdus Sattar family's affairs. At the time, Abdul Wahed Yunis employed four brothers of the Zackaria family, all British Indian subjects. In his father's absence, Abdullah went to Hudayda to check on a branch of the family business. Abdullah had a falling out with the Zackaria brother who was managing the Hudayda operations. Owing to his influence with Osman Nuri, Abdullah succeeded in having him arrested. As this feud escalated, the other Zackaria brothers resigned from the service of the Yunis family. Two of the brothers remained in the Hijaz, Eyub Zackaria in Mecca and Cassim Zackaria in Jeddah.

Meanwhile, the Abdus Sattar women had a disagreement with Abdullah Yunis and threatened to withdraw their money from his management. As it happened, the Abdus Sattars rented a flat from Eyub Zackaria and lived on the floor above his family. Allegedly this connection made Abdullah suspect Eyub Zackaria of influencing the widow Abdus Sattar into transferring her estate to his care. In retaliation, Abdullah accused Eyub Zackaria of carrying on a bizarre sexual affair with the Abdus Sattar women.[57]

As a result of these crude allegations, the governor forbade Zackaria from escorting the Abdus Sattar family on hajj, as was his family's custom. He also ordered Zackaria to discontinue living in the same building. Zackaria complied with the governor's instructions relating to the hajj, but he refused to move out of his family's residence. As a result, Osman Nuri had him expelled from Mecca. According to Osman Nuri, Zackaria stood accused of "maintaining illicit relations with the two ladies, both mother and daughter." As Consul Thomas Sampson Jago complained, from the evidence gathered from the Indian Muslim communities in Mecca and Jeddah, until this dispute occurred, "not a breath of suspicion had ever clouded their fair name." As he noted, even as the case exploded into scandal, only the most "foul-mouthed" among the Indian Muslim community "sought to attribute immorality to the mother"; most accusations were made only against the more eligible 24-year-old daughter. To support his contention, in a somewhat humorous (if deeply misogynistic) moment of bemusement, Jago declared that the mother's "age [only 40] and appearance necessarily precluded any such accusation."[58]

If Jago was unprepared to accept the first round of salacious accusations, the second further strained credulity. On hearing of Eyub Zackaria's plight, the consulate sent Cassim Zackaria to Mecca to retrieve his brother's family and goods from his home. When he arrived, however, a policeman promptly ordered him to leave the building. Cassim Zackaria also was accused of immorality with the mother and daughter.[59] As the plot thickened, Osman Nuri, who previously had favored the exile of the Abdus Sattar women from Mecca, reversed his opinion. He explained that the transfer of the two women to Jeddah constituted a threat to "peace and morality" on the grounds of their possible contact with the brothers Zackaria. As the consulate complained, at first Osman Nuri had called for the banishment of the women and their departure for India on the first available steamer. However, owing to the influence of Abdullah, Osman Nuri became determined to hold the two women under house arrest until he could secure the consulate's agreement to deport both families to India.[60]

With that, the Abdus Sattar women found themselves detained in Mecca in a legal no-man's land. According to the consulate, Osman Nuri's determination to hold the women in Mecca was a pointed demonstration of his policy that even those Indians registered with the consulate as British subjects would be considered subject to Ottoman jurisdiction and shari'a court justice while resident in Mecca. In this environment the financial and sexual coercion of Amna Abdus Sattar and her daughter devolved into a proxy war over Mecca's jurisdictional status.

After her release from Mecca, Amna Abdus Sattar's deposition detailed how Abdullah had verbally and physically abused her. When she forbade him from returning to her home, Abdullah and three other men came back and forced their way in. The men threatened to kidnap and forcibly marry her daughter. As Abdullah left he taunted: "I will put men at your door and then who will help you?" She defiantly replied, "God and the Consul." In response to the widow's invocation of consular protection, Abdullah violently grabbed her and warned, "the Consul of the Christians cannot help you." When Abdus Sattar emphasizd that she was a British subject, Abdullah was unfazed: "I have the power and will keep you in Mecca." He then demanded that the widow move into a house near him. When she refused his advance, he said that he would "take" her "by force."[61]

One of the two men sent to threaten the Abdus Sattars was Mohammed Saleh, a British Indian who recently had been naturalized as an Ottoman subject. He was the nephew of the widow and a rejected suitor of her daughter. As the consulate theorized, his desire to marry the daughter was merely a ruse to strip them of their property. Had he succeeded, according to the consulate, under Islamic law he would have been entitled to three-fourths of their estate.[62]

When Amna Abdus Sattar stated her intention to seek the protection of the consulate in Jeddah, Abdullah petitioned the shari'a courts and secured a fatwa prohibiting the women from departing Mecca without the protection of a *mahrem* (a legally acceptable male guardian, generally an unmarriageable relative), dramatically narrowing the possibility of their escape. As the situation worsened, the consul hatched a plot to rescue the two women. Consul Jago instructed Yusuf Kudzi to locate a suitable *mahrem*. The only man Kudzi could find was a cousin, Habib Omar. Although initially on the side of the Abdus Sattar family's captors, Habib Omar was tricked into cooperation. Kudzi held out the false promise that Habib Omar would be given the disputed power of attorney over the family's assets in the event of their success. With Habib Omar as *mahrem*, Kudzi successfully extricated the women from their persecutors.

On the women's arrival in Jeddah, the widow declared her intention to secure a new agent from her relatives in Bombay. However, as the consulate feared, Abdul Wahed and Abdullah Yunis signaled their intention to use Mecca's jurisdictional exceptionalism to hold onto the Abdus Sattars' property. For her part, Amna Abdus Sattar was most aggrieved by the damage done to her and her daughter's reputations, prompting concern that she might commit suicide.[63]

The tragic outcome of this case raised serious questions about the future position of vulnerable British subjects such as widows and orphans. It also was an indication of the growing determination on the part of the Ottoman state to keep (or pry) the Hijaz's real estate and wealth out of the hands of any non-Ottoman Muslims who might wish to avail themselves of consular protection.

Banning the *Umma* from Owning a Piece of the Holy Land

The Land Law of 1858 (*Arazi Kanunnamesi*) was the Tanzimat state's first substantive effort to consolidate its victories over wealthy provincial notables. The law's intent was to reassert state ownership of imperial possessions, which, over several centuries, had passed out of government control. The new law was meant to extend the central government's power into the provinces at the expense of notable families, the remnants of the Janissaries, tribal populations, and the *ulema*, all of which resisted the Tanzimat state's intrusions. As part of this process, older land taxes and Islamic categories of ownership were replaced and simplified. In order to enforce the law, a new Cadastral Regulation (*Tapu Nizamnamesi*) was prepared. Together these new regulations required all of the land and property of each province to be surveyed as it came under the jurisdiction of the new Tanzimat regime. Each person or institution claiming ownership henceforth would be required to prove their claims with appropriate legal documentation before they could acquire a new deed of ownership.[64]

These reforms were critical to the centralization and homogenization of Ottoman policies on taxation, land ownership, inheritance law, and the issuance of deeds. Although eventually Istanbul was able to impose these reforms in certain parts of Syria and Iraq, by contrast, the semiautonomous and tribal territories of the Hijaz, Trablusgarb (Libya), and Yemen remained beyond the reach of Tanzimat-style censuses, cadastral surveys, and land registration.[65] Apart from customs revenues, the Hijaz retained its customary exemption from taxes on land or individual persons. Thus Istanbul had no expectation that provincial revenues would constitute a substantial contribution to the state's traditional subsidies and gifts to the region. At the same time, this inability to account more precisely for the Hijaz's land ownership, inheritance patterns, and real estate transfers also meant that the state was poorly equipped to prevent Hijazi properties from passing into foreign hands.

In 1867, the Ottoman government formally recognized the rights of foreigners to purchase real estate throughout the empire (*Tebaa-yı Ecnebiyenin Emlake Mutasarrıf Olmaları Hakkında Kanun*).[66] In theory, this law should have clarified the Hijaz's exceptional status. Once again, the law explicitly exempted the Hijaz. Although this exemption was meant to prohibit Europeans from owning property in the Hijaz, it carried an ironic twist. After the 1869 nationality law redefined non-Ottoman Muslims as foreigners and bearers of European colonial nationalities, it placed real estate purchases by foreign Muslims under greater suspicion.

Against the backdrop of the British occupation of Egypt in 1882 and swirling rumors of British support for an Arab caliphate, Hamidian-era suspicion of the potential dangers posed by non-Ottoman Muslims in the Hijaz gained a new sense of urgency. In 1879, the British consulate counted the Hijaz's British Indian population at roughly 15,000.[67] In 1885, Dr. Abdur Razzack provided somewhat more conservative totals, estimating Mecca's Indian colony at roughly 10,000 residents, plus another 1,500 in Jeddah. In defining the Hijaz's British Indian residents, Abdur Razzack counted individuals who had resided there for as little as two years but also those who had settled in the area as long ago as thirty years.[68] Although no official censuses were carried out in the Hijaz, according to William Ochsenwald's estimates, in the first half of the nineteenth century, Mecca had a total population of about 40,000. By 1908, he puts that number at roughly 80,000. Between Jeddah, Mecca, and Medina, from 1840 to 1880, the Hijaz's major urban centers boasted a population of perhaps as many as 85,000. By 1908, that number rose to approximately 160,000.[69]

In 1882, Ottoman authorities estimated that at least one-eighth of the Hijaz's real estate was already in the hands of non-Ottoman Muslims, most notably British Indian and Dutch Jawi subjects.[70] As Osman Nuri Pasha lamented, however, even these estimates told only part of the story. As he pointed out, foreign subjects living in the Hijaz operated in a non-Tanzimat-compliant, tax-free environment and enjoyed a virtual monopoly over every sector of productivity and commercial resources in the region.[71] Although Osman Nuri's reasons for curtailing the sale of real estate to foreigners was couched partly in terms of fiscal responsibility and economic productivity, as he acknowledged, the other important motivation for the ban was driven by the constant threat of consular interference.[72]

Osman Nuri Pasha's repeated warnings coincided neatly with the Ottoman center's growing concern that the Hijaz's foreign Muslims were destined to become stalking horses for European political subversion and extraterritorial control. In 1882, a memorandum produced by the Council of State warned,

> If we remain indifferent to the accumulation of property by devious means in the hands of foreign Muslims, with the passage of time we may find that much of the Holy Lands have been acquired by the subjects of foreign powers. Then, the foreigners, as is their wont, after lying in waiting for some time, will suddenly be upon us at the slightest opportunity and excuse and will proceed to make the most preposterous claims.[73]

In response to these anxieties, between 1880 and 1883, the Ottoman state moved to ban the sale of land and other real estate to non-Ottoman Muslims, especially subjects of European powers.[74] The ban placed even transactions intended for pious and philanthropic purposes under scrutiny.[75] As the British consulate reported, this policy had been in the works since around 1876. However, these efforts were consistently resisted. It also appears that these measures were easily evaded through bribes.[76] Working through prominent local guarantors and legal proxies, foreigners continued to purchase and endow properties. Between 1877 and 1879, officials in Medina approved the sale of twenty-four houses and a mill, and Meccan authorities authorized the sale of ninety houses and 290 parcels of land to foreigners.[77]

As subsequent investigations revealed, because shariʿa court judges and officials counted fees and duties from real estate transactions as a significant
source of illegitimate profits, the prohibition was repeatedly overlooked.[78]

After 1880, however, judges came under increasing pressure to refuse
official assistance to Indians, Jawis, and other non-Ottoman Muslims unless
they produced proof that they had petitioned to seek refuge as Ottoman
nationals.[79] Owing to the persistence of the gentle corruption and benign
neglect surrounding the law, in 1882 it was proposed that noncompliant
judges be tried and punished and that their replacements be provided with
salaries sufficient to ensure that they would not flout the law to pursue
illegitimate revenue streams.[80] At the same time, the central government
refrained from ordering the confiscation of illegally purchased properties
because as it delicately expressed, such an aggressive step would not "suit
the glory of the exalted Caliphate." Instead of confiscating properties, the
Council of State asked for a register of all questionable transfers and recommended further deliberation. As Lâle Can points out, this bit of equivocation
"is an important example of how the need to maintain Islamic legitimacy
hampered the effective enforcement of the law."[81]

Such action also raises questions about the difficulty of imposing abstract
imperial-level regulations at the local level. Notions of legal nationality
needed time to germinate. For a judge in Mecca or Medina, it was hard to
adjust long-established local (*mahalli* or *yerli*) notions of belonging and Islamic
legal norms to accommodate newly minted, arguably un-Islamic forms of
imperial nationality and subjecthood.[82] Thus where Ottoman statesmen
in Istanbul saw non-Ottoman Muslims as "potential chinks in their armor
against the Capitulations," local authorities and elites continued to see nothing more than "pious Muslims engaged in everyday life." For officials on the
ground, one's status and identity as a local or a pious resident, regardless of
legal nationality, continued to trump imperial concerns over the potential
extraterritorial threat posed by foreign Muslims. And even among imperial
officials in Istanbul, it remained unclear whether the state itself was ever
fully convinced that such restrictions should apply with equal force to all
foreign Muslims. After all, the extraterritorial baggage carried by Bukharan
or Chinese Muslims was different from the more proximate threats posed by
an Indian, Malay, or Jawi brandishing British or Dutch passports.[83]

Again in 1885, Osman Nuri Pasha complained that because the government had not shown the necessary sensitivity in curtailing this corruption

and encouraging non-Ottoman Muslims to take up Ottoman nationality, real estate continued to pass into foreigners' hands.[84] In this context, even the prospect of property changing hands through marriages between Ottoman women (*nisvan-ı Osmaniye*) and non-Ottoman men in the Hijaz came to be viewed as a dangerous loophole.[85] According to the 1869 Ottoman Law of Nationality, Ottoman women who married foreign nationals would lose their subjecthood and be forced to take up their husbands' nationality. These anxieties mirrored similar concerns over "nationality miscegenation" in Iraq.[86] In an 1874 amendment to the 1869 nationality law, Istanbul reversed itself and exempted Iraq. The amendment revisited an 1822 prohibition on marriages between Ottomans and Persians. The amendment once again declared that Ottoman women who married Persians would not be allowed to take their husbands' nationality. In turn, any children born of their unions also would remain Ottoman subjects. Preventing these children from inheriting their fathers' nationality also meant that the male children of these mixed-nationality marriages remained subject to military conscription. Istanbul could ill afford to lose control over more subjects along another contested frontier.[87]

The Iraqi exemption to the 1869 nationality law is an instructive parallel to the situation in the Hijaz. As Karen Kern has shown, the ban on Ottoman-Persian marriages was central to the Ottoman state's efforts to hold onto a modicum of control over the eastern provinces of Baghdad and Mosul under less-than-ideal circumstances. The 1874 ban on Ottoman-Persian marriages clearly was meant to anticipate and prevent potential abuses of the Capitulations. Just a year later, in December 1875, the Ottomans and the Qajars signed a reciprocal treaty granting the same privileges to Ottomans residing in Persia as to Persians living in Ottoman territories. This Ottoman-Persian Convention confirmed that Persian consuls would have the same capitulatory rights as their European counterparts. This agreement permitted the Qajar state to appoint consuls to oversee the needs of Persian traders and pilgrims traveling to and from the shrine cities of the ʿatabāt in Iraq as well as Mecca, Medina, and Erzurum. Subsequently, civil and criminal court cases involving Persians and Ottomans would no longer fall under the jurisdiction of shariʿa courts. Instead, such cases were transferred to mixed tribunals, where Persian consuls and vice-consuls could extend extraterritorial assistance and protection. This was yet another demonstration of Istanbul's inability to fully control Iraq's eastern frontiers. Although the Qajars might not have been able to militarily threaten Istanbul itself, the Ottoman state could ill afford to go to war over the status of Persians residing in Iraq. However, this concession only further enflamed Ottoman anxieties over mass conversions from Sunnism to Shi'ism.[88]

Granting capitulatory privileges to Iran further compounded British India's already well-established consular reach into Iraq's Shi'i pilgrimage cities. Not only did numerous Shi'i Indians visit and settle in Iraq, the British government itself had a direct relationship with the Shi'i *mujtahids* (jurisconsults) via the Awadh (Oudh) Bequest. The bequest, established by the king of Awadh prior to that territory's annexation by the British government in 1856, funneled alms to Najaf and Karbala. Following Awadh's annexation, control over the bequest passed directly into British hands. As a result, the annual distribution of funds was conducted by the British consul-general in Baghdad and funneled to specially appointed *mujtahids* in Najaf and Karbala. Through the administration of these funds and the patronage they entailed, British colonial officials gained tremendous influence over both Ottoman Iraq and neighboring Iran.[89]

The question of marriages between Ottomans and foreign Muslims aroused similar fears in the Hijaz. However, unlike its Iraqi provinces, Istanbul's concerns over mixed-nationality marriages in the Hijaz and the *haremeyn* could not be resolved through an outright prohibition. In the Hijaz the state could not justify discouraging mixed-nationality marriages as a safeguard against mass conversion to Shi'ism.[90] Attempts to prohibit wholly legitimate marriages between Sunni Muslims of different nationalities likely would have aroused resistance among both Ottoman nationals and non-Ottoman Muslims. And unlike Iraq, which had become engulfed by the extension of both British and Persian consular systems, the Hijaz remained at least partly sheltered from the full impact of the Capitulations.[91]

As a result, the risk of Ottoman women becoming foreign nationals was less acute. In the Hijaz the Ottoman state had no compelling interest in prohibiting otherwise legitimate marriages between Sunni men and women of different nationalities. Rather, the central government's anxieties centered on landownership and the consolidation of real estate and immovable property in the hands of large colonies of Indians and Southeast Asians (including Jawis, Malays, and Hadramis with either British or Dutch nationalities). Again, anxiety over foreign nationals gobbling up property was a common thread running through all of the Ottoman Empire's major pilgrimage centers in the Hijaz, Iraq, and Palestine. In both Iraq and Palestine, for example, Yıldız Palace officials sought to shelter these vulnerable territories by acquiring huge tracts of land through the Sultan's Privy Purse (*Hazine-i Hassa*), a practice that effectively "nationalized" large swaths of land. In Baghdad and Mosul, this maneuver was aimed at nurturing construction of the Berlin-Baghdad railway project and keeping potentially lucrative oil-producing regions out of European hands.[92] In Jerusalem and Palestine, *Hazine-i Hassa* land acquisitions, Bedouin sedentarization efforts, and the resettlement of Muslim refugees from the Caucasus and Balkans played a similar role in Ottoman attempts to combat the growing threat of European land speculation and Zionist immigration.[93]

In the case of the Hijaz, as the Ottoman Foreign Ministry's (*Hariciye Nezareti*) Office of Legal Counsel (*Hukuk Müşavirliği İstişare Odası*) quickly came to realize that, in addition to acting through local proxies, one of the most obvious ways of subverting the state's newly imposed prohibition on real estate sales to foreign Muslims was by contracting marriages with Ottoman women.[94] In 1889, suspicions about the potential connection between mixed-nationality marriages and real estate transfers to foreign Muslims were raised in a query to the Office of Legal Counsel. In response, that office again warned that foreign/non-Ottoman Muslims were prohibited from purchasing immovable property. As the opinion stated, "whether in the *haremeyn* or in Jeddah," any "Ottoman women who marry Indian or Jawi foreigners, are to be considered nationals of the state to which their husbands belong."[95] In effect, by prohibiting Ottoman women from retaining their Ottoman nationality, the Office of Legal Counsel believed that it could prevent their husbands from legally purchasing real estate or legitimating previous illegal purchases performed by proxy. And given that the Office of Legal Counsel officially denied the applicability of the Capitulations to the Hijaz, technically foreign nationals—especially those who owned property outside Jeddah—would have little chance of availing themselves of consular legal remedies.

As the prohibition on real estate purchases by foreign Muslims provides insight into Istanbul's wariness of colonial extraterritoriality in the Hijaz, it also sheds light on the degree to which British officials gradually were becoming more realistic about the prospects of the hajj's potential as a conduit for seditious behavior. In 1896, the nizam of Hyderabad's brother-in-law wanted to purchase a pilgrimage hostel in Mecca. The nizam's British resident asked for Calcutta's assistance, and the government agreed to ask if the Ottoman state might be willing to relax its prohibition on foreign real estate purchases. As one official observed, whereas increased diplomatic and religious connections between Hyderabad and other Muslim princely states might prove "objectionable," ultimately the hajj already was providing countless avenues for the cultivation of such relationships. As he put it, the purchase of a guest house in Mecca by the nizam's family would make "little or no difference." As this episode suggests, by the close of the century, the British came to see the hajj as a relatively manageable security risk. Ironically, the Ottoman ban on foreign real estate purchases only worked in their favor. And if Indian Muslims found the policy irksome, it offered further opportunity for the British to malign the Ottomans for their maladministration of the pilgrimage.[96]

The ban on real estate purchases by foreign Muslims in the Hijaz was to remain in force through World War I despite the ongoing problems involved in enforcing it. At face value this law seemed to radically contradict the Hamidian state's attempts to cultivate loyalty to the caliphate among foreign Muslims. It is also clear that the ban did not go unchallenged on religious grounds. As one dissenting opinion submitted to the Council of State in 1903 pointed out, although the fundamental political concerns over Indian and Jawi colonial subjects were reasonable, the logic behind singling out these groups was unsustainable. As the author quipped, what of the territories recently ceded to Russia, Romania, Greece, and Serbia? Were Muslims from those territories not also foreign subjects? Whatever the possible dangers posed by a few Indians or Jawis, the author reasoned that it could not possibly equal the negative influence of this ban. As he chided, the right to settle in the holy cities is guaranteed under Islamic law. In any case, the vast majority of those who chose to settle in the *haremeyn* sought only "to collect a heavenly reward" and "have no other intention." Without the holy places, he worried that there would no longer be a place for the Islamic world to gather. Moreover, to prohibit settlement in the holy places would almost certainly break their ties to the center of the caliphate. After all, as the author challenged, did the caliph not claim leadership as the spiritual head of all Islam and not just Islam in his own domains, regardless of their nationality or subjecthood?[97]

As this dissenting opinion seems to ask, was the prohibition of land sales to foreign Muslims a case of the oft-cited, though rarely thoughtfully examined, "paranoia" of the Hamidian era? Had the state conjured an unrealistic demon? If not, what kind of "preposterous claims" did Osman Nuri and the Council of State fear? The petition's indignation at the growing chasm between the religious rhetoric of the caliphate and the Hamidian state's exclusionary policies reveals the contradictions inherent in the pursuit of Pan-Islamic universalism and territorial sovereignty at the same time. However, this paradox is an artificial one, an artifact of our insistence on thinking of Pan-Islam as a religious discourse. As the attempt to restrict real estate sales to foreign Muslims underscores, Pan-Islam often was a set of policies and discourses defined as much by sovereignty and international legal considerations as by Islamic legitimacy. The loftier foreign policy objectives of Pan-Islam were constantly being weighed against and frequently subordinated to projects designed to shelter Ottoman sovereignty from the corrosive effects of autonomy, extraterritoriality, international law, and their intersection.

Conclusion

The stalemate over protection dragged on until the end of Ottoman rule in Arabia. In 1910, four British subjects were tried and convicted of assault in Mecca. Once again the British Embassy claimed that Ottoman authorities had knowingly refused consular representation to their subjects, in blatant violation of the Capitulations. The embassy communiqué claimed that the authorities at the Sublime Porte "do not hesitate to admit" that no "exception of this sort" has ever been established, "neither through the text of the treaties in question nor through any subsequent agreement." The embassy's complaint pointed out that Istanbul already had "recognized more than one time that British subjects who find themselves in the Holy Cities have the right of protection from the Consulate of His Majesty in Jeddah."[98] The document cited precedents from 1884, 1888, and 1896 when the consulate's translator had been permitted to represent British subjects held in Mecca.[99] In light of these precedents, the embassy insisted that enforcement of the Capitulations "ought to apply to the Holy Cities just as the other parts of the Ottoman Empire." And in future cases, "a Muslim representative of His Majesty's Consulate in Jeddah" always should be invited "to assist in all of the proceedings" and be allowed to act in the "capacity of the Consular Authorities."[100]

The complaint was referred to the Ottoman Office of Legal Counsel. That office compiled a report on the status of the "Capitulations in the Hijaz" (*Hicaz'da imtiyazat-ı ecnebiye*) spelling out what might be regarded as the empire's final position on the matter. As the empire's most senior international legal experts reiterated, although it had long been the practice of the local Ottoman government to assist European consulates in Jeddah with questions pertaining to their subjects in Mecca and Medina, such assistance was merely a matter of "courteous procedure" (*muamele-i hatırşinasane*) and was undertaken in a strictly "non-official" (*gayri resmiye*) capacity at the discretion of the provincial government. They acknowledged that it had become customary for some Muslim officials of the consulates to visit Mecca during hajj season in order to attend to the civil and criminal affairs of their respective subjects, but the experts noted that the Ottoman government considered such individuals as acting "in a private capacity" (*suret-i hususiye'de*). Owing to this conceptual distinction, these individuals were not recognized as officially sanctioned consular agents. To emphasize this distinction between official and unofficial cooperation, the provincial authorities pointed out that all information given was "completely verbal" (*tamamiyle şifahen*).[101] More important, although the Office of Legal Counsel's interpretations underscored that these "unofficial" communications were carried out in a spirit of cooperation and in the best interests of the pilgrims, they cautioned that these niceties were observed "under conditions *unknown* in international law" and "without being bound by formal international commitments."[102] In short, such communications were not linked to any legally binding "exceptions" (*istisnaat*) or "privilege" (*imtiyaz*).[103]

In correspondence with the Foreign Ministry and the Office of Legal Counsel, the provincial administration in the Hijaz also articulated its perception of the threat posed by the British expansion of extraterritorial rights. As administration officials pointed out, the British consulate repeatedly attempted to employ Ottoman subjects in order to offer various forms of "intervention and protection" (*müdahale ve himaye*) to their subjects in Mecca and were trying to do the same in Medina. They also claimed that the British consulate frequently acted "outside the bounds of its official position" and involved itself in the "seizure and sale of goods and real estate," interfering "within the holy lands of the Hijaz." As officials on the ground saw it, giving in to British efforts to extend its exterritorial reach into the holy cities would only "facilitate the consulate's wide-ranging influence and lead to a further swelling of their demands."[104]

Taken in isolation, this kind of legal maneuvering might appear to be little more than a minor footnote. However, the British Foreign Office's persistent logic regarding the application of Article 42 provides a fuller context to the predicament that the Capitulations presented for Ottoman sovereignty in the Hijaz. As the Foreign Office's 1889 inquiry into the question of consular protection in Mecca concluded,

> as the Capitulations contain no provision to except the Hedjaz or the holy cities from their stipulations, Her Majesty's Government can admit no such exception. The only grounds on which Her Majesty's Government could be justified in renouncing at Mecca the rights of protection conceded by the Capitulations for the Ottoman Empire generally would be a distinct declaration from the Porte that that city had ceased to be (in the language of Article 42) "a portion of the Sultan's sacred dominions," *in which case it would be necessary to make such arrangements as might be possible with the Grand Shareef as an independent authority.*[105]

The stakes of these questions—and thinly veiled threats lurking behind them—extended well beyond the protection of pilgrims accused of crimes in Mecca. Rather, they are a reflection on how the Capitulations and the internationally binding character of the linkage between the Tanzimat reforms and the Treaty of Paris defined Ottoman sovereignty from Britain's perspective. Fair or not, by this logic, if the Ottomans claimed that they could not enforce the Capitulations in a given territory, the Ottoman state risked not being considered fully sovereign there. The inability to ensure extraterritorial protections provided a pretext for European intervention or, as the Foreign Office hinted, the search for an alternative sovereign. In this case, the independent alternative was the sharif of Mecca and ultimately a harbinger of things to come.

PART TWO

Ecologies of Empire

THREE

Microbial Mecca and the Global Crisis of Cholera

ON SEPTEMBER 19, 1891, the postal steamer *Nimet-i Hüda* arrived in Istanbul. The steamship had completed its return journey from the Hijaz after the conclusion of the hajj. One of the passengers was a man named Samsunlu Hacı Mustafa Efendi. The following day it was reported that Hacı Mustafa had been laid up in bed with a suspected case of cholera. Hacı Mustafa lived on a side street off Çeşme Meydanı Caddesi in Galata, placing him in the middle of Istanbul's second most populous district, home to some 220,000 souls, roughly a quarter of the city's urban population.[1]

In the span of three or four days, the panic induced by Hacı Mustafa's symptoms, whereabouts, and contacts attracted the attention of Ottoman officials of virtually every level and description, including the the municipal authorities in Beyoğlu; the police; *jandarma*; the international delegates on the Board of Health, the Health Ministry, and the Naval Ministry; the grand vizier; and even the sultan himself. As the case unfolded, an Austrian physician was dispatched to Hacı Mustafa's home to examine him. Cholera was suspected and the alarm was raised. Copies of the doctor's examination were forwarded to the Ministry of Health. Municipal authorities in Beyoğlu called in the police and *jandarma* to place the patient under guard, and a sanitary cordon was established. The guards placed outside the door would in turn discover that several women inside the home were suffering. The municipal government was then called in to provide welfare assistance for bread and other necessities.

Meanwhile, the Naval Ministry was instructed to tow the *Nimet-i Hüda* either outside Fenerbahçe or Yenikapı and place the vessel under a ten- to twelve-day quarantine. The crew of the steamship was to be rounded up and placed under quarantine as well. There was also the need to locate and examine as many of Hacı Mustafa's fellow passengers as possible. With the approval of the sultan, special instructions were sent to the *mutasarrıf* of Beyoğlu and the Ministry of Police urging that extreme care be taken in the event of the Hacı Mustafa's death. It was recommended that his corpse be taken far outside the city and buried in a deep grave lined with lime. In addition to the removal of the corpse, the order dictated that all of his personal items be disinfected or burned.[2]

In the midst of these frightening precautions, in his correspondence with the Ministry of Health, the grand vizier candidly spelled out his fear that this case might be the start of the next devastating epidemic in Istanbul. He reflected back on the devastation that Istanbul had suffered during the great cholera outbreak (*büyük kolera*) of 1865. As he explained, it had taken only one instance of negligence to allow an infected steamer to enter the Golden Horn, visiting "disaster and calamity" on the population.[3] In 1865, a cholera outbreak had ravaged the Hijaz. Steamers of returning pilgrims carried cholera across the Red Sea to Cairo and Alexandria. In turn, cholera made its way from Egypt to Istanbul aboard an Ottoman *korvet* (small warship) transporting a tuberculosis-stricken official, one Osman Pasha. Although communication between the infected ports of the Red Sea, Egypt, and Istanbul had been placed under strict quarantine measures, on its return journey the crew had thrown two cholera victims into the sea. The vessel went straight to the naval yard at Tersane, and that evening two soldiers were admitted to the Tersane hospital. Within days cholera had spread to the surrounding neighborhoods of Hasköy and Kasımpaşa.[4] The outbreaks would rage on for four months, killing as many as 1,000 per day at their height, leaving a death toll of as many as 30,000 by epidemic's end.[5] As Sadri Sema recounts, the 1865 outbreak was so devastating that for every eight or ten people attending the funeral of a cholera victim, five or six might die along the way to the original victim's funeral ceremony.[6] As Ahmed Cevad Pasha reviewed the precautions being taken, he could not help but wonder whether Hacı Mustafa and the *Nimet-i Hüda* were the source of the city's next great catastrophe.

In light of the anxieties produced by this case, a scientific committee composed of members of the Board of Health and faculty from the Imperial

Medical College (*Mekteb-i Tıbbiye-i Şahane*) were assembled to evaluate Hacı Mustafa. Despite all of the precautions requested by the Ministry of Health, according to the medical commission, Hacı Mustafa apparently did not have cholera after all. They argued that it was only a case of dysentery (*mezemmet-i disanteri*) and extreme exhaustion from the three-month journey to the Hijaz and back. As the committee pointed out, due to the impoverished and unsanitary state of the home, the patient could not be treated properly and should be transferred to a hospital for treatment. Within three days of their report, however, Hacı Mustafa was dead and buried in accordance with the protocols laid out for a cholera death. Although the Grand Vizierate later complained about how "very absurd" these measures had been even after it was determined that the victim had suffered only from a diarrheal illness, the confusion, bureaucratic infighting, international ramifications, and second-guessing surrounding this single suspected case of cholera provide us with a vivid sense of the epidemiological anxiety that must have hung like a fog over fin de siècle Istanbul.

The documentary record surrounding Hacı Mustafa, his body, family, home, and the preparations for his burial offers a succinct yet panoramic vignette of the social and administrative life of the Ottoman Empire during the multidecade reign of epidemic cholera. It also provides a starting point for unpacking the disciplinary mechanisms and modernizing public health reforms that cholera helped to produce.[7] The anxieties and memories of past mistakes dredged up by Hacı Mustafa's suspected cholera case concisely illustrate a pattern that was to become all too familiar to Ottoman and European physicians and officials during this period.

By the 1890s, both the Hijaz and Istanbul were living in perpetual terror of the next microbial disaster imported via the hajj from India, the endemic cradle of cholera. Between 1831 and 1914, cholera spread from India to the Hijaz on at least forty occasions.[8] After 1865, but especially between 1881 and 1895, a global cholera pandemic smoldered continuously from India to the Mediterranean. Throughout this period cholera remained in almost constant circulation, flaring up for extended periods in virtually every corner of the Ottoman Empire, especially along its Indian Ocean frontiers on the Red Sea and Persian Gulf.[9] By the 1890s, tragic scenes of human loss and the social and administrative confusion that came in their wake had been repeated with alarming regularity for more than half a century. The Hijaz had seen outbreaks of varying severity in 1831, 1834, 1836–40, 1846, 1851,

1856–58, and 1860. Then there was the great *Hacc-ı ekber* outbreak of 1865, which had killed between 15,000 and 30,000 pilgrims and sparked a global pandemic. The 1870s witnessed outbreaks in 1872, 1876, and 1877–78. In the 1880s and 1890s, cholera's visitations only continued to intensify. Cholera broke out during every hajj season between 1881 and 1883. In 1883, the outbreak once again spread to Egypt, killing approximately 50,000. Again, four of the six pilgrimage seasons between 1890 and 1895 produced outbreaks, reaching a gory crescendo in the *Hacc-ı ekber* season of 1893. Estimates of the death toll for that year range from 30,000 to as many as 50,000.[10] In the fallout from the carnage of 1893, cholera also afflicted Istanbul, claiming 1,340 souls between outbreaks in 1893–94 and 1895. Although that was nothing compared with the devastation visited on Istanbul in the 1865 epidemic, as we shall see, the outbreaks of the 1890s marked a critical turning point in the slow maturation of the sanitary reorganization of Istanbul, the Hijaz and the Red Sea, and the empire as a whole.[11]

As Alan Mikhail, Nükhet Varlık, and Sam White have pointed out, the early modern Ottoman Empire had its own particular "imperial ecology." Agricultural goods and raw materials were being extracted constantly to feed the imperial capital and sustain the Ottoman military's sprawling mobilization. At the same time, those same circuits that mobilized and circulated the empire's crops, livestock, people, and minerals just as easily could convey epidemic diseases such as bubonic plague. Likewise, the ecologies of Egypt, Anatolia, and the Balkans were inseparable from the whole of Ottoman environmental history, and vice versa. However, that larger Ottoman ecosystem also was overlapped and penetrated by environmental forces originating from well beyond its borders. Indeed, the "idea of the empire as an ecosystem" points to the "artificiality" of traditional political spatial distinctions.[12] In the case of cholera, as with plague before it, this point is made painfully clear. Time and again, cholera laid bare the Hijaz's newly vulnerable position as a transimperial nexus of the steamship era, which linked the imperial ecologies of Ottoman domains with British India into an almost seamless Indian Ocean "disease zone."[13]

Each time steam-powered cholera leapt across the Indian Ocean and struck the Hijaz, it exponentially raised the likelihood that the disease would bloom across the width and breadth of the empire and beyond as pilgrims returned to their homes, unwittingly carrying the devastating microbes. Returning pilgrims such as Hacı Mustafa had a way of bringing the instability of the Indian Ocean frontier home to the imperial center, laying its biopolitical and environmental insecurity at the feet of power. Chapter 3 explores how cholera annihilated the presumed difference between a modernizing Istanbul and the supposedly "backward" Arabian frontier. It examines how the infrastructures and procedures of sanitary and environmental discipline necessary to contain the death and destruction produced by cholera collapsed time and space and intimately bound the imperial capital to its unruly frontiers. Put slightly differently, cholera had a way of generalizing the frontier. Quarantine and medical surveillance measures were not a matter of merely building sanitary checkpoints on desert islands in the Red Sea. Rather, the defenses built up and directed outward against the Red Sea invasions of cholera-carrying Indian Ocean pilgrims were merely the most obvious physical manifestations of the disciplinary mechanisms that tracked, diagnosed, and treated suspected victims of cholera like Hacı Mustafa.

In this sense the multilayered practices and infrastructures of medical surveillance and environmental discipline being strengthened in Tanzimat- and Hamidian-era Istanbul were only as effective as their application and execution at the absolute geographical and logistical margins of the empire. As a result, from the 1860s onward—but especially by the 1890s—the Hijaz was by no means exempt from the increasingly invasive sanitary and envirotechnical interventions being imposed on the residents of Istanbul and the core of the Ottoman state. As chapter 3 shows, the new technologies of bacteriological science, urban sanitation, disinfection, and water safety tested and refined in Istanbul and elsewhere rapidly found their way to the Hijaz and the quarantine sites of the Red Sea and Persian Gulf.

Coping with India's Ecological Fallout

It is difficult to imagine a more gruesome or frightening death than cholera. Cholera is an acute diarrheal infection caused by exposure to unclean water that is contaminated with fecal matter containing the bacterium *Vibrio cholerae*. Although most of those infected will experience either mild or no symptoms, even these seemingly healthy individuals continue to carry the bacteria in their feces for seven to fourteen days after infection, unknowingly infecting others at every turn. For those who do develop acute symptoms, owing to cholera's rapid incubation time (ranging from a few hours to a few days), an otherwise healthy person can die in less than a day. Cholera kills by binding to the receptor cells in the small intestine that are responsible for the absorption and retention of chloride and, consequently, sodium. As a result, water rapidly drains from the body's cells and is dumped into the intestine. As victims succumb to the disease's characteristic "rice water" diarrhea, they can lose up to a liter of fluids per hour. The relentless diarrhea is followed by vomiting. The voiding of all of the body's fluids leads to catastrophic dehydration, crashing electrolytes, fevers, chills, severe cramping, and shock. Left untreated, roughly half of cholera victims will succumb to the disease.[14]

Over the course of the long nineteenth century, millions of Muslim men, women, and children crowded into the holds of slow-moving steamers bound for Mecca. Seasick, clinging to their belongings, and often deprived of even the most basic arrangements for clean water and sanitation, they endured weeks of misery en route from Bombay, Calcutta, or Singapore to Arabia. Along the way the claustrophobic spaces below decks provided a veritable petri dish for cholera's incubation, and it spread from one captive victim to another. And as cholera's regular visitations on pilgrimage steamers and in Mecca itself became increasingly predictable, solemnly enduring discomfort and bravely facing down an unimaginably horrific death became a normal, even integral, part of ordinary Muslims' hajj experience.

Just as individual pilgrims suffered and died under cholera's cruel reign, on a larger geopolitical and administrative scale, the Ottoman Empire was victimized by this distinctly colonial scourge. Since early modern times the Ottoman Empire had been managing the fallout from epidemic diseases and natural disasters, including plagues, droughts, famines, floods, fires, and earthquakes. Indeed, recent scholarship has pointed to the long evolution and resilience of the empire's disaster relief systems. In the context of the massive restructuring and modernization of the state undertaken during the Tanzimat and Hamidian periods, however, late Ottoman responses to natural disasters gained renewed significance. As tragic as an earthquake, flood, or fire might have been, these events also represented opportunities for transformation.[15] And although modernizing practices brought increased expectations for the immediate delivery of welfare relief, whether foodstuffs, medical care, or shelter, Ottoman authorities were emboldened to radically redesign urban landscapes. Repeated cholera outbreaks were no different. These tragic events brought new opportunities to test the latest technoscientific tools and infrastructures of bacteriological science, disinfection, quarantine, and urban sanitation, including the construction of new sewer systems and the reorganization of municipal water supplies. In other words, nineteenth-century disasters opened new spaces, living laboratories for the experiments of Ottoman modernization.[16]

At the same time, orchestrating the urban reorganization of Istanbul in the wake of an earthquake or fire, or even the overhaul of the capital's water and sewer systems, arguably represented more manageable challenges than the vexing interimperial puzzle of cholera prevention along the empire's vast and porous southern frontiers. From a purely fiscal and logistical perspective, reproducing the sanitary reforms being pioneered in Istanbul and the state's centralized core and transporting them to the empire's southernmost extremities was daunting it in its own right. To complicate matters, new notions of bacteriology, urban sanitation, quarantine, and disinfection were all met with varying degrees of suspicion and resistance by foreign pilgrims, urban Hijazis, and Bedouins. On the ground, sanitary reforms and quarantine measures frequently were framed as un-Islamic innovations and further evidence of Europe's growing influence over the administration of the Hijaz and the hajj. To a degree this was partly true. The Ottoman Board of Health was an international body subject to the capitulatory oversight of European representatives. However, it would be a mistake to view Istanbul's imposition of stricter sanitary and quarantine policies solely as a product of European pressure. As this chapter details, the medicalization of the frontier was well suited to the centralizing impulses of Istanbul's Tanzimat- and Hamidian-era statesmen and bureaucrats. Quarantines, increased border controls, and the sanitary reorganization of the Hijaz and wider Red Sea offered the Ottoman state critical opportunities to strengthen its administrative reach and underscore the empire's territorial sovereignty, while ostensibly doing so under the banner of diplomatic cooperation and international legal recognition.

Still, Istanbul's position on the frontlines of the international struggle against cholera was a lonely and deeply frustrating one. Unlike the case with earlier instances of disease and natural disaster, Ottoman officials no longer viewed cholera as an act of God. Istanbul had an increasingly clear understanding of cholera as a human-caused microbial crisis, produced and exacerbated by British colonial policies in India.[17] From Yemen, the Hijaz, and Iraq to Istanbul itself, the ecological fallout of British colonialism loomed like a monsoon cloud sweeping over Ottoman lands. Just as the Hijaz was increasingly subject to the extraterritorial political and legal influences radiating from the Indian Ocean, it was equally vulnerable to the explosion of human suffering, dislocation, and deadly microbes being unleashed by the predations of the British Raj. The deeper that India sank into its own ecological crises, the more the Hijaz and the broader Ottoman ecosystem bore the brunt of its steam-powered collateral damage.

Ottoman authorities did their best to leverage the weak mechanisms of international diplomacy to protect the empire and Europe itself from a disaster largely of Britain's creation. Yet even as international scientific opinion coalesced around India's position at the epicenter of the global cholera pandemic, Ottoman officials were confronted with a British colonial state that was virulently opposed to the emerging bacteriological consensus surrounding cholera's transmission and equally determined to deny its culpability in the creation of the crisis or further responsibility to mitigate the disease's tragic effects.

From 1865 through World War I, India experienced what Ira Klein describes as "a woeful crescendo of death." A staggering death rate of 4,130 per 100,000 in the 1880s—already high by contemporary European standards—eventually would rise to 4,860 per 100,000 between 1911 and 1921.[18] The causes of these appalling figures are multifaceted, but they collectively point the blame squarely at the environmental consequences of British imperialism. Much attention has focused on the balance of advancements and limitations in the way that Western medicine and sanitation were being applied to nineteenth-century Britain and India.[19] Others have stressed the colonial state's wholesale disregard for local environmental knowledge and the radical alteration of the Indian landscape and hydrosphere through the construction of massive irrigation networks, roads, and deforestation.[20] Similarly, disruptions to drainage systems created giant nurseries of mosquitoes in which malaria reigned unabated.[21] Still others have pointed to British military campaigns, the expansion of capitalism, and modern systems of trade and food distribution—reorganized by the introduction of rail and steam connections—as the primary sources of cholera's increased mobility.[22] Taken together, all of these dislocations played their part in setting the stage for colonial India's spiraling mortality figures.

In *Late Victorian Holocausts: El Niño and the Making of the Third World* (2001), Mike Davis attempts to capture the totality of colonial India's ecological and demographic implosion. He recasts India's exorbitant levels of mortality primarily as a function of the large-scale famines that resulted from the deteriorating economic, social, and environmental conditions created by Britain's exploitation of the subcontinent's land and resources. Davis argues that although environmental factors such as the failure of the monsoons certainly contributed to nineteenth-century India's catastrophic mortality rates, the synergistic relationships among drought, famine, malaria, plague, and cholera were human-caused crises born of colonial India's unjust agrarian, environmental, economic, and political systems.[23]

Regardless of whether one places more emphasis on human, technical, or environmental factors, colonial India's horrific death tolls are undeniable. Between 1896 and 1921, outbreaks of plague accounted for about ten million deaths. Malaria deaths during the same period accounted for probably twice that number. There was also the influenza pandemic of 1918–19, which wiped out another twelve to fifteen million. However, even these chilling statistics pale in comparison with colonial India's most consistent and prolific killer, cholera. According to David Arnold, between 1817 and 1865, rough estimates suggest that at least fifteen million Indians died from cholera. After 1865, more systematic—if politically tainted—mortality statistics began to be collected. From 1865 until 1947, a further twenty-three million deaths were recorded. Even these numbers are likely too low. Cholera deaths were consistently downplayed to avoid the threat that more stringent international quarantine measures would be imposed on Britain's lucrative India trade, or they were falsely recorded as dysentery or "famine diarrhea."[24]

Extended periods of monsoon failure and drought followed by intense famines ravaged the Indian countryside from the 1860s through World War II. Although statistics vary widely, it is estimated that the 1876–79 and 1896–1902 famines alone resulted in between twelve and twenty-nine million victims. In the midst of these repeated waves of drought and famine, India became fertile ground for the incubation of cholera, malaria, and a host of other epidemic diseases. Years of failed monsoons pushed villagers to seek water from contaminated sources. Chronic malnutrition combined with changes in diet and behavior worked to weaken immune systems and raise the risk of infection. Starvation led to desperate searches for sustenance, leading people to consume roots, leaves, and other marginal food sources, which resulted in diarrhea and other complications. Whether victims of famine or disease, many attempted to flee villages and towns, while others were concentrated in relief camps and emerging urban slums. As a result of both the mobility and concentration of victims, normal family and community standards of caretaking and hygiene collapsed into the maw of poverty and dislocation.[25]

Working in tandem, colonial India's vicious cycles of famine (and callous famine relief policies), impoverishment, and cholera set into motion a public health crisis that would assume global proportions for the better part of the nineteenth century. Although cholera had long been endemic in Bengal, over the course of the nineteenth century, it rapidly transgressed its previous boundaries. The disease first came to the attention of Britain and Europe in 1817, when there was an outbreak in the environs of Calcutta. Unlike the case with the outbreaks of precolonial times, new patterns of British trade and military movement allowed the disease to burst beyond its previous endemic range. Precolonial patterns of cholera outbreaks were thought to have revolved around Hindu pilgrimage and festival circuits. Large crowds of celebrants would contract the disease and carry the infection home, where it would run its deadly but still endemic course. From 1817 on, however, cholera transmission dramatically expanded its reach. By 1818, British troops had brought the disease overland to Nepal and Afghanistan, and by the 1820s, British ships had spread it to East Africa, Oman, the Persian Gulf, Iraq, Anatolia, China, and Southeast Asia.[26] This period would mark the first of five colonial-era global cholera pandemics: the first from 1817 to 1824, the second in 1829–51 (counted by some as three semi-distinct events), the third from 1852 to 1859, the fourth in 1881–95, and the fifth from 1899 to 1923 (see figure 3.1).[27]

By the second pandemic during the 1830s and 1840s, cholera seemed to fan out in all directions with little discernible pattern. For example, in 1830, cholera reached Moscow. The Russian army then spread it to Poland. The disease found its way to Istanbul for the first time, killing as many as 6,000. Between 1831 and 1833, cholera would spread across the Baltic to England and Paris and leap to Canada and the United States. In 1831, cholera also reached the Hijaz, killing an estimated 20,000 and spreading the outbreak to Egypt and Tunis. Without the benefit of clear bacteriological understanding of cholera's causal mechanisms and etiology, the disease seemed to jump

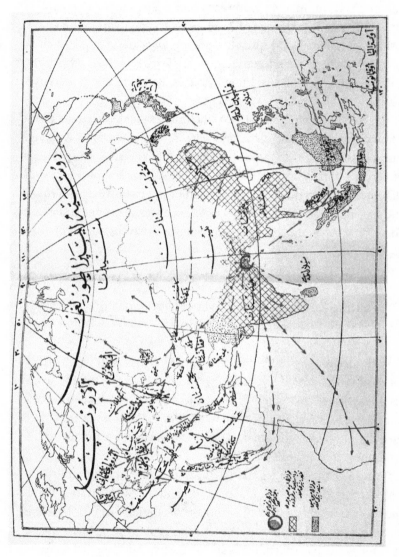

FIGURE 3.1 Ottoman map of cholera's spread from India, 1909. Reproduced from Akil Muhtar and Besim Ömer, *Kolera Hastalığında İttihazı Lazım Gelen Tedâbir ve Ettibaya Rehber* (Dersaadet: Arşak Garveyan Matbaası, 1909).

across land and sea in an almost untraceable pattern. When cholera devastated the Hijaz again in 1846, wiping out approximately 15,000 souls, the situation remained much the same. This time cholera likely made its way from Iran or Baghdad. In 1847, outbreaks had swept across Aleppo, Kars, Erzurum, and Trabzon. At the end of October 1847, cholera broke out among troops stationed in Mosul and spread to Aleppo, Diyarbakır, and Harput. In 1848 and 1849, cholera would continue to crisscross Anatolia, eventually making its way into the Balkans, Russia, Prussia, Belgium, the Netherlands, and Britain.

In all of these examples, cholera's globalization seemed so generalized and confounding that its exact pathways were impossible to track. Although the swamps of the Bengal delta had become widely known as the principal fount of cholera, through the 1850s, no special connection between cholera, Indian maritime traffic, and the hajj had been established. As a result, when the first international sanitary conference was convened in Paris in 1851, no specific recommendations or precautions were made to monitor pilgrimage traffic.[28]

Quarantine as Tool of Ottoman Sovereignty or European Extraterritoriality?

In the decades leading up to the great cholera outbreak of 1865, the thickening webs of railroads and steam navigation had transformed the world. Between the 1830s and 1870s, in many cases journey times between destinations were halved. Travel also became more direct. Railways in India were bringing pilgrims out of the subcontinent's interior more rapidly and in greater numbers than ever before. Likewise, even before the opening of the Suez Canal in 1869, the rail lines connecting Suez, Cairo, and Alexandria had melted all barriers between the Indian Ocean and the Mediterranean. Thus unlike previous pilgrimage-related outbreaks when the means of transmission had been slow and circuitous, the thickening sinews of steam and rail travel quickened the pace of cholera's spread to such a degree that its routes became all too legible.

As the hajj-driven pandemic of 1865–66 unfolded, Europe cast a wary eye toward what it considered the sanitary chaos of the Orient. In an age of sanitarian reform, Western Europe already had begun to take halting steps toward the environmental reorganization of cities, water supplies, and waste disposal. These projects, although operating without the benefit of proper germ theory, nevertheless began to push adult mortality rates downward. Conversely, European observers saw no such progress in the Ottoman Empire, Iran, and points farther east.[29] Istanbul had been ravaged by the 1865 outbreak, but that was only half of the story. Throughout southern Anatolia and greater Syria, there had been at least another 40,000 deaths. Beirut had seen 2,000 deaths out of a population of 80,000. In Jerusalem, 2,000 deaths struck a population of just 20,000. Jaffa and Nablus also had 2,000 deaths each. Tarsus and its surrounding villages lost more than 5,000 or one fifth of its population. Adana lost 5,000 too, roughly a sixth of its population.[30]

Owing to these appalling figures, to Europe the Ottoman Empire began to look less like a victim of India's repeated epidemic waves and more like an endemic disease pool in its own right. If Europe hoped to protect itself from cholera's predations, it would have to encourage new sanitary reforms along its Mediterranean frontiers, especially in Egypt and the Ottoman Empire. Moreover, if Europe wished to avoid the domestic application of stringent quarantines and embargoes, it needed to displace the burden of those precautions outward along its eastern frontiers.[31]

In 1866, Emperor Napoleon III of France attempted to breathe new life into the previous decade's inconclusive international conferences on quarantine and sanitation. In response to the French government's call for a conference to discuss the sanitary conditions of the East, Sultan Abdülaziz (r. 1861–76) agreed, but only on the condition that the conference be held in Istanbul. Thus the 1866 Istanbul international sanitary conference was hosted at the Galatasaray Lisesi (*Lycée de Galatasaray*). Tanzimat statesman and Foreign Minister Mehmed Emin Ali Pasha gave the opening and closing addresses. Invitations were extended to sixteen governments, all of which accepted except the United States of America. In total the conference would host thirty-nine delegates (including three Ottoman representatives) for a total of forty-four meetings spanning seven months.[32] During the deliberations at the conference, a new era of international sanitary interventionism emerged. The delegates took a strongly "contagionist stance," concluding that cholera was "communicable from the diseased to the healthy." Moreover, attendees "affirmed Asiatic cholera to be endemic in India, and in no other country." As for the mode of transmission, the delegates pointed to the squalid conditions of Hindu pilgrimage centers within India, as well as those of the "hajj to Mecca, seen as the second stage by which cholera was relayed from India to Europe."[33]

From an Ottoman perspective, the conclusions of this international body were meaningful in two respects. First and foremost, the 1866 conference established international consensus that India was the source of cholera and that the disease did not originate from within Ottoman domains. As the Ottoman bacteriology expert, Ḥamdī bin ʿAzīz (Hamdi Aziz), pointed out in his 1893–94 cholera treatise, mobilizing international consensus around this point had been a critical goal for Ottoman delegates from 1866 and at all subsequent sanitary conferences. Throughout this period the Ottoman state found itself in a desperate struggle to combat the claims of British physicians who put forward the alternative hypothesis that the 1865 outbreak had originated in Jeddah and subsequently been spread by returning pilgrims to Peshawar and Kashmir, moving via Afghanistan and Iran en route to Europe. Although international consensus rejected these claims, British denial of India's role in the crisis was to remain a key obstacle to Ottoman sanitary security for the remainder of the century.[34]

The second major result of the 1866 conference was the attendees' collective decision to adopt rigorous quarantine measures designed to inspect the health of all pilgrims arriving in the Hijaz and, if necessary, to restrict the movement of infected pilgrims and the vessels carrying them. Although it would take a decade and a half for these plans even to partly materialize, the proposals laid out in 1866 eventually led to the establishment of an archipelago of quarantine stations stretching from the southern mouth of the Red Sea to the Suez Canal, the Mediterranean, and Black Sea; eventually it was expanded to the Persian Gulf.[35] This system was to be anchored by a flagship quarantine station at the southern entrance to the Red Sea in the vicinity of Bab al-Mandab in order to intercept the growing influx of Indian Ocean pilgrims before they could reach Jeddah.[36] Although its staffing and administration were to be handled by the Ottoman state, it also would be subject to the international (extraterritorial) supervision of the Ottoman Board of Health.

Between 1831 and 1838, Sultan Mahmud II (r. 1808–39) had experimented with a number of temporary quarantine measures designed to protect Istanbul and Ottoman troops from cholera and plague outbreaks spreading from either the Mediterranean or the Black Sea. In 1838, Mahmud II moved to place quarantine measures on a more permanent footing. Based on a proposal prepared by Austrian physician Anton Lago, Mahmud II's creation of a Quarantine Board (*Karantina Meclisi*) signaled the Ottoman Empire's long-term adoption of European-style quarantine measures and a broad commitment to following the latest scientific advances in sanitation, public health reforms, and, eventually, the application of germ theory and bacteriology.[37]

Here it is important to emphasize that Mahmud II did not embrace quarantine measures under European pressure. Indeed, European officials harbored deep reservations about the Ottoman state's turn to quarantine. Although quarantine stations were meant to prevent cholera and plague, they also offered the emergent Tanzimat state new tools for controlling trade, customs, migration, and borders. Therefore it was no coincidence that many of the quarantine stations established in the 1840s doubled as customhouses. The proliferation of these dual-purpose customhouse-quarantine stations allowed the government to "intrude into the private spheres of its subjects, follow their movements, and know what they were buying and selling." In this sense, Ottoman public health policy facilitated the state's deepening reach into areas where previously it had been absent. It also had the virtue of making Ottoman sovereignty over the empire's ports and borders physically manifest to its European rivals.[38]

Ottoman efforts to impose quarantines on foreign vessels immediately encountered resistance from the European powers. Thus when the British set the liberalizing commercial terms of the Treaty of Balta Liman in 1838, they demanded that the Quarantine Board be placed under the supervision of a body composed of all major European powers. Under extreme duress from both Mehmed Ali Pasha's rogue Egyptian empire and the Russian Navy, Mahmud II had little choice but to consent.[39] The Ottoman Quarantine Board would be transformed into a foreign-dominated Board of Health, itself a capitulatory branch of the Foreign Ministry. Originally the board was composed of six Ottoman delegates and six foreign delegates. By the 1880s and 1890s, however, the board's European representation ballooned to as many as fourteen members versus just two to four Ottomans.[40] Over time the board morphed from a potential vehicle of imperial border control and sovereignty into an enduring symbol of the Capitulations, extraterritoriality, and foreign interference, right down to its abolition in Article 114 of the 1923 Lausanne Peace Treaty.[41]

Despite the repeated humiliations suffered by the board's Ottoman members and delegates at the international sanitary conferences of the late nineteenth century, at the 1866 Istanbul conference there was still much to be gained—or at least safeguarded—from an Ottoman perspective. Since signing the Treaty of Paris in 1856, the Ottoman state ostensibly gained begrudging acceptance as a member of the European family of nations. The Ottoman Empire also became the first non-European country to join intergovernmental organizations. From the 1850s on the Ottomans remained extremely active in such bodies, in part because their participation demonstrated that they belonged to European international society and had recourse to international public law.[42]

As in other diplomatic venues, Ottoman officials were at pains to present themselves as civilized, energetic modernizers capable of carrying out the necessary hygienic reforms to combat the spread of cholera. For the Ottoman Empire, so often derided as the "Sick Man of Europe," this delicate process of self-presentation was doubly magnified because it required financial support from the other governments in attendance.[43] To finance the ambitious quarantine project imagined at the conference, it was agreed that the Ottoman Board of Health would oversee the collection of a controversial tonnage-based quarantine fee.[44]

Apart from the immediate question of insulating Europe and the rest of the Ottoman Empire from pilgrimage-related cholera outbreaks, the 1866 international sanitary conference spoke directly to core Ottoman concerns over territory and sovereignty along the empire's southern frontiers. By taking primary responsibility for the sanitary policing of the Red Sea, Istanbul received a degree of international legitimation for its ongoing attempts to expand and reconsolidate its presence in the Arabian peninsula. The establishment of a quarantine station near Bab al-Mandab provided internationally sanctioned support for the Ottoman state's wider strategic goals to reconquer the coastal plains of Tihama and the Yemeni highlands, create a buffer between the Hijaz and British Aden, and ward off further British, European, and Egyptian designs on the Hijaz, Yemen, and the southern Red Sea. The construction of international quarantine facilities provided a clear material justification of Ottoman claims over some of the empire's most tenuously held territories. At the same time, these plans were highly dependent on the slow reestablishment of Ottoman authority over Yemen that unfolded from the late 1840s through the early 1870s. By the completion of the campaigns to subdue Yemen (1871–73), however, Ottoman momentum on the quarantine question had become mired in logistical challenges, hobbled by the glacial pace of international cooperation, and eventually overwhelmed by the wider military, financial, and political crises that consumed the empire in the latter half of the 1870s.[45]

Logistical Limits: First Steps and False Starts

In late 1865, the Ottoman Board of Health began contemplating preliminary responses to the horrific mortality of the 1865 pilgrimage season. The board adopted three main areas of reform. Because the outbreak was thought to have originated among pilgrims gathered in Mina, special attention was paid to locations associated with the sacrifice for *Kurban Bayramı* (*Īd al-Adhā*). It was argued that steps be taken to better handle the disposal of animal carcasses and the elimination of odors from their putrefaction. In addition to addressing the provision of sufficient pits for the disposal of the offal, initial reports also pointed to the cleanliness of the water supply at Mina. A second priority was the sale of potentially hazardous food and drink. For example, Ottoman authorities would attempt to prohibit the sale of certain raw fruits—especially melons—or drinks made from them. Finally, there was the larger question of how to monitor the health of pilgrims, especially those from India.[46]

Before 1865 there had been no public health oversight in Mecca and the Red Sea. From 1866 through 1868, however, annual public health commissions were sent to the Red Sea during each hajj season.[47] From reports produced by these commissions, the basic outlines of an ambitious project of environmental management and biopolitical discipline began to take shape. These efforts inaugurated a decades-long analytical process of breaking down the urban landscapes of the Hijaz and the hajj to their most minute parts. Thus even before the revolution in bacteriology unlocked the mysteries of cholera's spread, sanitarian questions of miasmas, waste products, and overcrowding had begun to suggest that efforts to combat cholera would lead the Ottoman state deeper into the day-to-day affairs of the Hijaz than ever before.

As with the sanitarian transformations taking place in Europe and, later, Istanbul itself, the commissions attacked the poor environmental conditions of Mecca's urban landscape and impoverished population, its congested and waste-strewn streets, and the poor state of pilgrimage-related housing.[48] In 1867, the commission advocated the widening of Mecca's streets and the demolition of ramshackle additions to shops and homes that clogged the city's thoroughfares. According to the commissioners' calculations, in Mecca and its environs there were something like 3,000 temporary huts and market stalls made of rush matting and lacking any toilet or water closet facilities. These temporary dwellings allegedly sheltered the city's vagabonds and unemployed. They also hosted large populations of Indians, Jawis, and Sudanese living cheek by jowl. The commission recommended that these huts be torn down and relocated a safe distance from Mecca in order to widen the streets and alleviate traffic congestion.[49] Another theme that would persist for the remainder of the century concerned Mecca's impoverished pilgrims and *mücavirin*.

As the 1867 commission complained, the pious foundations in Mecca and Medina that distributed bread and soup unintentionally encouraged the proliferation of vagrants lying about the streets and congregating around entrances to the *haremeyn*. In order to combat this problem, the commissioners reasoned that an examination performed in Jeddah or Yanbuʿ might be able to identify those with sufficient funds for the journey. Thus only those with enough funds would receive a *tezkere*, or visa, permitting them to continue inland. Another suggestion was that pilgrims not be given permission to make extended visits, which would increase their chances of falling into indigence. As we shall see in chapter 5, by the 1880s and 1890s, these and other questions surrounding indigent and destitute pilgrims emerged as the primary focus of international debate on pilgrimage regulation.[50]

In addition to reorganizing the Hijaz's urban landscape and disciplining its marginal populations, there remained the question of the Red Sea quarantine system. However, before the Ottoman state could implement the recommendations of the 1866 international sanitary conference, it would have to fend off a challenge from Egypt. Since 1831, Egypt had had its own capitulatory, mixed-membership quarantine administration, Le Conseil Sanitaire, Maritime et Quarantenaire d'Egypte.[51] Despite Egypt's continued status as an autonomous province of the Ottoman Empire, from the perspective of the international quarantine board in Alexandria, it was functionally independent. Thus in November 1866, the Egyptian board decided to move forward with its own Red Sea public health and quarantine measures.

The board proposed that all ships coming from India would require clean bills of health. If cholera was discovered in the port of departure or appeared during the journey, vessels would be diverted to Massawa for a fifteen-day quarantine. Even passengers traveling on vessels with clean bills of health would be required to spend a five-day quarantine at al-Tur (El-Tor) or Qusayr. If cholera was found among the pilgrims in the Hijaz, all communication with Egypt would be suspended immediately. Even pilgrims traveling by caravan would be required to complete quarantine at al-Wajh in the northern Hijaz.

The Egyptian board also prepared a report for the Khedive spelling out its plans to send doctors to Jeddah, Mecca, Yanbu', and even Mocha in Yemen. As the Ottoman representative to the Egyptian board reported, the plan to transfer the Hijaz's sanitary administration to Egypt was a flagrant violation of the Ottoman state's rights and political sovereignty. As the Egyptian proposal made its way to the Ottoman Board of Health and the Foreign Ministry, the plan was ardently opposed on the grounds that the Alexandrian board and Khedival Egypt had no right to send officials beyond their own borders.[52]

The quarantine question appeared to provide a new avenue for Khedive İsmail (r. 1863–79) to augment his expansionist policies in the Red Sea. In 1865, İsmail had negotiated the transfer of Massawa and Suakin from Jeddah's provincial administration to Egypt's in exchange for a modest lump-sum payment, a 5,000-*ardeb* wheat shipment, and certain considerations related to the slave trade.[53] In the end, Istanbul would retain control of quarantine operations in the southern Red Sea. However, this initial clash presaged the tense post-1882 divide between British-occupied Egypt's approach to quarantine arrangements in the northern Red Sea and the measures taken in the Ottoman-administered southern Red Sea.[54]

Another set of limitations that did not improve significantly until the 1880s revolved around questions of communications and transport. Particularly during the period prior to the opening of the Suez Canal in 1869, Istanbul's communications with the Hijaz and Yemen faced serious challenges. During the late 1860s, the Ottoman navy's Red Sea presence consisted of only one *korvet*, the *İzmir*, which had been transferred from the Basra docks in 1867 in a feeble attempt to assert the empire's claims of sovereignty over the Hadrami ports of al-Shihr and Mukalla and to maintain at least some presence to counter British naval dominance. In addition to patrolling for slave traders and gunrunners, the *İzmir* was placed at the disposal of the

Hijaz's health commissioners in 1868. The *İzmir* would remain the only permanent Ottoman naval presence until two gunboats arrived in 1883. As a result, frequently even the transport and supply of Ottoman troops in the region was achieved by hiring civilian ships. In 1868, Istanbul contracted with the Khedive of Egypt and the ʿAzīziyya steamship company to facilitate both regular steamship and postal services. An Ottoman imperial decree established the company's right to serve the ports of the Red Sea. In exchange the company agreed to provide grain transfers to the Hijaz at reduced prices.[55]

Following the 1866 conference, the Ottoman government realized that there was not enough time to set up a quarantine station near Bab al-Mandab before the next hajj season. Instead it opted for the imposition of temporary quarantine procedures in the principal ports of the Red Sea. By late 1868, however, the Ottoman Board of Health had collected enough information to put the Hijaz's public health administration on a more permanent footing. Fevzi Efendi, head of the Hijaz's sanitary operations, was tasked with the construction and staffing of a central quarantine station in Jeddah, with satellite branches in Mecca, Medina, al-Qunfudha, Rabigh, Lith, and Yanbuʿ. A further network of quarantines was planned for the Yemeni ports of Hudayda, Mocha, Luhayya, and Jizan.[56]

Despite the appointment of more than forty staff members to operate this makeshift quarantine system, it remained doubtful that quarantine procedures carried out in Jeddah and other ports would slow the spread of cholera. After all, one of the principal goals of the 1866 international sanitary conference had been to find a suitable location for a central quarantine station at the mouth of the Red Sea to intercept potential cholera victims at a safe distance from major Red Sea population centers. Originally conference participants believed that Perim Island (a British possession since 1857, later used as a coaling station) was the best site for the quarantine facility because it commanded the narrow entrance to the Red Sea at Bab al-Mandab. However, Britain's cool reception quickly killed the Perim proposal, forcing the Ottomans to fall back on the suggestion of Kamaran (Qamaran) Island, some 160 miles north of Bab al-Mandab.

In 1867, during the Ottoman sanitary commission's survey of potential quarantines sites, almost every port and island between Jeddah and Aden was ranked in terms of logistical convenience, climate, anchorage, water supplies, and isolation from population centers. The commission concluded that Kamaran Island, despite its limitations, was the best option due to its large, sheltered anchorage, its abundance of wells (all in disrepair at the time), and the ease of patrolling for any attempts at contact between quarantined pilgrims and the Yemeni mainland port of Salif. That said, there remained serious concerns that infected vessels would dock at Yemeni ports such as Mocha and Hudayda prior to arriving at Kamaran. Citing this concern, in 1868, the Ottomans pushed for an alternative site at Hisn al-Ghurab, located between Aden and Mukalla. In correspondence between Istanbul and Mecca, it was requested that the sharifate act as an intermediary and obtain the local shaykh's permission to erect a quarantine facility and agree to cede the territory formally to the Ottoman government. This bold gambit to push Ottoman territorial claims beyond the mouth of the Red Sea was doomed from its inception due to Britain's consistent refusal to accept any Ottoman claims farther south than the mouth of Red Sea or along the Hadrami littoral.[57]

As a result of the lingering lack of consensus among the Ottomans and their European counterparts on the Board of Health, it was decided that pending a decision on the permanent location of the quarantine station, contaminated ships would be sent to Kamaran Island. After 1869, however, plans for the construction of a more permanent Kamaran Island quarantine station were all but shelved until 1882. Throughout the 1870s, Istanbul opted to staff inexpensive quarantine operations along the Hijazi and Yemeni coasts on an ad hoc basis. In 1868, an additional 10-*kuruş* quarantine fee was imposed on each pilgrim. This additional fee was designed to augment the tonnage-based sanitary tariff, which was eventually passed by the Board of Health in 1872 but only after stiff resistance from Britain. Despite repeated British complaints that Ottoman quarantine measures were designed merely to generate new revenues, in reality these fees were wholly insufficient to cover the expenses of the Red Sea quarantine network.[58]

By the late 1870s, the Ottoman state could not bear any more financial burdens. As a result of the disastrous Russo-Ottoman war of 1877–78, the empire's ballooning debts precipitated a grave financial crisis. Battered and bankrupt, in 1881, the Ottoman state was forced to restructure its debts to stave off complete financial collapse. With the creation of the Public Debt Administration, Istanbul's European creditors assumed collection duties over numerous sources of Ottoman revenue in order to service the empire's debts. Only after this dramatic restructuring was the Ottoman state finally able to open the long-anticipated Kamaran Island quarantine station in 1882.

British India and the Science of Denial

Between 1866 and 1878, there were no outbreaks remotely comparable to the horrors of 1865. Thus in addition to the overwhelming logistical and financial challenges discussed earlier, there was also the creeping complacency that came with cholera's temporary absences. There was a sense— perhaps not wholly wrongheaded—that the basic sanitarian reforms, including street cleaning campaigns, improved hospital conditions, the increased presence of physicians, and safeguards surrounding the slaughtering pavilions and cisterns at Mina, had proven successful. However, there was also the ruthless resistance of Britain and India's medical establishments to all discussion of quarantine and cholera's communicability.

In 1874, another international sanitary conference was held in Vienna.[59] The conference aimed to adopt a "uniform system of preventative measures" applicable to all participating nations and their colonial possessions. However, little had changed since the previous sanitary conference. Despite the protests of British delegates, cholera was still considered by the majority of conference delegates to be contagious, and India was still blamed as its primary source. And though it was recommended that the controversial quarantine measures be adopted by all the participating nations, in the end it was recognized that individual states could opt for a less robust system of medical inspection.[60]

Under the system proposed in 1874, arrivals from an infected port were to be observed for one to seven days depending on the severity of the outbreak. In the ports of the eastern Mediterranean or under exceptional circumstances, the period of observation might be extended to ten days. If cases or suspected cases occurred while at sea, the period of observation for uninfected persons was set at seven days from the time of their isolation. The sick, however, were to be landed separately for medical care while the vessel and infected items on board were subjected to a rigorous disinfection process. Even arrivals from a port that was merely considered suspect, despite having no reported cases of infection or having been given free passage at another port of call, were subject to an observation period of five days. The boldest regulation of all, however, concerned "vessels considered particularly dangerous." This specifically targeted ships carrying pilgrims and emigrants. Any vessel carrying passengers labeled as such would be subject to "special precautions," which essentially meant that they could be held in quarantine for longer periods than for other vessels.[61]

Having left sanitary measures largely to "the discretion of individual states," it was proposed that the conclusions reached in Vienna be formalized as an International Convention. In the years following, however, representatives from Britain and British India repeatedly showed a preference for more flexible systems of medical inspection and intelligence sharing. British India also sought to implement its own package of sanitary and pilgrimage-related reforms unilaterally rather than assenting to any permanent agreements or surrendering any sovereignty to an international body. In 1876, the government of India formally declared that it "declined to be fettered in their legislation by any such Convention."[62] As the Foreign Office explained, Britain refused to allow any international sanitary conference or the international members of the Ottoman Board of Health to exercise authority over British subjects or ships beyond the terms outlined in the Capitulations.[63]

In addition to Britain's unilateralist approach to the quarantine question, there remained underlying questions surrounding the science of cholera's transmission. The precise cause and etiology of cholera remained hotly contested until at least the mid-1880s. Through his investigations of cholera in Egypt and India, German bacteriologist Robert Koch (1843–1910) eventually was able to discover the causal agent of cholera, the comma bacillus *Vibrio cholerae*, in a Calcutta water tank in 1884. However, Koch's findings would meet a ferocious campaign of denial and resistance from authorities in Britain and India.[64]

The government of India's sanitary commissioner, Dr. J. M. Cunningham, who served from 1868 to 1884, built his career around the denial of contagion theory and the obstruction of international quarantine efforts.[65] Cunningham, a disciple of earlier English sanitarians such as Edwin Chadwick and Thomas Southwood Smith, insisted that cholera was caused solely by local sanitary imperfections.[66] Cunningham remained convinced that some "miasma" or "mysterious influence" in the state of the atmosphere, a particular "season" or the "fermentative products of the soil" were responsible for cholera outbreaks. He held that such imperfections in India's environment were caused by the "unwholesome surroundings" or the "filthy habits" of Indians, not by any "specific communicable germ."[67] Throughout his tenure he repeatedly argued that quarantine measures based on "contagionist theory" were "no more logical or effectual than it would be to post a line of sentries to stop the monsoon."[68]

Cunningham's localist approach to the etiology of cholera had been popular among medical authorities in India since the early nineteenth century. However, their ideas also were reinforced from the 1860s on by the work of German miasma specialist Max von Pettenkofer. Pettenkofer, Koch's long-time rival, put forth a soil-based theory, which stated that the presence of a specific germ and susceptible victim could not alone produce cholera symptoms. Rather, cholera required the presence of specific soil conditions. Only then would the germ acquire its pathogenic qualities and produce an epidemic. As an anti-contagionist, unsurprisingly Pettenkofer was opposed to European and Ottoman calls for international regulations. As a result, despite their declining popularity among the European scientific community, his theories proved a valuable tool in British India's battle against quarantine regulation.[69]

Following Robert Koch's discovery of the cholera bacillus in 1884, his research was predictably attacked by his archrival. Although Koch was able to refute Pettenkofer's localist position publicly in 1885, Britain's deeply institutionalized opposition to contagion theory would survive for nearly another decade. Indeed, in his last days as India's sanitary commissioner, Cunningham expressed both "patriotic pique as well as professional chagrin that an outsider like Koch should presume to unravel the mystery which had baffled India's own medical service for more than sixty years."[70] Similarly, as Sir Joseph Frayer, surgeon-general at the India Office Council in London, put it: "I am also very anxious to avert the evil consequences that may accrue from the effects of this so-called discovery on our sea traffic and international communication." Frayer was determined that Britain not take Koch's discovery lying down, convincing the Indian government to engage its own team of scientists to refute Koch's claims. As a result of Frayer's campaigning, Drs. Edward Emanuel Klein and Heneage Gibbes were dispatched to conduct their own "independent" investigation. To the great relief of the government of India and the India Office, in 1885, Klein and Heneage reported that Koch's bacillus was innocuous and could not be the sole cause of cholera.[71]

Armed with these findings, Frayer managed almost single-handedly to derail the 1885 international sanitary conference in Rome.[72] Through Frayer's connivance with an Italian delegate, Koch was prevented from defending his research at the conference. In fact, it was even agreed that matters surrounding Koch's theory should not be discussed at all. By excluding Koch's work on cholera from the diplomatic conversation, Frayer and his Italian ally advanced a pro-British agenda calling for relaxation of the quarantine restrictions and fees being imposed at Suez and on Indian Ocean pilgrims. As a result of this aggressive strategy, the conference fell apart with no binding resolution.[73]

As a result of Britain's continuing denial of the overwhelming evidence in favor of cholera's communicability, by the 1880s, France and Germany had become increasingly frustrated with Britain's sanitary gamesmanship. Likewise, Ottoman public health officials, who had been early and enthusiastic adopters of germ theory and bacteriology, repeatedly expressed their dismay at the brazen intellectual dishonesty of their British interlocutors.[74] Despite these shared sentiments, however, no alliance of European states was able to fully counterbalance British obstructionism "through the weak apparatus of internationalism."[75]

As every Briton well knew, since the era of the Continental Blockade imposed by Napoleon, Britain's prosperity had depended on its mercantile fleet and the worldwide expansion of liberal free-trade policies.[76] Owing to the intermingling of these historical and ideological perspectives on cholera, quarantine, naval supremacy, and free trade, Britain remained decidedly less concerned with controlling cholera's transmission from India to Europe than with the protection of its Indian trade route against quarantine restrictions. Thus by the time the Ottoman state was finally prepared to open the long-awaited Kamaran Island quarantine station in 1882, British resistance to contagion and quarantine had reached the level of a nationalist paranoia. In the September 1883 edition of *The Lancet*, the fervor over pilgrimage-related quarantine was bluntly spelled out: "those who love quarantine and hate England fall back on the assumption that cholera comes from India, and although the links in the chain of communication cannot be discovered, they are perfectly willing to assume their presence."[77]

Kamaran: An Island of Discontent in a Sea of Suffering

Between December 24, 1877, and January 7, 1878, 845 people died from cholera in Mecca and Jeddah. The normal death rate in Jeddah ranged between five and ten per day under normal circumstances. During hajj season the death rate climbed to between ten and twelve. However, at the end of the 1877 pilgrimage, as many as 50 persons per day were dying in Jeddah and Mecca.[78] The outbreak coincided with severe flooding in Mecca, which dumped several feet of mud around the Kaʿba and filled Mecca's waterworks with sand and debris. Broken water pipes, a lake of standing water in the *Masjid al-Ḥaram*, and cisterns filled with brown, sediment-laden water turned Mecca into a veritable cholera incubator.[79]

Although the 1877–78 cholera outbreak was not nearly as a catastrophic as some past or future ones, it did begin to refocus Ottoman attention on sanitary reform, environmental management, and quarantine in the Hijaz. Efforts to ameliorate the region's ailing water infrastructure and impose tighter public health regulations would not achieve results immediately, nor would they come fast enough to avert further catastrophes. However, both Ottoman and global attention to pilgrimage-related cholera were reawakened in the late 1870s and early 1880s. In 1878 and 1881 alone, official British statistics from India tallied over 317,000 and 161,000 cholera deaths.[80] These outbreaks were only the leading edge. Between 1881 and 1895, the globe would be convulsed by its fourth global cholera pandemic. International sanitary conferences to address the reemergence of the scourge were held in 1881, 1885, 1892, 1893, and 1894. During this period Ottoman public health reforms in the Hijaz would also gain new levels of urgency, consistency, and continuity. And over the next two decades, Ottoman sanitary discipline would begin to mature and make its presence felt in the Hijaz and beyond as never before.

At the end of August 1881, during an outbreak in Aden, cholera made its way to Mecca just in time for the height of the hajj season. In what would become a running theme during these years, Ottoman officials repeatedly expressed their dismay as to why British officials were consistently allowing their vessels to leave Aden with clean bills of health.[81] By the time that Istanbul was informed of the outbreak in Mecca, it had already claimed 130 lives and was burning through the estimated 80,000 pilgrims assembled for hajj.[82] By the end of December the official numbers recorded by Gregory Wortabet, the chief Ottoman quarantine physician in Jeddah, counted some 4,500 deaths throughout the Hijaz.[83] However, as the British consulate speculated, the official statistics likely told only part of the grim tale. As they hypothesized, the real mortality was very likely in the vicinity of 8,000 to 10,000.[84]

As outbreaks of this magnitude and speed unfolded, terrified victims inevitably attempted to flee from the rising tide of morbidity and mortality. In their fruitless attempts to escape Mecca and Mina, many would be stricken and die along the way. Theoretically victims were supposed to be brought to the public health authorities in Mecca to be examined and receive an official death certificate. Under these extreme conditions, however, many victims were hastily buried by their friends, family, or pilgrimage guides.[85] During especially catastrophic outbreaks, often the mortality was so overwhelming that the normal procedures for washing the bodies of the deceased and their proper burial collapsed. Those responsible for handling corpses were among the most likely to be infected. As they also began to flee or die, bodies accumulated at the cemetery. And then there were those left unburied (and uncounted) along the roadsides, leaving the region's principal arteries strewn with decomposing corpses.

To make matters worse, as the carnage in Mecca unfolded, the Egyptian quarantine authorities announced that pilgrims traveling toward Suez would not be allowed to depart from Jeddah until fifteen days after the disease had completely died out there. The Egyptian restrictions slowed the departure of pilgrims, and shortages of food and water exacerbated the crisis. As the number of stranded pilgrims mounted, local Ottoman authorities pleaded with Istanbul to take the necessary steps to get traffic moving through the canal and to send steamships to speed the evacuation.[86]

As then-Governor Safvet Pasha correctly hypothesized, if the Ottoman state could not show that it was fully complying with the 1866 international sanitary conference's agreement that a sanitary official should be sent to the Hijaz each year, it would become increasingly likely that the European powers might seek to take more intrusive action in the name of public health. Although a decade and a half had lapsed since the disasters of 1865, much had changed since then. In 1881–82, the Hijaz was on the cusp of a dramatic spasm of state building and centralization under Osman Nuri Pasha's energetic governorship. The Hijaz and the Arab frontier more generally had begun to take on a greater strategic and symbolic value in the eyes of the Hamidian state. By the early 1880s, the post-1866 policy of sending an annually appointed public health commissioner to oversee the sanitary preparedness for hajj season was revived.[87] Likewise plans for the long-delayed Red Sea quarantine station also were also dusted off.[88]

In late 1881, the construction of the Kamaran Island quarantine station (*tahhafuzhane*) was finally under way. Kamaran is a barren strip of sand and rocks located off the northern Yemeni coast some 28 kilometers north of Hudayda and 180 nautical miles from the Straits of Bab al-Mandab.[89] It was sparsely populated by a handful of villages on the northern and southern ends of the island, and its well-sheltered port could accommodate up to twenty ships at a time.[90] At its height the station was capable of accommodating up to 30,000 pilgrims per year and up to 6,000 at one time.[91] However, in 1882, the number of completed shelters could accommodate only two shiploads at a time, leaving others to wait aboard their steamers.[92] Whatever its geographical attributes as a port, from the perspective of human comfort and environmental capacity, it is difficult to imagine many more miserable places.

Without British support for its establishment, the expenses for the construction of Kamaran fell squarely on the Ottoman government. The revenues generated by the sanitary tariff approved by the Board of Health in 1872 were insufficient to cover the 542,000-*kuruş* construction costs or its subsequent upkeep and improvement.[93] At the outset it was unclear whether Kamaran was even going to be a permanent operation. Responsibility for Kamaran's funding and upkeep was to become a running battle between the Ottoman Finance Ministry and the internationally controlled Board of Health. And although Kamaran was of enormous political concern to the Hijaz province and directly dependent on the medical expertise of the Board of Health, appropriations and oversight for construction, maintenance, and local workers flowed through the *sancak* of Hudayda.[94] However, Kamaran and Hudayda would not be linked by telegraph until 1893.[95] Owing in part to the muddled nature of Kamaran's financial and bureaucratic chains of command and poor communications links, for over a decade it operated without many of the human resources and physical infrastructure that it needed.

The problems began even before the pilgrims set foot on the island. The captains calling at Kamaran warned that the approaches to the island were unsafe for large vessels. Without buoys the passages between the treacherous reefs surrounding the island were invisible under windy conditions (see figure 3.2).[96] Almost immediately after the first Indian pilgrims landed, the British consulate in Jeddah received a deluge of protests. Pilgrims and

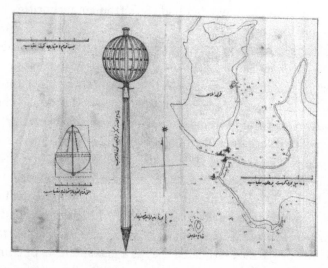

FIGURE 3.2 Ottoman map of Kamaran Island and its harbor with plans for the addition of safety buoys, 1889. *Source:* BOA, İ.DH, 1137/88763.

ship captains alike complained that the quarantine fees were excessive. Pitiful specimens of vegetables occasionally were procured from Hudayda but were wildly expensive. Supplies of dried vegetables, olive oil, butter, and other foodstuffs were generally shipped in from Port Said or Suez. Because all foodstuffs had to be imported, firewood and cooking fuel were prohibitively expensive. Pilgrims also complained about the island's scarce supply of brackish well water, which, although hardly palatable, was tightly controlled. Of particular annoyance was the closure of the station's water tanks from 10:00 a.m. until 4:00 p.m.[97]

As a result of the rationing of the water supplies, when water was distributed, it attracted large crowds. In the ensuing crush, the local guards, primarily drawn from fisherman living in the area, could not control the crowds and on several occasions resorted to beating them back with cane poles. As Dr. Abdur Razzack reasoned, the rough treatment of the pilgrims likely was not a product of any overtly malign intent on the part of the overzealous local staffers. Rather it was, first and foremost, a product of the mutual language barrier between the Arabic-speaking guards and their Indian charges. As he pointed out, all of this could have been avoided had the Ottoman authorities provided even one interpreter.[98]

The scarcity of food and water was further compounded by the island's deplorable accommodations. The pilgrims were herded into communal Tihama-style thatched sheds provided by the provincial authorities in Hudayda. The sheds were constructed from wood and date palm branches. Due to Kamaran's distance from Istanbul and its extreme climate, the costs and desirability of bringing in craftsmen and materials from Europe were deemed out of the question. As a result, brick and mortar construction methods generally were not available.[99] As pilgrims complained, the roofs were too thin to keep out the sun, and the openings for ventilation were too small. These thatched sheds also let in rain, dust, pests, and mice. They were nearly impossible to disinfect and easily damaged by hard rains and fire.[100] Dr. Abdur Razzack estimated that at a maximum, 40 pilgrims might be housed safely in each shed. However, up to 100 pilgrims at a time were being assigned to each of the seven structures.[101] The station's supervising physician optimistically calculated that each pilgrim would have had approximately 11.3 square feet of space. This cramped area offered essentially no relief from the similar conditions that pilgrims endured between decks while aboard the steamers that brought them there. Given the sizzling year-round temperatures for which Kamaran is infamous, this amount of space proved positively suffocating for healthy pilgrims, let alone sick or elderly ones.[102] As one physician who accompanied the pilgrims to Kamaran commented, "the shelter which is meant for their short imprisonment is totally unfit for such a place as Camaran, where sometimes the heat (sultry) is even greater than Muscat, and the poor pilgrims have to keep themselves half scorched under their cow-sheds until relieved."[103] As Yeniçeşmeli Hâfız Fâik Efendi, put it, The "bitterness of passing time [on Kamaran] is virtually like being punished in hellfire."[104]

In addition to concerns over the heat and flimsy shelters, there were repeated complaints about the woefully inadequate number and condition of the camp's latrines and the complete failure to consider the segregation of the sexes. Relaying the complaints of his fellow countrymen, Abdur Razzack expressed his astonishment at the total lack of forethought about any sort of separate accommodations for female pilgrims, many of whom he described as terrified, "all huddled together like sheep in a fold." The lack of separate housing for the better classes of female pilgrims, who were used to the security and seclusion of the *zenana*, was further exacerbated by the Ottoman (generally Christian) quarantine physicians' insistence that the women uncover their faces for the required medical examination. As Abdur Razzack complained, simply looking at the face of these women would yield little information to help one ascertain whether or not they might have contracted cholera. In any case, once the women became ill, the symptoms would be nearly impossible to conceal. As a compromise Abdur Razzack suggested that the Ottoman quarantine examination be conducted by checking the pulse or examining the tongue, neither of which would require female pilgrims to reveal their full facial features. From his perspective such problems were an unavoidable by-product of having European and Christian physicians staff the quarantine station. Abdur Razzack even coyly suggested the inherent contradiction between the Ottoman sultan's professed solicitude for the welfare of the pilgrims and their mistreatment at the hands of abusive local guards and Christian doctors on Kamaran Island. As he stated on behalf of his countrymen, "I only repeat their sentiments." Many pilgrims openly "wondered why he . . . who had toiled and travelled for six or eight months to reach the Holy place should be turned aside and brought to this uninviting island to sigh for the necessities of life even for a day by the servants of the 'Padishah' (sovereign) who called himself 'the servant of the Holy places'."[105]

In addition to the primitive conditions encountered by pilgrims during Kamaran Island's first pilgrimage season, the station disappointed in a more fundamental respect. It failed to stop cholera from reaching the Hijaz. Kamaran's poor performance seemed to provide more ammunition to the anti-quarantine lobby in India. Complaints were so numerous that the Indian government conducted an enquiry into the conditions on the island. The commission found that pilgrims had been "subjected to oppression and extortion amounting to positive cruelty." Moreover, the report argued that the sanitary measures ostensibly designed to protect the holy places from cholera would "only serve to predispose" pilgrims "to sickness and lay them open to the attacks of cholera generalized in the Hedjaz. . . . The whole of the arrangements at Cameran seem indeed to be devised for the pecuniary benefit of the Turkish authorities and can serve no other possible end."[106] Thus when cholera broke out in the Hijaz during the 1882 season, British observers attributed the outbreak to the local conditions on Kamaran Island and the Hijaz instead of to India.

Despite Kamaran's failure to stop cholera from entering the Hijaz, it did have a certain clarifying effect. The tighter tracking of India's pilgrimage vessels made it considerably easier for Ottoman and international observers to identify precisely where and when cholera was entering the Red Sea. However, even this evidence did little to combat Britain's entrenched miasma-based anti-contagionist ideology. In response to the obvious evidence that the 1882 outbreak had been transported from India to Kamaran and the Hijaz via Aden, as the British consulate in Jeddah cautioned, it would be "rash to assume its importation." Rather, the consul continued to argue that cholera was likely "latent" in Mecca and Mina "perennially, liable to excitement when the aggregation of unwholesomely living people occurs at the Haj."[107]

From the perspective of the Ottoman medical establishment, the situation looked very different. As in the case of the horrific 1881 outbreak, in 1882, cholera had again been detected in Aden prior to making its way into the Hijaz. By this point Ottoman officials had become increasingly wary of the veracity of the bills of health provided by Bombay and Aden. Ottoman officials accused British authorities of concealing cholera cases and sending vessels into the Red Sea with clean bills of health even though they had been detained in Aden. The pattern was clear. From Istanbul's perspective, the constant presence of cholera aboard vessels from Bombay was being downplayed through the issuance of intentionally misleading bills of health at Aden. Again, in 1890, the story remained much the same. That season cholera broke out on board the Indian vessel the *Deccan*. In the course of the *Deccan*'s hellish 72-day quarantine on Kamaran Island, 52 Indians died of cholera. During this period the disease spread to the local villagers on Kamaran as well as passengers from other steamers. And although the long-detained *Deccan* did not even make it to the hajj, the damage had been done. While the ship was in quarantine, the disease infected pilgrims traveling on the *King Arthur* and subsequently spread to Jeddah and Mecca.[108]

The "Pasteurization" of the Ottoman Empire

By the early 1890s, the Hijaz and Kamaran Island were ripe for change. The carnage of the early 1890s was a tipping point both within in the Ottoman Empire and internationally. For the 1890 pilgrimage season, the Hijaz's official death toll was estimated at 4,578. However, estimates ran as high as 10,000.[109] In 1891, the story was much the same. Cholera again broke out aboard a British steamer from Bombay and spread to Kamaran Island, Tihama, and the Hijaz.[110] The 1891 season claimed 2,942 victims in the Hijaz alone.[111] And although the 1892 season was quieter, it would prove to be the calm before the storm.

The 1893 pilgrimage season was approached with tremendous anxiety about the potential for food shortages, extreme overcrowding, and the increased potential for cholera. The 1893 season was again a *Hacc-ı ekber* season. With predictions that the hajj census would be multiplied several times above normal numbers, in the run-up to the start of the pilgrimage, the sultan called for the creation of a special commission to raise aid money for the Hijaz (*İane-i Hicaziye Komisyonu*). A one-percent draft was taken from military wages. The funds were earmarked for the transfer of basic supplies and foodstuffs such as bread, rice, butter, oil, and vinegar from Istanbul and Egypt.[112] Despite these efforts, once again the bill for the hajj season would be measured in human lives more than in treasury ledgers.

In the month leading up to the hajj in May 1893, cholera had already been reported among the Indians at Kamaran Island and, later, among a group of Yemeni pilgrims. Although in the months leading up to the hajj the Board of Health had imposed five- and even ten-day quarantines against communication with Yemen, the measures failed. And although the sultan authorized up to 150,000 *kuruş* for emergency sanitary expenses, by the time the pilgrims reached Arafat, the outbreak had begun. By the second day at Mina, pilgrims were informed that the shari'a rules mandating a three-day stay there had been suspended. On the request of the public health authorities, the sharif of Mecca ordered the caravans to remove the pilgrims early.[113] By then, however, there was little that could be done.

As Dr. ʿAbd al-Ḥamīd Shāfī, a physician who had witnessed the devastation firsthand, reported to the Egyptian Board of Health, the crisis had moved so rapidly that in Mina private residences were being converted into makeshift hospitals. Because the proper facilities and supplies needed to treat patients were nonexistent, such scenes quickly devolved from triage to hospice. In Mina alone the death toll was topping 1,000 per day. Shāfī speculated that the totals for Mina and Mecca might have reached 2,500 or 3,000 per day. As he reported, corpses were being buried without notifying the public health authorities. Local families had abandoned the cemeteries and were burying their dead in the courtyards and gardens of their homes. As the corpses multiplied the porters responsible for burying the dead either died themselves or fled (see figure 3.3). Those tasked with burying the animal sacrifices at Mina also deserted. The disgusting smell was pervasive.[114] In an attempt to clear the corpses and lift the fog of death, the Hijaz's commanding officer, Diyarbakırlı Osman Pasha, and his troops were left to bury the dead. As a result, he also succumbed to cholera just days later.[115]

As thousands of pilgrims attempted to escape, the disease fanned out in all directions with the Bedouins and on the caravans to Yemen, Najd, and Medina. Pilgrims attempting to make their way back to Jeddah also were stricken. In much the same fashion as in Mina, a handful of houses outside Jeddah were turned into makeshift hospitals in an attempt to keep the sick from entering the city. As Dr. Shāfī recounted, however, there was little that could be done. The sick were left waiting on rugs or on the ground, without treatment, waiting to die. Ravaged by severe diarrhea, vomiting, unquenchable thirst, and chills, victims might survive for days or expire within a few hours. Within hours victims' skin lost its turgor, producing wrinkles, sunken eyes, and an overall cadaverous appearance. As severe dehydration ensued, as Shāfī observed, the victims' skin, especially the fingernails, turned a characteristic bluish-purple.[116] It was if these men, women, and children were being transformed into living corpses before his very eyes.

Even before the 1893 outbreak, by this stage in the global pandemic of 1881–95, regardless of the international visibility of the hajj, it was by no means the only path of cholera's circulation. In 1892, cholera was raging in Yemen, Russia, Iran, Iraq, and Anatolia, and it had struck Istanbul as well.[117] The disease also had reached France and Germany and even spread as far as the Americas. That year also witnessed the iconic Hamburg epidemic. Hamburg has long been held up as the "good" epidemic, the one that made a difference and "forced" change.[118] That epidemic generally is thought to have produced a decisive victory for Robert Koch's laboratory-based bacteriological science over Pettenkofer's miasma-based theories. Hamburg helped to push forward a revolution in water safety, revealing the false consciousness of sanitarian prattle about fetid air and predisposing threats posed by impoverished and mobile populations. Rapidly the more general nineteenth-century sanitarian obsessions with street cleaning and relief for the poor no longer would be adequate. Rather, in the coming years the struggle against cholera would increasingly depend on disinfection

FIGURE 3.3 "Transports à la Mecque des cadavres des Musulmans." *L'Illustration*, August 5, 1893. *Source*: Khalili Family Trust, Hajj and the Arts of Pilgrimage Collection, ARC.PT 656.

technologies and safe, reliable supplies of drinking water and, more specifically, the technical expertise and infrastructure needed to support them.

With the benefit of historical hindsight, it might be more accurate to say that the 1892 Hamburg outbreak was the decisive battle over cholera prevention *within* Europe. However, for at least several more years, international attention and conflict over cholera prevention remained focused on the Hijaz and the archipelago of Red Sea quarantines from Kamaran to Suez, and belatedly it turned to the Persian Gulf. A simplistic reading of the 1890s attributes the reform of Ottoman quarantine and public health procedures to the withering pressure brought on by a succession of international sanitary conferences in Venice (1892), Dresden (1893), and especially Paris (1894).[119] In 1892, delegates at the Venice conference proposed different sanitary regulations for pilgrims as opposed to other travelers and commercial traffic. With the belated consolidation of scientific praxis surrounding Koch and Pasteur's bacteriological breakthroughs beginning to take root, at the 1892 and 1894 conferences, a degree of international consensus—albeit sharply critical of the Ottomans—finally was beginning to emerge.

After the carnage of 1893, the pilgrimage question reemerged as the principal source of international conflict. However, the battle lines had been redrawn. Fairly or not, it would be the Ottoman Empire, not British India, that would receive the lion's share of criticism for the catastrophic mortality witnessed during the 1893 pilgrimage season. Indeed, as the conference unfolded it became increasingly clear that the Ottoman Board of Health was on trial. Britain, France, and the Netherlands were increasingly eager to consider new steps to control maritime pilgrimage traffic, insisting that they had a right to intervene in the sanitary administration of Jeddah and the Red Sea. In particular British officials were quick to justify their newfound appetite for intervention by pointing out that pilgrimage matters concerned more British subjects than Ottoman ones, "lay[ing] stress on the fact that India contains within her borders more Moslems [roughly 60 million at the time] than any other country in the world."[120] And although the Ottoman delegation complained bitterly about the colonial powers' desire "to legislate on internal matters," infringing on Ottoman sovereignty, they were sharply rebuffed with a wildly hypocritical reminder that the issue at hand was "a question not of national sovereignty but of basic human rights."[121]

In 1894, the Paris conference revolved around three principal areas of concern: sanitary surveillance of pilgrims moving through the Red Sea, the imposition of new quarantine and surveillance measures in the Persian Gulf, and sanitary arrangements to be taken at ports of departure. Finally, after nearly three decades of dogged resistance, Britain acquiesced to virtually all terms regarding the Red Sea and Indian ports of departure. However, it would continue to fight against further restrictions in the Persian Gulf. The British delegation also refused to agree to calls for increased minimum space requirements aboard steamers, the mandatory imposition of passports, and introduction of means testing.

Despite Britain's continued refusal to assent to these measures, particularly out of deference to official opinion in India, the conference exposed a widening rift between London and Calcutta. Calcutta, which no longer was permitted to send a separate delegation, was outraged by London's acceptance of the conference's recommendations. Authorities in India were especially shocked by Britain's agreement to compulsory daily inspections aboard pilgrimage vessels deemed to be sailing from infected ports, forcefully remonstrating that such measures "would almost certainly be misconstrued by lower-class Muslims as a provocation."[122]

Aside from Britain's begrudging capitulation to decades of increasing pressure, the most important development of the 1894 conference was its prescription that pilgrims be subject to strict disinfection and control measures while advocating that quarantining other classes of travelers was unnecessary. Although this compromise assuaged Britain's long-held opposition to quarantine, it also constructed stark boundaries between European and Muslim/Asian mobilities. Thus as opposed to the European tourist, trader, or soldier, pilgrims, migrants, the poor, and non-Europeans were classified as dangerous. As a result, this recategorization of border crossers styled "some cross-border enterprises as cholera-free, linked with trade but also with the movement of troops." In turn "the singling out of the pilgrims as the main vector of cholera justified the lowering of restraints on other groups of travelers." As a result, the Suez Canal transformed into a kind of border, permeable for European colonial and commercial concerns but impermeable to Muslims and non-European migrants, a manifest injustice not lost on Ottoman and Egyptian officials, who were handed the thankless task of policing this imagined sanitary-cum-civilizational boundary.[123]

However, I argue that the Ottoman archival record tells a different side of this story. It shows that the administration of public health affairs in the Hijaz and Istanbul had their own antecedents, institution builders, timelines, and limitations. Between 1890 and 1895, Istanbul, the Ottoman Red Sea, and the empire more generally would experience their own sanitary turning points. With cholera reigning in the Hijaz, Istanbul, and Europe, local, imperial, and international sources of reform would converge and ping back and forth between metropole and periphery. In this period the clearly ineffectual reliance on lengthy quarantines would increasingly be revamped and paired with newer technologies and procedures of isolation, disinfection, and water filtration. Thus rather than merely reacting to European dictates, in many respects the Ottoman Empire emerged as a key proving ground for the newest methods of cholera prevention.

One measure of the gathering momentum for reform can be traced through a series of proposals and commissions, ultimately culminating in an overhauled and greatly expanded Ottoman sanitary administration in Mecca and the Hijaz emerging from the early 1890s. In 1890, Dr. Mehmed Şakir Bey (1851–97), an epidemiology expert at Istanbul's Haydarpaşa military hospital, had traveled to the Hijaz and produced a lengthy report on its sanitary conditions and the reforms needed to improve them.[124] His report was by far the most wide-ranging and detailed survey of the Hijaz's public health conditions to date. In a sense it was an encyclopedic summation of all the knowledge accumulated over the course of the previous three decades about the urban Hijaz's sanitary and infrastructural deficiencies. He outlined the need for permanent, segregated quarantine facilities in Jeddah and Mecca. He stressed the need for dedicated hospitals and shelters for indigent pilgrims. He outlined the urgent need for proper sewerage systems and secure sources of drinking water. In more remote locations such as Arafat and Mina, he again reiterated the need for constant vigilance in the placement and maintenance of latrines. For Mina he recommended the presence of a veterinarian to inspect all animals slated for slaughter. He made a number of suggestions on the need for new cemetery spaces and reformed burial procedures. He even called for the construction of a railway running from Jeddah to Mecca and on to Arafat. Taken together, a flood of new proposals from Mehmed Şakir, Dr. Kasım İzzeddin, and Charles Bonkowski Pasha read like a roadmap for the next two decades of infrastructure building and public health reforms in the Hijaz. In one form or another, the majority of these reforms would be implemented and refined between 1895 and World War I.[125]

In addition to a growing sense of coherency, confidence, and technical precision in the Ottoman dissection of the mechanics behind cholera's circulation in the Hijaz, Mehmed Şakir's reform proposal conveys the palpable frustration with the repeated importation of cholera from British India as well as the constant threat of European intervention in the region's intertwined sanitary and political affairs. As he warned, in addition to European oversight of the Kamaran Island quarantine station, by the early 1890s, the repetition of hajj-related cholera outbreaks had provided European states with the political cover to begin questioning whether Ottoman officials within the Hijaz proper were doing enough to prevent cholera from spreading overland via the caravans from Asir, Baghdad, Basra, Najd, Syria, and Yemen. Under the guise of protecting the masses of colonial subjects making the hajj each year, the French consul had proposed the formation of a mixed commission of doctors to monitor the hajj caravans each year. As in the case of Britain's use of Muslim consular agents, the French consul acknowledged that Christian doctors would not be able to travel inland to Mecca and Medina. Instead, he proposed that each year France, Britain, Russia, the Netherlands, and Austria should send a young, capable Muslim doctor from among their respective colonial subjects to accompany the hajj caravans. At the conclusion of their respective journeys, the consul thought it might be advantageous to have representatives meet and convey their suggestions to their home states. The consul even brazenly suggested that the doctors be accompanied and protected by a retinue of their respective governments' soldiers. In 1892, the consul forwarded the plan to the French ambassador. Not surprisingly, the Ottoman members of the Board of Health were virulently opposed to this radical attempt to internationalize the internal administration of the Hijaz.[126]

However, despite their effective resistance to this idea, as the Ottoman state prepared to import new technologies and procedures for biopolitical and environmental management, which previously had been applied only to pilgrim populations in quarantine settings, to Jeddah, and even to Mecca itself, their application to Hijazi locals increasingly was perceived as both an attack on local autonomy and the illegitimate product of European extraterritorial intervention. As a result, not unlike the violent resistance to the prohibition of the slave trade in the 1850s, in the 1890s, questions about sanitation and biopolitical surveillance quickly emerged as potent new symbols of Ottoman-Turkish alterity, Europe-ness, and anti-Islamic innovation in the Hijaz.

There was a kernel of truth in the Hijazi perception that public health reforms depended on the importation of new ideas and technology from Europe. However, this imagining of European extraterritorial manipulation of Ottoman policy was only partly a critique of Western power. It also was a reflection on the widening civilizational gulf between a modernizing

Istanbul and the empire's Arabian frontiers. In this sense, the man at the center of the tangled, overlapping projects of Ottoman sanitary reform from Istanbul to Kamaran and the Hijaz offers a perfect encapsulation of that gaping chasm. A Polish refugee born in Istanbul in 1841, Charles Bonkowski (Şarlo Bonkovski) Pasha (1841–1905) studied chemistry and pharmacy in Paris.[127] On returning from his studies, he taught at the *Mekteb-i Tıbbiye*. He became the first president of the Istanbul Society of Pharmacists. However, it was during Istanbul's struggle with cholera from 1892 to 1895 that Bonkowski would truly make his mark. During those years he emerged as something of an Ottoman equivalent of Koch or Pasteur.[128] As his star rose, in 1893, he was promoted to the rank of *mirliva* and given the title of pasha. In 1894, he was honored as the sultan's head chemist (*Saray Serkimyageri*). During this period Bonkowski also was named chief health inspector for Istanbul (*Dersaadet ve Bilad-ı Selase Sıhhiye Başmüfettişi*). He would work closely with the newly formed General Sanitation Commission (*Hıfzısıhha-i Umumi Komisyonu*) and Istanbul's municipal government to manage the environmental health and hygiene of the imperial capital. With cholera raging throughout the city, Bonkowski's mandate seems to have been almost limitless. His interventions ranged from issues as large as the inspection of housing, food safety, and trash removal to questions as minute as coffee shops' handling and disposal of dirty water from nargile pipes. He also was instrumental in the reorganization and modernization of Istanbul's sewer system and water supply.[129]

During this period Bonkowski Pasha served as an Ottoman representative at the 1893 Dresden and 1894 Paris international sanitary conferences. Thus in addition to his wide-ranging responsibilities in Istanbul, he was one of the moving forces behind the modernization of the Ottoman quarantine system during this period. As early as August 1891, Bonkowski began to point out the necessity of equipping quarantine stations with the newest tools, appliances, and methods for disinfection and water safety procedures. Working alongside the French representative to the Ottoman Board of Health, Dr. Jean-Baptiste Mahé, Bonkowski composed several reform proposals for Abdülhamid's consideration. Bonkowski and Mahé argued that the existing Ottoman quarantine system was inadequate. They pleaded that if the sultan wished to avoid cholera's increasingly annual damages to the empire's population, commerce, and agricultural output, it would be necessary to invest in rebuilding the empire's quarantine facilities.[130] But without raising more funds through sanitary tariffs, there was little likelihood of this plan's succeeding. With Mahé's assistance, however, their proposal managed to convince Britain to approve more funds for the quarantine system and a separate budget for Kamaran.[131]

With these additional funds, Bonkowski envisioned that Kamaran and the rest of the Ottoman quarantine system would be outfitted with cutting-edge disinfection stations equipped with large autoclaves or disinfection stoves (*etüv* or *tebhir makineleri*) designed to sterilize the pilgrims' clothing.[132] During this period Bonkowski would become intimately familiar with the latest disinfection techniques working alongside Dr. André Chantemesse (1851–1919), an assistant of Louis Pasteur's (1822–1895), who had been dispatched to Istanbul to assist with the 1893 cholera outbreak.[133] Through Chantemesse the necessary disinfection machinery and accessories were ordered from Paris. By late 1893 into 1894, Bonkowski and his colleagues in the *Hıfzısıhha-i Umumi Komisyonu* began establishing disinfection facilities across Istanbul.[134]

Thus contrary to previous studies, which have drawn a straighter line between the horrendous 1893 outbreak in Mecca and the application of international pressure at the 1894 international sanitary conference in Paris, it would be more accurate to think of the strengthening of the Ottoman quarantine system in the Red Sea as equally an outcome of the intense sanitary and environmental reorganization of Istanbul that had been sparked by the 1892–95 cholera epidemic there. Between 1892 and 1894, a special quarantine reform commission also was at work. Headed by Dr. Michel Cozzonis (Koçoni) Efendi, the commission strove to reorganize the Kamaran Island station and make it a model facility that could be reproduced in the empire's other Red Sea, Mediterranean, and Black sea stations.[135] Bonkowski and his colleagues stood poised to export the newly mastered technologies of Istanbul's sanitary revolution to the empire's cholera-riddled southern frontier.

As a result of the technical experience that Bonkowski and his colleagues had gained while battling cholera in Istanbul, by the time the 1894 international sanitary conference met in Paris, he was armed with a list of reforms for Kamaran Island. Among the highlights of this list, Bonkowski announced that the newly redesigned quarantine would be equipped with disinfection stoves, sterilizing machines, water filtration (condenser) machines, an ice-making machine, and mobile receptacles for the safe removal of feces from the camp. Bonkowski also promised the construction of a new bacteriological laboratory, allowing physicians to identify cholera accurately and constantly monitor the quality of the water supply. He called for the construction of some fifty or sixty shower stalls (complete with an adequate supply of soap). And in addition to reorganizing the camps and hospital facilities to keep the sick and well from commingling, Bonkowski called for the evacuation of Kamaran's local inhabitants to ensure that the island would not have a large permanent population to fuel further outbreaks.[136]

Between 1895 and 1902, Bonkowski's vision set in motion a complete overhaul of the Kamaran Island quarantine. The quarantine station was completely rebuilt and reorganized. The older thatched-roof structures were replaced by brick and iron accommodations, shops, a warehouse, a cafeteria, and even a mosque. To better facilitate further construction, a new brick factory was built. In addition to the renovated housing, two separate hospital wards were constructed to segregate patients suffering from cholera, plague, and/or typhoid fever. Built along the seashore, the hospital wards were positioned at a distance of approximately 500–600 meters from each other and all other facilities in order to minimize contact between healthy and infected persons. There were even new barracks for infected patients, completely fenced off from other housing sections. There were new staff quarters. Telephone lines were installed to facilitate communication between the residences of the sanitary inspectors and the physicians. Encircling the entire facility, an 11-kilometer tram line was built to transport pilgrims, supplies, and building materials more efficiently. In 1902, a new bacteriology lab (*bakteriyolojihane*) was established.[137]

Arguably the most important intervention of all related to the island's water supply and waste management. In 1894, Istanbul ordered its first condenser system from the Glasgow-based Mirrlees-Watson Company to filter the island's notoriously brackish well water.[138] This unit could process up to 60 tons of water a day and was accompanied by a storage with a further 160-ton capacity. Another major advancement for both hygiene and the comfort of the pilgrims was the installation of ice machines (*buz makineleri*) that were capable of producing five tons a day.[139] Perhaps most critical of all, Kamaran's pilgrims received flushable toilets and a totally revamped sewage disposal system.[140]

The results of these interventions were remarkable. After 1895, apart from a major outbreak in December 1907, when cholera victims did find their way to Kamaran Island, individual cases no longer metastasized into epidemics. According to Dr. Milton Crendiropoulo, director of the Kamaran station, after 1895, the average mortality among pilgrims on Kamaran plummeted from 3.37 per 1,000 to 1.04. As Crendiropoulo argued, for years Kamaran's wells and water tanks had been veritable cholera incubators. However, after the massive overhaul of the quarantine station that was set in motion in 1894–95, especially the addition of the island's water condenser system, cholera was more easily contained and isolated from the station's water supply.[141]

Despite the tremendous progress made by Ottoman public health authorities in both Istanbul and the Red Sea, even after 1894–95, their struggles with both British obstructionism and the larger issue of European capitulatory interference from within the Ottoman Board of Health were far from over. At the 1894 sanitary conference in Paris, Ottoman authorities faced a new round of international pressures to revamp and strengthen maritime quarantine procedures in the Persian Gulf and Iraq.[142] This period saw renewed Ottoman efforts to impose stricter quarantines on Persian pilgrims—both living and dead—crossing overland from Qajar Iran en route to Iraq's shrine cities. In the 1890s, quarantine authorities in Kermanshah, Basra, and Khanaqin imposed longer quarantine periods and even closed the border for seventeen months between June 1892 and November 1893. The Paris conference also prompted Ottoman authorities to more tightly regulate the transfer of corpses across the Iranian border to the cemetery sites of the ʿatabāt. Thus in order to avoid the potential risks of spreading cholera and plague via the corpse traffic, the Ottoman state imposed a prohibition on the transfer of any corpse buried for less than three years. By doing so Ottoman public health authorities sought to put an end to the importation of all "moist" corpses. Likewise, whereas living pilgrims were subjected to a 10-kuruş quarantine fee, cadavers slated for burial in Iraq's shrine cities were slapped with a 50-kuruş tax. As a result of these tightened quarantine and customs restrictions, an illicit trade in corpse smuggling across the Ottoman-Qajar frontier emerged to avoid the increased scrutiny.[143]

The glare of this international spotlight on the Persian Gulf and Red Sea would only intensify when bubonic plague spread from Hong Kong to Bombay in September 1896.[144] As had been the case for most of the previous three decades, British authorities would have to be coerced and cajoled to act in a forceful and fulsome manner. Once British India formally acknowledged the plague outbreak in October, Ottoman and European officials demanded that the hajj be suspended. Fearing that plague, as with cholera before it, might escape India's borders and find its way to Europe, the international community threatened to impose a total embargo on trade with not only Bombay but all of India unless British authorities agreed to take decisive steps to contain the outbreak. In January and February 1897, the duration of quarantine and disinfection periods at Kamaran and other Red Sea ports was raised from ten to fifteen and then eventually to twenty days.[145] As a result, further departures of Indian pilgrims during the 1896–97 season were forbidden. And for the first time, on February 20, 1897, India followed France and Russia in announcing that the hajj would be suspended as long as plague prevailed.[146]

Unfortunately, some pilgrimage vessels already had left India before the ban. The steamship *Pekin* arrived at Kamaran carrying two plague victims.[147] Despite having been discouraged officially from making the hajj, by June 1897, Foreign Office reports estimated that around 2,500 Indian pilgrims were present in Jeddah, 5,000 in Mecca, and 4,000 at Yanbuʿ.[148] Not surprisingly, by the end of the pilgrimage season, plague had landed in Jeddah. Although British officials opted not to impose a total ban on the hajj in 1898, pilgrims were publicly discouraged from making the journey.[149] As a result, only 893 Indians arrived at Kamaran Island.[150] Despite these precautions, plague struck Jeddah in 1898–99 and Basra in May 1899.[151]

As frightening as the global plague pandemic of 1894–1901 was, from the perspective of pilgrimage-related public health concerns, it was precisely the kind of shock needed to overcome British India's long-standing policy of obstructing the implementation of sanitary regulations. At the tenth international sanitary conference in Venice in February 1897, British India was forced to ratify the terms of the Paris convention.[152] The combined threat of plague and cholera had finally rendered British resistance politically unviable.

At the same time, Ottoman public health officials in the Red Sea and Persian Gulf were left bracing against a fresh wave of fallout from British India's seemingly endless string of public health disasters. Istanbul withstood yet another round of manifestly unjust accusations that its quarantine officials had failed to carry out their duties properly. In the midst of another disaster emanating from British India, this was tantamount to blaming the victim. As Dr. Michel Cozzonis pointed out to his European counterparts, "matters of quarantine in the Ottoman State are not in the hands of the government rather of the Europeans." If sanitary and quarantine services "are not functioning properly, the reality is that the cause is not Turkish incompetence." Rather the blame lay squarely with "the European physicians" who dominated the Ottoman Board of Health and "whose every desire is accepted by the government."[153]

Disinfection Insurrection

Although the 1890s marked a major turning point in the maturation of Ottoman sanitation, hard-won progress toward greater international sanitary cooperation, and the gradual erosion of British antiregulatory obstructionism, progress in the Hijaz itself remained elusive. As in the case of Kamaran Island, after the tragedy of 1893, Istanbul also attempted to impose a new level of sanitary discipline on the Hijaz proper. Unlike the controlled population and environment of the quarantine island, however, the Hijaz proved a more complicated puzzle of overlapping social, religious, technical, environmental, and biological challenges. Unlike the case with the internationally controlled quarantine system, Europe was not the primary obstacle. In the Hijaz itself Istanbul had to contend with resistance from urban Hijazis, the Bedouin, and the Sharifate of Mecca.

Prior to 1894, the principal axis of local Hijazi discontent with the tightening of Ottoman hygienic measures had revolved around attempts to restrict the sale of unsafe drinking water by local tank owners. During this period the Hijaz's water systems remained extremely vulnerable to cholera, drought, and profiteering. As we shall see in the next chapter, Ottoman attempts to revitalize the Hijaz's crippled water infrastructure and wrest its hydraulic economy from local hands would be confronted with a determined program of resistance and sabotage. Although Ottoman hydraulic interventions certainly upset powerful political and economic interests in favor of autonomy, they were not viewed as inherently alien or anti-Islamic innovations. After all, the use of state power for the construction and maintenance of hydraulic infrastructure, such as aqueducts and fountains, fit neatly into well-understood traditions with long and illustrious Islamic pedigrees. Conversely, the introduction of the kinds of disinfection technologies being applied in Istanbul and Kamaran lacked all such claims on Islamic credibility. Thus as the 1895 hajj season unfolded, Istanbul's stepped-up war on microbes quickly sparked a violent local insurgency.

The 1894 installation of disinfection machines at Jeddah and Mecca provided powerful new symbols for local resistance. What was different about these new disinfection measures was that unlike the remote quarantines enforced in the Red Sea, Ottoman disinfection procedures within the Hijaz did not distinguish between foreign pilgrims and locals or make exceptions for the Bedouin or women. Although for years foreign pilgrims had been subjected to the inconveniences and indignities of the state's medical examinations, this level of invasive biopolitical surveillance and discipline had never been attempted with Hijazi locals.

The object of the disinfection process was to sterilize clothing items, but the mysterious nature of the machinery and the culturally unthinkable notion of officials requiring men and women to undress stoked the imagination. As Dr. Adrien Achille Proust explained, this exotic procedure gave rise in short order to wild rumors that the victims of this process (rather than just their clothes) would be stripped naked and placed inside the disinfection machines. Even though two female attendants had been secured to oversee the process, on hearing these frightening rumors, many female pilgrims reportedly refused to travel farther than Jeddah during the 1894 season. As Dr. Proust warned, regardless of the desires of the international community, the Ottoman state could not do more than it already had. If Istanbul moved too far, too fast, he believed that the Hijaz might well turn into another insurgency-riddled Yemen.[154]

In 1895, local anger over disinfection procedures reached a boiling point. As Jules Gervais-Courtellemont narrated the events, a number of influential shaykhs went before Sharif ʿAwn al-Rafiq to address the public outrage surrounding the disinfection machines. They asked why the sharif had stood by while Ottoman officials dared to strip their women under the pretext of washing their clothes. They chided that if he could not stand up to this indignity, he did not deserve the title of sharif. Challenging both his legitimacy and manhood, they proclaimed that they had sharpened their daggers, were carrying their burial shrouds, and were ready to die for the cause.[155]

Aside from insulting the honor of Hijazi women, among both the Bedouin and urban populations of the Hijaz, the disinfection machines and newly reorganized quarantine hospitals had given credence to popular conspiracies surrounding cholera. As British Consul William Richards explained, there existed a "deep-rooted conviction" among the Bedouin that cholera was "introduced into the country by the quarantine doctors through the medium of the disinfecting machines!" Moreover, given that so few of those taken to the hospital "were ever known to come out alive again," the majority of Meccans believed that the victims "were purposely killed by doctors."[156]

Whatever the veracity of Gervais-Courtellemont's retelling of the confrontation between local shaykhs and the sharif and, by extension, his implied prior knowledge of said attacks, the threat of violence was real enough. On May 30, 1895, a mob of ʿUtayba tribesmen and local Meccans attacked the disinfection equipment and destroyed the offices housing it. That same evening a group of foreign consular officials had gone for a walk roughly half a mile beyond Jeddah's city walls. The group was attacked and shot by a Bedouin party, who quickly fled by camel. George Brandt, the acting Russian consul was seriously wounded. Richards and Charles Dorville, chancellor of the French consulate, were both slightly wounded. However, the long-serving British vice-consul, Dr. Abdur Razzack, was killed. Later Jeddah's disinfection facilities were ransacked by a party of Bukharan pilgrims, forcing the disinfection inspectors to flee in search of refuge aboard vessels in the harbor. Two days later Mecca's hospital was looted and vandalized.[157]

When word of the anti-sanitarian violence reached Istanbul, Abdülhamid was left to contemplate the real possibility of another bombardment of Jeddah as happened in 1858 or perhaps a more lasting international military occupation. The situation was so sensitive that the sultan's War Cabinet (Divan-ı Harb) had to be convened to discuss the possibility of European military intervention. There was also concern that any action to punish the local population might provoke further international attention. Taking punitive measures against Hijazi locals was deemed too dangerous because of the difficulty in anticipating precisely which locals were Ottoman subjects and which could claim foreign protection or nationality.

In the meantime, sanitary operations within the Hijaz ground to a halt. Construction on the new hospitals in Jeddah and Mecca were suspended. It was even suggested that the unfinished buildings be demolished to appease the mob. European consuls and foreign subjects were taken aboard a British cruiser to ensure their security. Jeddah's harbor was rapidly populated by British, Dutch, French, and Russian warships. In light of the inadequacy of the local garrison, troops had to be called in from Yemen. Citing the nightmare scenario of a foreign occupation of Jeddah during hajj season, the sultan implored Governor Hasan Hilmi Pasha and the sharif to reestablish public safety in Jeddah immediately.[158]

In the wake of the violence, the true identities of Abdur Razzack's murderers were never determined. Despite an onslaught of diplomatic pressure from the British and French embassies, weeks turned into months. Neither the sharif nor the authorities in Istanbul caved to foreign pressure. Indemnities were paid for the casualties and their dependents. However, justice remained elusive. Hasan Hilmi was relieved from his governorship. Likewise, the *muhtesib* was dismissed for allegedly spreading anti–public health propaganda citing the Ottoman state's impotency in the face of the European-dominated "mixed" Board of Health.[159]

As the British ambassador argued, responsibility for the investigation should have rested with the governor. However, because the culprits were allegedly Bedouins, the affair conveniently fell under the jurisdiction of ʿAwn al-Rafīq. The sharif placed the blame on the Ṣaḥḥāf branch of the Ḥarb tribe and launched an ineffectual campaign of collective punishment. As the British consulate theorized, however, given the enmity between ʿAwn al-Rafīq and the Ṣaḥḥāf, their implication in the attack was merely an expedient way to settle old scores.[160] The consulate believed it considerably more likely that the Bedouin culprits operated on behalf of the sharif. Though the consular community could marshal no proof other than rumors from the bazaar, they remained convinced that Abdur Razzack had been targeted by the sharif.

As the investigations unfolded, two competing narratives emerged. As Hasan Hilmi concluded, the alleged Bedouin assailants had mistaken the consular officials for Ottoman quarantine officers, who were the focal point of local anger over the new disinfection procedures. However, from the perspective of the European consular community, this theory did not hold up. They believed that the attack had been premeditated. As proof, they reasoned that the attackers would have required specific intelligence about the consular officials' evening walks outside the city walls. Thus those responsible for feeding this intelligence would have known very well that the quarantine officials did not frequent the location where the shootings took place. Rather, it was the opinion of the consuls that the attack was overtly "political, prompted and organized by the Grand Shareef of Mecca." As the consul explained, Abdur Razzack had "incurred the hatred of the Grand Shareef," who "would have himself shot Mr. Razzack had opportunity offered." Abdur Razzack had served the consulate for over a decade, during which time he had energetically worked to expose and contest ʿAwn al-Rafiq's brazen extortion and abuse of British subjects and pilgrims more generally. These actions placed him at odds with the most powerful financial interests in the province, a string of Ottoman officials, and the sharif himself.[161]

Conclusion

During his first visit to the Hijaz in 1879, Dr. Abdur Razzack surreptitiously made the hajj as a British spy. At the time, he had predicted that had his covert mission been discovered, very likely he could have been murdered for secretly working on behalf of a Christian government.[162] In the end, after over a decade and a half of service in the Hijaz, at just forty-five years of age, Abdur Razzack's morbid premonition of his own demise was finally fulfilled. In the interim Abdur Razzack became one of the longest-serving officials in the Hijaz. During that time he had seen scores of Ottoman governors and European consuls come and go, and even the deposition of a sharif. If ʿAwn al-Rafiq was responsible for Abdur Razzack's death, in a sense it would have been fitting. Despite their very different roles, they were arguably the most influential avatars of the late Ottoman Hijaz's two dueling political forces, autonomy and extraterritoriality. The different but often mutually reinforc- ing challenges posed by the clash between local and interimperial dynamics illustrates the insoluble dilemmas facing Ottoman modernization along the empire's southern frontiers.

It is a great irony that the events that ultimately precipitated the doc- tor's murder did not directly involve any European intervention or great scandal involving a British subject arrested in Mecca. Despite the popular imaginings of Hijazi locals, the implementation of disinfection procedures could not be attributed solely to the European powers or the "mixed" Board of Health. If anything, an equal case could be made that the reforming energies of Ottoman technocrats such as Bonkowski Pasha had pushed the conflicted parties of the Board of Health toward more aggressive measures rather than vice versa.

Although it is clear that international pressure played an important role in the evolution of Ottoman public health controls in the Hijaz and the empire more generally, as this chapter has argued, extraterritorial interfer- ence in the Ottoman Empire's sanitary statecraft also was a considerably more complicated story than most English-language studies previously allowed. Just as the erection of Red Sea quarantines had suited the centralizing impulses of the Tanzimat state and lent international legitimacy to a revitalized Ottoman presence in the Hijaz and Yemen in 1866, the Hamidian-era overhaul of the Hijaz's sanitary administration from 1894–95 on should not be read exclusively as a product of capitulatory international pressure. Instead, it would be more useful to think of disinfection machines, quarantine hospitals, and the increasing visibility of public health officials in the Hijaz as a natural manifestation of Istanbul's maturing program of technoscientific modernization reaching into the empire's Arabian frontier and reproducing itself. As the next chapter further reinforces, those same infrastructural interventions also supplied Hijazi locals with the very technologies that they would redeploy to resist the advance of Ottoman modernization.

FOUR

Bedouins and Broken Pipes

IN 1881, James Zohrab, the British consul in Jeddah, had samples of Zamzam water sent to London for chemical analysis. The samples were tested by Dr. Edward Frankland, a professor at the Royal College of Chemistry. His gruesome findings were published in *The Times* and later reproduced by *The Lancet* in 1883. Frankland put forward the shocking claim that the holy water of the Zamzam well was six times more contaminated by animal waste than London sewage. He also claimed that Mecca's system of waste removal was responsible for the contamination of the groundwater feeding the well. As he explained, "These latrines empty themselves into pits dug outside the houses. When these get filled they are emptied into other pits, which are made in the streets or any convenient spot, and then covered over with earth. . . . This system of burying foul matter in every direction has been pursued for centuries; it is not, therefore, surprising that the ground in and around Mecca is surcharged with excrementitous matter." Frankland concluded, "there can be no doubt" that due to its "surroundings," Zamzam water "is the most potent source of cholera poison." Thus "it would scarcely be possible to devise a more effective means for the diffusion of this poison throughout Mahomedan countries." He even called for the closure of the Zamzam well to protect "the health of Europe and Asia" from "this abominable and dangerous pollution."[1]

Later that year the Dutch representative to the Ottoman Board of Health, Dr. C. Stekoulis, published a treatise in French and Ottoman Turkish on cholera and the hajj featuring Frankland's results. This attack on Zamzam water was perceived as a deeply offensive work of anti-Islamic propaganda by the Ottoman medical establishment. Mehmed Şakir Bey was so outraged that he enlisted Bonkowski Pasha and Ahmed Efendi, professor of chemistry at the Ottoman War College, to conduct their own chemical tests.[2]

Bonkowski wrote a scathing letter to Frankland admonishing him for his "mistakes and quite bizarre conclusions" and expressing deep dismay at the professor's obliviousness to the "most severe indignation" that his comparison of these holy waters with London sewage would arouse among the world's three hundred million Muslims. He reported that his own sample of Zamzam water was colorless, odorless, and slightly saline and had a slightly basic pH value. In short it was harmless. Bonkowski even noted that the well water could be bottled for up to a year without spoiling. Bonkowski cited a long list of chemical differences between his sample and Frankland's, explaining that the salinity observed in Frankland's results was so high that it resembled seawater. He attempted to explain to Frankland the difference between the sources of Zamzam water and Mecca's main supply of drinking water, the 'Ayn Zubayda aqueduct. He also tried to disabuse Frankland of the idea that pilgrims bathed anywhere near the Zamzam well and concluded with a pointed question: "If Zamzam were cholera's source, wouldn't one suppose that cholera would appear in Mecca every year?"[3]

Bonkowski and Mehmed Şakir were convinced that the sample provided to Frankland could not have been authentic, or it had been tampered with prior to testing. In his *Lancet* article, Frankland alluded to his concerns over the sample's authenticity and even included Consul Zohrab's reply to his inquiries. As Zohrab explained, the sample was procured by a "Mahomedan gentleman in whose good faith I have implicit confidence."[4] Bonkowski and Mehmed Şakir suspected that Zohrab's Muslim associate was Yusuf Kudzi, the translator for the British consulate in Jeddah. Kudzi was a British-protected person of Russian-Jewish origin born in Jerusalem. Prior to surfacing in Jeddah in 1870, Kudzi claimed to have spent years in India and China and to have converted to Islam.[5] However, as Bonkowski and Mehmed Şakir's mention of his conversion suggests, the Ottomans were highly suspicious of Britain's use of Muslim consular employees—most notably Kudzi and the vice-consul, Dr. Abdur Razzack—as intelligence operatives in Mecca. The nature of their work aroused suspicions that these men were not "genuinely" Muslims. Kudzi likely raised further suspicions on account of his notorious reputation for corrupt dealings in the pilgrimage steam-ship industry. Thus as Mehmed Şakir explained, they theorized that Kudzi had introduced some sort of contaminant in order to produce the embar-rassing test results. Although Bonkowski and Mehmed Şakir's accusations are impossible to prove, their skepticism regarding the objectivity of Frank-land's analysis was well founded.[6]

As discussed in the previous chapter, in the wake of repeated pilgrimage-related cholera outbreaks, at the 1866 international sanitary conference in Istanbul, the hajj had leapt to the center of European hygienic conscious-ness.[7] Taking a strongly contagionist stance, conference delegates identi-fied the steamship-going hajj from India as the primary conduit for the globalization of cholera.[8] Following their recommendations, the Ottoman state was tasked with organizing a Red Sea quarantine system to halt chol-era's progress before it could reach the Suez Canal and Europe's Mediter-ranean shores.

For the next three decades, British officials struggled to deny India's image as an exporter of cholera and worked to obstruct the imposition of quarantine regulations. They feared that interference with this pillar of the Islamic faith would spark a backlash in India and that strict quarantine mea-sures might be applied punitively to vessels from India, threatening the free flow of trade. Britain and the Anglo-Indian medical establishment became deeply invested in anti-contagionist or localist theories of cholera's etiol-ogy, which blamed cholera on mysterious influences in the atmosphere, fer-mentative products of the soil, miasmas caused by festering human waste, or other predisposing causes.[9] According to localists, the presence of a spe-cific germ and susceptible human victim could not alone produce cholera symptoms. Rather, they hypothesized that cholera required the presence of specific soil or groundwater conditions. This idea was especially attractive because it offered an environmental explanation for spontaneous outbreaks of disease, which were seen as evidence of the inefficacy of quarantines.[10] These were the theories that formed the intellectual backdrop to Frank-land's findings.

In 1883–84, at the same time that Frankland was attacking Zamzam water as a source of "cholera poison," German bacteriologist Robert Koch was conducting research in Egypt and India that would provide definitive proof of cholera's causal agent, the comma bacillus. Koch's discovery of the role played by the human intestinal tract in the life cycle of the bacterium, and his confirmation of cholera's waterborne transmission through infected human waste products, should have brought the scientific debate surrounding cholera's spread to a screeching halt.[11] Yet throughout the 1880s and into the 1890s, British scientists remained stubbornly wedded to their anti-contagionist views. Anti-contagionist Zamzam articles continued to circulate in Britain and India as late as 1895.[12] In the context of the simultaneous struggles to control the repeated cholera outbreaks in Istanbul from 1892 to 1895 and the devastation of the 1893 outbreak in the Hijaz, even some Ottoman officials briefly embraced the Zamzam theory. Ottoman army and navy physicians sent to inspect Mecca's health conditions proposed a temporary ban on drinking Zamzam water. However, the proposal was vetoed by the sharif of Mecca, who ultimately controlled access to the well.[13]

What are we to make of this duel of experts? In light of Koch's discoveries, the ideological character of anti-Zamzam polemics becomes more evident. But are we to read this episode as a footnote in the struggle between advocates and opponents of contagion and quarantine? Or are we missing an opportunity by allowing water to be reduced to a proxy in Britain's anti-contagion campaign? In a sense Frankland's sanitarian concerns were not unfounded; Mecca's water systems were on the verge of a massive overhaul. However, we shall see that the ways in which Ottoman administrators understood and prioritized the management of Mecca's water resources suggests a story vastly different from the one Frankland imagined.

Although European observers viewed Mecca primarily through the international lens of cholera and quarantine, for Ottoman administrators an additional, yet inextricably linked, responsibility was the provision of enough safe, potable water for both pilgrims and permanent residents. As a result, Ottoman analyses of the Hijaz's public health often moved along a more localized set of axes, dedicating as much or more attention to the Hijaz's water supply and the repair and upkeep of the region's aqueducts, water tanks, cisterns, pipes, and fountains. Ottoman reporting also conveys a much stronger sense of the mutually reinforcing relationship between the region's susceptibility to water scarcity and its vulnerability to waterborne disease.[14]

In many respects potable water was a microcosm of Istanbul's incomplete projects of modernization and state building on the empire's Arab peripheries. Water questions sat at the intersection between international pressures surrounding cholera, drought, Wahhabi and Bedouin disorder, and the inability of the state to impose its will on the semiautonomous Amirate of Mecca. To be sure, Ottoman public health reforms and increased attention to water infrastructure were partly a product of the intense international attention generated by cholera and the capitulatory nature of the Ottoman Board of Health. However, as with other projects with more overt military and strategic implications—most notably the Hijaz telegraph and railway (see chapter 6)—the Ottoman state also saw an opportunity to harness the increasing medicalization of the hajj to serve a broader set of efforts to consolidate the empire's most vulnerable frontier provinces.

Frontier Anxiety: Osman Nuri Pasha and the Birth of the Hamidian Hijaz

The Hijaz's role as a symbol of Hamidian Pan-Islamic legitimacy has been well documented, but less attention has been paid to its role as a laboratory for the state's shifting approaches toward its tribal frontiers. In the midst of the early crises of his reign, Abdülhamid flirted with the idea of wresting power from the sharif of Mecca to subordinate the semiautonomous Amirate of Mecca to the will of the Ottoman center. In the end, however, the sultan became convinced that any direct attempt to subdue the sharif of Mecca and his Bedouin levies would prove expensive, foment unrest, and increase the potential for European intervention in the Hijaz.[15] Nevertheless, the career arc and ideas of Osman Nuri Pasha (1840–98), the man to whom this aborted centralizing mission was entrusted, are no less illuminating (see figure 4.1). Throughout the 1880s and 1890s, he would serve as governor of Yemen, Aleppo, and twice in the Hijaz, garnering a reputation as arguably the premiere expert on the empire's Arab tribal frontiers. Osman Nuri's successes and failures would inform the sultan's delicate balancing act in the Hijaz long after the governor's stormy tenure.[16] Here a brief digression from our discussion of the Hijaz's water crisis is needed to more fully introduce the governor who first attempted to address the province's overlapping environmental and constitutional frailties.

Osman Nuri's rise to prominence and his centralizing style were byproducts of the confluence of domestic and international anxieties converging on the Hijaz at the beginning of Abdülhamid II's reign. In 1876, Sultan Abdülaziz had been deposed in a coup orchestrated by Midhat Pasha

FIGURE 4.1 Osman Nuri Pasha, governor of the Hijaz, 1885. Photograph by Christiaan Snouck Hurgronje/al-Sayyid ʿAbd al-Ghaffār. *Source*: BL: IOR, 1781.b.6/8, in *Qatar Digital Library*.

(1822–84) and his allies and sanctioned by the *Şeyhülislam*. Although Abdülhamid was allowed to replace Murad V on August 31, 1876, on the grounds of the latter's poor mental health, he did so under duress and was forced to agree to the promulgation of Midhat Pasha's proposed constitution. In 1878, Abdülhamid eventually was able to consolidate enough power to prorogue the constitution indefinitely. However, Abdülhamid harbored deep suspicions of Midhat's seditious aspirations. He also continued to view Abdülaziz's ouster and subsequent suicide as a "murder" plotted by Midhat and his associates. Following the closure of the second parliament in 1878, Midhat was arrested and put on a ship destined for Brindisi. However, eventually he was brought back and appointed governor of Syria. But in 1881, he was arrested again and tried at Yıldız Palace for the murder of Sultan Abdülaziz.[17]

Another element of the backdrop to Midhat Pasha's arrest and conviction were the swirling rumors surrounding the threat of a rival Arab caliphate. According to the theory presented by Gabriel Charmes, Midhat and the constitutionalists had intended to separate the caliphate from the sultanate and the Ottoman dynasty.[18] According to intelligence collected by the British consulate in Jeddah, after Abdülhamid came to the throne, Midhat and his coconspirators had designs on deposing him and transferring the caliphate to the infamous but elderly former sharif, ʿAbd al-Muṭṭalib.[19] Midhat and his fellow conspirators allegedly believed that if the caliphate were transferred to the Amir of Mecca, the sharifate would take on the ecumenical duties as spiritual head of the Muslim world and the Ottoman Sultanate would be forced to base its authority on constitutional legitimacy. To accomplish this dramatic transfer and consolidate a new constitutional regime, Midhat reportedly supported granting more autonomy for the Hijaz and other Arab provinces.[20]

In 1880, Sharif Ḥusayn ibn Muḥammad ibn ʿAwn (r. 1877–80) was assassinated by an Afghan pilgrim, ostensibly resentful of the sultan's support for British policy in Afghanistan. Alternatively, some have speculated that the assassination was plotted from within the Ottoman state in reaction to revelations of the sharif's secret correspondence with the British.[21] On receiving news of the sharif's assassination, the sultan saw an opportunity simultaneously to balance the competing claims of the Zayd and ʿAwn branches of the Hashemite family, reduce the political significance of the sharifate, and dispose of a would-be rival. To do so, Abdülhamid appointed the ninety-year-old ʿAbd al-Muṭṭalib to a second term as sharif. ʿAbd al-Muṭṭalib previously held the position in the 1850s but had led an open revolt against Ottoman rule in 1855–56. He had been deposed and exiled to Salonica and later Istanbul, where he remained until his reappointment in 1880. British consular reports reasoned that the sultan had reinstalled him as sharif as "a reward for his loyalty, but also perhaps partly . . . to keep him out the way."[22] Despite his past disloyalty and advanced age, the irascible sharif suited the sultan's motives perfectly. Initially ʿAbd al-Muṭṭalib was paired with a new governor,

Ahmed İzzet (Erzincanlı), who also had served as governor in the 1850s. The appointment of this duo of nonagenarians was hardly an accident. As would rapidly become clear, real control of the region and Istanbul's interests was intended to reside solely in Osman Nuri Pasha's capable hands.

Due in part to the sharifate's alleged role in Midhat's scheme to transfer the caliphate, Abdülhamid was understandably anxious to avoid having the Hijaz's governor or military command compromised by the exiled Midhat and his coconspirators.[23] There also was considerable anxiety that the British consulate in Jeddah was engaged in a plot to assist Midhat in escaping from his confinement in Ta'if.[24] The sultan required someone who had no relationship to these principal figures and who professed total loyalty to him. Owing to these needs, Osman Nuri was chosen for a special mission. On October 31, 1880, he was informed that he would be brought to Istanbul for a personal audience with the sultan. During their meeting Osman Nuri was given verbal instructions regarding the unique duties of his new posting. Abdülhamid explained that Osman Nuri would have complete responsibility for the conditions and movements of Midhat and his associates.[25] Henceforth this responsibility would be taken completely out of the hands of the sitting governor and sharif of Mecca.[26] Within just two years, in 1882, Osman Nuri Pasha was given the governorship of the Hijaz and promoted to marshal (müşir), the empire's highest military rank.

Armed with the personal confidence of the sultan and an almost limitless mandate to stamp out the specter of internal conspiracy and foreign intervention, Osman Nuri set out to bring the Hijaz under his direct control. In pursuit of this mission, in February 1882, he dispatched a detailed report outlining the sharif's tyrannical behavior and the need to take drastic steps to limit his powers.[27] The governor recommended that the sharif be stripped of all judicial power. He argued for disbanding the sharifate's private security forces and the removal of his responsibility for the affairs of the Ḥaram, the appointment of its personnel, and the management of its endowments. Even the management of the Bedouin shaykhs was to be transferred to the governor. This would have left the Amir of Mecca with just two functions: the mediation of disputes between Bedouin tribes and the local organization of the hajj. As the British consulate saw it, the governor's intention was to "do away with the Sherifate altogether or, if that was not possible, to deprive the Grand Sherif of all secular powers and leave him to enjoy his title as a sort of high priest."[28]

As it turned out, Osman Nuri was prepared to go even further. In June 1882, ʿAbd al-Muṭṭalib asked to be excused from his reduced position and be allowed to take up residence in Medina. Osman Nuri cautioned against allowing this, claiming that the sharif's true design was to join forces with Muḥammad ibn Rashīd of Haʾil in order to return to Mecca and declare himself under British protection. Although the likelihood of this scheme is dubious at best, this narrative exacerbated previous rumors of the sharif's involvement in Midhat Pasha's alleged caliphate conspiracy. Despite the flimsiness of these allegations, authorities in Istanbul were prepared to take precautions against them.[29] To support his accusations, in August 1882, Osman Nuri reported the interception of a messenger carrying alleged letters of sedition verifying the sharif's conspiratorial communications with the British consulate. Armed with this likely falsified evidence and possibly even a forged *ferman*, Osman Nuri deposed the sharif and placed him under house arrest.[30]

Having disposed of ʿAbd al-Muṭṭalib, between 1882 and 1886, Osman Nuri continued his consolidation of power. From the British consulate's perspective, Osman Nuri appeared to have been chosen specially by the sultan to "reduce the Hedjaz, so far as local independence goes, to the condition of a third-rate Turkish province." In just a few years "Osman Pasha's word" had become "law in all matters great and small" and "his summary proceedings and despotic powers are naturally feared."[31] Eventually, however, the governor's alienation of Bedouin and urban notables swelled the ranks of Sharif ʿAwn al-Rafiq's supporters. This growing sense of local discontent with the governor's performance gave the sharif precisely the leverage he needed to campaign for Osman Nuri's removal in 1886.[32] In their dueling letters to Istanbul, the two men laid out the high stakes of the conflict between an aggressively centralizing governorship and the continued autonomy of the sharifate. As ʿAwn al-Rafiq complained, Osman Nuri was waging a rogue campaign to strip away the long-standing privileges of the sharifate.[33] In turn Osman Nuri claimed that if left to his own devices, the Amir of Mecca would harbor a desire (*meyl ü arzu*) to revolt and establish independence (*tefferüd ve istiklal*) for himself. Whatever the veracity of either man's claims, as the grand vizier concluded, this level of persistent conflict could not continue in a place as sensitive as the Hijaz.[34]

In the end, Osman Nuri's aggressive assault on the Sharifate of Mecca's independence led to his removal as governor in 1886. However, his dismissal cannot be interpreted as a total repudiation of his ambitious policies, nor did it erase the long-lasting legacies of his tenure. Rather, Osman Nuri's governorship appears to have been a formative learning experience for the sultan. Having experimented with a more direct confrontation with the sharifate and the Bedouin, from 1886 on the sultan pursued a more cautious and indirect strategy of technopolitical development, building new infrastructures—new material facts on the ground—intended gradually to bind the frontier to the Ottoman center and narrow the parameters of the province's autonomy. And instead of abolishing or dramatically changing the constitutional status of the sharifate, Abdülhamid opted to slowly build up new technologies of Ottoman rule around it. Thus although the sultan abandoned Osman Nuri's openly confrontational approach, over the next two decades he did embrace many of his proposals, particularly his vision of tribal education and his strong advocacy for technological and infrastructural development.

The Hijaz and Other "Hot Provinces": Technopolitics on the Tribal Frontier

In 1885, Osman Nuri wrote a report, a kind of blueprint, outlining his plans for provincial reforms in the Hijaz and Yemen.[35] In it, he attempted to adapt Istanbul's vision of modernity and civilization to better suit the Bedouin profile of these provinces. His main priorities included political and administrative divisions, taxation and revenue, educational and legal reform, the construction of government buildings and infrastructure, and transportation and communications. He argued that without this slate of reforms, there would be "no way the state can bring any executive power to bear" on the Bedouin. Further, he claimed, "they will continue to live according to their savage old customs which are against Sharia and modern laws." He lamented that the state's failure to provide appropriate access to "imperial" education had left the population "like so many lifeless corpses of no benefit to humanity."[36] Eventually his ideas on Bedouin education would have empire-wide implications. In 1892, Osman Nuri wrote the curriculum for the Aşiret Mektebi (Tribal School).[37] Rather than forced sedentarization programs, the Tribal School aimed to foster allegiance to the state by training the sons of tribal notables for government service.

Osman Nuri observed that tribal populations hindered Istanbul's ability to project force along its Arab frontiers. He conceded that Muslims from Arab, Kurdish, and Albanian tribal areas remained in "a state of nomadism and savagery" (*hal-i bedeviyet ve vahşet*). They represented a massive untapped reservoir of military recruits, agricultural and economic productivity, and tax revenue. This problem was not limited to Bedouins; rather, it was the autonomous status of both the urban and tribal populations of these regions that most hampered provincial administration. In the Hijaz, Yemen, and Trablusgarb, the Bedouin question was compounded because even the settled Muslim populations were "exempt" (*muaf*) from military service. Therefore the burden of the "blood tax" (*kan vergisi*) shouldered by Anatolian Turks or the "fundamental element" (*unsur-ı asli*) was exacerbated. Difficulties in forcing soldiers to go to these provinces also were tied to environmental factors. The high mortality facing troops came not only from local resistance but also from disease, poor water and sanitation, and extreme climate. Owing to these dangers, Osman Nuri proposed that this trio of "hot provinces" (*vilayat-ı harre*) be considered as a special administrative unit earmarked for reforms to reduce the burden placed on soldiers from the more temperate climes of the Balkans and Anatolia.[38]

On one hand, Osman Nuri succinctly expressed Istanbul's desire to assert modern notions of territorial power in previously autonomous frontier regions. As Timothy Mitchell argues, Bedouin territories constituted a "geographical margin, partly within and partly beyond government control." By the standards of modern governmentality, these "forms of marginal political life, where allegiance to the central authority was graduated or variable," demanded elimination and replacement by "more uniform and rigorous methods of control."[39]

On the other hand, Osman Nuri reframed the assumed civilizational gap between center and periphery in environmental terms. Just as colonial expertise represented tropical environments as "strange and defective" in comparison with western Europe's supposedly "normal" climates, Osman Nuri's reporting demonstrates how Ottoman modernization discourse resorted to similar forms of "environmental orientalism" when describing the Arab periphery. Bedouin disorder was seen as a defining element of the frontier's "foreign nature" and the underlying impediment to the eventual Ottomanization of these "hot provinces."[40] Given this slippage between human and natural objects of development, Ottoman efforts to address the region's water supply, aridity, and disease profile often were indistinguishable from efforts to tame "unruly" autonomous populations, both Bedouin and urban.[41]

If Osman Nuri diagnosed Bedouin disorder as the Hijaz's primary ailment, infrastructural development was his panacea. His prescriptions display an almost magical faith in the construction of government buildings, military installations, courts, schools, and other desired infrastructure as a means to "reflect the glory of the state" and bind the local population to it.[42] Not surprisingly, Osman Nuri was an early advocate for the construction of telegraph (1899–1902) and rail lines (1900–8) in the Hijaz.[43]

Osman Nuri pointed to the critical need for better communications and transport, both within the Hijaz and between the Hijaz and Istanbul. At the most basic level, he stressed the need first to draw a proper physical map of the Hijaz.[44] Power would be derived through topographic knowledge and command of space and nature. In turn "power over persons was to be reorganized as power over space."[45] He argued that in order to command the Hijaz as a space, basic road construction and military outposts were needed to connect the various administrative centers throughout the province. As he complained, the connection between Mecca and Medina was essentially an imaginary one. Due to the distance between them and the slowness of communications, they were administered in almost total isolation from each other. Thus without the completion of telegraph lines linking the major commercial and administrative centers of the province, security would continue to suffer. However, the centerpiece of Osman Nuri's plan to revolutionize transportation and communications in the region was a railroad link between Syria and the Hijaz, complete with secondary lines connecting Jeddah and Mecca, Yanbuʿ and Medina, ʿAqaba and Jerusalem, and perhaps even a link to Hudayda.[46] To complement these rail links, Osman Nuri argued that government concessions might be established to promote a more robust steamship service connecting the ports of the Red Sea. In order achieve the improvements in transportation and communication that he desired without opening this sensitive region to foreign interests, the governor also suggested that it would be advantageous for the concessions for their construction to be reserved for "Muslim companies."[47]

Conventionally, the story of Ottoman technical expertise in the Hijaz has been narrated through the construction of the Hijaz Railway as the "physical embodiment" of Abdülhamid's Pan-Islamic ideology.[48] However, Pan-Islam is an inadequate container for the broader technopolitical aims of modern governmentality and state-building efforts that were being applied across the empire's Arab frontiers at the same time. These projects were meant to ameliorate the negative effects of autonomy and accelerate the frontier's integration with the Ottoman center. Particularly in light of the British occupation of Egypt in 1882 and the Scramble for Africa, overland telegraph and rail links were seen as essential to insulate the Hijaz and Yemen from British naval dominance.[49] Telegraph and rail construction also played a similar role in strategies to integrate Eastern Anatolia and Iraq more effectively and stave off British expansion via the Persian Gulf.[50]

This infrastructural turn served multiple audiences. Following the 1884–85 Berlin Conference, Istanbul reacted to new developments in international law. The Berlin Conference had stipulated that international claims to territory demonstrate "effective occupation." These conditions were supposed to define the methods by which European powers could claim "spheres of influence" within Africa. From that point forward, mere "discovery" or the process of surveying the land by a citizen or subject of an empire would not provide sufficient grounds to claim control. As the Ottoman state internalized this concept, in provinces such as Libya and, later, the Hijaz, its construction of large-scale infrastructure projects was meant to serve as physical proof of Ottoman sovereignty and compensate for the state's inability to demonstrate fuller territorial control over the autonomous Bedouin spaces these projects traversed.[51]

As these projects attest, Osman Nuri's recommendations proved startlingly clairvoyant. Indeed, they were signature statements of Hamidian technopolitical approaches to the tribal frontier. One area where the governor's wide-ranging report remained curiously silent, however, was on the subject of water infrastructure. One explanation for Osman Nuri's silence on the subject was that his reconstruction of the Hijaz's water systems was already well under way.

Repairs Needed: Environmental Imaginaries of Wahhabism and Water Infrastructure

An "environmental imaginary" is "a constellation of ideas that groups of humans develop about a given landscape, usually local or regional, that commonly includes assessments about that environment as well as how it came to be in its current state." Environmental imaginaries often assess blame and reveal "who wins and who loses when that imaginary is operationalized."[52] Thus although European observers might have seen Mecca through the prism of their own hygienic concerns, from an Ottoman perspective the decline of the Hijaz's urban water systems was imbedded in environmental imaginaries of the empire's tribal frontiers.

In June 1880, Eyüp Sabri Pasha, an Ottoman naval officer and avid historian of the Hijaz, Wahhabism, and the wider Arabian Peninsula, wrote a series of articles in the semiofficial newspaper *Tercüman-ı Hakikat*.[53] In both these articles and an expanded version in his magnum opus, *Mirat ül-Haremeyn* (1883–88), he alerted readers to the plight of Mecca's ʿAyn Zubayda water system and attempted to publicize the recent efforts of a partnership between Hijazi notables and the Ottoman administration, known as the ʿAyn Zubayda Commission, formed to restore the aqueducts.[54]

For Eyüp Sabri this was more than a public-works project; it symbolized the exorcism of the ghosts of the Wahhabi occupation of the Hijaz.[55] In the wake of that occupation and the wider crises set in motion by Mehmed Ali Pasha's empire building at the expense of the Ottoman center during the 1830s, Ottoman control would not be restored until 1841, when Mehmed Ali's Egyptian troops were forced to withdraw from the Hijaz and Syria in accordance with the terms of the 1840 Convention of London. During these occupations the region's water systems were badly damaged and their upkeep neglected. The damage sustained during this period formed the backdrop to a decades-long struggle to repair and expand the province's water supplies to meet the increasing demands posed by the greater accessibility of the steamship-era hajj.

In Eyüp Sabri's narration of the environmental and infrastructural history of the Hijaz, the Wahhabi occupation of Mecca and Medina represents the beginning of an era of overlapping social, technical, and natural collapse, providing an alternative reading of the uneven restoration of the Ottoman Hijaz. This construction of the past provides a blameworthy old regime against which he favorably compared the "civilizing" zeal of the Hamidian-era reassertion of Ottoman power in the Hijaz in the late 1870s and early 1880s. From this perspective, interest in the region's water infrastructure cannot be understood solely as a response to water scarcity; it was also as a measure of the provincial administration's increased capacity.

The waterworks were named after Zubayda, wife of the great Abbasid Caliph Hārūn al-Rashīd, whose philanthropy funded the network of aqueducts needed to bring the waters of Wadi Nuʿman and Wadi Hunayn to Mecca to provide a reliable source of potable water for both the local population and pilgrims. Completed in 810, the project was said to have cost some 1.75 million dinars, or, as Zubayda is said to have remarked with only slight exaggeration, "a gold dinar for every stroke of the pickax" (figure 4.2).[56] After the Hijaz came under Ottoman control in the sixteenth century, a major effort to repair and expand the ʿAyn Zubayda system was undertaken by Sultan Süleyman I's daughter Mihrimah Sultan.[57] After recounting this overhaul, Eyüp Sabri provided a detailed summary of the Ottoman state's subsequent efforts to maintain the aging watercourses and repair damages sustained during the occasional floods experienced

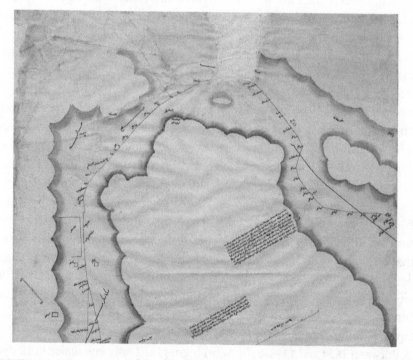

FIGURE 4.2 Ottoman map of the ʿAyn Zubayda aqueduct system, 1848. *Source*: BOA, HRT.h, 541.

in Mecca and its environs. He explained that the last major repairs to the system before the Wahhabi occupation were carried out in the late 1760s. The next maintenance did not take place for nearly a half century, until Mehmed Ali expelled the Wahhabis from the Hijaz.[58]

In Eyüp Sabri Pasha's narration of the environmental history of the Hijaz, the Wahhabi occupation of Mecca and Medina represents the dawn of a new era of water insecurity. Due partly to this prolonged neglect and partly to the "destruction and devastation" (hedm ü harab) directly attributable to the Wahhabi occupation, the aqueduct system was severely damaged and "broken in many places." As a result, Mecca's local population began to suffer from "water scarcity," which was only compounded during the hajj season. Around 1820, Sultan Mahmud II ordered Mehmed Ali to repair the crippled waterworks. However, due to the extent of the damage and the considerable cost of the renovations, "the repairs were [only] of a partial sort."[59]

On this point Eyüp Sabri Pasha's narrative is corroborated by Johann Ludwig Burckhardt's account of his three-month sojourn in the Hijaz in 1814–15. Burckhardt also provides support for Eyüp Sabri's claim that the damage to the waterworks was not merely a product of decay and neglected maintenance but a direct result of the Wahhabis' intentional cutting of the water supply during the occupation of Mecca.[60] Wahhabi attacks on Mecca's water system were not an isolated incident. Although most sources dwell on the Wahhabi vandalism of tombs and sacred spaces, little attention has been paid to their exploitation of the Hijaz's water infrastructure as a tool to terrorize the local population into submission during the 1805 siege of Medina. According to Eyüp Sabri Pasha's Tarih-i Vehhabiyan (1879), as soon as the Syrian pilgrimage caravan and its accompanying soldiers departed and distanced themselves from Medina, the Wahhabis promptly laid siege to the city's fortifications, occupied several surrounding villages, and fortified and sealed off access in and out. After the Wahhabis thoroughly surrounded the city, the final blow was their destruction of the ʿAyn Zarqa (Zerka) watercourse, which subjected the city's people to "calamitous famine and drought."[61] Again, however, the Ottoman center could do little more than promise to send assistance via Egypt's Mehmed Ali Pasha.[62]

Between 1820 and 1878, Eyüp Sabri highlighted only one major initiative to improve Mecca's water supply. In 1847, Elmas Agha, an Indian philanthropist, oversaw a project to connect the waters of ʿAyn Zafran to the ʿAyn

Zubayda system to increase its output.[63] Despite Istanbul's efforts on several occasions to raise the necessary funds for a permanent solution, however, annual allocations from the imperial *evkaf* (pious endowments) for "cleaning the ducts" were insufficient to tackle a project of this scale. There is also evidence to suggest that these funds were not always used for their intended purpose.[64]

According to Eyüp Sabri Pasha, due to the combination of the long periods during which the aqueducts were "neglected and left completely without cleaning or repair" and Mecca's vulnerability to "frequent flooding," more and more of Mecca's water supply was leaking away. Although Mecca receives only around four inches of annual rainfall, torrential downbursts are not uncommon. And because of the region's aridity, there is little soil to absorb the runoff. Local wells were inadequate substitutes. Thus seasonal and hajj-related shortages became a regular occurrence, inspiring "fear and dread" (*havf ve dehşet*) among the locals that "the waters of ʿAyn Zubayda would completely run dry."[65] Although Eyüp Sabri did not provide specific examples of floods or assign them the same agency or weight as Wahhabi predations, it is likely that the cumulative damages caused by severe floods in 1861 and 1877 exacerbated the earlier blockages and leaks incurred during the Wahhabi occupation and its aftermath.

In 1861, Mecca experienced its most "disastrous flood" (*sel felaketi*) of the century. The flooding destroyed or damaged hundreds of homes, particularly affecting the flimsy dwellings inhabited by the city's poor, sparking a drive to collect charitable donations to aid the flood victims and their families in rebuilding their homes. Both the Ḥaram and the city's water system were "filled" with debris. In the flood's immediate aftermath, the need to repair the Ḥaram was obvious, but there also was grave concern that if the city's damaged pipelines were not quickly repaired, they would be "completely filled with sand" in the event of further rain.[66]

Flooding also was a trigger for waterborne epidemics. John F. Keane, in his 1877–78 pilgrimage narrative, told of one flood that struck Mecca just after the conclusion of the hajj. Although Keane described the flood as an ordinary event by Meccan standards, the extent of the damage was still horrific. According to Keane, the whole of the Ḥaram was "turned into a lake, the water lying about three feet deep in the western arcades, six feet around the Kaʿba." The next morning, "in every place where the water had been it left a layer of about six inches of tough springy earth cutting like clay—in many places it was much thicker: round the Ka'ba it was eighteen inches deep." Keane said that the pollution of the water supply was the most dangerous aspect of the flood. "For many days after the flood the water in all the wells was brown and muddy, and if left standing all night would not be more than half settled in the morning." As a result of the contamination of the water, "cholera, smallpox, and typhus epidemics broke out and raged wildly for about three weeks."[67]

By the late 1870s, it was clear that dramatic steps would be needed to ensure Mecca's future water security. In 1878, the Indian shaykh 'Abd al-Raḥman Sirāj, the Hanafi Mufti of Mecca at the time, took on the enormous task of restoring 'Ayn Zubayda. Each day for two months he was able to raise a workforce of 200 to 300 men composed of Indian pilgrims and Bedouins. Following the positive results of Sirāj's initial efforts, later that year Abdülhamid issued a decree calling for the formation of a "repair commission" (tamirat komisyonu) to raise money and oversee a thorough overhaul of the aqueducts.[68] Initially headed by 'Abd al-Raḥman Sirāj, the commission was composed of local notables from Mecca and Jeddah, ulema, Ottoman officials, and local Indian notables.[69] Not surprisingly, members of the commission and other local elites were enthusiastic contributors to the effort, but as the composition of the commission itself suggests, the largest donations came from India. Kalb Ali Khan Bahadur, the nawab of Rampur, gave 100,000 rupees in 1880 and later would contribute a further 70,000 for restoration of the pipeline connecting 'Ayn Zafran with the main 'Ayn Zubayda aqueduct. The nawab of Dhaka, Khwaja Abdul Ghani Bahadur, and his son contributed 40,000 rupees.[70] The ruler of Bhopal, Shah Jahan Begum, added 20,000. In addition to these large donations from the rulers of Indian princely states, the Indian agent for the pro-Ottoman newspaper, al-Jawāʾib, was able to solicit smaller donations, bringing the total collected from India alone to 1,625,000 kuruş.[71]

This fundraising effort provides a perfect example of the interimperial miscomprehension surrounding the colonial-era hajj. At first British surveillance, constantly on the lookout for Muslim anticolonial plots, misinterpreted 'Ayn Zubayda fundraising as an effort to fund a jihad in the name of Mecca and Medina. This episode undoubtedly points to the enduring strength of fraternal bonds between the Ottomans and South Asian Muslims, but, as John Slight has argued, the "official mind" was far from uniform in its views of Indian charitable donations to the Ottoman Empire.

As a result of this influx of pious donations, Dr. Abdur Razzack, the British official best positioned to comment, saw pious donations from Indians as an invaluable advertisement of British influence and benevolence to the rest of the Islamic world.[72] He repeatedly touted the indispensable contributions of Indian notables to the reconstruction of Mecca's hydraulic infrastructure. By doing so he sought to combat the perception that cholera was an Indian import to the Hijaz. In his reframing of the issue, Indian merchants and princes were positioned as the real heroes of the Muslim holy land, defending Mecca against both its sanitary woes and Ottoman mismanagement.[73] Here Indian enthusiasm for this earlier round of pilgrimage-related infrastructure building offered a blueprint that foreshadowed later fundraising appeals to Pan-Islamic solidarity surrounding the Hijaz railway project.

In 1880, once the fundraising began to yield such impressive results, the sultan promised to make up the difference should the cost of the repairs exceed the total donations. As the repairs continued throughout the 1880s, the project's funding continued in much the same manner. Donations from local and foreign (mostly Indian) notables constituted the core of the commission's revenues, while contributions from the imperial treasury were used as a backstop to ensure completion of the various construction projects.[74] Despite the important role played by local notables in launching the ʿAyn Zubayda Commission, given the technical and engineering challenges involved, as the project progressed a construction committee (inşaat kısmı) composed of the then governor of the Hijaz, Osman Nuri Pasha, the commission's chief engineer, Sadık Bey, and a number of other members of the Ottoman military's general staff (erkan-ı harbiye), eventually emerged as the commission's driving force.[75] However, it was Osman Nuri's name that ultimately attained an almost mythical status across both the empire and the wider Islamic world for having rescued the Holy Places from their looming water crisis. For Osman Nuri, however, the pious purposes of the project were perhaps secondary. The reconstruction of ʿAyn Zubayda fit neatly into his far-reaching technocratic vision for simultaneously taming and respatializing the Hijaz's environment and making its inhabitants into proper Ottoman subjects.

Beginning from ʿAyn Zubayda's source at Wadi Nuʿman, approximately 30 kilometers northeast of Mecca, more than 3,000 workers labored for four years to refurbish the ancient waterworks. Work began by opening a new channel roughly 400 meters from the old one. The new duct was more durable and wider, making it easier for workers to move freely and carry out the needed repairs. Following the original channel toward Mecca, the sections that could be salvaged were repaired, the exterior of the duct was resealed, and in those places where the damage was too severe, new channels were opened. In some sections along the way, pools and access shafts were opened for easier access and repair.

As a result of the restoration of the ducts, Mecca's water output was greatly enhanced, yielding 5,000 *kıyye* or approximately 6,140 liters per minute, leading to a dramatic drop in the "exorbitant price" being charged for fresh water during hajj season. Taking advantage of the restored flow, nine reserve cisterns and several other storage depots were built, new ablution facilities were established around the perimeter of the Ḥaram, and new fountains were built across all quarters of the city. The improved water supply also ensured that the hospital and soup kitchens for the poor, the pharmacy, government offices, military barracks, printing press, police stations, laundry facilities, and bathhouses all had taps installed.[76]

The Milieu of Tanks of Toilets

Despite these improvements, the ʿAyn Zubayda system remained extremely vulnerable to microbial contamination. Although repairs also were made to smaller branch pipelines and basins serving Arafat and Mina, the aqueduct was not a closed system. In a number of places the Bedouins had opened sections of the main pipeline to draw water. The main aqueduct also first had to pass through the stations of the pilgrimage at Arafat and then Mina before arriving in Mecca.[77]

Even before the revolution in bacteriology yielded the secrets of cholera's etiology, sanitarian questions of miasmas and filth associated with overcrowding and human waste had placed the nonurban portions of the hajj circuit in Arafat and Mina under suspicion. Although the 1880s was a decade of flux between older miasmic understandings of human waste and more precise bacteriological analyses of contagion, Ottoman and European colonial officials had begun to map cholera's movements through Mecca's water supply.[78]

In 1885, Osman Nuri ordered a thorough cleaning of the open tanks and basins at Arafat and Mina, which had been implicated as potential cholera hotspots.[79] At Arafat he ordered a military cordon to protect the basins and open sections of the watercourse from being fouled by pilgrims bathing or washing clothes in the water. However, as Mehmed Şakir noted, preventing pilgrims from bathing in the basins remained a perennial struggle. He cited Bedouins, Indians, and Yemenis as frequent offenders.[80]

The need to police this behavior becomes clearer in light of the inadequate latrines in both locations. In 1878, the government of India appointed Abdur Razzack to join the hajj surreptitiously and report on the sanitary conditions in the Hijaz. He was stunned by the omnipresence of human waste in Arafat. "Except taking care of the drinking water, there was no other arrangement for the pilgrims. Everyone had a temporary privy near his tent, while the poorer people, having nothing of the sort, did not hesitate to answer the calls of nature wherever they found it convenient." His depiction of the situation in Mina was even grimmer. The latrines consisted of shabbily stacked rock partitions enclosing sand pits "with no arrangement for the water to run off, every particle thereof being supposed to be absorbed by the sand." In short order the pits were saturated until the latrines were abandoned and "then the space around the body of the building itself was made use of, not to speak of all the nooks and corners formed by the tents and litters in every part of the field." Owing to this, "[i]nside the town it was the same thing again; excepting the main street, all along the walls of the houses in every lane and corner there was human excrement lying and covering the whole place, which made it almost impossible to walk through." The danger posed by Mina's latrines was compounded by their proximity to the ritual slaughter of animals performed in accordance with the hajj.[81] Despite the obvious questions raised by Abdur Razzack's status as a British agent, ultimately the substance, if not the accusatory style, of his claims was supported by subsequent Ottoman efforts to reform the water and waste systems in Mina and elsewhere.

Osman Nuri ordered that the water tanks at Mina be filled no more than a week prior to the hajj.[82] To bring in fresh water, he had a steam-powered pump installed about 150 meters above the main water ducts.[83] Despite his efforts to provide clean water and guard against its contamination, ʿAyn Zubayda water was not the only source in circulation. Stagnant rainwater also was sold. As Mehmed Şakir explained, before the repair of ʿAyn Zubayda, a deeply exploitative system of water profiteering had taken root across the Hijaz, but especially in Mina and Jeddah.[84] Privately owned tanks and cisterns (*sahrınçlar*) were used to collect rainwater and distribute it to water carriers (*sakalar*) to sell to pilgrims at inflated prices. In Mina tanks housed in local homes were ubiquitous. Often water was stored in tanks for up to six months or a year before hajj season. Tanks placed beneath ground level were especially dangerous. Although some tanks were housed on rooftops, others were vulnerable to organic debris from flash flooding and runoff carrying excrement and refuse from the streets. In addition to all this, the water was served from unhygienic water skins (*kırbalar*) that the town's water carriers used to transport it (see figure 4.3). Invariably these skins or bags remained in circulation for long periods. In order to preserve the water and keep it from spoiling, sesame oil, lime blossom, and a sweet-smelling oil were added. As a result, however, the water's taste was altered and reportedly produced a "disgusting smell" (*rayiha-i kerihe*).[85] As Ottoman officials lamented, the product provided by Mina's water carriers was invariably "fetid" (*müteaffin*) and "microbe-filled" (*mikroplu*).[86]

FIGURE 4.3 Postcard depicting Jeddah's water carriers. *Source*: Khalili Family Trust, Hajj and the Arts of Pilgrimage Collection, ARC.PC 307.

As Ottoman officials discovered, their attempts to manage and sustain human life in the face of water scarcity and cholera necessitated new and more precise understandings of water as a complex milieu of social and biological pathologies.[87] Even after the supposed victory of bacteriological science in the 1890s, older sanitarian efforts to alter the "pathogenic terrain" of cholera continued to play their part.[88] Mecca's water supply presented a tangled web of hybrid processes that blurred any assumed boundaries between technical, natural, and human elements. Thus efforts to provide potable water were not merely public works. They were radical restructurings of the existing social and economic organization of the hajj, which would be met by local elites with an equally determined campaign of resistance.

"Tyrants in Fear of Civilization": Profiteering and Pipeline Sabotage in Jeddah

In addition to Abdur Razzack's attention to Arafat and Mina, his account paints a grim picture of Jeddah's almost total dependence on rainwater. In 1853, Faraj Yusr, the prominent Indian merchant and banker who had been at the center of the controversies leading to the violence in Jeddah in 1858, had raised funds and successfully rehabilitated a Mamluk-era well and canal bringing water from a spring twenty kilometers east of town. By the 1880s, however, it had fallen into disrepair, leaving Jeddah without a reliable source of running water. This dependency on rainwater concentrated enormous power in the hands of the city's rainwater tank owners, giving rise to an ugly system of water profiteering. As Abdur Razzack explained, the population of Jeddah suffered at the "caprice and whims of those who are the owners of the *sehreejes* or tanks for collecting rainwater." Large stone tanks dotted the landscape just outside the city's walls. Their "proprietors" were among the "first men in the place." Each tank owner was allotted "a certain number of tanks[,] and a plot around a particular set is hollowed out, and the earth that is thus dug up is formed into banks all around, so that the rain that falls over one hollow does not run off into another man's tanks, but flows in those around which the embankment is formed." The water was either sold by slaves or the tanks were leased to water carriers. As a result of this system, during times of drought "the owners of these tanks make immense profits, and they can whenever they choose cause the townsmen the greatest sufferings."[89]

The landscape outside Jeddah en route to Mecca was dotted with these mounds or hills, some rising as high as eighty meters. This system of "reservoir hills" (*sahrınç tepeleri*) was the province of Jeddah's elites. Not only was their control over rainwater collection lucrative, it became a representation of their social identity. As Eyüp Sabri related, the area came to function as something of a hill station for Jeddah's wealthy. Owing to the mountain views and lower humidity, many of the *tepe* system magnates summered in this area and built lavish apartments, kiosks, and gardens. According to Eyüp Sabri, the leading figure in this trend was Sayyid ʿUmar al-Saqqāf (al-Sagoff).[90]

The al-Saqqāf family owned a Hadrami trading outfit and had made their fortune in the transition from sail to steam in Singapore.[91] In the process they also cornered the Southeast Asian market on pilgrimage transport and financial services.[92] In the early 1880s, ʿUmar al-Saqqāf emerged as one of the leading figures in a sophisticated pilgrimage services monopoly operating in the Hijaz with the blessing of the sharif of Mecca. The monopoly aimed to control every aspect of the pilgrimage travel experience, including steamships, boatmen, pilgrimage guides, and camel brokers. With the organization of this system competition was restricted, prices were rigged, and the resulting profits were shared among the members of the pool. Another notable tank owner was ʿUmar Nasīf,[93] who also was a principal in the pilgrimage transport ring. In light of Saqqāf and Nasīf's wide-ranging operations, to which we will return in the next chapter, the constellation of local interests lurking behind the commodification of Jeddah's water resources and their resistance to Ottoman interference comes into sharper focus.

As Mehmed Şakir recounted, Abdur Razzack's investigations caused considerable embarrassment for the Ottoman government. Following the release of his report in 1879, Dr. Edward Dalzel Dickson, the British delegate on the Ottoman Board of Health, drew on it in his scathing indictment of Jeddah's water supply in the *Gazette Medical D'Orient* (*Ceride-i Tıbbiye-i Şarkiye*). In the years following Abdur Razzack's damning report, Jeddah's water security became a top priority. As Mehmed Şakir explained, great pains were taken to "silence the foreigners' objections" by preventing "the sale of the harmful and infested waters of the local profiteers' tanks and basins to the pilgrims and local residents at high prices."[94]

On the heels of the restoration of Mecca's water supply, Osman Nuri Pasha set Jeddah's water supply as the ʿAyn Zubayda Commission's next project. To provide Jeddah with a reliable and safe supply, he proposed bringing water from a well sunk at ʿAyn Waziriyya (Ayn-ı Veziriye), located approximately ten kilometers (or two and a half hours' distance) from Jeddah. Construction began in 1885.[95] However, because many of the potential sources of funding had been exhausted during restoration of the ʿAyn Zubayda aqueduct, the ʿAyn Waziriyya project's funding proved somewhat more difficult. In addition to funds raised from local notables, Osman Nuri received permission to solicit donations from average pilgrims. Ottoman documents referred to these funds as charity (*iane*), but British consular reports reveal that these contributions were made compulsory by Osman Nuri.[96]

Despite the aggressively obtained collections from pilgrims over the course of four hajj seasons, as late as 1887, the project remained stalled with only two-thirds of the pipeline completed.[97] Although less difficult than the ʿAyn Zubayda restoration, Jeddah's waterworks required a workforce of more than 3,000 and took roughly three and a half years to finish.[98] It also eventually required additional funds from the sultan to complete the port's new ornamental fountain, ablutions station, water depot, and distribution reservoir.[99] When the project was finally completed in 1888, it appeared that Jeddah had been rescued from the clutches of the city's water profiteers.

Writing just two years later, during his visit to prepare a report on the public health conditions of Hijaz, Mehmed Şakir Bey described his first impressions of the improvements to Jeddah's water infrastructure, which he had seen on a previous trip en route to Yemen. He recalled how the port's main square featured a beautiful octagonal fountain bearing the name of the sultan, complete with taps on all sides. On his return in 1890, however, the fountain's previous flow had been greatly diminished, and it was becoming increasingly difficult to fill the recently established water depot and distribution reservoirs. As Mehmed Şakir made clear, the rapid decline of ʿAyn Waziriyya's output was not the result of any ordinary malfunction. Because the local tank and cistern owners had been prevented from selling their stagnant, disease-infested rainwater, they had hatched a plot to "cancel" (*iptal etmek*) the benefits brought by Jeddah's new source of fresh water by purposely "clogging the water pipes."[100]

Mehmed Şakir Bey's accusations of sabotage were far from isolated. Writing in 1907, the British representative to the Ottoman Board of Health, Dr. Frank G. Clemow, observed that the drought-stricken Jeddah of 1906 was again limited to tank water and the brackish water from wells dug just outside the city walls. As Clemow pointed out, there were four springs nearby, but only one was serviceable. However, its water had to be transported by camel or donkey. The pipes leading from the other three, including ʿAyn Waziriyya, were constantly sabotaged. As Clemow suspected, the city's influential tank owners, whose interests had been damaged by the construction of the water pipes, had directed Bedouin agents in a campaign to cripple the pipelines and retain their monopoly.[101]

El-Hac Hüseyin Vassaf's narrative of his 1905–1906 pilgrimage paints a vivid picture of the Ottoman center's frustration with the locals' stubborn refusal to accept the gifts of the civilizing mission started during the governorship of Osman Nuri Pasha:

The now deceased Osman Pasha brought water here from a far-away source. He established a thriving fountain providing sweet drinking water for the pilgrims and the locals free of charge. However, the Arab notables who own the tanks were financially harmed by the establishment of the waterworks, and are suspected of damaging the watercourses. They extort heavy fees from the people and the pilgrims. They are ignorant and oppressive men. For personal gain they prefer to harm the general welfare. They are tyrants in fear of civilization and public health. As a result of the water here, there is unbearable drought. Due to the worm-infested and microbe-filled water and the brackish water of the wells, diseases and infirmities, especially cholera and diarrhea, are endless.

The capable and much-celebrated governor called "Topal Osman [Nuri] Pasha" made the Arabs tremble. However, with his passing away, the Arabs have gotten out of control; what he built up, they have destroyed.[102]

Drinking the Sea, Distilling Empire

The region that is now known as the Middle East partly owes its "middleness" to the carbon storage networks designed to fuel the age of steam.[103] In the late nineteenth century the British Empire depended on the even spacing of coaling stations spread across the Red Sea and Persian Gulf to service the increasing flows of steamship traffic between India, the Mediterranean, and England itself. Although coal is the obvious centerpiece of this transportation story, water has remained a neglected part of this history. Advances in desalination methods went hand in hand with the rise of oceangoing steamships. The first steamers, originally used for river navigation, could supply their boilers with the rivers' freshwater. When oceangoing steamships were built, they encountered new technical challenges. Crews either had to carry freshwater supplies with them or they would use seawater to operate the ship's boilers. However, the use of saltwater resulted in the accumulation of saline scales on the flues and bottoms of the boilers. In addition to reducing the lifespan of iron boilers, saltwater required more fuel to heat, yielded inferior steam power, and increased the risk of boiler explosions. In order to overcome these problems, between the 1830s and 1860s, the development of surface condensers and seawater evaporators eventually made it possible for crews to convert seawater into freshwater for both the boilers and the crew's consumption. As a result, the condenser became a standard part of the steamship.[104]

However, the condenser did not remain stranded at sea. Over time condensers made their way into the ports of the Middle East. From as early as the late 1850s and 1860s, the British Empire began to experiment with the installation of coal-fired condenser units in eastern Mediterranean and Red Sea ports such as Malta, Suez, and Aden, where local water supplies were unable to keep up with the new demands of industrial steamship traffic.[105] In the 1880s and 1890s, lengthy military engagements in Egypt and Sudan tested Britain's ability to supply water to its troops. At first steamers were kept in ports such as Suez and Suakin solely to generate freshwater from their boilers.[106] Over time, however, these kinds of "emergency" security operations became normalized as permanent features of the region's infrastructure, leading to the installation of land-based systems with larger daily capacities. By World War I, these British condensers formed a desalinated archipelago from Suez, Port Sudan, Suakin, Perim Island, and Aden in the Red Sea to Muscat, Bahrain, Kuwait, Bushehr, and Kerman in the Persian Gulf.[107]

As this British chain of condensers began to dot the Red Sea, by the early 1890s, the sabotage of Jeddah's pipelines once again reduced the city to dependence on rainwater. The magnitude of this setback was made painfully clear as the 1890s emerged as a decade of escalating drought in Jeddah and Yanbu'. Recognizing both the severity of the drought and their inability to protect their freshwater pipelines from tampering, as early as 1894–95, Ottoman officials began to adapt and co-opt the British turn toward desalination. As discussed in the previous chapter, Ottoman authorities began to explore the feasibility of importing European equipment to distill seawater.[108] In 1894, Istanbul first ordered a condenser system to filter brackish well water for steamship-going pilgrims from the Indian Ocean who were quarantined on Kamaran Island.[109]

In hindsight, the turn to desalination represented a critical turning point in the long struggle for water safety along the cholera-stricken Indian Ocean and Red Sea pilgrimage routes. However, unlike the Kamaran quarantine station, the Hijaz was not a small, self-contained island. It presented a vastly more complicated mix of logistical, social, and ecological challenges.

Although local authorities had identified a source of spring water located six hours' distance from Yanbu', the severity of the drought facing the town rendered long-term planning obsolete. Without rain it was feared that the town was headed for disaster during the upcoming hajj season. The Hijaz *vilayet* requested that the Naval Ministry import two machines capable of producing freshwater from seawater (*denizden tatlı su yapmak üzere iki makina*).[110] In the meantime they pleaded that a steamship capable of producing desalinated freshwater (*su yüklü bir vapur*), similar to those located at Suez, be sent to Yanbu' as soon as possible. As an additional precaution, all hajj traffic for the upcoming season was prohibited from landing in Yanbu' and rerouted to Jeddah.[111]

Throughout the 1890s and 1900s, emergency operations became the new normal. As the situation worsened, pilgrims arriving in Jeddah were transferred to the nearby Ebu Saad quarantine station to ease the strain on the city's resources. A tugboat equipped with a distillation machine capable of producing five tons of drinking water per day was ordered from Geneva. This vessel, aptly named the *Zülal* (meaning "pleasant to drink"), became the coastal towns' emergency reserve. In 1899, this floating desalination unit provided relief to pilgrims arriving in Yanbu' from Medina. A 50-ton iron container was shipped in so that it could be filled with potable water produced by the *Zülal*. Concerned that even this action would not stave off a catastrophe, each of the Ottoman *İdare-i Mahsusa* steamship service's three departures between Jeddah and Suez were ordered to bring drinking water to Yanbu'.[112]

In 1900, a twenty-four-hour burst of rain half-filled the town's tanks, rescuing Jeddah from the brink of disaster. However, during the protracted crises in Jeddah and Yanbu', the European consuls had grown increasingly concerned for the safety of their colonial subjects and demanded a more permanent solution. In light of the tremendous improvements that resulted from the installation of a water filtration machine (*su taktir makinası* or *filtre makinası*) at the Kamaran quarantine station near the mouth of the Red Sea, it was decided that a similar machine could solve the chronic shortages facing the Hijaz's port cities. The cash-strapped Ottomans were unable to finance the 9,000-lira cost of the two filtration machines requested by the Hijaz *vilayet*. In 1900, the Grand Vizierate requested that the Board of Health loan the necessary funds but was refused on the grounds that the money would be better spent on the quarantine system. Again in 1903, the sultan approved the amount, but in 1905 his *irade* was nullified. The bureaucratic infighting in Istanbul continued until the Board of Health finally relented in 1907 and decided to install filtration machines at Jeddah and Yanbu'.[113]

By 1907, Britain's representative to the Board of Health, Dr. Clemow, also had thrown his support behind Ottoman efforts to import new British-manufactured condenser machines to process brackish well water and purify rainwater. As Clemow reasoned, the switch to distilled water would break Jeddah's reliance on local tank and cistern profiteers. It also meant that Jeddah's locals and foreign pilgrims no longer would be wholly reliant on the Ottoman state to secure the Hijaz's easily sabotaged pipelines supplied by wells outside the city. However, Ottoman officials remained wary of the tank owners' seemingly unshakable grip on the city. They worried that the tank owners, acting in cahoots with the sharifate and the Bedouin, might be tempted to wage a campaign to prevent the sale of distilled water. And recalling the attacks on disinfection and hospital facilities in 1895, both British and Ottoman authorities feared that the opening of a new condenser plant might provoke another spate of violent machine smashing. As Clemow predicted, a further obstacle would be to convince Jeddah's locals, "strongly conservative by nature," to get used to distilled water.[114] As had been the case in Aden, Oman, and other Persian Gulf ports, where the British introduced condensers, local humans and even animals often refused to drink "dead"-tasting condenser water unless some seawater was added to reconstitute the salt and mineral content of the conventional water supplies to which they were accustomed.[115]

The Ottomans' first experiment with condenser water netted mixed results. As Kasım İzzeddin recounted, the original machine purchased in 1907 was a disaster. The water that it produced had a disgusting smell and was hardly palatable. In any event, the machine's capacity was insufficient and quickly broke down. Despite this initial setback, however, the Ottomans' turn to British-built condenser technologies helped forge a collegial working relationship between İzzeddin and Clemow. At the twelfth international sanitary conference in Paris in 1911, İzzeddin and Clemow found common ground, collaborating on both water questions and arrangements for a new quarantine station connected to the Hijaz Railway. Thus in a curious twist, after decades of pitched diplomatic battle between Ottoman delegates and their British opposites, in 1911, İzzeddin and Clemow forged an unlikely technocratic partnership to solve Jeddah's perennial water woes.[116] With Clemow's support, in 1911, İzzeddin and the Hijaz's sanitary administration secured a 5,000-lira loan from the Board of Health to cover the cost of a new condenser machine and the facilities to house them.[117] Under İzzeddin's direction, a filtration machine capable of producing one hundred tons per day was purchased for Jeddah from Glasgow's Mirrlees-Watson Company (see figure 4.4).[118] The condenser machine arrived in Jeddah on September 20, 1912. After numerous delays to the installation of the condenser and construction of the plant, on November 10, 1913, the new facility produced its first water for pilgrims returning from Mecca.[119]

In the midst of the long struggle over Jeddah's condenser plant, empire-wide changes were on the march in Istanbul. In 1908–1909, the Young Turk Revolution of the Committee of Union and Progress (CUP; İttihad ve Terraki Cemiyeti) swept into power and eventually deposed Sultan Abdülhamid II. Between 1894 and World War I, Dr. Kasım İzzeddin had overseen the erection and gradual reform of Ottoman public health services and quarantine, crisscrossing the empire from Mecca and Jeddah to Baghdad, Basra, Damascus, and Sinop. Throughout his tenure Dr. İzzeddin had been forced to endure countless frustrations and setbacks at the hands of the Ottoman Board of Health's foreign representatives. And not unlike Abdur Razzack's clashes with ʿAwn al-Rafīq prior to his murder in 1895, from 1908 on İzzeddin repeatedly clashed with the sharif of Mecca, Ḥusayn ibn ʿAlī (r. 1908–16 as sharif, 1916–24 as king of the Hijaz). From İzzeddin's perspective, the sharifate and its local authorities, whether in the guise of urban

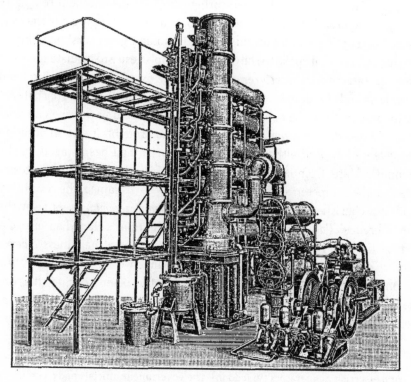

شكل — ١

حجاز صحیه اداره‌سی طرفندن جده‌ده وضع ا‌لنان صو تقطیر ماکینه‌سی

FIGURE 4.4 Water distillation machine installed in Jeddah in 1914. Reproduced from Kasım İzzeddin, *Hicaz'da Teşkilat ve Islahat-ı Sıhhiye ve 1330 Senesi Hacc-ı Şerifi: Hicaz Sıhhiye İdaresi Senevi Rapor* (İstanbul: Matbaa-ı Amire, 1914/1915).

notables or the Bedouin, represented the principal obstacles to his work. However, he also placed considerable blame for the Hijaz's sanitary woes on the nonchalance and sluggishness of the Hamidian regime. In the wake of the revolution, the Hijaz's public health services underwent a final burst of centralizing reforms. In 1910, a new Hijaz Board of Health (*Hicaz Sıhhiye Meclisi*) was created. This new body was separated from the Health Ministry and transferred to reside under the budgetary control of the Interior Ministry (*Dahiliye Nezareti*). As the administration's new inspector general, Kasım İzzeddin worked in the name of Interior Minister Talat Pasha (1874–1921).

The move was a statement underscoring the CUP's commitment to a more energetic approach to public health reform and to stamping out the perceived corruption and ineptitude of the Hamidian governors' handling of the hajj. Likewise, it spoke to the CUP leadership's desire to insulate the Hijaz from extraterritorial interference—constantly exacerbated by hajj-related scandals—and simultaneously to further impose its will on the sharifate.[120]

In January 1914, the condenser plant's grand opening was the culmination of a decades-long war against cholera and drought. It was an occasion for celebration. And although that struggle also had been waged by the Hamidian state, from İzzeddin's perspective this achievement was a testament to the competence of the new regime. As he explained, the revolution and "our cherished Constitution" (meşrutiyet-i muazzezemiz) swept away the "indifference" (lakaydi) and "oppression" of the Hijaz's Hamidian-era governors (istibdad-ı valileri) and ushered in a new "era of happiness" (devr-i saadet), earning the gratitude of the entire Islamic world.[121]

On that long-awaited day, the opening of the plant housing the condenser, filtration apparatus, ice machine, coal depot, and electric generators was marked by a joyful ceremony:

In January 1914 [Kanun-i Sani 1329], they completed installing the ice machines and electricity generators [in Jeddah]. The government officials had a ceremony with the consulates of the foreign powers, local notables and steamboat agents. They slaughtered rams and prayed that the Caliphate of Islam's glory may be increased. They also wished for the prosperity of the Hijaz sanitary administration. The opening day of the ice and electric generators was a joyful one for the people of Jeddah. They opened the doors of the factory to the public and all the people around came to see the machines and were happy.[122]

The carnival-like atmosphere surrounding the introduction of distilled water and the technological marvel of an ice maker in Jeddah was reminiscent of similar celebrations associated with the construction of the Hijaz Railway. These machines conveyed the empire's sovereignty and the CUP's modernizing prowess in concrete material terms that the average man could appreciate. Although the machines were undoubtedly a novelty, the plant itself was of equal import. Pipeline sabotage was partly overcome by relocating water production to a secure site or "technological zone" that could be policed in ways that Jeddah's watercourses had not been.

A technological zone is "a space within which differences between technical practices, procedures or forms have been reduced." Thus the plant represented a "border" distinguishing between an outpost of internationally accepted technical expertise and the unwanted corruption of the local economy and society outside.[123]

In much the same way that the overhaul of the Kamaran Island quarantine station, complete with its own condenser system, had dramatically reduced the risks of major cholera outbreaks and slashed mortality rates, Jeddah's shift to condenser water coincided with the tapering off of cholera's deadliest outbreaks. Although cholera lingered through 1907–1908 and returned in 1911–12, the last major cholera outbreak during hajj season occurred in 1912.[124] Following the advances in Ottoman sanitary policy and water safety and security and the overall maturation of international sanitary regulation from the mid-1890s on, the kinds of catastrophic hajj seasons witnessed in 1865 and 1893 finally were relegated to the past.

Conclusion

As Timothy Mitchell argues, "Infrastructures arrange the interaction of human lives with nature." Even the most mundane public works deploy the "politics of nature." It is through these infrastructures that "nature is produced" and experienced. The "spaces, flows, measures, and calculations out of which infrastructures are built create the most common forms in which humans encounter and measure the reserves of nature—or experience their lack."[125] Bearing this basic dictum in mind, was it drought or increased demand from the steamship-era pilgrimage or water profiteering and pipeline sabotage that produced water scarcity? Put slightly differently, was it nature itself or the nature of the state's approach to infrastructure, centralization, and governmentality that produced resistance and exacerbated scarcity? Although the late Ottoman state embarked on a series of ambitious water projects, which produced tangible results in the state's long microbial war on cholera, ultimately the state was unable to fully instrumentalize that infrastructure in the service of Ottoman centralization.

Ottoman hydraulic projects, much like Ottoman disinfection procedures featured in the previous chapter, were hobbled and reshaped by local resistance. Although Ottoman administrators were unable to provide sufficient fresh water to eliminate demand for rainwater, they remained in open conflict with the Hijaz's tank owners and water carriers. Not unlike their Bedouin counterparts, who frequently attacked the Hijaz's rail and telegraph lines (a subject to which we will return in chapter 6), these urban elites waged their own campaign of sabotage against Ottoman water infrastructure. In a sense all of these technologies represented "points of vulnerability" providing the "infrastructure of political protest" for locals to resist Ottoman centralization.[126] Ultimately, the Ottoman state proved incapable of adequately governing the spaces that these projects traversed. Thus although the state was able to execute ambitious technological feats, it was never able to leverage its expertise fully as a means to produce the intensity of territoriality or the thickness of biopolitical control over the population, whether Bedouin or urban, that was necessary to eliminate or effectively manage autonomous forms of frontier political life.

And just as Ottoman technopolitics could not fully overcome Hijazi resistance, nor could it fully escape its inherent dependence on and vulnerability to European technology, expertise, transport, and energy systems. In their quest to quash local resistance to sanitary centralization and quell the international concerns that had dogged the Hamidian-era administration of the hajj, İzzeddin and the CUP's reorganized public health services were forced to seek foreign technical support. Thus although Jeddah was temporarily saved from its water crisis, its water supply had been thoroughly ensnared in the infrastructures of Britain's empire of steam. This meant that the plant's construction and operations required continual supervision by British engineers and mechanics.[127] Those condenser and ice machines had to be imported through Red Sea shipping lanes that Britain controlled. And given that construction of the Hijaz Railway ultimately stalled in Medina, even the coal needed to fire the plant's electric generators had to be shipped along those same routes. As a result, with the opening of hostilities between Britain and the Ottoman Empire in November 1914, British technical support, spare parts, and fresh shipments of coal—all vital to the upkeep of Jeddah's condenser plant—were completely cut off.[128]

Such was the fate of the empire's eleventh-hour technopolitical surge. When Jeddah's condenser plant officially opened in 1914, Kasim İzzeddin could not have known that Ottoman rule would be swept away in just a few years. Nor could he have predicted that this marvel of transimperial ingenuity was destined to lead such a distinguished postimperial afterlife, emerging as a critical inspiration for the Ottoman Hijaz's ultimate successor state, the Kingdom of Saudi Arabia. In the century since World War I, from Jeddah's first Ottoman desalination operations, Saudi Arabia has emerged as the world's largest producer of desalinated water. Even today, pilgrims are still drinking the sea.[129]

PART THREE
Managing Mobility

FIVE

Passports and Tickets

IN 1892, a delegation representing the Muslims of Madras presented the following petition (*arzuhal*) to the Ottoman consul-general (*başşehbender*) in India, Hacı Mehmed Kadri Bey.[1] The petition's authors declared their utter devotion to the Ottoman sultan-caliph before turning to the thorny matter at hand:

> We venture to take this opportunity to lay before your Honor, certain facts connected with the annual pilgrimage to Mecca, which cause much inconvenience and suffering to the Indian pilgrims, with the sanguine hope that Your Honor will be pleased to bring them to the august notice of your Imperial Master with a view to steps being adopted for prevention. The troubles of Indian pilgrims commence from Bombay. The pilgrim vessels are allowed to be so much thronged with passengers and the sanitary arrangements are so defective and unsatisfactory that not occasionally Cholera breaks out in the ships as soon as they leave Bombay . . .
>
> The appearance of Cholera necessitates the vessels being placed in quarantine, the period of which sometimes exceeds the Haj season,—with the result that the pilgrims return to their homes disappointed, dejected in mind and broken-hearted.
>
> Although our British Government with its usual sincerity of action and solicitude for the welfare of its subjects has framed rules regulating the traffic of pilgrim vessels, yet for obvious reasons they are not acted upon either by the

owners and charterers of the vessels, who wish to promote their own interests regardless of the convenience and comfort of the passengers, or enforced by those responsible for the rules being carried out. The only remedy therefore lies in such vessels being carefully inspected on reaching their destination, by Turkish Officials, and any violation of the rules or shortcomings adequately dealt with.

The whole Moslem world is aware that His Imperial Majesty the Sultan spends annually crores of dollars from his own pocket and from the Imperial Treasury for the well being and comfort of the pilgrims and that the Turkish Officials spare no pains in contributing to the same, but owing to the unfortunate malpractices of the Sheriff of Mecca, his interference in every matter of administration, and above all his hostile attitude towards all reforms introduced by the Turkish Government of Hejaz,—all of which are prompted by motives of pure self interest—disturb the administration and peace of the Hejaz and cause considerable suffering to all the pilgrims.

Those who understand the situation know that the Sheriff is responsible for such state of affairs, but others, who form the majority of pilgrims and who are not acquainted with the Sheriff's tactics, form an unfavorable impression of the local Turkish Government which is prejudicial to the reputation of His Imperial Majesty's rule.

The Indian Mussalmans alone number about 60,000,000 and those from other parts of the world exceed this number. We are sure that His Imperial Majesty will not allow such a large body of the Faithful to entertain other than the most loyal and respectful sentiments towards his Government and that the 'Ameerool Momineen,' whose kindheartedness, foresight and desire to do good to all, are proverbial, will order the adoption of necessary remedial measures, which may tend to secure for the pilgrims all necessary safety and convenience.

At first glance this petition seems a perfect example of the Ottoman state's successful cultivation of the Pan-Islamic cult of personality surrounding Abdülhamid II. Despite the petition's reverential tone, however, there is a thinly veiled warning that Indian Muslims' attachment to the caliphate was far from unconditional. Although the petition acknowledges positive steps taken by both the British and Ottoman administrations, it nevertheless raises the question: ultimately, who was responsible for the perilous conditions of the steamship-era hajj? Although the lion's share of their complaints are leveled at the sharif of Mecca, the petition makes it plain that if the public health crises, security risks, and naked corruption plaguing the pilgrimage experience were not remedied, the situation would likely taint Indian perceptions of the Ottoman administration in the Hijaz and the sultan-caliph would shoulder the blame.

As this document demonstrates, the Hamidian regime's emphasis on Abdülhamid's role as protector of the holy places created some unintended consequences. The crafting of this image succeeded in imbuing Abdülhamid with greater spiritual significance in the eyes of Indian and other non-Ottoman Muslims. However, this public persona also was meant to convey a sense of temporal power in the Hijaz and competence in securing the health and safety of pilgrims. Thus it also raised expectations for material, infra-structural, legal, and administrative changes that the Ottoman state found difficult, if not impossible, to fulfill.

The petition's authors paint a vivid picture of the failure of all parties involved to regulate the pilgrimage transportation industry, both at sea and on land. Despite the deplorable conditions of the steamship-era pilgrimage having been an issue of international concern for nearly three decades, the question of how to guarantee the health and safety of the masses of pil-grims moving across imperial and administrative borders remained unre-solved. Despite Indian calls for the Ottoman sultan-caliph to act decisively, by the latter half of the nineteenth century, the Ottoman state could no longer make decisions as the sole protector of the hajj. The conduct of the steamship-era hajj had become a globalized, deeply interdependent market-place and mobility regime requiring coordination and cooperation among the Ottoman Empire, the Sharifate of Mecca, British India, and the rest of the European colonial world. The hajj had become ensnared in an interim-perial web of conflicting regulations and practices governing passports, quarantines, shipping firms, pilgrimage guides, camel drivers, and even the legal interpretation of Islamic ritual itself.

In this internationalized climate, Pan-Islam was a double-edged sword for pilgrims. Rather than inspiring dramatic reforms, Pan-Islamic rhetoric and symbolism often undermined Ottoman efforts to impose modernizing reforms, safeguard the empire's territorial sovereignty, and fully apply the kinds of documentary practices and border controls needed to combat the omnipresent threat of pandemic cholera. For the Indian Ocean pilgrims caught in middle, it was precisely this Gordian knot of legitimacy, binding the two great "Muslim" empires of the colonial era, each vying to burnish their credentials as protectors of the faithful and patrons of the pilgrims, that ensured caution and mutual inaction. Neither side was willing to mandate reforms that might have been perceived as preventing pilgrims from fulfilling their sacred obligations to perform the hajj.

Chapter 5 catalogues how the interconnected failures of Ottoman oversight and interimperial mobility regulations combined to provide the space for the institutionalization of suffering and corruption on local, imperial, and global scales. By the early 1880s, the sharif of Mecca, ʿAwn al-Rafiq, had consolidated his position at the center of a vast Indian Ocean syndicate affecting virtually every aspect of the pilgrimage experience, whether steamship ticketing and boatmen or pilgrimage guides and camel brokers. With the advent of this monopoly, competition was restricted, prices were inflated, and the resulting spoils were shared by the pool's principal participants. Here I trace how the fissures between Ottoman and British approaches to passports, documentary practices, and steamship regulation facilitated the metastasis and institutionalization of this monopoly system. This chapter demonstrates how these fractured systems of interimperial regulation were evaded repeatedly and even conditioned through the collaboration of the sharif of Mecca, Ottoman provincial officials, European steamship companies, elements within the European consular community in Jeddah, and the transoceanic networks of Indian and Hadrami commercial interests that controlled the pilgrimage transport and brokerage industries linking Mecca and Jeddah with India, Singapore, and Java.

The Pauper Pilgrim Question

From the 1860s on, the mechanics of an "industrializing" pilgrimage transportation sector emerged as a major concern for European empires with large Muslim populations.[2] This was especially true of the British and Dutch administrations in South and Southeast Asia, from which the largest contingents of pilgrims hailed. Ever since the 1866 conference in Istanbul, international attention had focused heavily on the squalid conditions of Hindu pilgrimage centers in India, as well as the hajj, which it was argued was the second stage by which cholera was spread from the subcontinent to Europe. In particular, India's "pauper pilgrims" were singled out as the most likely carriers of cholera.

Here a word of caution is in in order. As both Nile Green and Radhika Singha have warned, one of the most obvious pitfalls of reading the steamship-era hajj exclusively through the medical case files of the colonial archive is the omnipresent danger of uncritically accepting their racialized terminologies and the colonial hubris that it entails. One way to partly guard against this Orientalizing tendency is to remember that indigent and destitute pilgrims were not so different from other migrants and long-distance travelers of their time.[3] Between 1840 and 1940, global port and customs statistics estimated roughly 150 million long-distance voyages. This number would have been composed mostly of passengers traveling in third class or steerage, ordinary men and women variously categorized as migrants and laborers.[4] These millions of lower-class mobile bodies, whether Chinese and Japanese crossing the Pacific or Europeans making their way across the Atlantic, were similarly stigmatized and subjected to new regimes of border, passport, and biomedical controls.[5]

Between 1853 and 1953, an accounting of all hajjis, arriving by either land or sea, supports a rough estimate of around 12 million pilgrims.[6] When set against the backdrop of this larger picture of long-distance travel and migration during the age of steam, the pilgrimage to Mecca looks less exceptional. Thus instead of imagining an Irish, Italian, or Eastern European immigrant arriving at New York's Ellis Island as the quintessential steamship experience of the period, it might be useful to reimagine the journey to Mecca as one of the most common and congested steamship circuits of the era. Likewise, the much-maligned "pauper pilgrims," who "begged" their way to Mecca and back, were less the uniquely Muslim products of religious "fanaticism" or "tradition" imagined by colonial administrators. Rather, they were remarkably similar to the vagabonds, beachcombers, hobos, and railway tramps of European and American steam-age lore. Poor pilgrims were an Islamic variation, a category partly forged and expanded by the depravation of colonial oppression but simultaneously part of a wider global trend of subaltern mobility unleashed by steamship capitalism and industrialization. In other words, they were products as much of imperial bureaucracies and the marketplace as of the mosque or the *waqf*.

In this brave new era of mass pilgrimage and subaltern mobility, a new class of ordinary pilgrims—the poorest of whom set out for Mecca with less preparation and spare cash than ever before—found themselves negotiating a volatile new system precariously balanced between the commercialization of steamship travel and pilgrimage-related charity. On the one hand, increased competition among shipping agents put the cost of a steamship ticket to the Hijaz within reach of the poor. On the other hand, the emergence of this new market brought a wave of exploitation and scandal. To be clear, this exploitation played out on both ends of the hajj in the Hijaz and in colonial ports of departure. In Bombay pilgrimage brokers were accused of luring prospective pilgrims to the docks with the promise of inexpensive fares, only to delay embarkation and raise prices as the hajj drew closer. In other cases larger vessels, eager to pack as many passengers as possible on board in order maximize profits, would sell off their excess tickets at bargain rates just before departure. Coupled with the notoriously disorderly embarkation procedures at Bombay, this system allowed brokers and steamship operators to load numbers well in excess of the legal limits imposed by the government of India.[7]

Many of these pilgrims were dependent on the munificence of prosperous Muslim merchants and shipping agents seeking to acquire merit by helping their less fortunate brethren. In some cases this assistance took the form of small amounts of cash, but often it came in the form of special discounted or free tickets provided by Muslim shippers. As this pattern emerged more clearly during the 1870s and the 1880s, the much-maligned figure of the impoverished pilgrim became a stock character in the correspondence of Indian newspapers, government officials, and Muslim charitable organizations. They were consistently described as backward illiterates duped by rapacious brokers and ignorant of the complexities of the brokerage schemes with which they were dealing. To be sure, many of them were cheated and taken advantage of. According to Singha, however, there also is a competing strand of colonial argumentation suggesting that many of these pilgrims were attracted by rumors of the commercial and charitable practices surrounding the pilgrimage industry and actually were savvy consumers who were prepared to pursue whatever means were necessary to make their hajj as cheaply as possible.[8]

Another dimension of the question of charity that has seldom been highlighted is the practice of hajj by proxy (*bedel haccı*). According to these Islamic legal provisions, pilgrims who cannot perform the hajj themselves due to lack of physical or financial ability (*istitaat*) may send a proxy (*vekil*) to perform the rituals on their behalf. However, from a strictly legal perspective, this practice is highly circumscribed. The grounds for sending a proxy must be permanent infirmity, generally due to old age or chronic disease. Likewise, to qualify as a proxy, the person elected to make the hajj must have performed the pilgrimage on his or her own behalf.[9] As Dr. Kasım İzzeddin explained, however, in practice pilgrimage by proxy frequently failed to satisfy those conditions. As he suggested, this was less a question of actual ability to make the hajj and more an expression of class divisions. From his perspective this practice was a major contributor to the rising numbers of destitute pilgrims because it was commonly mishandled by "men of wealth" who elected to send their "poor coreligionists" as representatives to "get the rewards of the hajj."[10]

In many respects İzzeddin's analysis agreed with long-standing complaints lodged by the British consulate in Jeddah. As early as the late 1870s, the British consulate had become convinced that wealthy Indian Muslims had begun sending their poorer coreligionists on hajj with insufficient funds. In particular, Dr. Abdur Razzack singled out India's Muslim princely states—Bhopal, Hyderabad, and Rampur—as the principal sources of this well-intentioned but sometimes dangerous practice. For a sense of the scale of this charity, during the 1880s, the nizam of Hyderabad alone issued at least 500 free return tickets each year. At the time this would have meant that roughly 5 percent of all Indians traveling on a steamship from Bombay received a free ticket from just one benefactor.[11]

Another part of the problem was that the economics of inexpensive steamship tickets had divorced hajj-related charity from the theoretical rules governing *bedel haccı*. Another contributing factor was that the suffering of pilgrims financed by India's booming marketplace of hajj-related charity happened on the other side of the Indian Ocean. As the Jeddah consulate complained to the authorities in India,

These Mahomedan gentlemen who distribute free tickets think that as soon as they have give[n] away the tickets their duty is finished. Charity it certainly is to facilitate the journey of those who want to go on religious mission, but a more mistaken, misapplied, and misguided charity than the one in question cannot be conceived. The distributors of these free tickets think not and care not how these poor creatures, whom they have loaded in a ship without any money, provisions and clothing, are going to keep themselves alive for about 20 days on board the ship and 10 days at Cameran in quarantine. The suffering and troubles which await their arrival in the Hedjaz and the difficulties experienced by these poor wretches for going back to India are matters which happen on the other side of the seas and therefore cannot tax the brains of the Indian charitable Mahomedans.[12]

Of equal concern for both European and Ottoman administrators was the significant number of pilgrims who were able to muster only enough cash to purchase a steamship ticket for their outgoing journey from Bombay to Jeddah. In addition to begging their way to Mecca and back, a more serious problem emerged when these pilgrims could not afford the cost of a return ticket once their hajj was completed. As a result, Indian pilgrims gained a reputation for professional mendicancy, marking them as a public nuisance in the eyes of Hijazi locals, British and Ottoman officials, and even many of their wealthier Indian coreligionists.[13]

This reputation led British officials, elite Indian Muslims, and the press to stigmatize poor pilgrims. Their harsh rhetoric is exemplified by the *Times of India*'s 1885 exposé, "The Pilgrim Trade":

Many people leave India with a passage ticket (obtained by begging), a few dirty rags, and perhaps two days' food. What becomes of these people? may be asked. Why, they starve to death. That many pilgrims die every year through starvation is a well-known fact. And again, there are amongst the pilgrims the very old and weak—people who are hardly able to come on board. Why should these people be allowed to undertake a voyage they are totally unfit for? All this is against the Koran.[14]

As a result of the pathogenic danger posed by this subset of pilgrims, states across Europe and the Islamic world sought to discourage "beggars trusting to the charity of their richer brethren" from undertaking "so long and expensive a business as the Haj."[15] According to Radhika Singha, supposedly "Enlightened Muslims" also were encouraged by the government to repeat the basic logic of this argument. Because British officials were keenly aware of their severe legitimacy deficit when it came to religious issues, they invited Muslim elites to instruct their poorer brethren that making the hajj without being physically and financially able was a violation of Islamic law. This oft-repeated legal justification for restricting the mobility of the poor was instrumental in securing support from Muslim elites, many of whom sympathized with the zeal of their coreligionists but still agreed that their actions were not permissible.[16]

In 1886, the government circulated a letter outlining Ottoman complaints about "the large influx into the Hedjaz of destitute British Indian Muhammadan subjects." The letter was distributed to Muslim notables to solicit their opinion regarding what steps might be taken to alleviate the situation. Writing on behalf of the Central National Muhammadan Association, Ameer Ali wrote a blistering condemnation:

> from the experience of many of the members of this Association who have themselves been to Hedjaz, there appears to be considerable truth in the complaint of the Turkish Government. A large majority of the destitute Indian Muhammadans who go to Mecca are actuated more by the worldly motive of making a livelihood from the charity of the richer pilgrims; and in many cases they prove themselves a nuisance to their well-to-do fellow compatriots. Under the Muhammadan law no person is entitled to make the *huj* unless he has the means of paying for the journey to and fro, and maintaining himself at the same time.[17]

In his response Maulvi Abdul Jubbar gently attempted to refute the most outrageous accusations leveled against India's poor pilgrims. Nevertheless he also urged both imperial governments to impose a means test to curb indigence:

> It is true that many destitute Indian Muhammadans yearly proceed to the Hedjaz on pilgrimage, but I do not think that they go there with the object of subsisting on the public charity. Arabia is a poor country, and the Indian Muhammadans know it well that its inhabitants expect gifts from foreign pilgrims. The latter therefore do not go there in the hope of obtaining any pecuniary help. They are led to the holy shrines in that country by religious enthusiasm, which prevents them from looking into the difficulties of a journey undertaken without sufficient means to pay the travelling charges. The ecclesiastical law of the Muhammadans does not make pilgrimage obligatory upon an individual who is not able to pay the costs of a journey to and from Mecca. I think every pilgrim may, before embarkation, be required to satisfy the authorities that he possesses the means of travelling. What minimum amount will be sufficient for the purpose may be determined by correspondence with the Turkish Government.[18]

In 1890, Dr. Mehmed Şakir Bey recorded his first-hand observations of the problem in a *layiha* prepared for the sultan. In his report he could not help but express his sympathy for the zeal and religiosity of the Indian pilgrims, which, as he pointed out, was at least partly a product of their devotion to the Ottoman sultan-caliph. He also praised Indian Muslims for the bravery and dignity with which they bore their poverty and misfortunes. Nevertheless Mehmed Şakir remained convinced that their behavior was unacceptable from both a religious and a sanitary point of view. From a religious perspective, he conceded that their begging was not technically a sin given that it was necessary for their survival. That said, he believed that India's poor pilgrims were clearly unable to satisfy the conditions of shariʿa law that intending pilgrims should have both the "financial and physical means" (istitaat-ı maliye ve kudret-i bedeniye) to complete the journey.[19]

Mehmed Şakir could not completely conceal his technocratic disdain for the pathogenic risk the poor pilgrims posed to the Hijaz. He described the disembarkation of Indians as if Jeddah were being besieged by "a mob of beggars and a naked and needy gang of the infirm." Once the authorities were satisfied that they could not produce the landing or visa fee (ayak bastı or mürur tezkeresi), the pilgrims were allowed to proceed to Jeddah. Armed with an "old tin mug" or a "dervish's bowl," they immediately begin to beg, crying out for mercy, "their voices fill[ing] the spaces of the neighborhoods and markets." But the "people of the Hijaz's ears became so accustomed to their voices that from the cradle they become indifferent and just observed rather than helping them." As he concluded, "their wasting away in the streets and their fouling the markets and the town, day and night, with their natural needs [i.e., their bodily functions], exposes many people to epidemic and deadly diseases." He lamented that these indigent pilgrims constituted a danger to the Hijaz that no amount of "Islamic piety" or "Ottoman medicine" could ever "silence" (see figure 5.1). At the same time, Mehmed Şakir admitted that Istanbul's unwillingness to take more meaningful steps to prevent indigent pilgrims from making the hajj was motivated partly by fears that such measures might weaken non-Ottoman Muslims' attachment to the caliphate.[20]

In a candid visit with the British vice-consul at Jeddah, Dr. Abdur Razzack, Mehmed Şakir bluntly outlined his concerns. As he complained, not only was the manner in which India's poor pilgrims made the hajj against shariʿa law and immoral, but their mendicancy rose to the level of corruption. He then pressed Abdur Razzack for suggestions on how best to solve the problem. Here Abdur Razzack explained that although he had raised the

FIGURE 5.1 Postcard depicting "beggars" in Jeddah, November 13, 1913. *Source:* Khalili Family Trust, Hajj and the Arts of Pilgrimage Collection, ARC.PC 308.

issue with the then viceroy, Lord Dufferin, four years earlier, the response he had received was merely a restatement of Britain's commitment to religious freedom, which prevented the government from restricting poor pilgrims' access to the hajj. Here Mehmed Şakir noted that the viceroy's position had little to do with religious freedom. Rather, it was motivated by post-1857 fears of provoking a "great rebellion." British officials were convinced that any attempt to interfere with a fundamental Islamic tenet such as the hajj likely would be perceived as a violation of Queen Victoria's 1858 promise of noninterference in Indian religious affairs (given in the wake of the Indian Revolt of 1857) and might incite another violent uprising among Indian Muslims. As a result, rather than restricting access to the hajj to ensure public safety, Mehmed Şakir believed that the British in fact were doing just the opposite, offering their Indian subjects "every kind of welfare assistance" to facilitate the hajj.[21]

In his 1892 pilgrimage narrative, Süleyman Şefik Söylemezoğlu arrived at much the same conclusion. However, Söylemezoğlu interpreted that a much more sinister, practically eugenic, program of social engineering was behind British pilgrimage policy. As he observed, European colonial regimes had begun to take note of the growing spiritual prestige and influence of the caliphate. In particular the British had begun to take special care and attention to address this question. In an almost cartoonish comparison, he noted that in other colonial settings, such as Australia, the British treated the aborigines like dogs (*ahali-i kadimeye köpek muamelesi ettiği*), and he did not believe there to be any favorable treatment of Parsis (*Mecusiler*) in India. By contrast, the rights of Indian Muslims aroused ceaseless anxiety. The British found it necessary to lavish Indian Muslims with all manner of honors in order to keep the populace contented. Thus promoting the hajj "killed two birds with one stone." In addition to tamping down the potential of Muslim social unrest, such promotion made it possible for the "useless and lazy" to be "sent on hajj with their entire families." On the one hand, this was a means of "cleansing the country of a pack of invalids" (*memleketini bir takım amelmandelerden tathir*); on the other, it served as a means to make "many a happy fool." As a result, Söylemezoğlu believed that the Hijaz was being inundated with thousands of beggars (*dilenciler*), who were responsible for the spread of all manner of "epidemic diseases" (*enva-ı ilel ve emraz*) and "vermin" (*haşerat*) to Ottoman domains.[22]

Although annual estimates vary, it appears that between the 1880s and World War I, the percentage of Indian pilgrims classified by either the Ottoman or Indian government as "paupers" (*fukara*: those claiming to have insufficient funds for quarantine fees, landing fees, and/or return transportation) fluctuated between 20 and 50 percent.[23] However, even these appalling figures might have been too low. Although the Ottoman Board of Health found that between 1882 and 1888, the number of pilgrims unable to pay their quarantine fees at Kamaran Island rose from 8 to 26 percent, by 1896, official Ottoman statistics recorded that the number of pilgrims landing at Jeddah who were unable to pay for the required Ottoman *mürur tezkeresi* (landing fee or visa) had risen to 48 percent.[24] Even this figure was likely a poor indication of the pilgrims' overall financial health and a poor predictor of whether or not the pilgrims would have enough money to feed themselves and finance their entire journey. According to Mehmed Şakir's estimation, from among the roughly 10,000 Indians landing in Jeddah in 1890, approximately "two in three were found to be in need of bread money and starving" before their eventual departure.[25]

The culmination of the pilgrims' suffering came at the end of the hajj season. Each year at the conclusion of the hajj, crowds of stranded Indian pilgrims, sometimes numbering as many as 1,500, descended on the British consulate in Jeddah pleading for assistance. Despite the considerable consternation and embarrassment caused by these stranded pilgrims, generally consular officials were able to rely on the assistance of steamship agents to offer reduced or free tickets for destitute pilgrims at the end of every hajj season. Over time this ritual gained a level of predictability. Wealthier pilgrims would pay a premium to depart early and the poor would wait until free or discounted fares became available. As Singha explains, "Having creamed off the solvent customers, shipping agents would give reduced or free return passage at the very end of the season. This made business sense—it maintained goodwill and the shipper's reputation for piety and encouraged pilgrims to come out again." British officials on both sides of the Indian Ocean complained bitterly about this systematized fusion of commercial gamesmanship and "reckless" charity, but they could do little to stop it. In fact, on some level they ultimately came to embrace it because neither the Jeddah consulate nor the government of India wanted to give the impression that it would provide free transport back to India, thereby encouraging even more pilgrims to expect repatriation free of charge. British officials in Jeddah repeatedly stated that they were under no international legal obligation to repatriate stranded pilgrims. Eventually the government of India began printing this warning on pilgrimage passports.[26]

In the wake of the devastating cholera outbreak of 1893, the debate on indigent pilgrims took center stage at the 1894 international sanitary conference in Paris. Surveying Ottoman sanitary reforms and hajj policies from the 1850s through the reforms recommended in 1894, Kasım İzzeddin recounted both the Ottoman's state's vision of the Islamic jurisprudence underpinning hajj regulation and the opinions of its European counterparts. In his view Islamic law, as defined by the conference attendees, raised serious questions about the legality of the poor pilgrims' attempts to make the hajj. Since as early as the 1866 international sanitary conference, the idea of imposing a "means test" to restrict the mobility of poor pilgrims had been posited as the most obvious solution to the problem. As Dr. Adrien Achille Proust, the French delegate, reminded the 1894 delegates, "the aforementioned conference demanded that some measures be taken concerning pilgrims moving by steamship and that special local modifications be made to the law and applied particularly to India." Furthermore, "it might be made mandatory for each pilgrim going on the hajj to have enough funds for their departing and return journeys and enough money to sustain their families during their absence." Finally, he added, "the Islamic shariʿa recommends this anyway." Thus if intending pilgrims fail to meet the minimum deposit required by their home government, they would be prohibited from making the hajj.[27]

As İzzeddin pointed out, as early as 1851, the Dutch administration in Java had applied a deposit system. Similar schemes also had been imposed in French Algeria, Austrian-controlled Bosnia, and Russian territories in Central Asia.[28] Eventually France, the Netherlands, and Russia adopted mandatory systems of return tickets in order to prevent indigent pilgrims from becoming stranded in the Hijaz without enough cash for their passage home.[29] Even other British possessions, including Egypt and the Straits Settlements, eventually adopted similar deposit and ticketing systems to those pioneered by the Dutch.[30]

In response to this proposal, the government of India's delegate, Dr. J. M. Cunningham, cunningly replied that if such a financial requirement were considered consistent with Islamic jurisprudence, the government of India would be willing to investigate whether the measures could be applied. However, he thought that this would be possible only if the "Sultan and Caliph of all Muslims" agreed to "declare it to be necessary and proper." As he explained, without the sultan's approval the Indian government would hesitate to accept such measures. And "since the government of India gives complete freedom to every religious community in every colonized land, I have no doubt that they would not have a law which would put its Muslim subjects in a lower position than Muslims in any other countries." In response, the Ottoman delegate, Turhan Pasha, could do little more than recite a list of the sultan-caliph's recent benevolent acts to alleviate the sufferings of poor pilgrims in Mecca. Turhan Pasha pointed to sanitary reforms already being imposed and the construction of a pilgrimage guesthouse (*misafirhane*) and improved hospital and pharmacy facilities dedicated to indigent pilgrims. After citing these precautionary measures, he went on to make it clear that the Ottoman state could not legally (or politically) justify preventing pilgrims from meeting their religious obligations.[31]

Once again the British handcuffed the Ottomans with their own Pan-Islamic rhetoric and framed the government of India as the defenders of Muslim freedom of religion. By emphasizing Sultan Abdülhamid II's role as caliph and spiritual leader of all Muslims, Cunningham set him up as the ultimate arbiter of Islamic jurisprudence. In the event that the Ottomans agreed to the proposed financial restrictions on poor pilgrims, the British were well prepared to lay the blame at the feet of the sultan.

Passport Optional?

Although the failure of the Ottoman and British Empires to circumscribe the mobility of the poor was partly conditioned by debates over Islamic law governing the hajj and the mutually constructed fears produced by Pan-Islam, it also was intimately tied up with the vexed questions of the pilgrimage passport and the omnipresent threat of European extraterritorial jurisdiction. During the late nineteenth century international passport regulations were still in their infancy.[32] However, the hajj emerged as a critical interimperial arena of passport experimentation. By demanding the biopolitical data that passports and visas ideally provided, the Ottoman and British Empires sought to identify risks posed by certain categories of travel and limit entry to nonnationals deemed to pose epidemiological, political, or financial threats.[33] Despite compelling arguments from both Ottoman and British officials in favor of the erection of hajj-related passport and visa regimes, for both empires the emerging pilgrimage passport system was fraught with political risk and often insurmountable practical and logistical challenges. Although states were increasingly intent on defining and "monopolizing the legitimizing means of movement" both within and across their borders, in the late nineteenth century this international system was still very much a work in progress.[34] Ultimately it would not mature and fully take root until after World War I.[35] And yet understanding the logic behind these unfinished projects and the deep ambivalence surrounding pilgrimage passport proposals and regulations helps us to better understand the intractable limitations of interimperial mobility controls for both the Ottomans and their European rivals.

From the 1860s on, British consular officials in Jeddah had repeatedly suggested the need for a compulsory passport linked to some sort of means testing or prepaid deposit system. From their perspective the potential benefits were clear. This system could have provided a more accurate means of accounting for or calculating the number of pilgrims making the hajj each year. It also would have provided a firmer statistical basis for tracking epidemic outbreaks and detecting the overloading of pilgrimage vessels. Once in the Hijaz, a compulsory passport would have provided pilgrims with documentary proof of British nationality, which in turn could have been used to extend the extraterritorial protection of the consulate in Jeddah in the event that pilgrims ran afoul of the law. In addition, it held great potential as an instrument of political surveillance. As Vice-Consul Abdur Razzack put it, "To know with something like exactness how many of its Muhammadan subjects leave India every year, how many return and the number of those who do not; besides which Government will be able to keep a check on the movements of those who are suspected or disaffected."[36]

Despite its potential as a technology for colonial surveillance, curiously, the pilgrimage passport was never fully embraced by the government of India. Instead it was the Ottoman state that first sought to impose passport regulations on the hajj. In 1880, British officials were informed that henceforth passports would be required of all pilgrims. During the Tanzimat period the Ottoman state gradually erected a series of internal and external passport regulations: the 1841 *Men'-i Mürur Nizamnamesi*, the 1844 *Memalik-i Mahruse-i Şahane'de Mürur ve Ubur*, and the 1867 *Pasaport Odası Nizamnamesi*.[37] Effectively, all of these laws demanded that foreign travelers carry passports and apply for what might equate loosely to a visa or "document of passage" (*mürur tezkeresi*) from an Ottoman consul in order to gain entry into Ottoman domains (see figure 5.2).[38] The *mürur tezkeresi* provided an internal passport system meant to render domestic mobility within the Ottoman Empire visible to the state, allowing it to delineate more clearly between legitimate forms of mobility such as pilgrimage, trade, and labor migration and those that it saw as illegitimate, such as banditry, smuggling, and vagrancy.[39] At the same time, it provided the basic identity documents needed to differentiate more clearly between Ottoman subjects and foreign nationals. In turn these documents undergirded Ottoman reforms that sought to curtail European practices of extraterritorial protection and minimize the kinds of uncertainties and abuses surrounding Ottoman nationality and subjecthood that were highlighted in chapter 2.[40] Prior to 1880, these Tanzimat-style requirements had not been applied to pilgrims traveling to the Hijaz from abroad. Suddenly, however, British officials were

FIGURE 5.2 Ottoman *mürur tezkeresi*, 1885. *Source*: BOA, Y.PRK.HR, 8/15.

warned that articles 7 and 8 of the 1844 passport law would be enforced. Under these rules pilgrims traveling without passports and visas theoretically were subject to expulsion.[41]

In practice, however, the enforcement of these Tanzimat passport regulations proved impossible. As Abdur Razzack pointed out, the notion that visas should be secured by Ottoman consuls at the ports of embarkation was absurd. This plan "overlooked the fact that except in Bombay there is no Turkish Consul in any of the ports of India whence pilgrims start for the Haj."[42] Thus when pilgrims showed up for the 1881 hajj season without visas and many without passports, none of them were turned away. By 1882, the law appears to have "existed only in name and the passports were not thought of."[43] Instead, the Ottoman *mürur tezkeresi* was made readily available when pilgrims landed in Jeddah.

The Ottoman state's failure to enforce its own regulations raised puzzling questions as to what the Ottomans had hoped to achieve in the first place. The consulate in Jeddah theorized that the sale of the *mürur tezkeresi* was likely the law's "chief object" and "was evidently designed to make this a source of income." With these documents available at 8 *kuruş* per head, the consulate estimated that the charges totaled some 40,000 rupees per hajj season, providing the provincial administration with a much-needed revenue stream.[44] However, as the British consulate complained, this ad hoc visa system did not function as an effective instrument of border control, nor did it provide any additional guarantee of safety. From Abdur Razzack's vantage point, the passports should have been used as a policing tool, allowing the Ottoman administration to offer pilgrims greater protection from the Hijaz's other mobile population, the Bedouin. Instead, he argued that these documents proved "of no service to the pilgrims" once they had "passed through the gates of Jeddah." Likewise, the Bedouins "have so very little reverence for the Turks themselves, outside of the towns, that the Tezkireh is not likely to prove a safeguard to the pilgrims."

In 1884, a new Ottoman passport law (*Pasaport Nizamnamesi*) was again promulgated.[45] Again, the law called for pilgrims to furnish passports complete with visas from Ottoman consuls. European consular officials were given a detailed schedule of fees for the visas as well as a series of fines and punishments for those in violation of the law, sparking years of running objections from the British, Dutch, and Russian embassies.[46] The European powers repeatedly complained about what they considered exorbitant prices that targeted largely poorer travelers. They lobbied for a reduced price of six *kuruş* and even that free (*ücretsiz*) visas be granted to pilgrims traveling to Mecca and Jerusalem.[47] Again, however, the procedures described in the law were not implemented fully, despite repeated attempts.[48] Ottoman authorities continued to charge for the *mürur tezkeresi* but did not expel or punish pilgrims who could not (or claimed to be unable to) pay the visa fees.[49] Ottoman documents show that over time, the state even came to understand these visa-less or even passport-less (*vizesiz* or *pasaportsuz*) pilgrims as a category unto themselves. As Abdur Razzack put it, Ottoman administrators on the ground readily admitted "that it is impossible to repulse a person simply for not having a passport when he is dressed in the pilgrim's garb and sings out 'Allah hooma labaik' (Oh God I am here)."[50] Moreover, in his capacities as sultan-caliph and Servant of the Two Holy Places, Abdülhamid could not afford to be perceived as responsible for turning away intending pilgrims landing in Jeddah. As this dilemma suggests, the maintenance of the Hamidian state's Pan-Islamic image and the imposition of more rigorous forms of territorial sovereignty and biopolitical surveillance were irreconcilably conflicted.

The Ottoman state's attempt to erect firmer border controls and documentary practices turned out to be a double-edged sword. As the British consul in Jeddah at the time, Lynedoch Moncrieff, read it, the Ottoman state's volte-face on the compulsory nature of the passport was intimately connected to fears of European extraterritorial claims. Moncrieff reasoned that passports would only enhance the ability of foreign states to offer protection to their subjects, a practice that would represent a contradiction to the sultan's "well-known policy" of centralization in the Hijaz. Although Moncrieff recognized that passports might provide British subjects with a modicum of protection against potential abuses at the hands of the Ottoman justice system or the Sharifate of Mecca, if the Ottoman state was treating the passport as "optional," he questioned "whether there were any advantages in maintaining it." Sensing an opportunity, he recommended that intending pilgrims "be most clearly made to understand that his own Government does not *oblige* him to take a Passport."[51] Moncrieff suggested that the Indian administration issue pilgrimage passports "unconditionally" and "without any fee or deposit." By doing so, "the entire odium of passport regulations" could be laid at the feet of the sultan (figure 5.3).[52]

Taken together, Pan-Islam and European consular extraterritoriality fundamentally altered and inverted the ideal logics of border maintenance and governmentality. Thus legally reserving the right to demand passports, but not actually doing so, appeared to better serve the interests of Ottoman sovereignty. And yet the ceremony of admission through

Form A.]

Registered No.

BRITISH CONSULATE,
JEDDAH.

PILGRIM'S PASSPORT.
GOVERNMENT OF INDIA.

Name (in English and Urdu).	Father's name.	RESIDENCE.			Occupation.	Age.	* Distinctive marks.	Names and places of residence of nearest relations in India.
		Town or village.	Pargana or taluka.	District and province.				

* To be filled up for male pilgrims only.

This passport, issued by the authority of the Viceroy and Governor General of India in Council, requests and requires all those whom it may concern to afford the person above named going on pilgrimage to the Hedjaz all needed assistance and protection.

By Order of the Governor General of India in Council,

Countersigned at_____

this_____ day of_____190__

(Sd.)_____

Magistrate or Commissioner of Police, or Political Agent.

Secretary to the Government of India

~~in the Home Department,~~

in the Department of Education.

NOTICE TO PILGRIMS.

1. Although the authorities in the Hedjaz will allow pilgrims from British India to land without a passport, this passport is issued to enable pilgrims to obtain the advice and assistance of the British Consul at Jeddah, and every pilgrim is recommended to provide himself or herself with one.
2. A passport is supplied on request made by or on behalf of the intending pilgrim, but no fee is charged for issuing the same. It is intended only for the Hedjaz and, if a pilgrim desires to travel beyond Medina, he should procure a regular passport, which is granted on the production of a certificate of identity and which should be vise by the Turkish Consul at the port of embarkation.
3. The British Government does not undertake to bring back pauper pilgrims from the Hedjaz.
4. The British Government has no desire to interfere with the liberty of the pilgrim, but warns them that they should not undertake the pilgrimage if they have not sufficient pecuniary means for the expenses of the journey to the Hedjaz and back to India.
5. On arrival at Jeddah the holder of this passport should deliver the duplicate copy to the Agent of the British Consulate before leaving the ship.
6. This passport is granted solely for the convenience of the pilgrim. The holder thereof should apply to the British Consul at Jeddah for advice in case of difficulty.
7. Pilgrims are warned not to risk their money by depositing it with untrustworthy persons in Jeddah or Mecca and are recommended to deposit it in the British Consulate in Jeddah, where they can obtain facilities for the purchase of cheques from respectable merchants for any amounts which they may require in Mecca or Medina.
8. For the convenience of pilgrims not knowing English, this passport is accompanied with a full translation of this notice in Urdu, Arabic and Bengali.

FIGURE 5.3 Pilgrim's passport issued by the government of India, c. 1900. *Source*: Khalili Family Trust, Hajj and the Arts of Pilgrimage Collection, ARC.MX 439.

which pilgrims presented themselves before a representative of the "Exalted Caliphate" remained, preserving at least the illusion of the state's sovereign rights of exclusion.[53] Ultimately this dynamic would prove one of the most intractable paradoxes of the colonial-era hajj.

Despite the seemingly obvious desires of both Ottoman and European states to impose more intrusive forms of biopolitical surveillance and documentary practices, the Ottoman state stopped checking passports, and the government of British India continued issuing them but refused to make them compulsory.

Breaking the Brokers

For nearly three decades following the 1866 international sanitary conference, Britain declined to submit to any international agreements proposing stricter quarantine procedures or an integrated system of compulsory passport and ticketing practices. Instead the government of India pursued an entirely separate package of reforms. Because of British officials' discomfort with the possibility that international quarantine regulations might be manipulated by foreign powers to harm British commercial interests as well as their concern that fees attached to either passports or mandatory return tickets might be interpreted by Indian Muslims as a government attempt to bar poorer Muslims from making the hajj, the British sought a less direct path to pilgrim reform.

In an attempt to thread the needle between these seemingly irreconcilable concerns, the government of India formulated a doctrine of "indirect" intervention. Rather than imposing restrictions on individual pilgrims, British officials attempted to reform the business of the hajj. Such reform efforts were aimed primarily at cleaning up the pilgrimage shipping industry and its associated networks of ticketing brokers. On one hand, colonial administrators hoped that by tightening their regulation of the pilgrimage transportation industry, they could eliminate the worst instances of overcrowding and squalid conditions, which had been identified as one of the greatest factors contributing to the spread of cholera en route to Mecca. On the other hand, by licensing ticketing brokers, they hoped to provide pilgrims with a measure of consumer protection against aggressive touts, pricing scams, and coercive monopolies. This strategy required shipowners to make major capital investments in their vessels to meet the legal requirements imposed by the government.

Requiring cleaner, larger, and better-equipped steamships necessarily would lead shipowners to raise ticket prices. Whether or not colonial officials admitted it, raising and fixing prices was the cornerstone of their doctrine of so-called indirect intervention. If direct measures prohibiting poor pilgrims from setting out for Mecca were deemed too dangerous, the only other option was to raise the standards of travel in such a way that either unsanitary conditions were eliminated or the poorest pilgrims were priced out of the market altogether. Although poor pilgrims were certainly victims of this strategy, they were not the enemy in this equation. The true targets of this plan were the intertwined Muslim shipping firms and their allied networks in the pilgrimage brokerage industry.

The centerpiece of British India's steamship legislation was the Native Passenger Ships Act of 1870 and its subsequent amendments in 1872, 1876, 1883, and 1887, culminating in the 1895 Pilgrim Ships Act.[54] These regulations were designed to restrict the number of passengers per vessel in the hope that by alleviating instances of overcrowding, the risk of cholera outbreaks would be mitigated. These acts established clear limits on the maximum number of passengers according to each ship's registered or estimated tonnage. Likewise, they set guidelines that gradually increased the minimum superficial space per passenger according to their accommodation in the upper or lower decks. In addition to addressing the most basic question of overcrowding, these acts stipulated mandatory provisions for the safety and welfare of passengers and the obligations of the shipping company and crews to their passengers. These included access to cooking fuel, clean water, proper ventilation and fresh air, clean latrines, and medical supplies. To ensure the compliance of shipping companies and in order to allow for easier surveillance of sick pilgrims during their journey, the acts also required that ships carrying more than one hundred pilgrims have a qualified medical officer.[55]

In 1880, the Ottoman Board of Health drafted a similar piece of legislation, the *Hacı Nakleden Sefaine Dair Nizamname* (Law Concerning Pilgrim-Carrying Vessels). The law was framed to agree with the recommendations of the 1866 Istanbul and 1874 Vienna sanitary conferences. It also was explicitly modeled on British India's Native Passengers Act.[56] At that time all of the European representatives shared their own governments' regulations with the Ottoman Board of Health. This marked the beginning of the board's efforts to forge a unified set of internationally recognized standards for pilgrimage vessels. In many respects, however, the Board of Health's legislation counted for little. A decade later, in 1890, both the

British Foreign Office and government of India still viewed such efforts with a wary eye. The Foreign Office feared that laws drafted by the Board of Health, composed of both European and Ottoman members, were in a sense "international and intended to be binding on the Powers."[57] It was the opinion of the Foreign Office that foreign ships and the subjects they carried should not be bound by Ottoman legislation unless they were in Ottoman territory.

Without the strong cooperation of the states producing the most pilgrims, Ottoman legislative efforts were doomed to fail. For example, in 1882, 45 of the 75 pilgrimage vessels arriving in the Hijaz sailed under British flags, and roughly the same ratio of pilgrims originated from either India or Southeast Asia.[58] In light of the dominance of British shipping, if the standards of the pilgrimage transport industry in the Indian Ocean were not addressed at their point of origin, Ottoman legislation governing the ports of the Red Sea was unlikely to make a dramatic impact.

With the 1883 Native Passengers Act, sailing vessels, which long had been in decline, were officially banned from the pilgrimage trade. Although the prohibition on sailing vessels might have been a redundancy, the ban may be taken as indication of the long-term direction of British regulation. The most dramatic example of this process came when Britain, relenting to decades of international pressure and against the government of India's vehement protests, signed the convention produced by the 1894 Paris international sanitary conference. The convention stipulated that the minimum space for each adult pilgrim be raised from 9 to 21 superficial feet. In order to meet the new international standards for superficial space, India's 1895 Pilgrim Ships Act required that all vessels be at least 500 tons and be able to achieve a speed of at least 8 knots under monsoon conditions.

As government standards for shipboard fittings, anchors, cables, nautical instruments, safety equipment, overall tonnage, and speed during monsoon conditions gradually were raised, shipping companies were forced to either update their existing vessels or obtain newer ones. Although the government framed these reforms as the products of international pressure or their own promotion of the best interests of pilgrims, scholars generally have underemphasized the extent to which this legislation was at least partly designed as a challenge to Muslim-owned shipping companies. European shipping companies had little problem meeting the progressively tightening standards, but Muslim shippers, with comparatively limited access to capital and correspondingly older, less well-appointed, and smaller vessels, struggled to comply with these regulations. During this period Muslim shippers made several strategic adjustments. First, they found a niche in the market by catering to a lower-end clientele. Second, smaller individual or family-owned firms pooled their resources either to charter a ship for the pilgrimage season or to raise enough capital to stave off European competitors. By consolidating their resources, Muslim shippers were able to acquire larger, second-hand ships from European shipping companies such as Peninsular and Oriental and Lloyd's.[59]

At the same time, the government of India was engaged in a parallel attack on Bombay's and Calcutta's pilgrimage brokers. Shipowners depended on large networks of touts and petty brokers to attract business and sell tickets. Working for a commission, these brokers were accused repeatedly of fleecing pilgrims through a mixture of misinformation, intimidation, and bait-and-switch pricing scams. Worse still, they conspired with shipowners to pack in more pilgrims per ship than was legally permitted.[60] The rapacious broker became the most ubiquitous villain in official descriptions of the pilgrimage trade. As one government official put it, pilgrims are "entirely at the mercy of a class of men very like the Liverpool crimps who charge them extortionately and rob them at all ends."[61]

In an attempt to protect pilgrims from these unscrupulous brokers, in 1883, Bombay passed the Pilgrim Protection Act. It required all brokers to obtain a license from the Bombay police commissioner and created a new position called the Protector of Pilgrims. Stationed at the port, this Muslim official was instructed to act as a special advocate, providing information and assistance to intending pilgrims.[62] In addition to the measures taken in Bombay, British officials also began to understand that they needed better consular representation on the other side of the Indian Ocean. In 1878, Dr. Abdur Razzack was sent to accompany India's pilgrimage contingent for that year. Eventually he was appointed as the Muslim vice-consul of Jeddah in 1882. Two years later additional Muslim vice-consuls were stationed on Kamaran Island and the nearby port of Hudayda.[63]

Despite these timid first steps toward reform, the 1880s emerged as a decade of pilgrimage-related scandals, exposing the dark underbelly of the Indian Ocean pilgrimage shipping industry and the virtual paralysis of the government. Undoubtedly the best-known scandal occurred in August 1880. The steamship *Jeddah*, which belonged to Muḥammad bin Aḥmad al-Saqqāf, the managing partner of the Singapore Steamship Company, set sail under a British flag carrying nearly a thousand Malay and Indonesian pilgrims. In addition to the pilgrims, Muḥammad's nephew Sayyid ʿUmar al-Saqqāf was headed to the company's Jeddah branch. After enduring some difficult storms, the ship began taking on water and sprang a major leak just off Cape Guardafui, at the mouth of the Gulf of Aden. With the water rising rapidly, al-Saqqāf, the captain, and the ship's European officers panicked and abandoned the passengers to their fate, an apparently certain death. Escaping with one of the ship's few emergency crafts, al-Saqqāf and the Europeans were picked up by another vessel and taken to Aden. Astonishingly, however, the *Jeddah* arrived in Aden some twenty-four hours later, having been towed by a French vessel. The pilgrims had courageously worked the pumps and kept their vessel afloat until help arrived, while the Hadrami steamship magnate and European crew showed great cowardice in abandoning their charges to die.[64] The official inquiries that followed sparked an international scandal, which effectively shamed British authorities from Aden to Singapore. In 1898, this great "scandal of the Eastern seas" would eventually provide the basis for Joseph Conrad's famous novel *Lord Jim*.[65]

However, even the *Jeddah* incident did not immediately move British officials in India to take drastic steps. Some five years later the issue of overcrowding and the plight of the indigent pilgrim remained unresolved and returned to the public eye with a vengeance. In November 1885, *The Times of India* ran a scandalous eyewitness account of the entire ordeal endured by India's poor pilgrim masses, titled "The Pilgrimage Trade." Like Conrad's fictional account, the article's harrowing scenes of seasick men, women, and children, clinging to their belongings, "all packed like sardines in a box," conjures images reminiscent of the "Middle Passage."[66] Confronted with these graphic details, many observers came to see the disorder of the pilgrimage industry and government's refusal to intervene directly as further proof of the government's indifference to the suffering of the poor rather than an expression of Britain's commitment to religious freedom. As *The Times of India*'s reporting made clear, the underlying flaw in both the Native Passenger Ships Act and the Pilgrim Protection Act was the government's refusal to impose any fees or conditions directly on the mobility of pilgrims themselves.

Not surprisingly, however, poorer pilgrims continued to prefer the cheapest available fares. Despite the government's increased regulation of the hajj, a strong correlation persisted between low prices and the unsanitary and overcrowded conditions that the government had sought to eliminate in the first place. Because the government feared imposing passport fees, mandatory deposits, or return tickets, it could not directly deter intending pilgrims regardless of how poor they might be. The only avenue that remained was to manipulate the price and quality of pilgrimage services by introducing an outside stimulus into the market. Having arrived at the conclusion that the entire complex of indigenous shipping interests and brokers was responsible for widespread and often deliberate neglect of the government's evolving pilgrimage-shipping regulations, the government of India sought a private partner willing to enforce its legislation and documentary practices, raise the overall conditions of the industry, and wrest market share away from the competition.

"The Infidel Piloting the True Believer"

On January 4, 1886, the government of India passed a resolution making Thomas Cook and Son the official travel agent of the hajj. As the conditions of the agreement between the two parties made clear, British officials in India attempted to foster a government-backed monopoly over the pilgrimage transportation industry for Thomas Cook and Son while also ceding responsibility for the regulation of that industry to the firm.[67] The effect of this ambitious privatization scheme was that Cook's employees were given the authority to act "precisely the same as though they were in service of the Government." In addition to the enormous operational latitude given to Thomas Cook and Son, the company also was indemnified against any losses that it might incur in the first three years while administering the hajj.[68]

Between 1886 and 1890, Thomas Cook's growth was remarkable. The government expressed its satisfaction with the progress that Cook's shipboard representatives made in ensuring that the ships it chartered met all legal requirements for medical surveillance and sanitation. Cook's introduced a fixed-price system for the journey from Bombay to Jeddah, allowing for no reduced-price tickets. The firm's dates of departure were fixed and publicized in advance and were generally observed. This allowed pilgrims making their way from inland destinations to purchase all-inclusive tickets for rail and steamship travel in advance (see figure 5.4). Even as the Cook's experiment soured in subsequent years, the government continued to claim that

FIGURE 5.4 Thomas Cook Mecca pilgrimage ticket, 1886. *Source*: Thomas Cook Group Archives.

the company's presence in the pilgrimage market had encouraged greater competition, forcing Muslim shipping agents to take measures to better their services, which in turn had raised the overall safety and comfort of the industry and led to an overall reduction in opportunities for extortion.[69]

With regard to the question of the so-called pauper pilgrim, the firm's indirect intervention did precisely what the government wished to accomplish but feared doing itself. Cook's entrance into the pilgrimage-shipping industry immediately altered the price structure, ticketing procedures, and flexible timetables on which Muslim shipping agents, brokers, and poor pilgrims depended. For wealthier pilgrims, fixed fares likely did place limits on extortionist pricing schemes. However, fixed prices dramatically narrowed the options of poorer pilgrims, who preferred flexible timetables that enabled them either to arrive at Bombay early to secure a cheap fare or to hold out until the last minute to take advantage of reduced or even free fares offered by Muslim shipping agents. Likewise, although the government and Cook's discouraged extended stays in Bombay, for poor pilgrims this was often a critical stage in their journey. Often, Bombay was where pilgrims generated enough funds to purchase a one-way ticket or where they replenished their funds after purchasing a ticket through labor, selling petty goods, or begging. In other words, fixed prices and departure times impeded poor pilgrims' access to the kinds of charitable structures, sliding-scale pricing, and reduced or free fares on which they had come to rely.[70]

Bearing these questions in mind, it is doubtful that Cook's services were actually an attractive option for customers or if the firm's gain in market share between 1887 and 1890 was simply the by-product of the overwhelming government support that it received. It is also difficult to tell whether Cook's fixed-price system absorbed any appreciable share of the indigent population it aimed to eliminate or if the firm's increasing market share was merely a matter of attracting those pilgrims who could already afford full-price fixed fares and round-trip tickets. Leaving aside these unknowns, the firm's results were undeniable. In Cook's first year of operation, it was able to attract nearly 20 percent of the market. That figure rose steadily to 29.3 percent in 1888 and to 38.6 percent in 1889, and it peaked in 1890 at 44.5 percent. It appeared that Cook's was on its way to dominating the pilgrimage trade.[71]

Despite the initial promise shown by the Thomas Cook project, these early gains proved illusory. In the final years of its collaboration with the government, Cook's was accused of overbooking its ships.[72] There were complaints that the firm had been unwilling to provide the necessary privacy for "respectable" women.[73] Worse still, as many customers pointed out, the difference between ships chartered by Cook's and those captained by the company's competition was increasingly negligible. In fact, since Cook's contracted with companies such as Hajji Cassum & Co., customers began to note that Cook's steamers rarely offered advantages over other steamship offerings.[74] Most damaging of all, however, was the outbreak of cholera on the Thomas Cook–chartered steamship the *Deccan* in 1890. As Mehmed Şakir explained, due to severe overcrowding on the *Deccan*, some 50 pilgrims passed away during their quarantine on Kamaran Island. While they were in quarantine, the disease infected pilgrims traveling on the *King Arthur* and subsequently spread to Jeddah and Mecca.[75]

Despite Cook's confidence that he could not only reform the pilgrimage industry but also achieve profitability, the profits never materialized. Despite all of the advantages of state sponsorship, the firm failed to monopolize the pilgrimage travel industry and marginalize indigenous Muslim shipping interests. At peak of its intervention in 1890, the firm chartered four of the eleven steamships making the journey to the Hijaz, carrying 4,220 of the 9,953 pilgrims leaving from Bombay that year. Despite achieving approximately 45 percent of the market share that year, in 1892–93 the firm's share dwindled to just 14 percent.[76]

Although it is tempting to attribute Cook's plummeting market share to these embarrassing incidents, as John Mason Cook understood, the firm's problems were more systemic. In his final reports to the government in 1894, he identified two areas that were likely the sources of his troubles in Bombay. First, Cook's chartered the appropriate number of steamships to accommodate the pilgrims it booked each year, but the firm did not own its own fleet. As Cook would complain once the project began to break down, "nothing short of a special service of steamers would enable them to compete successfully with the shippers who had controlled the pilgrimage traffic before they themselves had come on the scene."[77] This leads to the obvious conclusion that although Muslim shipowners' market share initially had been damaged by the tremendous advantages conferred on Thomas Cook by the government, in subsequent years they made the necessary changes to compete and undercut Cook's prices and successfully rallied to recapture their customers. In addition to owning their own steamers, Muslim shipping agents could still count on their superior networks of brokers in the districts to steer business away from Cook's.[78]

In November 1893, the agreement between Thomas Cook and Son and the government came to an acrimonious end. In his final report to the government, John Mason Cook complained bitterly about the forces that had conspired against his firm.[79] And although one Muslim correspondent for the *Bombay Gazette* explained that the waning of Cook's "popularity was owing to the fact that a Mussulman has sentimental objections to being helped by 'unbelievers' in his pilgrimage," as John Mason Cook's allegations make clear, it was not so much the pilgrims themselves as the complex web of Indian Ocean shipping, brokerage, and political interests that Thomas Cook and Son had failed to conquer.[80] Cook felt that the resistance of local officials in Bombay led to collusion between Muslim members of the Governor General's Council with interests in the shipping business to set prices at a level that would force him out of the market. Although there might be an element of truth in Cook's accusations, such claims ignore the question of whether or not Cook's was equally successful in imposing its will on Ottoman officials in Istanbul, Jeddah, and Mecca. They also overlook the degree to which India's Muslim shipping and brokerage industries were anchored to and dependent on the Hijaz's pilgrimage guilds.

Perhaps the most basic problem posed by the Ottoman administration in the Hijaz revolved around passports. When the Ottoman state reversed its demand that pilgrims carry a passport, it gravely undermined the utility and necessity of British Indian efforts to impose passport controls. Although the government of India continued to issue pilgrim passports, Thomas Cook and Son was disappointed to learn that the government of India stubbornly refused to make the passport compulsory. As John Mason Cook complained in 1887, "I always understood that *every* Pilgrim from ports of British India to the Hedjaz *must* take a passport." Yet as his report for the 1887 pilgrimage season indicates, only 6,555 of the 9,389 pilgrims departing Indian ports were issued travel documents.[81] Originally Cook had expected that by making passports compulsory, even if they were given unconditionally, intending pilgrims would be funneled to his agents, who had been granted the authority to issue them. This would ensure that eventually the firm would gain a majority of the trade. Without this critical element, there was nothing to stop pilgrims from avoiding Thomas Cook–chartered ships altogether.

In addition to this critical flaw in the agreement between Cook's and the government, the Hijazi side of the arrangements proved considerably more difficult than John Mason Cook had expected. In 1887, the company touted its pilgrimage reforms in *The Excursionist*, the company's official publication, predicting that "in years to come the firm will secure concessions from the Turkish Government; in which case the world may witness the astounding spectacle of the *Infidel piloting the True Believer* through the dangers that beset the former's path to salvation."[82] Cook believed that he would be able to negotiate the same kind of exclusive concessions that his tourist operations had concluded so successfully with the Khedival government in Egypt or Ottoman authorities in Palestine.[83] Cook vastly underestimated how sensitive Istanbul had become to the threat of European extraterritorial encroachment on the Hijaz. An early indication of the frosty reception that awaited the Cooks in Jidda came in October 1886 when the firm's representative in Istanbul attempted to get the Ottoman Board of Health to endorse their plans. After multiple attempts by the British Embassy and the British delegate to the board, Cook's failed to secure a letter of introduction. In the end, Cook received a cold reply stating that the Ottoman state would instruct the governor of the Hijaz to assist the British consulate but flatly refused to work directly with Thomas Cook and Son.[84]

The Sharif's Share

Despite British efforts to grapple with the pilgrimage shipping and brokerage industries in Bombay and the government's attempts to better represent pilgrims once they arrived in the Hijaz, British officials in India continually failed to fully grasp the interconnected nature of the brokerage systems and their links to the highest levels of Hijazi society, the Ottoman administration, and the even European consulates in Jeddah. In the Hijaz pilgrimage guides known as the *mutawwifin* (Ottoman Turkish: *mutavvifler* or *deliller*) exercised almost total control over the hajj experience. At the most basic level, they were responsible for guiding non-Arabic-speaking foreigners through the required prayers and rituals of the hajj. From the moment that the pilgrims disembarked in Jeddah until the time they returned home, they were under the constant supervision of their guides. As soon as the pilgrims arrived in Jeddah, they were met by the *mutawwif*'s agent. The agent arranged for their camel transport and protection from marauding Bedouins and delivered them to their guide in Mecca. Once in Mecca the *mutawwifs* instructed the pilgrims on how to perform the rituals of the hajj properly, acted as interpreters, arranged their lodging and access to water, and facilitated their purchases. As a result, pilgrims generally found themselves at the mercy of their guides' exorbitant charges for virtually all basic needs.[85] As Süleyman Kâni İrtem, governor of Istanbul from 1917 to 1918, lamented, "for the Arabs there is no difference between the pilgrims and milk animals [*sağmal hayvanlar*]." They are nothing more than a "source of revenue." Thus even if the pilgrims survived the plundering Bedouin along the road from Jeddah to Mecca, they were unlikely to escape the "second assault" on their wallets at the hands of their guides.[86]

The *mutawwifin* were organized by a guild system subdivided along national, regional, and/or linguistic lines. Each branch of the guild was headed and policed by a shaykh appointed by the sharif. With the help of pilgrims from foreign lands (*mücavirin*) who had settled in the Hijaz, each branch of the guild system gained expertise in the language and culture of its assigned region. In addition to their duties in the Hijaz, guilds also sent their deputies to India to advertise, recruit, and act as intermediaries between rural Indians in the subcontinent's interior, the pilgrimage industry in Bombay, and their operations in the Hijaz. Because the expertise of the *muṭawwifīn* and their local deputies was so specific to each language and region they served, generally membership in this professional guild was passed from generation to generation. These agents possessed an enormous genealogical knowledge base of who had or had not performed the hajj. Working in concert with local religious leaders, these recruiters sought not only to attract new clients but also to inspire more members of families that they had previously served to make the journey. Thus as the government of India eventually would discover, regulating steamship agents and pilgrimage brokers in Bombay attacked only one link in a much larger chain.

In 1886, when John Mason Cook sent his son, Frank Henry Cook, to Jeddah to plan the firm's operations in the Hijaz, they quickly discovered that their own official ticketing scheme in Bombay paled in comparison with the massive monopoly on pilgrimage services being run from Jeddah. At the top of this pyramid sat the sharif of Mecca, ʿAwn al-Rafīq (figure 5.5); a handful of the Jeddah's commercial elites; and a rotating cast of Ottoman and European consular officials. This group controlled every aspect of the pilgrimage experience, including steamships and boatmen, pilgrimage guides and camel brokers.

In 1883, the principals of this scheme approached the sharif to gain his cooperation. In order to ensure the system's dominance, the sharif was asked to force pilgrimage guides and camel brokers (*mukharrij*) to impel Southeast Asian (Jawi) pilgrims to book their return passage at Mecca, where neither European consular authorities nor rival steamship interests could intervene. ʿAwn al-Rafīq waged a determined campaign to tighten his control over the *muṭawwifīn* guild system as a monopoly or syndicate to which only he could grant admission.[87] Prior to his tenure as sharif, theoretically anyone was free to purchase a lifetime license for a particular region. From the mid-1880s on, ʿAwn al-Rafīq instituted a new licensing procedure, known as the *taqrīr* system. Under this system individual guides were no longer free to compete for pilgrims from a particular region. Instead, ʿAwn al-Rafīq began auctioning licenses for control of each region. Rather than issuing lifetime licenses, the sharif forced the guides competing for control over their respective regions to renew their claims whenever the amir's administration declared a new round of bids.[88] As a result, licensing dues that previously cost 30, 40, or 50 lira ballooned to upward of 3,000 *altın* (gold coins).[89] As the bids for control of the Jawi and Indian divisions of the guild became more expensive, it became necessary for the guides to pass the cost on to

FIGURE 5.5 Sharif ʿAwn al-Rafiq, 1888. Photograph by Christiaan Snouck Hurgronje/
al-Sayyid ʿAbd al-Ghaffār. *Source*: BL: IOR, 1781.b.6/7, in *Qatar Digital Library*.

the pilgrims, leading to inflated prices for boats, housing, camels, tents, and
almost every other necessity.

With the organization of this system in 1883, competition for transporting pilgrims was restricted, prices were inflated, and the resulting profits
were shared among the members of the pool. Once the sharif's cooperation
had been secured, pilgrimage guides and camel brokers began to funnel all
steamship business to the monopoly. Owing to the restricted competition,

prices quickly doubled. The extra profits were divided as follows: 25 percent went to the sharif, 40 percent went to the guides and brokers, and the remaining 35 percent went to the founders of the monopoly. (In subsequent years a more substantial share would go to the Ottoman governor.) The original principals included J. S. Oswald (Lloyd's agent in Jeddah) and his partner, Hasan Jawhar (a wealthy Indian merchant); ʿUmar al-Saqqāf (the so-called native agent for the Ocean Steamship Company or Stoomvaart Maatschappij Nederland); P. N. Van der Chijs (the Jeddah agent for Holt's and its subsidiary, the Ocean Steamship Company) and his business partner, Yusuf Kudzi (the British consulate's translator); and J. A. Kruijt (the Dutch consul). In addition to this core group, a rotating cast of governors and other representatives of the central government were brought into the scheme or sufficiently bribed to look the other way.[90]

In order to secure the sharif's cooperation in the monopoly, all non-Ottoman citizens were excluded from the Jawi guild of the muṭawwifīn. In this way he was able to exercise complete control over the pilgrimage guides without the prospect of Dutch or English interference. Each guide was instructed to collect 40 Straits dollars from every pilgrim, preferably before leaving Jeddah. This amount secured the pilgrim's passage home. The muṭawwif would collect a commission of as much as 9 dollars and then turn over the remaining amount to the shipping agents for the pilgrims' return fare.[91]

From the perspective of Ottoman officials on the ground, however, this monopoly achieved far better results than the flood of stranded pilgrims produced by British India. In a revealing passage from Mehmed Şakir's report to the sultan, he compared pilgrims traveling through Singapore with their Indian coreligionists. He cited the role of the Jeddah-based Hadrami businessman, ʿUmar al-Saqqāf. As Mehmed Şakir enthused, if by chance a Dutch Jawi subject runs out of money, al-Saqqāf would cover their expenses. Thanks to this access to credit, Mehmed Şakir claimed that no Jawi indigents ever found themselves stranded in the Hijaz.[92] Certainly al-Saqqāf was not acting merely for the sake of pious charity. He was arguably the most important figure in the Indian Ocean–spanning pilgrimage syndicate that dominated the market that Thomas Cook and Son were charged with "cleaning up." Ottoman officials lavishly praised al-Saqqāf for his generous charity, but in reality, Jawi pilgrims never became stranded because they paid for their return passage in bonded plantation labor.

Benevolent Banker or Unscrupulous Steamship Broker?

Although it is often assumed that the transition to steam navigation virtually killed indigenous shipping interests across the Indian Ocean, the history of the al-Saqqāf family shatters this stereotype. In many respects Hadrami shipping enjoyed its golden age as European colonists steadily suppressed piracy in Southeast Asia. In the 1820s, Sayyid ʿAbd al-Raḥman al-Saqqāf established the family in Singapore. In 1848, the family trading firm, Alsagoff and Co., was established. By the 1850s, the Saqqāfs had started transporting pilgrims using sailing vessels. By the early 1870s, Sayyid ʿAbd al-Raḥman's son Sayyid Aḥmad successfully transitioned into steam navigation. On Sayyid Aḥmad's death in 1875, his son, Muḥammad bin Aḥmad al-Saqqāf, took over the Singapore Steamship Company. By the mid-1870s, the Saqqāfs were making their presence felt in the pilgrimage shipping industry on both ends of the Indian Ocean.[93]

Sayyid Muḥammad sent his nephew ʿUmar to Jeddah to look after the family's stake in the pilgrimage trade. ʿUmar al-Saqqāf's handling of the family business seemed ill-fated in the wake of the infamous *Jeddah* episode in 1880. But by the mid-1880s, ʿUmar had become, perhaps aside from the grand sharif in Mecca, the most powerful person in the hajj services industry. Although the sharif's influence over the pilgrimage industry within the Hijaz should not be diminished, in many respects it paled in comparison with the Saqqāfs' multiregional role in the coordination of labor migration, money-lending services, and steamship brokerage. The sharif had the market cornered by sheer virtue of Mecca's sacred geography, but by comparison, al-Saqqāf was an ocean-bestriding magnate whose operations resembled a global octopus. First and foremost, al-Saqqāf had positioned himself as the primary money-lender associated with the Indian Ocean pilgrimage system.[94]

Probably the single greatest contributor to Indonesian migration to Singapore and the Malay Peninsula was the desire to make the pilgrimage to Mecca. The vast majority of pilgrims traveling from Indonesia to Mecca came via Singapore. There were several reasons for this. First, the Dutch government was distrustful of what it perceived to be the subversive political influence of returning hajjis. Even before concerns over cholera emerged in the 1860s, the Dutch had pioneered predeparture means testing and an examination system on return. However, would-be pilgrims soon learned that they could avoid Dutch restrictions by traveling via Singapore.[95]

Many Jawi pilgrims engaged in an indentured labor scheme not unlike the Chinese credit-ticket system, constituting of a kind of hybrid category of *hajji-coolie*. Typically these bonded laborers or indentured pilgrims were accompanied to Mecca by a shipping agent. On their return, the agent would hand the pilgrims over to a shaykh, who would find work on plantations across the peninsula so they could pay off their passage debts. Al-Saqqāf perfected this system, creating a monopoly that integrated all of the overlapping functions of pilgrimage services, banking, and labor migration under the al-Saqqāf banner. Given that most pilgrims could afford only a one-way ticket from Singapore to Jeddah, when they became destitute and stranded in Jeddah on completion of their pilgrimage, ʿUmar al-Saqqāf would advance them money in exchange for a promissory note in which they undertook work as agricultural laborers on the Saqqāf family's plantation on Kukup Island, the Constantinople Estate.[96]

From the perspective of the British consul at Jeddah and the authorities in Singapore, however, the Saqqāff hajji-coolie system was an exploitative racket. According to the Jeddah consul, a pilgrim contracting with the Saqqāfs would "seldom [be] able to free himself from the clutches of his employers at the end of the two or three years named in the contract.... On one occasion inquiries conducted at the request of the government revealed that men had been detained at Kukup Island beyond the maximum period allowed by their contract." Starting in 1896, the government refused to recognize the contracts for servitude concluded by pilgrims at Jeddah. Following the tip-offs from Her Majesty's consul at Jeddah concerning ships due to arrive at Singapore conveying hajjis under contract to al-Saqqāf plantations, the British Protector of the Chinese looked out for these hajjis to explain that their contracts were not binding as far as the government was concerned.[97] With the direct cooperation of the Jeddah consulate and the Protector of the Chinese, in a sense the interconnected nature of pilgrimage and labor mobility regulation across the Indian Ocean had come full circle.

Despite British claims of exploitation, the Dutch consul-general in the Straits Settlements painted a very different picture. In 1889, he claimed that "out of 200 pilgrims from Indonesia who entered into such a contract with Alsagoff all but ten redeemed their debts within a fortnight. The ten pilgrims who had not paid their debts left for Kukub to redeem the debt by working on the estates, but within a couple of months they had paid what they owed with the assistance of their countrymen."[98] This assessment lends credence to the enthusiastic endorsements of Ottoman officials in Jeddah and a fair number of historians, who have argued that the Saqqāfs filled a critical niche as the Indian Ocean pilgrimage economy's most important moneylender. The contract-tickets served as security for the money that had been lent to the pilgrim; particularly when the labor force on the estates increased, the function of moneylender became the main function, and the contract was seldom carried into effect.[99]

Powerful Hadrami families in Singapore—especially the al-Saqqāf and al-Kāf, both of which had strong genealogical ties to the Hijaz—were critical to the organization of pious endowments, which extended financial benefits to ordinary Southeast Asian pilgrims. These endowments provided loans, paid for steamship tickets, extended cash advances or credit for housing in the Hijaz, and offered a network of brokers and handlers. Ideally this system was meant to insulate pilgrims from the most "rapacious groups of capitalists in Singapore, both foreign and indigenous." Despite repeated investigations by colonial administrators into abuses connected to these operations, many Southeast Asian Muslims felt that arranging their pilgrimages through these endowments would ensure that they would not fall prey to cheats and other coercive schemes.[100] In the eyes of Southeast Asian pilgrims, these benefits might very well have been real.

Monopolizing Mecca

In 1888, the sharif attempted to extend the monopoly on Southeast Asian pilgrims to Indians. He instructed the head of the *muṭawwifīn* not to allow any Indian pilgrims to leave Mecca for Jeddah without having booked their return ticket with one of the members of the monopoly. As a result, the price of return tickets increased by 60 percent.[101] Not coincidentally, in 1888–89, Indian Muslims holding return tickets issued by Thomas Cook and Son began to complain that on their return from Mecca to Jeddah, they were unable to obtain passage home. As Ata Mohammed, then the British vice-consul at Hudayda, and Acting Consul Abdur Razzack in Jeddah reported, the trouble originated within the British consulate itself. Yusuf Kudzi, the consulate's translator and the local ticketing agent for Thomas Cook, had begun pushing Indian pilgrims to book their return tickets with steamship companies tied to the sharif's monopoly.[102] Even more disturbingly, the

Indian *muṭawwifīn* were forcing pilgrims, even illiterate ones, to purchase special Ottoman-printed Qurʾans at inflated prices. If the pilgrims refused either to book their return tickets through the monopoly or to purchase their Qurʾans, they were not allowed to secure a camel for the return to Jeddah or continue on to Medina.[103]

As it turned out, the sharif had overreached. He had failed to include the new Ottoman governor, Nafiz Pasha, and J. S. Oswald. Oswald had long since fallen out with the monopoly and had tried repeatedly to draw attention to the nefarious acts of the pool's main actors. As a result of having overlooked these key figures, the sharif exposed the monopoly to greater scrutiny from the British consulate and the Ottoman governor. On August 11, 1889, Nafiz Pasha issued a public notice in the name of the sultan guaranteeing absolute freedom of choice to all pilgrims.[104] On August 23, 1889, the governor arrested the Indian pilgrimage guides in Mecca. He moved to dismantle the monopoly on Javanese and Malay pilgrims by abolishing the post of chief pilgrimage guide (*shaykh al-mashāʾikh*) for Jawi pilgrims. With the Indian and Southeast Asian monopolies crashing down, Van der Chijs, then acting as the consul for Sweden and Norway, committed suicide and his company went out of business.[105]

Despite the governor's apparent victory, the collapse of the monopoly would be brief. The attempt to extend the monopoly to Indian pilgrims exposed new depths of corruption not only in the Hijaz but also in Istanbul. The Indian pool and Qurʾan extortion scheme included Yusuf Kudzi, ʿUmar Nasīf, and ʿAbdullāh Bā Nāja. Nasīf and Bā Nāja represented two of the most prominent members of the Hadrami merchant community in Jeddah. Bā Nāja was an agent of the Ocean Steamship Company. The Bā Nāja family owned one of the region's most important shipping houses. It also was a major lender for the Ottoman administration in the Hijaz.[106] Nasīf, on the other hand, had long served as the sharif's agent in Jeddah and on the provincial administrative council.[107]

Nafiz Pasha's attempt to dismantle the Indian and Jawi monopolies enraged the sharif and his allies. ʿAwn al-Rafiq reached out to his father-in-law, Ahmed Esad Efendi, who held the ceremonial post of Sweeper of the Prophet's Mosque in Medina (*Feraşet-i Şerife Vekili*).[108] Just as he had done to rid himself of Osman Nuri Pasha a few years earlier, working through Ahmed Esad, the sharif successfully lobbied the sultan to dismiss the governor.[109] Following Nafiz's removal, the monopoly was reconstituted under the leadership of al-Saqqāf, Nasīf, and C. R. Robinson, who had taken over the late Van der Chijs's role as agent for Holt's and the Ocean Steamship Company. Having learned from past mistakes, the new group modified its prices and began to farm a percentage of the overall trade to other companies in order to avoid further inquiries from the Ottoman state or the European consulates.[110]

Between December 1892 and June 1894, Ahmed Ratib (Ratip) Pasha assumed the Hijazi governorship and command of its military forces. He was an imperial aide-de-camp and former minister of the Navy and was deeply familiar with British India and the geostrategic threat that it posed to Ottoman Arabia. In 1889 and again in 1892, he made official trips to India, experiences that apparently helped to forge strongly anti-British sentiments.[111] Even before taking up this position as governor, Ahmed Ratib quickly proved himself useful to 'Awn al-Rafiq's interests. During his investigations prior to taking office, 'Awn al-Rafiq gave Ahmed Ratib a bribe of at least 14,000 lira. In exchange Ahmed Ratib ignored the complaints of local notables against the sharif. Indeed, Ahmed Ratib even went on the offensive, writing to Istanbul, not to complain about the sharif's corruption but, rather, to lodge complaints against Osman Nuri for his alleged interference in the amirate's internal affairs. Thus at Ahmed Ratib's urging, Osman Nuri was dismissed and Ahmed Ratib was appointed as his replacement. It was the beginning of a long and fruitful collaboration between governor and sharif.[112]

Following the arrival of Ahmed Ratib, in 1893, the pilgrimage transport monopoly reached altogether shocking levels of inhumanity and exploitation. In the midst of a cholera outbreak estimated to have struck down more than 30,000 souls, a new monopoly emerged.[113] Prior to the 1893 pilgrimage season, Messrs. Knowles and Company of Batavia had bribed 'Awn al-Rafiq to oust the old al-Saqqāf monopoly on Jawi pilgrims. The new operation was headed by a certain I. G. M. Herklots, a Dutch subject described as a "Javanese half-caste," who, on his arrival in Jeddah, purportedly converted to Islam and took the name Abdülhamid. In exchange for a lump sum of 60,000 Mexican dollars 'Awn al-Rafiq and the governor, Ahmed Ratib Pasha, agreed to instruct all of the Southeast Asian pilgrimage guides to funnel their charges to Herklots and Messrs. Knowles and Co. To achieve this, pilgrims were not allowed to leave Mecca without first having obtained written permission from Herklots. Without this receipt, the camel drivers were forbidden to supply transport back to Jeddah. Worse still, Knowles did not have the capacity to handle the numbers that they had booked. As a result, despite excess capacity and reduced fares being offered by other providers, British and Dutch subjects from Java and the Straits Settlements were trapped in a cholera-stricken Mecca. Although British pressure eventually forced the governor to break the monopoly, many pilgrims were detained for weeks or were swept away by the raging epidemic before the conspiracy was broken up and Herklots was arrested.[114] However, Ahmed Ratib was barely chastened. He flatly rejected the notion that the pool was exploitative, pointing out that the system had been in place for a decade. And in his correspondence with the British consul, he even went on the offensive, questioning why the European consulates had never raised their concerns before. From Ahmed Ratib's perspective, the revolving door of European consular employees, shipping agents, and colonial subjects from the monopoly's inception rendered European complaints hollow, even hypocritical.[115]

In the wake of these naked and flagrant abuses, in April 1894, the sultan once again issued a proclamation guaranteeing complete freedom of choice to all pilgrims, and the positions of the chief pilgrimage guides were eliminated.[116] By July of that year, however, Dr. Abdur Razzack again protested the reinstitution of the chief pilgrimage guides, who were responsible for arranging camel hires and steamship ticketing. As he complained, Yousuf Kattan, charged with Malay and Javanese pilgrims, and Hassan Daood, responsible for Indian traffic, were acting as agents for the sharif. He claimed that both men were complicit in the sharif's extortionate inflation of prices for camel hires.[117] At the same time, Abdur Razzack's accusations against the sharif failed to acknowledge that the flow of recommendations, nepotism, and kickbacks reached back to India too. As subsequent investigations revealed, even the British Protector of the Pilgrims in Bombay, Abdul Hussein, had been complicit in funneling pilgrims to Hassan Daood and the sharif's camel and steamer monopolies.[118] Although Abdur Razzack's protests against the sharif were mostly well founded, as we learned in chapter 3, it is highly likely that his repeated public challenges to the sharif's authority ultimately cost him his life.

The 1890s also saw multiple commissions sent to investigate the region's health conditions and extortionate camel prices and to explore the numerous claims of malfeasance against 'Awn al-Rafīq.[119] In the midst of the international uproar generated by the catastrophic 1893 hajj and the subsequent international sanitary conference in Paris, in 1894, Marshal Asaf Pasha arrived in Jeddah with 40,000 lira and a staff of 150 tasked with the construction of a new hospital and the investigation of the province's latest public health collapse. Eager to rid themselves of Asaf Pasha, ʿAwn al-Rafīq and Ahmed Ratib conspired to ensure his swift return to Istanbul. Before that occurred, however, Asaf Pasha found that Ahmed Ratib Pasha had failed to take adequate measures to safeguard the province from cholera and was able to bring about his dismissal.[120]

However, as Mahmud Nedim Bey explains, inevitably these commissions were corrupted by bribery and influence pedaling before those appointed to investigate the situation in the Hijaz had even departed from Istanbul.[121] Having been dispatched to Istanbul on a similar mission in 1892, Ahmed Ratib was intimately familiar with how best to defend against Istanbul's probes.[122] Thus when Hasan Hilmi replaced Ahmed Ratib as governor in June 1894, he was immediately paid some 2,000 lira in return for his willingness to allow the shipping monopolies and pilgrimage guild system to continue. In turn, Hasan Hilmi spread this largesse to officials in Istanbul so that they would continue to tolerate the syndicate system. Just a year later, in 1895, Ahmed Ratib returned to the Hijaz's governorship, where he would remain ensconced until 1908. And although ʿAwn al-Rafīq eventually succumbed to diabetes in 1905, Ahmed Ratib and Amir and Sharif ʿAlī ibn ʿAbdullāh (r. 1905–8) would continue this alliance until the Young Turk Revolution in 1908.[123]

Even in the face of consistent diplomatic pressure on the grand vizier, the monopoly system endured and continued to reinvent itself with each pilgrimage season. By 1896, the sharif and his associates seemed to have worn down their opposition, foreign and domestic. On arriving in the Hijaz in 1896, incoming British consul George Pollard Devey promptly announced that the monopoly had become part of the customary organization of the hajj. In his opinion, "the pilgrims were not fleeced any more than tourists would be elsewhere in the world."[124] In any case, with Ahmed Ratib serving as governor, consular officials had no one left to complain to.

Despite the well-known excesses of ʿAwn al-Rafīq, the sultan understood that any direct confrontation between the Ottoman state and the sharifate would increase the likelihood that the sharifate might forge an alliance with a foreign power or that open conflict between the central government and Mecca would provoke a violent crisis that also might lead to foreign intervention. Thus in addition to securing the Hijaz and the hajj against external colonial threats, Hamidian prestige depended on the internal stability of the province. Between 1882 and 1886, Osman Nuri Pasha's aggressively centralizing policies and combative style marked a low point in relations between the Ottoman center and the sharifate. After ʿAwn al-Rafīq was able to orchestrate Osman Nuri's dismissal in December 1886, however, Yıldız Palace officials struggled for nearly a decade to find equilibrium in the power struggle between governor and sharif. Between 1886 and July 1895, the Hijaz saw seven brief and largely ineffectual governorships. In their short tenures, each of these governors found themselves bested and ultimately dispatched by the increasingly well-entrenched ʿAwn al-Rafīq.

In the wake of the scandal-riddled 1893 cholera outbreak and the alleged Bedouin attack on Jeddah's European consuls in 1895, in 1896, the *Meclis-i Vükela* (Council of Ministers) considered detailed proposals for the reorganization of the Hijaz's administration.[125] As Ahmed Muhtar Pasha warned the sultan on numerous occasions, this problem was not merely a matter of conflicting personalities. Indeed, the issue was entirely systemic, wholly independent from the individuals in question. As long as the Hijaz's sovereignty and administration "remained two-tiered, problems are inevitable, no matter who is appointed as amir or assigned as governor."[126] He was right to assume that the long-standing pattern of conflict between governor and amir likely would continue unabated. However, as the sultan had learned from previous experience, a policy of supporting an overzealous governor bent on dominating the sharif of Mecca or the Bedouin ran the risk of pushing them into the arms of Istanbul's British rivals.

Thus as much as Yıldız Palace might have wished to exert a stronger influence over the Hijaz and the administration of the hajj, it also needed a modicum of stability in its relations with the sharifate. Given the checkered track record of Osman Nuri Pasha and his weaker successors, it is unlikely that anyone could have predicted that ʿAwn al-Rafīq would find common ground with any official dispatched from Istanbul. In 1892–93, however, the sharif did just that, forging a notorious and enduring partnership with Ahmed Ratib Pasha, who would serve as governor of the Hijaz from 1892 to 1894 and again from 1895 to 1908. Instead of warring over their overlapping responsibilities, the sharif and the governor bonded over their shared pecuniary interests in divvying up the spoils of the steamship hajj. Working in tandem, they leveraged their positions to squeeze more and more revenue from the pilgrims. Through official corruption, graft, and coercion, they would amass the power and revenue streams to bribe or co-opt any official Istanbul might dispatch to investigate their crimes.

But why did the Yıldız Palace tolerate this behavior for so long? As Butrus Abu-Manneh hypothesized, Abdülhamid II very well might have seen an abusive and reckless ʿAwn al-Rafiq as a useful prop. ʿAwn al-Rafiq's despotic tendencies and gross abuses of power over the course of his two decades as sharif—especially his extortion of money from pilgrims through his coercive organization of the pilgrimage transportation industry—effectively would have neutralized him as a potential rival claimant to the caliphate and served as an instructive lesson in the sultan's promotion of loyalty among non-Ottoman Muslims. In turn the sultan's own well-advertised demonstrations of concern for the welfare of pilgrims were meant to stand in stark contrast to the sharif's rapacity.[127]

Conclusion

As this chapter has shown, the mutually constructed discourses of Hamidian Pan-Islamic legitimacy and British guarantees of nonintervention in Muslim religious affairs deeply compromised the potential policing of the hajj's steamship mobility system. Although the Hijaz and hajj generally have been framed as fundamental assets of Hamidian Pan-Islamic legitimacy and accepted as prime outlets for Ottoman anticolonial propaganda, in the context of the debate on poor pilgrims, steamship regulation, and passport controls, Pan-Islam proved an enormous liability. The expectations raised by the sultan-caliph's public image made it virtually impossible for the Ottoman state to impose the kind of documentary practices and border exclusions that could have strengthened public health protections while further incorporating the Hijaz into the wider empire's post-Tanzimat nationality and mobility regimes. The imposition of passport controls revealed deep tensions between the universalizing goals of Pan-Islam and the secular imperatives of governmentality and territorial sovereignty. The end result was an almost total inversion of Ottoman sovereignty. The threat of turning away intending pilgrims landing in Jeddah without passports and visas was deemed spiritually unjustifiable and a grave political risk, and demanding passports only strengthened European claims of extraterritorial jurisdiction over pilgrims. In the end, the Ottoman state was left with a hollowed-out pilgrimage visa system, little more than a rubber stamp.

Certainly, these failures were not limited to the Ottomans or the Hijaz. Rather, the interimperial collapse (or even failure to launch) of effective passport and border controls had a cascading effect felt throughout the Indian Ocean pilgrimage services market. Even British efforts to regulate the interlocking steamship transportation markets and their intimate connections with the webs of brokers, financial services, labor migration, and pilgrimage guides on both ends of the Indian Ocean turned out to be deeply dependent on the imposition of passports and round-trip tickets. Without these instruments, individual pilgrims remained imbedded in a continuous supply chain of pilgrim services that spanned the entire length of their journey. These market systems were integrated, but the government regulations devised to check the abuses of the marketplace were not. The pilgrim's journey was segmented between British, Dutch, Ottoman, and sharifal administrations.

The wide autonomy granted to the sharifate placed most of the on-the-ground pilgrimage services industry beyond either the tenuous grasp of the Ottoman center or the influence of the European consulates. Although traditionally the Hijaz's autonomous status has been framed primarily as a problem of Bedouin disorder, both the monopolization of water discussed in the previous chapter and the pilgrimage transport schemes dealt with here also point to the autonomy of the Hijaz's urban elites. The Hijaz's pilgrimage services economy became a partnership anchored by Hijazi political elites, elements of the Ottoman government, Hadrami financial concerns (both Ottoman and non-Ottoman), and a mixed cast of European subjects with the ability work both within and around the political, financial, and legal frameworks of the Ottoman, British, and Dutch empires.

As Osman Nuri Pasha had warned in 1885, the presence of large numbers of non-Ottoman Muslims in the Hijaz's urban spaces—especially in Jeddah—not only opened the door to European extraterritorial influence, it also placed the province's commercial and financial resources beyond Ottoman control and taxation. By the time the Ottoman center began to take serious steps to bring the Hijaz and the sharifate under more centralized control in the early to mid-1880s, the mechanisms governing the industrializing steamship hajj already had begun to crystalize. And the enormous profits generated by this system proved more than sufficient to bribe any governor or commission intent on dismantling it.

SIX

The Camel and the Rail

WITH THE ADVENT of coal-fired transport, the older preindustrial rhythms of monsoon sailing, camels, and caravansaries were transformed into an "itinerary of steam nodes," moving pilgrims seamlessly from railheads connecting colonial hinterlands to steamship ports. As Muslims made their way to Mecca, they were funneled through ports such as Alexandria, Port Said, Odessa, Aden, Bombay, and Singapore. These cosmopolitan steamship hubs were at once microcosms of nineteenth-century globalization and exhibits of colonial modernization. In the process, pilgrims were exposed to a new kind of hajj experience, a mechanized pilgrimage that was punctuated increasingly by encounters with the non-Muslim world and highly distinct from the "memory space" of a preindustrial Muslim world.

Yet in the face of these sweeping transformations, the Hijaz itself has been described consistently as a world *almost* beyond the reach of steamship globalization. According to this logic, once pilgrims disembarked in Jeddah, they all but left the age of steam and colonial modernity behind. And for the final forty or so miles from Jeddah to Mecca, pilgrims found themselves transported back in time to an unchanging landscape of Bedouin camel transport "virtually untouched by mechanization." Although "encompassed by the industrial underpinnings of a non-Muslim world," the Hijaz itself remained stuck, "as though in a kind of ritual quarantine," leaving Mecca as "the last place on the journey to retain the old sacred space-time of the hajj."[1]

Following this line of thinking, the Hijaz's integration into the world of industrial communications began in earnest only with the Ottoman construction of the Hijaz telegraph and rail lines between 1899 and 1908. Ultimately this process would not come to fruition until Saudi Arabia's petroleum dynasty began to emerge from the 1930s on. As a result, the deceleration from modern steamship to the seemingly archaic world of camels and caravans was a jarring, often unwelcome transition for most colonial pilgrims. Numerous travel narratives and hajj diaries from the period make at least some comment on the experience—or at least the perceived risk—of Bedouin raiding, banditry, robbery, and extortion. Until the Saudis gained dominance in 1924–25, this threat was well documented by individual pilgrims, European consular letters, and Ottoman state archives.[2] For Ottoman administrators, Bedouin disorder was perhaps the most galling and embarrassing feature of the late Ottoman hajj.[3] Unlike cholera, which the Ottomans could, with confidence, blame on British India, Bedouin violence and mistreatment of pilgrims were undeniable symptoms of the limitations of Ottoman sovereignty. On the one hand, securing pilgrims from Bedouin violence was a traditional metric of the caliph's responsibilities to the hajj and the holy places. On the other hand, Ottoman and colonial frustration with Bedouin violence also reflected the ways in which both parties' expectations of centralization and sovereignty had shifted. The Ottoman state's traditional practices of seasonal negotiation with the Bedouin, balanced between subsidies and military force, no longer lived up to the ideals and expectations of post-Tanzimat officialdom, European observers, or Muslim colonial subjects. As a result, the Bedouin and their camels became powerful symbols of the dissonance between the perceived administrative and infrastructural order of the steamship route and the underdeveloped disorder, disease, squalor, and violence of the Hijaz. Here, though, it is worth noting that Indian and other non-Ottoman pilgrimage writings often echoed official colonial critiques of Ottoman maladministration. And even when appropriate technological solutions were applied in the Hijaz, as was the case of the disinfection and condenser machines featured in chapters 3 and 4, Ottoman development efforts were not always universally appreciated by pilgrims either.

Although there is considerable truth in pilgrims' assessment of Mecca's relative underdevelopment, such criticisms nevertheless were grounded in certain assumptions about which forms of transport counted as industrialized, modern, and safe and those deemed traditional, backward, and unsafe. Given the often grisly health and safety record of European-owned and -operated steamships, which also received their fair share of complaints from pilgrims, this sharp division between the perceived safety of caravan and steamship transport seems questionable. Even if we accept all of the derision heaped on the hajj's final caravan leg, should we assume that preindustrial forms of desert mobility, such as Bedouin-controlled camel caravans, actually stood apart from the industrialization and commercialization of steam? This chapter argues that neither the camel caravan industry nor its Bedouin laborers escaped the changes wrought by steam transport. As Valeska Huber points out, though it is often assumed that camel caravans and Bedouin mobility could be decelerated, circumscribed, or even made obsolete by the onslaught of steam and rail, often the opposite was true. The construction of the Suez Canal and the expansion of steamship routes, railways, and telegraph lines in Egypt, the Red Sea, and, eventually, the Hijaz were deeply entangled with—even dependent on—preexisting circuits of camel transport and labor.[4]

As On Barak cautions, historians often have been too keen to depict the advent of fossil-fueled transport as a kind of immediate revolution that rapidly overturned previous forms of energy such as those derived from human muscles or beasts of burden. In reality, the transition to coal and steam was, for many years, deeply dependent on older energy and mobility regimes. In other words, the infrastructures needed for the introduction of steam included sailing ships that stocked coal stores and the camel caravans that did so from land.[5] Thus, although Richard Bulliet, Dawn Chatty, and Alan Mikhail have all noted how steam power and, eventually, automobility gradually decreased the economic importance of animals as muscle power in Egypt, Arabia, and the broader Middle East, these transitions also tended to temporarily increase the importance and visibility of animal power.[6] Initially railways required camel caravans to offload their goods or to supply them with water or materiel for track construction. Thus camel caravans would continue to linger as critical appendages to steamship and rail routes until well into the next global energy transformation from coal to petroleum. As a result, the Bedouin and their camels were definitely not functioning in a world apart from industrialized transport. Their labor either could extend and facilitate the advance of steam and rail transport or hobble and halt it.[7]

For obvious reasons, most scholarship on the relationship between steam transport and Bedouin camel traffic has tended to emphasize the pressures that steam and rail placed on nomadic populations and the caravan trade on which they depended. In the long term this was certainly true. However, the impacts of steam technologies were not evenly distributed. For example, with the opening of the Suez Canal, caravan traffic through and from Egypt declined as the transport of both goods and pilgrims shifted to steamers. Previously insignificant port cities blossomed while older inland hajj stations saw comparatively fewer pilgrims. Nevertheless, not all locations along the steamship hajj route experienced its arrival as an economic loss.[8] Although the steamship robbed long-distance caravan routes of many thousands of customers, certain segments of the hajj route—particularly those attached to major ports—experienced dramatic economic growth. Nowhere was this increased demand more concentrated than in Jeddah. As the number of pilgrims arriving from the Black Sea, Mediterranean, and Indian Ocean exploded, the Hijaz's camel industry experienced an unprecedented spike in demand for transit between Jeddah and Mecca and on to Medina.

As we learned in the previous chapter, between 1883 and 1908, Sharif ʿAwn al-Rafiq and Ahmed Ratib Pasha oversaw the erection and perpetuation of a system of monopolies, price fixing, and graft that integrated steamship ticketing, pilgrimage guides, and camel transport into a seamless commercial and political web. As the sharif, governor, and their allies quickly came to understand, camel caravans were still an unavoidable part of the steamship hajj, an obligatory ritual on which all pilgrims, whether arriving by land or sea, would depend. As a result, Hijazi animal labor and the Bedouins who managed it were critical to controlling all other pilgrimage transport and service industries. Unless pilgrims acquiesced to the terms of the monopoly that the group had created, they could restrict or withhold access to camel rentals and guides. Working in tandem, increased demand and official corruption drove camel prices higher and higher. Because of their critical role in this system, not unlike their urban counterparts in Jeddah and Mecca, Bedouin camel drivers (deveciler) also experienced something of a golden age of steamship-driven demand.

It is well documented that this monopoly system played a key role in undermining Ottoman and colonial efforts to manage the protracted logistical, environmental, and public health crises sparked by steamship-era cholera outbreaks. However, the story of vulnerable pilgrims fleeced by pilgrimage brokers and camel drivers told in both the Ottoman and colonial sources invariably fails to consider how the rapid commercialization of the steamship hajj affected and incentivized the economic and political behavior of Ottoman officials, the sharif of Mecca, and the Bedouin and their ungulate companions. Both this increased demand and the monopoly system that grew up around it were paradoxically tied to—not separate from—the use of steam technology at sea. Thus the material interface between the roaring Indian Ocean steamship market and Bedouin camel transport provides a fresh angle for rethinking Bedouin and urban Hijazi resistance to the Ottoman construction of telegraph and rail lines in the Hijaz. Rather than viewing resistance to these projects as atavistic, backward responses to Ottoman modernization and centralization, this chapter contends that Istanbul's relatively late-arriving communications and transport technologies represented a grave threat to the lucrative marriage between Bedouin animal labor and the already well-established economic and political structures that had grown up alongside the steamship-driven Indian Ocean pilgrimage market.

Speeding Past the Bedouin: Infrastructural Imaginings of the Hijaz Railway

From the 1860s on, the globalization of steam and rail technologies encouraged numerous Ottoman and non-Ottoman observers to reimagine the Hijaz's transportation and communications systems. Over the course of the final decades of the nineteenth century, the steamship-era hajj helped to catapult the once isolated imperial backwater of the Hijaz into the heart of international public health consciousness and the European colonial imagination. As the annual hardships facing Muslim colonial subjects making the hajj became ever more notorious, the Ottoman state's modernizing technocrats, military men, engineers, and physicians became increasingly anxious about the relationships among the Hijaz's compromised sovereignty, the hajj's insecurity, and the potential for European intervention. In this sense the colonial hajj—and the new risks that it entailed—simultaneously acted as a midwife and an obstacle to the penultimate expression of Ottoman frontier technopolitics, the construction of the nearly 1,500-kilometer Hijaz Railway.

Although the Hijaz Railway project rightfully has been associated with Hamidian Pan-Islamic symbolism, foreign policy, fundraising, and propaganda efforts directed toward India and the rest of the Islamic world, it is important to recall that this massively ambitious infrastructure project was not conceived entirely within the walls of Yıldız Palace, nor were these later symbolic uses chief among its original driving forces.[9] Rather, the project bubbled up from the technocratic experiences of officials on the ground who were grappling with the practical and material challenges of provincial rule and pilgrimage administration on the empire's tribal frontier. It was seen as a "technological fix," a kind of shortcut through which the Hijaz and the sharifate's traditional constitutional statuses could be remolded and renegotiated, not through direct military confrontation with the sharif and the Bedouin or an aggressive program of legal and administrative reforms to consolidate power in the hands of the province's governor, but through the construction of new material facts on the ground.[10]

In 1864, Charles F. Zimpel, a German American civil engineer, was the first to suggest a railway connecting Syria and the Red Sea. Ultimately Zimpel's idea would be realized four decades later. However, initial reactions to this first proposal were telling. As the French consul in Jeddah pointed out, the sharif flatly opposed the advance of any railway project in the region. As would continue to be the case decades later, the Amirate of Mecca feared that the railway would disrupt its control over camel transport, which would diminish its income as well as its political power over the Bedouin. Although Zimpel had anticipated this criticism, expert opinion was overwhelmingly convinced that even if Bedouin resistance could be overcome, the likely cost of the project was prohibitively high.[11]

The first senior Ottoman military official to propose a rail link with the Hijaz was Ahmed Reşid Pasha. Following his participation in the reconquest of Yemen in 1871–73, in 1874, Ahmed Reşid lamented the extreme difficulties that he had experienced in the deployment of Ottoman soldiers to the Red Sea. He came to believe that the only way to overcome these challenges was to build a railway from Damascus to Mecca and on to Jeddah. As he noted, the ability to defend the Hijaz and the empire's Arabian possessions was a critical underpinning of the caliphate and the House of Osman's legitimacy.[12]

In 1880, then Minister of Public Works Hasan Fehmi Pasha also suggested a rail link to the Hijaz in a long memorandum submitted to the grand vizier.

Hasan Fehmi's wide-ranging proposal laid out a comprehensive vision of the Ottoman state's future infrastructural needs. In many respects Hasan Fehmi's proposed grand railway line, connecting Anatolia and the empire's Arab lands, anticipated what became the Berlin-Baghdad project but also included a secondary Hijaz line.[13]

By 1882, the collective process of imagining how a railway might function in the Hijaz gained and sustained momentum. As the glare of the international attention focused on the safety and security of the hajj intensified, British, Indian, and Ottoman observers speculated on the potential benefits of rail links to or within the Hijaz. In 1882, Wilfrid Scawen Blunt proposed British imperial support for construction of a railway from Jeddah to Mecca as part of a wider project to demonstrate London's commitment to the efficient regulation of hajj transport and the protection of the Queen's pilgrim subjects.[14] In the 1892 Madras petition, featured at the beginning of the previous chapter, Indian pilgrims had lobbied for the construction of a 74-kilmoter rail link that would have eliminated the dangerous two-day (18–24-hour) camel journey between Jeddah and Mecca. Indeed, the 1,400-kilometer Damascus-Medina line—with an estimated price tag of 4 million lira, equal to roughly 15 to 20 percent of the total Ottoman budget—that the Ottoman state eventually built bore little connection to the much simpler project for which Indian Muslims had lobbied but ultimately never received.[15]

However, British and Indian observers were not alone in their calls for a rail link to connect Jeddah and Mecca. Among the earliest Ottoman proposals there was equal recognition of the need to build a rail link from Jeddah to Mecca (or Arafat) in order to speed the pace of the hajj experience. By modernizing the transportation infrastructure of the Indian Ocean hajj's final leg, it was hoped that the duration and costs of the hajj circuit would be driven down. In 1890, Dr. Mehmed Şakir drew a clear connection between the reduction of the financial and physical strains of ground transport and the sanitary defense of the Hijaz against cholera. He believed that by eliminating the camel transport leg of the hajj, the Ottoman state simultaneously could improve the health and safety of the pilgrims and remove a perennial source of European colonial complaint.[16] As Osman Nuri, then serving as the Hijaz's military commander, argued in 1892, by eliminating camel transport between Jeddah and Mecca, the sharifate's domination of the camel rental industry, exploitative pricing, and the associated dangers of caravan banditry could have been alleviated.[17]

Taken together, these proposals suggest a kind of segregation by speed, separating the fast steam and rail mobilities of foreign pilgrims from the camel caravan's slow-moving, protracted window of opportunity for Bedouin violence and the manipulation of the sharifate. As Osman Nuri suggested, a local company with Muslim shareholders, engineers, and managers easily could have been established for the construction of a light rail link without overburdening Ottoman coffers. However, when he brought his proposal to Sharif ʿAwn al-Rafiq and then Governor İsmail Hakkı Pasha, suggesting that they submit a joint report to the sultan, both men showed little enthusiasm, offered a series of contrived excuses, and generally dragged their feet.[18] It was a harbinger of future rounds of resistance over the next decade and a half.

Despite the wall of resistance that Osman Nuri encountered locally, his proposal was reviewed favorably in Istanbul. In 1892, a commission composed of Derviş Pasha, Ahmed Şakir Pasha, and Mehmed Şakir Pasha recommended that the project was worthy.[19] As Tahsin Pasha's memoirs outline, the positive recommendations put forward by this commission made a lasting impression on the sultan.[20] Between 1892 and 1900, numerous Ottoman officials would put forward similar proposals promoting and gradually fleshing out the strategic logic and practical plans for what the Hijaz Railway ultimately became. Although centralizing critics of Hijazi autonomy such as Osman Nuri Pasha and Ahmed Muhtar Pasha failed to convince the Hamidian regime to directly confront or even abolish the sharifate, this did not mean that their concerns completely fell on deaf ears. A growing chorus of Ottoman officials warned of the need to bolster the Hijaz's territorial sovereignty, limit the sharifate's autonomous privileges, and better protect foreign pilgrims from the harsh Hijazi environment and the predations of the Bedouin. In their respective reports and proposals, Osman Nuri Pasha (1884, 1892), Dr. Mehmed Şakir (1890), Süleyman Şefik Söylemezoğlu (1892), İzzet Pasha (1892), and Ahmed Muhtar Pasha (1897) all came to similar conclusions.[21]

As these proposals made clear, the construction of a railway linking Anatolia, Syria, and the Arabian Peninsula was the only way to bring Ottoman military power to bear on the Hijaz and Yemen, build up modern forms of governmentality and territorial sovereignty, and shelter the peninsula from the growing dangers of autonomy and foreign intervention. Particularly in light of the British occupation of Egypt in 1882, the ensuing Scramble for

Africa, and the intensification of European colonial interest in the Red Sea, both overland telegraph and rail links were seen as essential to insulate the Hijaz and Yemen from British naval dominance in the event of a future war in which communications via the Suez Canal likely would be cut.[22] As Abdül-hamid eventually would make explicit, the interior positioning of the telegraph and rail lines was ultimately a conscious choice on his part. Despite the potential benefits to oceangoing pilgrims, the sultan firmly believed that rail lines built too close to the Red Sea coast would have made them a prime target for hostile European powers, making the rapid occupation of the region that much easier.[23]

As İzzet Pasha, who rose to become one of Abdülhamid's closest advisers and the point man for the Hijaz's telegraph and railway projects, explained in his 1892 proposal (written from Jeddah while he served as the local *waqf* administrator, or *evkaf müdürü*), the traditional methods of Ottoman rule in the Hijaz were becoming increasingly obsolete. In his opinion "sovereignty" in its fullest meaning never had been achieved in the Hijaz. Thus Ottoman rule remained bogged down in an antiquated strategy designed for the premodern provisioning of public safety for the caravan-based hajj.[24] İzzet Pasha and other Ottoman administrators increasingly understood that the traditional relationships among the Ottoman state, the sharifate, and the Bedouin had been "episodic, contractual, and seasonal." In the precolonial, pre-steamship, or pre-Suez Canal era, Istanbul's seasonal projection of military force along the caravan routes was enough to signify its imperial claims over the Hijaz. By the end of the nineteenth century, however, this kind of episodic, uneven projection of force no longer was sufficient. It signified a weak, incomplete sovereignty both in European eyes and increasingly in the eyes of post-Tanzimat officials who were trained to venerate the centralization and homogenization of governmental reach. This failure to suppress Bedouin violence also failed to live up to the rising expectations of foreign pilgrims, who were comparing their hajj experience in the Hijaz with the relative convenience of the rest of their rail and steamship journeys under colonial rule.

Likewise, Abdülhamid's Pan-Islamic image-making further encouraged such comparisons, risking the sultan-caliph's status in the eyes of the Muslim world even more if the material conditions of the hajj experience remained poor. In decades and centuries past, if the Bedouin failed to provide safe passage through their territories, the Ottoman state would have withheld its annual subsidies or waged a bloody military campaign. In the late nineteenth century, however, the threat of tribal punishments was no longer effective. Unrest in the region and the potential that colonial subjects would wind up as either spectators or collateral damage only further contributed to the risk of European pressure and even intervention. In this sense Ottoman-Hijazi relations were no longer strictly an internal matter. In the age of steam there was always an international audience that had to be considered.[25]

Because European empires now were deeply involved in monitoring and regulating the safety and security of the hajj, formerly localized lapses in Ottoman-Bedouin relations carried increasingly internationalized risks. Whereas in early modern times periodic lapses in Ottoman-Bedouin negotiations over the payment of food and cash subsidies resulting in Bedouin raiding and banditry had been an accepted feature of life on the desert frontier, by the latter half of the nineteenth century, the increased expectations of European empires and their Muslim subjects rendered the traditional rhythms of hajj security increasingly untenable. This left the sultan with two choices: either he could maintain the existing system of Bedouin integration, or he could try to reform or replace it.[26] To address this new dilemma, the Ottoman state needed to deploy modern infrastructures of transport and communications to renegotiate the traditional terms of this relationship gradually. In order to install the telegraph poles and railway tracks to do so, however, the nature of Ottoman-Bedouin security agreements no longer could be seasonal and temporary. The construction of these infrastructures required local tribesmen to accept the Ottoman state's "permanent" occupation of tribal spaces that traditionally had been considered beyond Istanbul's authority. To an outside observer, the impact of erecting rails and telegraph poles on the vast, seemingly empty expanses of the Arabian desert might seem negligible. By contrast, as the Ottoman state was well aware, the Bedouin—and, by extension, the sharifate—were very likely to "read" these infrastructural "changes in the desert landscape as a sign of Ottoman colonization of their space," alterations that ultimately posed an existential threat to their way of life.[27]

As numerous Ottoman strategists considered these questions, they understood that this project would require a delicate approach tailored to multiple constituencies. On one hand, telegraph and rail links across the Hijazi deserts were considered essential for the rapid projection of Ottoman materiel and military force along the frontier. Likewise, from an international legal perspective, the mere physical presence of these infrastructures was considered evidence of the empire's "effective occupation" of its territories, providing at least a modicum of protection to forestall potential European colonial claims. These infrastructures needed to "send conflicting messages to different audiences." To its European rivals, "the message was that the Ottoman imperial government controlled the desert." Similarly, the message that the sultan-caliph was striving to modernize the hajj and improve safety and security was tailored to maintain the spiritual and political allegiance of non-Ottoman Muslims living under colonial rule, a factor that also further disincentivized European powers from aggressive intervention in the Hijaz. Similarly, for fundraising and propaganda purposes, the railway's potential to ease the hardships faced by steamship hajjis was critical to its appeal. Although, as the Ottomans' prioritization of the Damascus-to-Mecca line over the considerably shorter, less difficult, and less expensive Jeddah-to-Mecca line makes clear, reforming the caravan sections of the ocean-going hajj, which accounted for the largest, most concentrated flows of pilgrims each year, was of secondary importance to the military and strategic goals of integrating the Hijaz with the Ottoman center.

On the other hand, Istanbul had to strike a more delicate, conciliatory note in its approach to the Bedouin. These projects would be slow moving and vulnerable to Bedouin resistance and sabotage. Thus they would require Bedouin tolerance, cooperation, and even a tenuous sense of "partnership."[28] As we shall see, however, neither the Bedouin nor the sharif were ever fully convinced of the genuineness or permanence of this would-be partnership. As they rightly surmised, once the telegraph and railway were completed, the Hijaz's traditional privileges and economic way of life would be subject to an entirely new set of material realities.

The Price of Security: *Sürre*, Salary, or Sabotage?

Officials in Istanbul were not naive to the challenges facing their proposed intrusions into Bedouin territories. Nearly all of the proposals advocating for the construction of telegraph and rail links to the Hijaz addressed Bedouin tribes as the primary obstacles to their technopolitical reimagination of Arabia. In light of this recognition, as these projects moved from proposal to reality, authorities understood that they were moving into uncharted territory with the Bedouin. Thus before embarking on construction of the Hijaz Railway, the Ottoman government used the construction of the Hijaz's overland telegraph connection with Damascus as a trial run. This decision was both a practical matter of infrastructural scaffolding for the more complex railway project and a test of the state's ability to integrate the Bedouin into its plans.[29]

In his recommendations to the Telegraph Commission, Şakir Pasha warned that even if the project's technical and logistical plans were flawless, the telegraph line's success hinged on the state's relationship with the Bedouin. Şakir Pasha put forward three basic guidelines. First, the Ottoman state would have to wage a concerted diplomatic effort to integrate Bedouin chiefs into the administration of the telegraph and rail lines. He argued that chiefs should be granted state honors and positions commensurate with their status and importance to the success of the central government's plans. Second, Bedouin workers should be treated well and paid their full wages at all times. And third, above all else, the state must honor all of its financial obligations in a timely and consistent manner.[30]

Based on these recommendations, eventually the Telegraph Commission began granting Bedouin chiefs monthly salaries of up to 2,500 *kuruş*, a handsome salary that was comparable to the highest-paid Foreign Ministry officials in Istanbul. The shift from the state's episodic distribution of *sürre*-style or *atiye* gifts or bribes in exchange for safe passage of Ottoman troops and pilgrims to a more regular salaried position was illustrative of the central state's more sensitive posture toward the Bedouin. The granting of these positions also offered the state a new way to control the Bedouin. Tribal leaders who cooperated with the state's infrastructure projects were included in the state's hajj-related security arrangements, and those who failed to do so were excluded. As Mostafa Minawi's research illustrates, Şakir Pasha's gentler ideals of Ottoman-Bedouin partnership achieved, at least at first, some success in ensuring Bedouin cooperation in the territories between Damascus and Medina.[31]

However, the Ottoman state was not a monolith. The view from Mecca was quite different. Even as far back as 1892, Sharif ʿAwn al-Rafīq had shown a distinct lack of enthusiasm for Osman Nuri's advocacy for rail links to Mecca. As government planning for the construction of telegraph and rail lines gained momentum, a clearer pattern of delays, criticism, and even outright hostility emerged from Mecca.[32] In 1896–97, Ahmed Ratib wrote to

Istanbul to criticize the Council of Ministers' plans to build the telegraph line along the caravan route from Syria to Medina and onward to Mecca. The governor suggested that the government would be better off running a submarine cable from ʿAqaba to Yanbuʿ with overland spurs from Yanbuʿ to Medina, Mecca, and Jeddah. Ahmed Ratib claimed that by relying on submarine links, Istanbul could shrink its overland exposure to Bedouin resistance.[33] Echoing Osman Nuri Pasha and a variety of other "frontier experts" who preceded him, Ahmed Ratib painted a vivid picture of a region gripped by savagery and ignorance and populated by men who were unable to grasp the civilizing benefits of the telegraph project. It was a well-worn script sure to be understood in Istanbul.

However, Ahmed Ratib's correspondence with Istanbul contained what in retrospect seems to have been a veiled threat. As the telegraph's construction continued in the direction of Medina, he warned that the government undoubtedly would encounter Bedouin resistance. He chided that the money the government had set aside to ensure the Bedouins' cooperation would provide no real guarantees against attack. As the governor recommended, the only way to insulate the telegraph from Bedouin violence was to avoid the desert expanses and opt for a submarine line. As he contended, the only routes appropriate for overland construction were the roads linking Medina, Mecca, and Jeddah because these were well trafficked and patrolled by Ottoman troops. Reading between the lines, we find that his exaggerated claims of Bedouin "ignorance" and "savagery" were meant to dissuade Istanbul from constructing telegraph and rail links that would have enabled the government to move information, troops, and materiel rapidly from Syria to Medina and onward to Mecca.

Ironically, for all of his bluster about Bedouin savagery, Ahmed Ratib's own financial interests in the Hijaz and the hajj were built on the backs of Bedouin labor, labor that he and the sharif intended to keep under their exclusive sway. Thus by speaking as an authority on Bedouin affairs, Ahmed Ratib was not acting in earnest to protect the government's interests. Instead, he and the sharif were actively working to protect the Hijaz's autonomous status quo and their own pecuniary interests from Istanbul's interference.[34]

Despite the ardent resistance of Ahmed Ratib and ʿAwn al-Rafiq, in 1898, the Ottoman state decided to build the telegraph line along the interior Syrian caravan route (see figure 6.1).[35] In the end, the external geopolitical

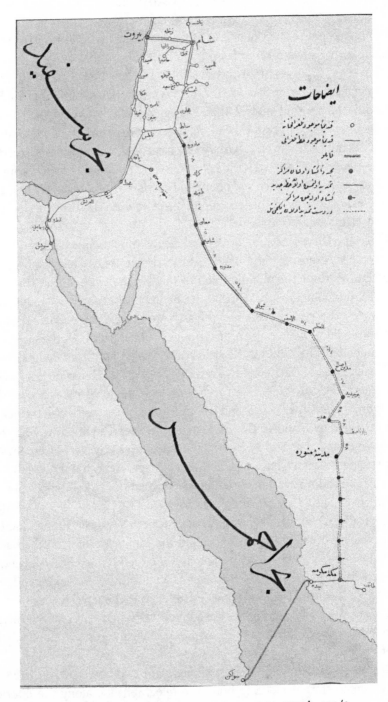

FIGURE 6.1 Map of the Hijaz telegraph route. *Source*: BOA, HRT.h, 475/2.

threats posed by European naval power along the Hijaz's Red Sea coasts overshadowed Istanbul's concerns over the challenges of the interior route's harsh environment and Bedouin resistance.[36] Despite the duplicitous motivations behind Ahmed Ratib's attempts to redirect Istanbul's telegraph construction away from the Medina-Mecca road—the core of his and the sharifate's power base—the governor's warnings proved prophetic. There was no stable Ottoman-Bedouin partnership to be struck. Or, perhaps more accurately, the partnership being proposed by Istanbul offered insufficient incentives for the Bedouin to turn their backs on their preexisting relationships with the Ottoman governorship and sharifate.

As construction of the telegraph line proceeded from southern Syria into the northern Hijaz, Ottoman visions of a collegial relationship with the Bedouin gave way to the realities of the desert environment. Despite the telegraph authorities' best intentions to treat the Bedouin as partners and salaried laborers, in reality much of the telegraph's progress depended on coerced labor from Bedouins and villagers along the project route.[37] Without the benefit of rapid rail transport, which would arrive later, Ottoman officials found themselves deeply dependent on Bedouin labor and camel transport to haul the telegraph's wooden poles and wires.[38] As Ottoman officials took up permanent posts in telegraph stations in Ottoman fortifications along the Syrian caravan route, they also found ruined water basins, which could not support their continual presence. Here again they were forced to employ camels to replenish their water supplies in these remote locations.[39]

In addition to the most obvious issues surrounding the Ottoman state's dependency on Bedouin camel labor, there were also more mysterious issues. Bedouin reports that the presence of operational telegraph lines caused their animals to behave strangely were dismissed by both Ottoman and British observers as manifestations of "native superstition." As scientific research later proved, however, the Bedouins' complaints were well founded. Extremely low-frequency electromagnetic fields such as those created by high-voltage power or telegraph lines have been shown to disrupt large mammals' electromagnetic orientation, causing them to display unusual, confused, and excitable behaviors.[40]

In July and August 1900, as conflicts between Ottoman officials and Bedouin laborers mounted, the relative calm of the first few months of construction gave way by 1901 to a more enduring pattern of sabotage and resistance. At first poles and wires were stolen, but eventually Bedouin sabotage progressed to cutting lines and pulling down poles.[41] Despite these mounting challenges, the Telegraph Commission's work proceeded at a blistering pace of nearly three and a half miles per day. By January 1901, the line reached Medina. However, in the months following the commission's first telegraphic communications from Medina, progress ground to a standstill. Bedouin violence along the road from Medina to Mecca rapidly escalated, likely at the sharif's instigation. As a result of the uptick in violence, work was halted. By April and May of 1901, a Bedouin campaign of sabotage came into clearer focus along the completed sections between Biyar Nasif and Medina. However, as telegraph officials rushed to repair the damage, fresh waves of attacks repeatedly undid their work.[42]

As the work stoppage along the Medina-Mecca road dragged on, officials in Istanbul directed their inquiries to Ahmed Ratib Pasha and 'Awn al-Rafiq, calling on the governor and the sharif to take swift action to investigate and punish the culprits behind the thefts and sabotage. In the face of the mounting threat to their autonomous fiefdom, Ahmed Ratib unleashed a series of blistering replies to the Interior Ministry and the Grand Vizierate. According to Ahmed Ratib, both he and the sharif had been nothing but solicitous in their administrative and financial support of the project. The governor went on the offensive, attacking İzzet Pasha, Sadik Pasha el-Müeyyed Azmzade, and the Ministry of Teleraph and Post for what he claimed was a woefully misguided strategy of rewarding with wages and medals of honor the "ignorant" Bedouin tribesmen who sabotaged the project. In a display of faux exasperation, Ahmed Ratib even wrote that he hoped that the Bedouin would cause the entire project to fail so that he would be blamed and "finally sent back to Istanbul."[43]

Here Mostafa Minawi rightly sees through the governor and the sharif's bluster and bluff. Despite their bravado, the governor and the sharif were deeply anxious that the advance of the telegraph and eventually the proposed railway soon would bring their dominion over the Bedouin and the business of the hajj to an end. Istanbul's traditional worry always had been that the sharif of Mecca would be tempted to partner with a foreign power, most likely Britain. As Minawi points out, no one could have imagined that the sharif would be able to so thoroughly co-opt an Ottoman governor dispatched from Istanbul and turn him against the central government. In the previous chapter, we saw the origins of their alliance. However, to understand the full extent of their brazen resistance to the extension of the Hijaz telegraph and rail lines, we also have to appreciate how the old systems of Bedouin subsidies and hiring of caravan camels were being reconfigured by the brave new world of mass steamship pilgrimage. By doing so we find the lucrative ties that bound these unlikely allies together.[44]

Oppressor of the Pilgrims: The Rise and Fall of the House That Camels Built

In the first decade following the formation of ʿAwn al-Rafiq's pilgrimage services syndicate in 1883, the lion's share of colonial outrage at the sharif's price-fixing schemes revolved around steamship ticketing and the abusive practices of pilgrimage guides. From 1894–95 through 1905, however, the sharif's monopoly increasingly made its presence felt through the pricing of camel hires. Unlike the restriction of steamship competition, the sharif's control of camel hires was less subject to European consular oversight and intervention. After the scandals and investigations of 1893–94 following the Herklots affair, the sharif's pivot toward the camel business represented a second phase in the evolution of his pilgrimage transportation monopoly. This phase also coincided with the favorable conditions produced by Ahmed Ratib Pasha's roughly fifteen-year run as governor.

Most historians of the colonial hajj have focused primarily on the steamship's revolutionary impact, but what generally has been overlooked is that the preindustrial rhythms of Bedouin-led caravan transport did not simply vanish. Though diminished by comparison with past times, the caravans from Egypt and Syria continued (see figure 6.2). Likewise, the ceremonies of the *mahmal* and the traditional Ottoman presentation of the *sürre* purse to the sharifate also continued.[45] In turn, the sharif was free to distribute or withhold the central government's gifts from the Bedouin as he saw fit. As ʿAwn al-Rafiq and Ahmed Ratib Pahsa came to understand, steamship transport remained yoked to the camel. The two systems—the old and the new—intersected and required coordination to coexist, but without Bedouin cooperation and camel labor, the steamship hajj would have amounted to little more than a long boat ride to Jeddah.

As the steamship hajj grew, so did demand for camel rentals. By way of comparison, prior to the 1860s, rough estimates of annual pilgrims hovered

FIGURE 6.2 *Tadhkira*: Document of safe passage for a camel traveling with the Egyptian caravan to the Hijaz (1282/1866). *Source*: Khalili Family Trust, Hajj and the Arts of Pilgrimage Collection, ARC.MX 136.1.

somewhere between 50,000 and 80,000.[46] By World War I, those numbers grew to between 150,000 and 200,000 with some years cresting at over 300,000.[47] As a result of this overall expansion in the hajj's human participants, by the twentieth century the average number of camel rides hired in the Hijaz leapt to more than 100,000 annually.[48]

In his memoirs, Süleyman Kâni İrtem painted a dark portrait of how ʿAwn al-Rafîq and Ahmed Ratib Pasha amassed mind-boggling fortunes on the backs of the pilgrims and the Bedouin and their camels. Prior to Ahmed Ratib's era, the amirate extracted 2 or 3 kuruş from each camel working between Jeddah and Mecca and 20 kuruş (equal to a mecidiye silver piece) for the Mecca-Medina trip. During Ahmed Ratib's era, however, those charges increased to 10 kuruş for the Jeddah-Mecca road and up to 4 "İngiliz lira" (presumably referring to a gold guinea or pound sterling) for the Mecca-Medina leg. As a result of the increased extraction from the camel traffic, the prices set by the chief camel brokers rose to keep pace. The camel fees paid by the pilgrims rose from 3 mecidiye (60 kuruş) to 1.5 or 2 gold pieces (altın or lira) for the Jeddah-Mecca journey and from 4 to as many as 10 gold pieces for the Mecca-Medina trip.[49]

Although the exact figures fluctuated from season to season and differed among the various caravan legs, there is ample evidence to suggest a sustained rise in camel prices from year to year and rapid departures from stated prices within a single season. For example, in 1893–94, we find that Indian and Jawi pilgrims were charged more than 60 percent more than the originally stated price for camel rentals between Mecca and Medina.[50] In 1901, the Emir ül-hacc for the Egyptian caravan, İbrahim Rifat Pasha, reported even more dramatic increases. He recounted how the price of a camel rental between Jeddah and Mecca had been approximately 2.75 riyals in 1885. After a decade and half under ʿAwn al-Rafîq's control, that figure had more than doubled. At the beginning of the 1901 hajj season, the fee for camel rentals from Jeddah to Mecca was supposed to be 6.5 riyals. However, when the Egyptian caravan arrived in Jeddah, the price was raised to 10 riyals and would continue to rise until it reached 30 riyals. According to İbrahim Rifat's calculations, at the time, 30 riyals equaled roughly 5 English guineas. By 1908, he reported that a pilgrim traveling from Jeddah to Mecca, on to Arafat, Medina, and leaving via Yanbuʿ was being charged a total of 17.5 English guineas.[51] Even these expenses paled in comparison with the longer journey between Damascus and Medina, on which an average hajji might spend up to 50 lira on services and supplies.[52]

However, as İbrahim Rifat complained, these price increases were not finding their way into the hands of the Bedouin camel handlers. Instead, roughly 50 percent of the price paid by pilgrims was being distributed to the pilgrimage guides, brokers, the sharif, and the governor. As İbrahim Rifat put it, this was nothing like a normal tax. Rather, the system robbed both the camel driver and the pilgrim and was clearly oppressive.[53]

Working hand in glove, the sharif and the governor forged a remarkably durable agreement to share the revenue extracted from each camel rented.[54] By the end of his term as governor, the scale of the annual camel revenues being diverted into Ahmed Ratib's hands was staggering. According to Murat Özyüksel, for each camel rented, Ahmed Ratib received a 5-lira kickback. With roughly 100,000 camels rented per year, this meant that Ahmed Ratib could have earned up to 500,000 lira annually.[55] For a sense of the scale of this figure, in the late nineteenth century and early 1900s, the total cost of the Syrian caravan and direct and indirect subsidies to the Bedouin along the pilgrimage routes ranged from 70,000 to 135,000 lira annually. During this period estimates of the sharif's annual income were only about 150,000 lira.[56] Even if we accept that the estimates of the governor's income might be inflated, the scale of Ahmed Ratib's graft appears to have been vast.

A deep excavation of Ahmed Ratib's lavish lifestyle reveals a long list of luxury purchases commensurate with these eye-popping figures. As Süleyman Kâni İrtem detailed in his graphic exposé of the governor's gilded existence, Ahmed Ratib Pasha "lived like a Khedive" (bir hidiv gibi yaşardı). The governor spent lavishly on nightly entertaining, reportedly running up monthly household bills of up to 5,000 lira in Mecca and upward of 6,000 lira when in Istanbul. He also is alleged to have been extremely fond of luxury furniture and household goods. His purchases included imported English armchairs, furniture crafted from Coromandel ebony, Indian fabrics, silver candlesticks, and bejeweled oil lamps.[57] While traveling in India in 1892, he returned home from Bombay with a flamboyant haul of silk fabric, doves, and a parrot.[58]

As his fortune grew, Ahmed Ratib also became something of connoisseur of fine jewelry. During hajj season he had access to jewelers from across the Islamic world. However, even this selection could not fully satisfy his sartorial appetites. The governor maintained a lively correspondence with fabric brokers, purveyors of luxury home furnishings, tailors, jewelers, and diamond brokers in London, Paris, Lyon, and New York. Such were the volume of his purchases that he was able to summon jewelers from Europe and North America to Jeddah, from whence a Muslim agent would arrange to transfer the goods for private showings in Mecca. With this kind of concierge service, Ahmed Ratib turned camel revenues into an assortment of rubies, diamonds, and pearls, showering gifts of necklaces, bracelets, and rings on the women of his family. Likewise, he spared no expense in the elaborate customization of gifts and clothes for his son's wedding.[59]

Not all of Ahmed Ratib's largesse was spent on himself. Considerable sums were devoted to the bribes needed to maintain favor in Istanbul. The governor and sharif were careful to make regular demonstrations of their affection for and obedience to the sultan. In addition to sending well wishes on the anniversaries of Abdülhamid's accession to the throne, they took full advantage of their access to luxury imports from across the Indian Ocean.[60] Each year they would send a shipment of Yemeni coffee accompanied by 40 or 50 dirhems (roughly 120 to 150 grams) of ambergris. Ambergris is a waxy substance produced by the intestinal secretions of the sperm whale and is used in perfumes and to add spice to coffee. At a cost of roughly 3 to 4 altın for just 3 grams, it was literally worth more than its weight in gold. As was his custom, the sultan enjoyed taking his coffee perfumed with this rare Indian Ocean luxury.[61]

On another occasion, in 1904, a delegation representing Ethiopian Emperor Menelik II (r. 1889–1913) presented Abdülhamid with a collection of gifts that included a pair of elephant tusks. When Ahmed Ratib learned how pleased the sultan was with this gift, he took the idea a step further, engaging a European craftsman to design a pair of ivory candlesticks.[62]

To get a better sense of the scale and severity of Ahmed Ratib's misappropriation of funds and lavish spending, a comparison with the Hijaz province's overall fiscal health and security situation is useful. In the 1890s, the Hijaz experienced a string of troop mutinies and strikes. In 1894, Istanbul had granted a one-year reduction from the standard tour of duty for soldiers serving in the Hijaz. In part the government's sensitivity to this question stemmed from fear that mutinies and strikes would be visible to foreign pilgrims and the European consulates. Again in 1896, soldiers in Jeddah seized the Akkash Mosque and demanded payment of their back salaries, dismissal from service, and immediate return home. Although their demands were met when new troops arrived, the problem remained. In 1901, more than half of the 3,000 soldiers stationed in the Hijaz had already fulfilled their term of service but were being detained there indefinitely. Provisions for food, clothing, and housing were so bad that some soldiers even sold their rifles to the Bedouin for bread money. The situation reached a climax when the soldiers mutinied and forced the closure of the Meccan Ḥaram.[63]

The military instability in the Hijaz had a negative impact on the region's security. During this period the confluence of sustained ecological and military disturbances appears to have taken a cumulative toll. As a result of the plague pandemic and the serious restrictions imposed by colonial governments between 1897 and 1899, the number of pilgrims arriving by sea dipped to roughly 35,000 per year and began to rebound only from 1904 on. At the same time, during the late 1890s, the Hijaz experienced a severe drought. As a result of the weakness of pilgrimage attendance, the Bedouin were deprived of revenue. Not surprisingly, robberies and raids along the caravan routes skyrocketed. However, even in the face of this increased violence, the governor and sharif continued to extract more and more income from the camel trade and to embezzle substantial chunks of the *sürre* subsidies and food aid that were intended to pacify the Bedouin.[64]

Therefore, it is no wonder that Bedouin tribesmen attacked the telegraph line as it advanced from northern Syria to Medina. Despite the Ministry of Telegraph and Post's attempts to address Bedouin grievances and incorporate them into its construction plans, the Ottoman state in the Hijaz was divided against itself and entirely unreliable. The telegraph authorities hoped to buy Bedouin cooperation while the governor and the sharif were lining their pockets with funds that were meant to reach Bedouin hands and mouths. Long experience also had taught tribesmen that the distribution of the *sürre* subsidies, no matter how arbitrarily or selectively applied, would continue to flow through the sharif's hands. As Sadik Pasha el-Müeyyed Azmzade had advised the Ministry of Telegraph and Post, in addition to receiving regular salaries, those tribes willing to cooperate with the central government's telegraph project should be given control of hajj transport and security, while those that chose not to cooperate should be frozen out of the caravan business. As he saw it, Istanbul's rapid development of a direct financial relationship with the Bedouin tribes was the only way to break the sharif's monopoly on the caravan business and reorient their loyalties. While Sadik Pasha el-Müeyyed Azmzade had diagnosed the problem accurately, as we shall see, he was powerless to overcome the weight of tradition and the ferocious resistance of the sharif and the governor.[65]

Perhaps even more than his taste for jewelry, rare imports, and lavish gifts, the most conspicuous symbol of Ahmed Ratib's ill-gotten gains was the handsome fifty-plus-room mansion (köşk) that he commissioned in Istanbul's Acıbadem neighborhood. The Art Nouveau mansion, built by Mimar Kemaleddin Bey between 1904 and 1908, also became an enduring monument to his disgrace.[66] As it turned out, Ahmed Ratib never got the chance to enjoy his planned retirement in Istanbul. In July 1908, the Young Turk Revolution and restoration of the 1876 Constitution would undo everything that he had built. At first Ahmed Ratib and Sharif ʿAlī tried to suppress the news from Istanbul. The sharif ordered those speaking in favor of the revolution to be whipped. Working together the governor and the sharif tried to mobilize the Bedouin to oppose the revolution. By the middle of August, however, the ground had shifted beneath their feet. On August 19, 1908, military officers at Taʾif openly proclaimed the reinstatement of the constitution. The officers forced the sharif to publicly swear on the Qurʾan his loyalty to the new regime. In addition, he was forced to promise to stop all illegal extortions from pilgrims immediately and to redouble his efforts to maintain the security of the hajj routes. The sharif promptly blamed the oppression of the pilgrims on Ahmed Ratib and was allowed to maintain his position until November.[67] As word came down from Istanbul that the governor had been dismissed, on August 21, he was arrested and taken to the Jeddah barracks.[68] In the jubilation following his downfall, crowds stormed his residence. In the aftermath of his arrest and subsequent investigation, Ahmed Ratib was stripped of his titles and eventually exiled to Rhodes.[69]

In the months prior to the revolution, Kazım Pasha and Arif Pasha had been dispatched to negotiate with Ahmed Ratib Pasha and Sharif ʿAlī the advance of the railway from Medina to Mecca. As Arif Pasha explained to Ahmed Ratib, the railway's progress was of the utmost importance to the sultan. However, as had been the case during the construction of the telegraph line nearly a decade earlier, Ahmed Ratib and the sharif stubbornly avoided declaring their support for the railway's advance. Again, the sharif prevaricated and played for time, asking that the construction be delayed for a year on the grounds that he had been in ill health. Kazım Pasha was livid. As he pointed out, for six years he had been camped in the desert, enduring miserable conditions to make the sultan's dream a reality.

By contrast, the governor and the sharif had played games and shown themselves to be disloyal to the sultan's cause.[70]

In the end, Kazım Pasha's suspicions were well warranted. When Ahmed Ratib's papers were examined after his overthrow, his correspondence with Yıldız Palace favorites, including the minister of the interior, revealed that he had been encouraged by enemies of İzzet Pasha to continue to stall and oppose the extension of the telegraph and rail lines south of Medina.[71] Likewise, as the British consulate reported, İzzet Pasha was convinced that Ahmed Ratib was guilty of covertly fomenting Bedouin resistance, even raising the possibility that he was personally responsible for a Bedouin ambush on Kazım Pasha outside Medina in January 1908.[72] Despite their mutual emnity, Ahmed Ratib and İzzet Pasha found themselves on the wrong side of the revolution. In an ironic twist of fate, both men wound up on the same list of most-wanted Hamidian loyalists hunted by the Committee of Union and Progress. But unlike the fugitive İzzet Pasha, who fled abroad, Ahmed Ratib would not escape CUP justice.[73]

In the end, Ahmed Ratib's long history of systematic corruption, embezzlement, and gross misappropriation of funds finally caught up with him.[74] Thus, even if we acknowledge the hint of sensationalism in İrtem's damning critique of Ahmed Ratib's alliance with the Amirate of Mecca, it remains remarkably well supported by both British and Ottoman archival sources.[75] Ultimately Ahmed Ratib's fortune, jewels, lavish furnishings, and properties were seized by the state.[76] In 1908, his infamous Istanbul mansion, which had become something of a monument to his corruption, passed into the hands of the Ottoman Ministry of Education. In 1915, it was repurposed in service of a considerably nobler cause as the Çamlıca İnas Sultanisi, one of the empire's first high schools for girls, which lives on today as the Çamlıca School for Girls.[77]

As the full measure of Ahmed Ratib's corrupt practices spilled out into public view, he became something of a villainous caricature symbolizing the excesses and failures of the Hamidian regime. He was precisely the kind of official against which the new CUP regime wished to compare itself. As the great Ottoman-Turkish historian and archivist İbnülemin Mahmud Kemal İnal (1870–1957) noted, Ahmed Ratib's long record of abuses against innocent pilgrims had earned him the fittingly ignominious nickname of *Haccac-ı Hüccac*.[78] Roughly translated, it marks him as the "Oppressor of the Pilgrims."[79]

Although fascinating in their own right, the stranger-than-fiction details of Ahmed Ratib's life and career provides a critical illustration of how Sultan Abdülhamid II's deep reluctance (or inability) to sever the amicable working relationship forged between the governor and sharif affected other aspects of the Ottoman state's wider frontier strategy. In turn, an audit of Ahmed Ratib's deep financial and political entanglements with the sharifate, the Bedouin, and the business of the hajj also enables us to better understand his motivations for resisting and delaying the advance of Istanbul's telegraph and rail lines into the northern Hijaz and onward to Mecca and Jeddah. Over the course of his long tenure as governor, Ahmed Ratib became an increasingly sly and formidable guardian of Hijazi autonomy even in the face of Istanbul's determined efforts to bring the region closer to the Ottoman center. Thus when forced to choose between the profits of the Indian Ocean hajj and the advance of Istanbul's frontier policy, the governor and the sharif repeatedly sided with the profits and privileges of the steamship and camel over the centralizing potential of the telegraph and rail.

Moving Down the Tracks

Although a comprehensive overview of the Hijaz Railway's planning, finance, construction, and operations is beyond the scope of this study, a brief discussion of the Hijazi resistance efforts that hobbled this project represents a logical terminus point for this study. The decision to build the railway was the culmination of the Hamidian technopolitical plan to reach deeper into the region. Likewise, it was the Ottoman state's final and most decisive effort to bolster its defenses against foreign attack and bring the semiautonomous Hijaz more directly under Istanbul's legal and military authority.

On May 1, 1900, Abdülhamid II announced his government's decision to build the Hijaz Railway. The project was to be a "sacred line," a Muslim project built by Muslim engineers with Muslim capital. The entire project was to be a material demonstration of Ottoman competence, capacity, and technical and economic independence from Europe. Construction would commence on September 1 to coincide with the twenty-fifth anniversary of the sultan's ascension to the Ottoman throne.[80]

Although the railway was more formalized than the more experimental telegraph line, there remained strong continuities between the two projects. Again, Damascus would constitute the starting point and principal node of the railway's operations. Nazım Pasha, the governor of Syria, would chair the railway's Damascus commission. In late 1901, Marshal Kazım Pasha, commander of the Fifth Ottoman Army in Syria, was appointed to head the railway's Construction Ministry. In 1902, Sadik Pasha el-Müeyyed Azmzade, a Damascus native and the man responsible for the telegraph's extension to Medina, was appointed his chief assistant. Ultimately the men on the ground in Damascus would be tasked with translating the will of the Istanbul-based supreme commission (*Komisyon-ı Ali*) into action at the local level. At the heart of the chain of command in Istanbul sat a coterie of the empire's most important cabinet ministers. However, for better or worse İzzet Pasha would remain the sultan's right hand, the heart and soul of the commission and the project. İzzet Pasha would have the opportunity to learn from (and, it was hoped, correct) the failures of the telegraph project. He would have a second chance to bring Medina and the rest of the Hijaz into Istanbul and Damascus's orbit, to finally render it less exceptional.[81]

Although Abdülhamid long had resisted the idea of a full-scale military occupation of the Hijaz, in many respects the military workforce that was deployed to construct his railway came close to being just that. By 1902, approximately 5,700 soldiers had been deployed to work on the railway. As in the earlier telegraph construction campaign, diplomacy and financial incentives remained critical to the government's outreach to the Bedouin. As the project progressed, however, the railway also took on a more militaristic posture. As construction moved farther south, rail stations increasingly took on the appearance of armed garrisons bristling with barbed wire. As in the earlier sabotage inflicted on the telegraph lines, Bedouin vandalism also forced administrators to switch from wooden to iron crossties. As a result, by 1907, Istanbul made the decision to reinforce the railway's defenses. It was decided that each train would be supplied with an armored wagon at the back, complete with machine guns to protect the trains from Bedouin assault. Eight new fortifications were planned for the Medina–Mecca road, each containing two cannons and two machine guns. Likewise, the number of soldiers patrolling between Damascus and Medina was upped from 300 to 500.[82]

Apart from the omnipresent specter of Bedouin resistance and the project's inherent engineering challenges, the desert itself proved a formidable obstacle. In recognition of the hazards of the work, soldiers were promised reductions in the duration of their service commitments. Three years of work on the railroad counted as four elsewhere, and after two years on the railway, officers could expect special promotions. It was an attractive offer but one that cost many soldiers their lives. Apart from the Bedouin resistance that they encountered, soldiers were subjected to extreme temperature swings from daytime heat soaring above 50°C (122°F) to chilly desert nights. Soldiers and civilian workers on the line were especially vulnerable to the persistent lack of adequate supplies of clean water and good nutrition. As a result, troops suffered repeated bouts of scurvy, dysentery, and typhoid. And not unlike the scores of pilgrims who had succumbed before them, in 1902–03, some 400 railway workers operating near Amman died from cholera, prompting a wave of desertions. By 1906, another 2,000 men were transferred from the Sixth Army in Iraq to replace them. By 1907, some 7,500 men were working their way south while another 1,800 advanced north from Medina.[83]

At the same time that the influx of workers helped to maintain the project's progress from Syria into the northern Hijaz, their presence created nearly insurmountable demands for fresh water, taxing the region's ancient hajj-related infrastructures beyond what they could support. As work progressed south, sufficient water reserves were available only in Damascus, Dara'a, Amman, Ma'an, al-Hasa, and Mudawwara. As a result, workers encountered stretches of 100 and even 200 kilometers lacking adequate wells and reservoirs.[84]

As the project moved to al-Akhdar and Mada'in Salih, administrators unsuccessfully tried to dig artesian wells. When their efforts failed, camel contractors from Damascus were employed to haul water.[85] When these measures proved insufficient, however, officials were forced to import German-made tanker wagons.[86] In addition, German water experts were brought in to identify potential well sites.[87] Even these were only partial solutions. The mobile water tankers could move only as far as the rails had been installed. From there water, food, and railway materiel had to be transferred by camels along the unfinished sections of track. At first railway officials tried renting from Damascene contractors and the local Bedouin. However, as rental costs and camel thefts bloated the budget, they decided to buy 400 camels, but without dedicated Bedouin handlers, many of those camels died. By 1905, the *Komisyon-ı Ali* was forced to bring in its own salaried camel expert to tend to the railway's animal workforce.[88]

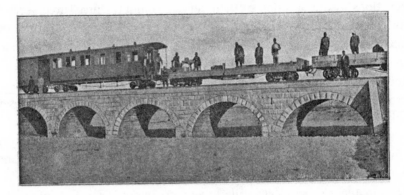

FIGURE 6.3 Hijaz Hamidiye Railway postcard. *Source*: Khalili Family Trust, Hajj and the Arts of Pilgrimage Collection, ARC.PC 433.

As the project progressed southward past the Yarmouk and Jordan River valleys, most of the railway's biggest topographic and engineering challenges had been surmounted, and there would be no need for major bridges and tunnels. However, in the deserts between Ma'an and Medina, there were a number of dry wadis that were subject to flash flooding after rainfall. These physical features required the construction of small bridges and culverts to channel the water so that it would not destroy the railway's embankments (see figure 6.3).[89] Flooding that could wash away sections of track was the biggest threat to the railway's northern reaches, and farther south the railway also would need clay and stone walls to protect against sandstorms.[90]

After completion of the more difficult terrain of the Yarmouk Valley and the Haifa branch, between 1906 and 1908, construction leapt across the map. In 1906, construction of the 233-kilometer section from Ma'an reached Tabuk. In 1907, another 288 kilometers were laid en route to al-'Ula, and by 1908, the final 323 kilometers to Medina had been traversed.[91] As construction drew nearer to Medina, a series of meetings were held there to promote the railway. The city's guild of pilgrimage guides decided to encourage its clients to patronize the railway. At the suggestion of city's religious functionaries, local notables volunteered their time in the construction efforts. In 1907, a delegation of merchants traveled to Damascus for a tour of the railroad's operations. In the run-up to the railway's arrival in Medina, a celebration was planned to mark the inauguration of the Medina train station.

Perhaps most exciting of all was the electrification of the station and the Prophet's Mosque.[92] The festivities were specially planned for September 1, 1908, the thirty-third anniversary of the sultan's ascension to the throne.[93]

Journalists from Ottoman and foreign outlets were on hand to cover the occasion. Kazım Pasha, the organizer of the festivities, and Hacı Muhtar Bey, the engineer who had overseen the completion of the final section of track, were hoisted onto the shoulders of local residents and feted for their accomplishments. As news made its way to Bombay and Calcutta, Indian Muslims read prayers in Sultan Abdülhamid II's name, celebrating the materialization of his visionary spiritual leadership.[94]

However, across the Ottoman Empire this anniversary of Abdülhamid II's enthronement had become pregnant with new meaning. The Young Turk Revolution had stripped him of his authoritarian powers. Likewise, leading members of the old regime—including İzzet Pasha, the mastermind of the railway itself—were now fugitives and exiles. And although the Committee of Union and Progress embraced the Hijaz Railway, the revolution cast the railway's extension in a new light. If the railway was viewed as a central pillar of the Hamidian regime's technopolitical approach to the Arabian frontier, it was doubly so for the sultan's successors in the more aggressively centralizing CUP. Aside from the most obvious changes that the railway promised to bring to the business of pilgrimage transport, it also meant that Medina was about to become a contested borderland between direct CUP rule and the still autonomous territories of the sharifate and the Bedouin who lay beyond its tracks to the south.

The End of the Line

Although the railway arrived successfully in Medina in the summer of 1908, tensions in the city and its environs were reaching a boiling point. Local sensitivities to the uptick in the central government's activities in the region were not confined to questions surrounding the telegraph and rail projects. Like the rest of the Hijaz, Medina was a non-Tanzimat-compliant space. There was no conscription or land registration, and the city, as with the rest of province, remained exempt from taxation. In 1903, Ottoman authorities attempted to impose a sanitation tax in Medina, sparking a riot. In 1904, disturbances in the city also revealed the Ottoman garrison to be unreliable due to its pattern of intermarriage among soldiers and women in the local population.[95]

Against this backdrop it is no surprise that tensions came to a head as the full freight of the Ottoman state came barreling down the tracks from Tabuk to Medina. In January 1908, Kazım Pasha, still supervising the railway's construction, arrived in Medina with a retinue of some 1,300 soldiers, engineers, and laborers. Believing himself virtually untouchable, Kazım foolishly arrested a handful of Bedouin tribal leaders who had refused to support the railway. In the wake of these arrests, he set out from Medina for Rabigh with a 1,000-man escort with the intention of negotiating with tribal leaders in the surrounding area. Just outside the city his party was ambushed. The attack left 7 soldiers dead and another 13 injured. Although Kazım escaped the attack, the Ḥarb tribe effectively closed the road to Yanbuʿ. The road would be reopened only after Istanbul had ordered the arrested tribal leaders be released. But the damage was done. Even after order was restored temporarily, the Egyptian *maḥmal* was attacked near Medina.[96]

Kazım Pasha's punishment of the tribesmen set off a full-fledged Bedouin rebellion. By May 1908, the region was plunged into a cycle of arrests and Bedouin attacks, culminating in attacks on Medina itself. A force of some 3,000 Bedouin fighters attacked the Biyar Nasif station north of Medina, killing 72 people, including two officers. Another guerilla-style night raid resulted in the slaughter of some 300 Ottoman soldiers. Fighting along the railway spread as far as 170 kilometers north to Hadiyya. As the violence escalated, more than 2,400 soldiers were transferred from Dedeağaç, İzmir, and Trabzon.[97]

Despite the troop reinforcements, however, most of the Medina garrison remained tied up in the frantic railroad construction. Work was being carried out in armed groups of 20 to 50.[98] A rolling perimeter was established to keep the Bedouin beyond firing distance from all construction sites. As a result of the military labor tied up in the railway, civilians in Medina were pressed into service to defend the city from Bedouin attacks.[99] By July the rapidly approaching railway and the reinforced garrisons eventually were able to beat back the Ḥarb tribe's attacks and arrest the rebel leadership.[100]

Between July and November 1908, a fragile pause in the fighting was brokered. As Kazım Pasha had tried to convince tribal leaders at the beginning of the conflict, the primary purpose of the railway was to make the hajj more comfortable for intending pilgrims (a claim that was only partly true). Moreover, he had stressed that Istanbul would not discontinue the traditional *sürre* subsidies and gifts on which the Bedouin depended. At the same time, the Bedouin could not help but question what was to become of their traditional livelihood. As British agent Arthur John Byng Wavell explained in 1912, the continuation of the traditional *sürre* payments formed the absolute crux of the problem.

> For many years past the Turks have found it less trouble to pay a certain sum of money to the sheikhs of the Bedou tribes through whose country the pilgrim caravans have to pass, in return for immunity from attack, rather than to send large escorts with them. Though it may well be considered undignified for a civilized Government to submit to such extortions in their own country, there is really no help for it. To occupy and police Arabia in such a manner as would make it safe for travellers, would be at present about as practicable as an invasion of the moon. Neither the Turks nor any one else can hope to accomplish it. . . .
>
> With the completion of the Hedjaz railway the Turkish Government made a precipitate and, in the circumstances, an ill-advised attempt to stop further payment of tribute for safe conduct to the tribes en route. This as a matter of fact did not amount to very much, as the part between Syria and Medina never gave the caravans any great trouble. The news however spread through Arabia and alarmed the more important tribes between Medina and Mecca, and Medina and Yembu. If they were not allowed to plunder and not paid to refrain from doing so—they would be in a bad way.[101]

Although the government and the railway's promoters had proposed a variety of alternative means to maintain the *sürre* subsidies, share ticket revenues, and compensate for the lost income from camel hires and hajj security, often these suggestions amounted to visions of the Bedouin working to haul carts, transfer baggage, or service the railways in some other capacity.[102] In many ways these imaginings breezily conjured a tamer, more sedentarized Bedouin population, but officials failed to articulate adequately how such a dramatic transition would be accomplished. As a result, the tribes were understandably nervous about both their revenues and the permanent presence of Ottoman forces in the region. Owing in part to the Ottoman government's vacillations between the carrot and the stick, fears turned into wild rumors that once the railway was completed, a prohibition on camel transport would be imposed. Thus when the government failed to deliver and even tried to suspend *sürre* payments, the Bedouins' worst fears were confirmed.

In an attempt to end the sporadic violence witnessed in 1908 and 1909, the Ottoman government was forced to try and forge a more durable peace with the Bedouin. In the negotiations, presided over by Sharif Ḥusayn, tribal leaders voiced their grave concerns about the financial distress they would face once the railway was completed. In order to build trust, the government once again vowed to continue paying the traditional *sürre* subsidies in exchange for a nonaggression pact. And for the time being, all construction work on the Mecca and Jeddah extensions was suspended. To continue payments to the tribes, the government also was forced to impose security fees of 50–100 *kuruş* on railway passengers.[103] As a result of this settlement, relative peace was maintained until the launch of Sharif Ḥusayn's Arab Revolt in 1916. This fragile peace did not mean that the CUP government had simply given up its plans to assert its will.

As the sharif's eventual rebellion suggests, the Bedouin were not the only ones worried about the onslaught of change that the railway promised. In the summer of 1910, the CUP government announced that it had changed the administrative status of Medina from a *sancak* of the Hijaz *vilayet* to an independent *sancak*. The separation of Medina from the rest of the Hijaz was a powerful demonstration of the railway's potential to integrate the Hijaz into the mainstream of Ottoman provincial administration, threatening finally to usurp the sharifate's centuries-old privileges and exemptions.[104] When Ḥusayn protested, he was flatly told that "since communication with Medina and the capital by telegraph and railway is now direct, the governorship of Medina may now be considered independent, and directly under the Ministry of Interior and not the Province of the Hijaz."[105]

From 1910 on, the battle lines were drawn between the CUP's desire to end Hijazi autonomy and the sharif's desperate struggle to maintain his traditional privileges. Between 1910 and 1913, the CUP repeatedly tried and failed to relaunch construction of the railway. Having given up on the idea of proceeding directly from Medina, they revived plans for the much shorter Jeddah–Mecca line, calculated at a cost of only 180,000 lira. After its construction, the government believed that the remaining Mecca–Medina segment could be funded easily by ticket sales from Indian Ocean pilgrims. However, without the cooperation of the amirate, the project proved impossible. External forces also intervened. With war in both the Balkans and

Libya, and the looming threat of Italian attacks in the Red Sea, construction planning on the Jeddah line ground to a halt (see figure 6.4).[106]

In 1914, the railway's extension was revived for a final time by the Hijaz's new governor, Vehib (Vehip) Bey. A radical centralizer, Vehib took an openly

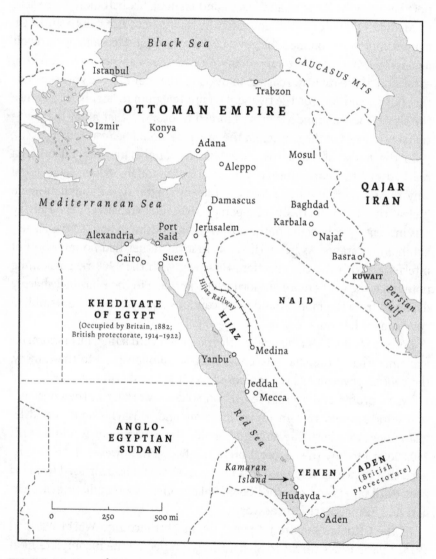

FIGURE 6.4 Map of Ottoman Empire and Arabian Peninsula, c. 1914. Map created by Erin Greb.

authoritarian line with the sharif and the province's inhabitants. He set about bolstering the region's military presence, fired a number of officials, and openly declared his intention to bring the Hijaz under the Law of Vilayets, threatening the imposition of taxes and effectively abolishing all of the province's traditional privileges. In response, the Bedouin blocked transport between the Red Sea and Mecca and Medina. Six battalions were sent to Medina to reinforce the governor. In turn Mecca burst into anti-CUP rioting. A mob surrounded the governor's mansion in Mecca in open revolt against the governor's attempted imposition of the Law of Vilayets and the extension of the railway. Fearing an uprising that neither the governor nor the sharif could control, the two sent a joint telegram to Istanbul. To defuse the situation, the grand vizier was forced to promise that all of the traditional privileges of the sharif and the province would be restored.[107]

In the midst of the crisis, CUP Minister of the Interior Talat Pasha reached out to Sharif Ḥusayn via his son, ʿAbdullāh. When Talat asked why the sharif refused to allow the railway's extension, ʿAbdullāh made it clear that from the Hashemite perspective, the extension of the railway was intimately connected to the government's desire to abolish the Hijaz's autonomous status. As he clarified, at first his father had no intention of interfering with the construction. However, with the 1908 revolution, he noted that the CUP's more authoritarian approach to the Hijaz had sharply departed from the motives and more cautious methods that the Hamidian government had pursued.

Despite ʿAbdullāh's resistance, Talat persisted with a final ultimatum. He explained that if the sharifate could quell local opposition to the railway, the central government was prepared to offer the sharif one-third of the railway's profits and a promise that all soldiers working in the construction efforts would remain under its command. Ḥusayn's sons would be guaranteed to inherit the amirate. Finally, the government would furnish 250,000 lira to buy the cooperation of the Bedouin. However, Talat threatened that if the sharif refused this final bid, he would be dismissed from his post. Both father and son considered Talat's offer as a humiliating bribe at best and insincere trickery at worst.[108]

As the Ottoman Empire prepared for its entrance into World War I in 1914, Talat Pasha's threat to Sharif Ḥusayn reflected the incomplete final status of the empire's long technocratic campaign to integrate the Arabian frontier. After all their efforts, Hijazi autonomy had been battered and narrowed but not stamped out. The Hijaz Railway and the CUP's fever dreams of a centralized Hijaz remained stranded in Medina. For his part, the sharif of Mecca no longer saw a viable future under the banner of the House of Osman. Thus even before the British Empire moved in to secure the ultimate demise of Ottoman rule in Arabia, the long war in the peninsula had already been lost, not to British intervention but to the stubborn endurance of Hijazi autonomy.

Conclusion

On November 14, 1914, the chief Muslim cleric of the Ottoman Empire, the Şeyhülislam, issued a fatwa declaring jihad. It called on the Muslim world to rise up against its Christian imperial rulers. The declaration specifically called out the British, French, and Russian Empires and their allies for their attacks on the faith, colonization of Muslim lands, and hostilities toward the Ottoman Caliphate. He ruled that all Muslims living under colonial rule were obligated to join the Ottomans and their German allies in jihad.[109] The CUP government's declaration of jihad did not reflect a sudden outpouring of Pan-Islamic sentiment. Rather, it was a reflection of the empire's increasingly desperate strategic position. Battered by Italy's 1911 invasion of Libya and the crushing defeats of the Balkan Wars in 1912–13, the CUP viewed its alliance with Germany as the only way to forestall the empire's dismemberment. Likewise, Germany's principal decision makers understood the Ottoman state's strategic weakness and sought to leverage the Ottoman Caliphate's symbolic power to mobilize anticolonial sentiment throughout the Muslim world for its own purposes.[110]

The Pan-Islamic influence that Sultan Abdülhamid II had so adeptly wielded had given the Ottoman Empire a means to remonstrate against and restrain at least some of Europe's darker inclinations toward the global Muslim community. However, as Abdülhamid had well understood, the implied threat of his influence over Europe's Muslim colonial subjects always had been most powerful as a force of restraint. By deploying Pan-Islam in its maximalist form, the CUP declaration of anticolonial jihad had confirmed Britain's and other European colonial powers' darkest, most floridly "racist imaginings" of what Muslim internationalism entailed. In the long term, both the CUP-led Ottoman state and the British Empire would suffer different kinds of consequences stemming from their delusional Pan-Islamic fantasies.[111] In the immediate context of the war and its implications in the Hijaz, however, the Ottoman declaration of jihad would have dramatic effects. Its rhetoric played into decades of British fears and reactivated radical ideas of transferring the Ottoman Caliphate to a Hashemite sharif and imposing a British imperial protectorate over Mecca, ideas that repeatedly had been dismissed as too dangerous by nearly a half century of British colonial policy makers.

In 1913, with Sharif Ḥusayn increasingly wary of the CUP's radical designs, his son ʿAbdullāh was the guest of the khedive of Egypt. During that meeting he met with British Consul-General Horatio Herbert Kitchener. Ostensibly their conversation was supposed to revolve around the improvement of hajj administration. However, it became the prelude to the Arab Revolt. Kitchener and ʿAbdullāh met again in February 1914. During this meeting ʿAbdullāh more directly broached the subject of an Anglo-Hashemite alliance, inquiring whether Britain would be willing to prevent Istanbul from deposing his father. In the event that Istanbul did try to depose the sharif, ʿAbdullāh hoped that Britain would ensure that Ottoman reinforcements could not reach Mecca by sea, leaving the Ottoman garrisons in Mecca and Medina to contend with a full-scale Bedouin uprising.[112]

In November 1914, Lord Kitchener moved to assure Sharif Ḥusayn that if he rebelled against Istanbul, the British Empire was prepared to guarantee his independence against any external aggressors. Reviving the old fantasies of James Napoleon Zohrab and Wifrid Scawen Blunt, Kitchener dared to go a step further to encourage the sharif. As he noted: "till now we have defended and befriended Islam in the person of the Turks; henceforward it will be that of the noble Arab. It may be that an Arab of the true race will assume the Caliphate." In much the same vein, when Kitchener addressed the War Committee in February 1915, he warned that Britain should be prepared to take all necessary measures to secure an Arab kingdom under British protection that encompassed Mecca, Medina, and the shrine cities of Iraq. As he argued, the security of the Muslim holy places would be critical to the maintenance of British prestige among its millions of Muslim subjects. At the highest levels of British government, from London to Cairo and Delhi, the fate of Islam's holy sites, both Sunni and Shiʿi, were considered central to the empire's plans for a post-Ottoman future.[113]

At the same time, however, British administrators in India were nervous about how Cairo's actions in the region might be interpreted in the sub-continent. Kitchener's cavalier language prompted a sharp rebuke from the India Office. As both India Office personnel in London and officials in Delhi were well aware, any British attempts overtly or even covertly to interfere with the caliphate or the Muslim holy places was likely to present grave risks to British-Muslim relations in India and elsewhere. In recognition of the divergent opinions emerging from Cairo and Delhi, in November 1914, the viceroy of India, Lord Hardinge (Charles Hardinge), proclaimed that Mecca and Medina would be "immune from attack" by British forces as "long as there is no interference with pilgrims from India." Moreover, at the war's conclusion the viceroy promised that the holy places of the Hijaz would be guaranteed independence. As he put it, the British Empire would not "annex one foot of land in it nor suffer any other power to do so."[114] In a subsequent 1915 proclamation, the viceroy repeated these sentiments and carefully expanded them to include not only Mecca and Medina but also "the Holy Shrines of Mesopotamia and the port of Jeddah."[115]

However, the die had been cast. In the months following Kitchener's initial suggestion, a clique of British officials serving in Egypt and Sudan became fervent advocates of an Arab caliphate. Reginald Wingate, governor-general of the Sudan; Sir Henry McMahon, British high commissioner in Egypt; and Ronald Storrs, Oriental secretary in Cairo would all come to support an emerging vision of a post-Ottoman Arab caliphate. Thus when, in July 1915, Ḥusayn sent a letter to McMahon proposing the conditions under which he might be persuaded to enter into an alliance with Britain, McMahon and the Cairo-based Arab Bureau responded eagerly. This marked the beginning of the infamous Ḥusayn-McMahon correspondence (July 1915–March 1916), an exchange of ten letters that would spark bitter postwar disputes and permanently reconfigure the map of the entire Middle East.[116]

In June 1916, with British support secured, Sharif Ḥusayn and his son Fayṣal launched the infamous Arab Revolt. On June 5, Fayṣal and his brother ʿAlī, launched their attack against the largest concentration of Ottoman forces in the Hijaz in Medina. There the Hashemites were met by General Ömer Fahreddin Pasha.[117] Fahreddin Pasha had arrived to take command of more than 11,000 Ottoman soldiers. With just 1,500 tribal irregulars, the Hashemites were in no position to take Medina's railhead. Instead they kept

Fahreddin's forces surrounded, leaving Sharif Ḥusayn and his British allies free to operate in Mecca and the rest of the Hijaz.

Mecca fell in only three days. British cannon fire from the sea and bombing from the skies forced Ottoman troops in Jeddah to surrender less than a week later, on June 16. Although Fahreddin Pasha's forces put up a spirited fight for Yanbuʿ throughout 1916, in the end they were some 150 miles from their base in Medina and surrounded by British naval forces at sea and Hashemite tribal fighters on land. With the arrival of British air support near the Red Sea coast, Fahreddin's fighters were forced to retreat to Medina. Ottoman troops were pinned down by an Arab force that was too small to take the city by force but just big enough to keep Fahreddin's men occupied for the remainder of the war.[118]

Despite Fahreddin Pasha's determination to hold onto Medina at all costs, his garrison was wholly dependent on the Hijaz Railway's continued operation. Unable to dislodge Fahreddin Pasha from his garrison or attack the much larger, 25,000-man Ottoman force near Amman, Sharif Ḥusayn's Bedouin irregulars and their British advisers adopted a strategy of attrition and guerilla tactics. Between Medina and southern Jordan, Fayṣal and T. E. Lawrence famously turned the Hijaz Railway tracks and stations into their battlefield. At the beginning of the revolt, an average of two trains per day made their way between Damascus and Medina. However, with Ottoman forces unable to venture far beyond Medina, Arab raids on the railway began to take their toll, and only two trains per week made it to Medina.

Throughout 1917, Arab saboteurs waged a withering campaign, uprooting tracks and destroying bridges and culverts. By January 1917, all passenger service was suspended for the remainder of the war. Beginning in October 1917, entire trains were being captured and a string of stations began to fall to Arab hands. April 1918 would mark the last time that a train completed the entire journey from Damascus to Medina. And with the fall of Damascus in October 1918, the Ottoman administration of the Hijaz Railway was abolished.[119]

Despite his ultimate defeat, Fahreddin Pasha proudly withstood a three-year siege. He steadfastly defended the Prophet's Mosque and the adjoining Jannat al-Baqīʿ cemetery. More controversially, he collected many of Medina's holy artefacts and manuscripts and spirited them back to Istanbul by train. When the Armistice of Mudros was signed on October 30, 1918, the general was expected to surrender. Instead he rejected the armistice and refused to hand over the sacred city. Eventually he was arrested by his own men and handed over to the Hashemites on January 9, 1919. For his stubborn defiance, Turkish historians have lionized him as the "Tiger of the Desert" (*Çöl Kaplanı*) and the "Defender of Medina" (*Medine Müdafii*), a fittingly heroic foil for Britain's villainous Lawrence of Arabia.[120]

With the surrender of Medina in January 1919, four centuries of Ottoman rule over the Hijaz came to an end. By cutting the Hijaz Railway, Sharif Ḥusayn and T. E. Lawrence painfully illustrated the fragility of Istanbul's rail-based frontier centralization in the face of the powerful gravitational pull that Britain's Indian Ocean and nascent Middle Eastern empires exerted over the late Ottoman Hijaz and the hajj. As the sharif understood, at the conclusion of World War I, Britain was destined to emerge as the new imperial power on which his and Mecca's fortunes would depend. Thus in the end, the preservation of Hijazi autonomy and the continued presence of an alternative sovereign and rival claimant to the caliphate came back to haunt the Ottoman dynasty. To be sure, the existence of an Ottoman caliphate around which Muslims from all corners of the *umma* could unite held tremendous spiritual and political significance for many millions of Ottoman and non-Ottoman Muslims during the empire's final decades. However, as this book has argued, the Ottoman caliphate and the legitimacy that it conferred was more than merely an idea. It had always had material and temporal manifestations in the real world. The Hijaz Railway was a powerful but fragile symbol of transimperial Muslim modernity, Muslim internationalist solidarity, and the Ottoman state's ability to administer the hajj effectively and shelter the Muslim holy places from colonial interference. By severing the Hijaz Railway, the British-backed Arab Revolt hollowed out all of the claims that it was meant to convey. Those broken tracks represented the last physical connection, the very umbilical cord of spiritual legitimacy, binding the Ottoman state to Mecca and Medina. Once it was severed, the central pillar of the Ottoman dynasty's claim to the caliphate collapsed.

Epilogue

Legacies and Afterlives

Laying Down the Caliph's Burden

In 1918, a secret memorandum, "The British Empire and the Mohammedans," was produced for the British high commissioner in Egypt.[1] It succinctly laid out the strategic and legal logic underpinning British plans for the transfer of the caliphate to the sharif of Mecca. Playing on British fears that the German kaiser was sponsoring jihad and manipulating the Muslim world through his controlling influence over the Ottoman Caliphate, the report reads like it could have been ripped from the pages of John Buchan's spy thriller, *Greenmantle*.[2] It pulls together a number of British anti-caliphal fantasies and contingency plans for a post-Ottoman future, threads that had been in circulation, though generally discarded as too reckless, since the publication of Wilfrid Scawen Blunt's *The Future of Islam* in 1882. With the Ottoman entrance into World War I, however, British imperial fantasies about controlling or reshaping the Muslim world that repeatedly had been dismissed in the past moved from fantasy into the realm of the possible. When viewed as part of this decades-long intellectual tradition, the report would have been a fitting conclusion to an almost comically ambitious half-century project aimed at nothing less than the destruction of the Ottoman Caliphate and the establishment of British control over the hajj, Mecca, and, by extension, the Islamic world.

What is most notable about this report is that it was not written by a British propagandist or colonial official. The document was produced by a Polish émigré, Count Léon Ostrorog (1867–1932). Between 1909 and 1914, Ostrorog had been a key figure in the development of the CUP Ministry of Justice's secularizing judicial reforms and the abolition of the Capitulations. Before leaving behind his much-decorated career in Ottoman government service in 1914, Ostrorog became the empire's highest-ranking legal counsel (*Bab-ı Ali Birinci Hukuk Müşavirliği*).

Wielding the authority of his Ottoman, international, and Islamic legal expertise, the same tools that he had used to defend Ottoman sovereignty against colonial aggression, Ostrorog turned them against his former masters. After leaving Istanbul, Ostrorog eventually took up an appointment at Oxford University, where he offered lessons on Islamic public law and Ottoman/Turkish law. Ostrorog, like many other pieces of infrastructure and Ottoman expertise, was an asset to be collected and redeployed in service of Britain's expanded postwar dominion over the Islamic world.[3]

And yet, despite his decisive break with his former employers, there is an element of continuity in his work. Even after leaving Ottoman government service, Ostrorog remained intent on advancing the work of disentangling the Ottoman state from the extraterritorial spiritual and political responsibilities entailed by the caliphate. As he mused, "His Brittanic Majesty is the greatest Ruler of Mohammedans in the world." In light of this, Ostrorog believed that Britain was in a position to definitively reshape the Islamic world to suit its needs. He believed that the most beneficial sequel to Britain's military achievements in the Arab Revolt would be to permanently "displace the centre of gravity of Islam from the Turkish to the Arab race," offering them the caliphate as a "token of their reintegration in their ancient state of independence and dignity." Unlike the "dangerously spurious [Ottoman] Caliphate," which rested precariously "on a State secret," an Arab caliphate would, from the perspective of "Mohammedan public law," constitute a "legally genuine Caliphate above any discussion." Although Ostrorog was careful to point out that such a scheme would require considerable caution to avoid the inevitable accusation that crafting an Arab caliphate was merely a trick of "Christian diplomacy," he still believed that the British could simultaneously orchestrate its "restoration" and a "Reformation of Islam" consistent with British values of "human liberty and enlightenment." As he recommended, "it would be possible and easy for intelligent British agents in India and in Egypt to enlist able Mohammedans in this double campaign, Mohammedans exclusively appearing on the stage, although inspired by British statesmen."[4]

Ostrorog believed that stripped of the Hijaz—and, by extension, the basis of his claims to the caliphate and global leadership of the Muslim community— "the Turkish Sultan would be reduced exclusively to his territorial importance." Without the Hijaz and the caliphate, "the Sultan of Turkey would fall to the degree of the Emeer of Afghanistan, of no moral importance whatever in Islam." In turn, "German Pan-Islamism would become impossible, and would be replaced by a Pro-Ally Pan-Islamism." With "Great Britain and France controlling a majority of Moslems and practically the whole of Mohammedans of Arab blood, an Arab Caliphate thus restored and organized, would practically find itself in the hands of the Allies, with incalculable consequences."[5]

This chimerical project of building a Hashemite caliphate was seen almost universally as an illegitimate colonial plot. Between 1918 and 1924, India's Khilafat movement fought valiantly to preserve the Ottoman Caliphate and thwart British attempts to promote Sharif Ḥusayn as a legitimate alternative.[6] From the moment that news of the Arab Revolt reached India in June 1916, Muslim public opinion had been strongly opposed to the Hashemite betrayal of the Ottomans. For the leaders of what grew into the Indian Khilafat movement, Sharif Ḥusayn was a usurper and a selfish collaborator who had acted in pursuit of personal gain and aided the British Empire in simultaneously undermining the caliphate, destroying the territorial integrity of the Ottoman Empire, and bringing Islam's sacred spaces under non-Muslim control. The Khilafat movement channeled a feeling of deep betrayal that Muslim loyalty and sacrifices during World War I were not being repaid with respect for their religious sensibilities, particularly with regard to Mecca and Medina. Unlike the strategic instrumentalization of Pan-Islamic jihad deployed by the wartime CUP government, the Pan-Islamism of the Indian Khilafat movement "reflected genuine anxiety about the destiny of the Muslim world and the Muslim race, which could no longer be represented by an independent empire ruled by a caliph." Khilafat leaders' rejection of Sharif Ḥusayn was a repudiation of Britain's brazenly cynical attempts to manipulate and control the Muslim world. Their attempts to protect the Ottoman Caliphate and the Muslim holy places from colonial machinations reflected their belief in the Ottoman Empire's critical role as a bulwark against the racial inequality and injustice of European colonial rule.[7]

On the one hand, Ostrorog and his British interlocutors were badly mistaken in their hopes that India and the rest of Muslim world would embrace a British-engineered Arab caliphate. On the other hand, his call for the separation of Ottoman territorial power from the extraterritorial spiritual power of the caliphate contained a kernel of truth that, although unpalatable to Indian Khilafat supporters, was clear to both British and Turkish observers. Since Abdülhamid II's time, in addition to its religious and spiritual dimensions, the caliphate gradually had accumulated an international legal personality with critical implications for Ottoman and, subsequently, the Turkish Republic's sovereignty.[8]

On November 1, 1922, Mustafa Kemal Atatürk's government in Ankara moved to abolish the Ottoman dynasty. Just seventeen days later, the last Ottoman sultan, Mehmed VI Vahideddin (Vahdettin), boarded the British warship *Malaya* and sailed into exile. Following his departure Turkey's Grand National Assembly (*Türkiye Büyük Millet Meclisi*) voted to elect the exiled ex-sultan's cousin Abdülmecid II (r. 1922–24) as caliph. With this step Turkey's new leaders were preparing for a radical departure from the Ottoman past. In 1923, the new Turkish Republic was well on its way to the military victories that it needed to force Britain to revise the onerous terms of the 1920 Treaty of Sèvres. With the Lausanne Treaty of 1923, the reimagined Turkish state secured full sovereignty over the remaining territories under its control. In return Turkey renounced all rights, claims, and privileges in the former Ottoman territories of Egypt, Sudan, Iraq, and Syria. Here "the implicit bargain was that Turkey could be a Westphalian sovereign nation so long as the Ottoman Empire was relegated to the past." As the Lausanne Treaty made clear, the new Turkey that rose from its ashes would have no transnational or extraterritorial spiritual authority.[9]

The only remaining vestige of that kind of authority was the caliphate. Despite the Khilafat movement's earnest determination to defend the remnants of the Ottoman Caliphate, for the nascent Turkish Republic the diplomatic leverage that Pan-Islam once had offered the Ottoman Empire in its relations with Europe's imperial powers was now a spent force. For Atatürk and the Turkish Republic, the caliphate and its Pan-Islamic baggage posed only potential dangers. The caliphate continued to enjoy profound spiritual influence over hundreds of millions of Muslims worldwide, most of them living under European colonial rule. However, Turkey no longer had any claims to sovereignty over the Hijaz. The caliphate had been severed from both the Ottoman sultanate and its physical jurisdiction over Mecca and Medina. Even the caliphate's material responsibilities as Servant of the Two Holy Places were now beyond Turkey's capabilities. Indeed, such responsibilities directly conflicted with the spirit of the Lausanne Treaty. As Atatürk would later note, it simply was no longer reasonable to expect that Turkey's Muslim population of just eight million could presume credibly to host a still globally potent caliphate that was "capable of interfering in the affairs of British colonial domains," which were "home to about one hundred million Muslims." Turkey simply could not move forward as a "normal" nation-state without laying down the unique extraterritorial spiritual and political burdens of the caliphate. Nor could this new Turkish nation hope to move closer to Western civilization without decisively shedding its responsibilities as the leader of the global *umma*.[10]

Thus on March 3, 1924, the Turkish Grand National Assembly voted to abolish the caliphate.[11] Only two days after the Turkish move to abolish the caliphate, Sharif Ḥusayn proclaimed himself as the new caliph. Outside the Hijaz itself, however, Ḥusayn's bid for the caliphate attracted more opposition than support. In light of his blatant collaboration with the British, Muslims from Afghanistan to Southeast Asia remained virulently opposed to his candidacy. On March 10, Egyptian religious scholars called for a future conference to decide the fate of the caliphate. Even Abdülmecid, the deposed Ottoman caliph, supported the notion that such a congress might be able to achieve the democratic election of a new caliph by representatives from across the Muslim world.[12] In July 1924, Sharif Ḥusayn organized just such a congress in Mecca, but he failed to attract the support that he and his British supporters once had imagined possible. Although Ḥusayn plotted another conference for the 1925 pilgrimage season, he would find himself increasingly isolated, simultaneously denounced by Muslims everywhere and discarded as a liability by his erstwhile British allies.[13]

On September 4, 1924, ʿAbd al-ʿAzīz ibn Saʿūd (1875–1953) and his Najdi-Wahhabi tribal warriors, the *Ikhwān*, descended on the Hashemite summer residence in Taʾif. However, Ḥusayn's desperate pleas for assistance were met with deafening silence from London. Rather than risk becoming entangled in an armed struggle for the Hijaz, which would have been met with explosive resistance in India, Britain decided to leave the Hashemite king to his own devices. As a result, the Najdis seized Mecca and Medina and then laid siege to Jeddah. Britain limited its assistance to escorting Ḥusayn out of harm's way and into exile in Cyprus and eventually Transjordan.[14]

Decades of British imperial fantasies about the manipulation of the Islamic world through the control of a weak Arab caliphate lay in ruins. And although decades of Indian attachment to the Ottoman Caliphate had been unable to save the institution from the new realities of the Turkish nation, the energy and organizational experience that the Khilafat movement gained on the international stage ultimately was redirected into joint Hindu-Muslim activism, Muslim participation in Mahatma Gandhi's Indian noncooperation movement, and ultimately, the anticolonial struggle for independence.[15] In the short term, the Allied victories of World War I had left the British Empire in an indisputably dominant position throughout the Muslim world. In the longer run, however, it was a pyrrhic victory. In India the Khilafat movement exposed the callousness with which Indian bonds of religious sentiment for the Ottoman Caliphate had been disregarded by British imperial policies. The British had won the battle for the caliphate but lost the war for the continued loyalty of its Muslim subjects. As British colonial officials came to understand, complete ownership of and responsibility for the fate of the caliphate and the administration of the Hijaz was an enormous political liability. Without the Ottoman sultan-caliph to blame, the British Empire finally felt the full weight of the responsibilities for which it had clamored for so long.[16]

Still, Britain had achieved one of its most coveted strategic objectives: the hajj had been severed from Ottoman military and temporal power. The nascent Kingdom of Saudi Arabia was poor, weak, and largely untrusted by the rest of the Muslim world. For the Saudis who ousted Ḥusayn, the caliphate held little appeal. For more than a century, the Ottoman Caliphate had been a symbol of everything that the Saudis had fought to overturn. The Ottoman Caliphate represented the kind of "cosmopolitan Muslim culture that Wahhabi ideology denounced as a deviation from the true principles of Islam."[17] Likewise, due to their violently anti-Shiʻi and anti-Sufi ideologies, evidenced by their desecration of tombs and other sacred sites in the Hijaz, Indians, Persians, and many other groups across the Islamic world voiced their strong opposition to the idea of a Saudi caliphate.[18]

With the Hashemites and the Saudis removed from the equation, no other candidates for the caliphate were able to capture the imagination of

the Muslim world. None could claim ownership of a great, truly independent Muslim empire. Even the custodianship of the holy cities now resided
in the hands of Saudis. Thus when pilgrims arrived in Mecca in 1925, the
new Saudi ruler of the Hijaz and the Najd shifted Muslim attention away
from the caliphate and sought to redirect it toward the material safety and
security of the hajj. In his 1925 welcome address to the pilgrims, Ibn Saʿūd
sought to contrast his stewardship with the corruption and malfeasance of
his Ottoman and Hashemite successors. As he put it, "You are aware that
the previous rulers of the Hejaz used to treat pilgrims badly and despoti-
cally; but, by the grace of God, we shall try as far as possible to put an end to
everything based on bad treatment." As Ibn Saʿūd understood, Saudi legitimacy would be forged and preserved not by the caliphate but through the
safe and efficient administration of the hajj, a policy that sought both to
allay the fears of foreign Muslims and to ward off the interventions of their
European colonial rulers.[19]

Slow Decolonization

Although the Arab Revolt's sabotage of the Hijaz Railway provides the most
dramatic illustration of how the physical and legal bonds linking the Hijaz,
the caliphate, and the Ottoman dynasty were irreparably damaged and
eventually severed, this did not mean that all of the Ottoman infrastructures and procedures surrounding the modern hajj simply vanished. There
were continuities, too. In the absence of the Ottoman Empire, the organization and administration of the hajj ostensibly devolved to the Hashemite
Kingdom of the Hijaz and eventually to the Saudi kingdom, which replaced
it in 1924–25. In reality, however, neither the Hashemites nor the Saudis
were truly capable of overseeing the transoceanic, international, and global
dimensions of the postwar pilgrimage. To varying degrees, both were client
states, extensions of British India's Persian Gulf archipelago of indirectly
ruled or semiautonomous native and princely states, treaty shaykhdoms,
and residencies.

As Susan Pedersen points out, Britain found postwar Wilsonian principles
of national self-determination surprisingly "easy to accommodate." This
was "because they dovetailed so nicely with British imperial practice. British statesmen had always hunted diligently for 'native rulers' with whom

they could ally and trade." After all, "a preference for 'indirect rule' marked the imperium at many turns." Thus although these native princes might run their own internal affairs, they still would be guided by the oversight of British residents or consuls, and their external relations would remain under the British Navy's imperial security umbrella. In the case of Arabia, as Colonial Secretary Alfred Lord Milner explained to David Lloyd George in 1919, "native states" such as the Hashemite Kingdom of the Hijaz or their Saudi rivals in the Najd "should be kept out of the sphere of European political intrigue and within the British sphere of influence: in other words her independent native rulers should have no foreign treaties except with us."[20]

Although, in deference to Muslim sensitivities, the Hijaz was never formally colonized or placed under control of the League of Nations' Mandate system, in the aftermath of World War I, it emerged as an ambiguous space of internal sovereignty and external protection. British officials might have had to admit that Husayn was technically sovereign, but they did not necessarily see the Hashemite Kingdom of the Hijaz as a separate or wholly independent entity from the British Empire. There was a recognition that short of "something like an annexation," Britain could not maintain the kind of capitulatory consular protections that it had come to expect in Ottoman times. And yet the whole point of installing Husayn had been to absorb the Hijaz and the hajj more fully within Britain's sphere of influence. Even sorting out which subjects belonged to the British Empire and which belonged to the Hashemite Kingdom was problematic. Given that at least a third to a half of Mecca's population was of Indian descent and that much of the rest of the population was composed of Yemenis, Hadramis, Somalis, Afghans, Sudanese, and Egyptians, Husayn complained that if the British Empire claimed them all as subjects, he would be left with no one to rule beyond the "Qoreish Bedous [sic] and the pariah dogs of the streets." And although the British admitted that they could not simply "spread the Union Jack over all of the residents in the Hejaz who have any colour of British nationality or protection," they also found it nearly impossible to distinguish Hashemite subjects from "persons who might, by a more comprehensive definition, be considered as entitled to British protection."[21]

In a sense the British Empire's postwar position of de facto suzerainty over a subsidy-dependent, minor sovereign in the Hijaz mirrored that of the Ottoman Empire before it. In the empire's final decades, Istanbul had been unable to fully manage and regulate the rapidly evolving transoceanic hajj on its own. During this period administration of the steamship hajj had evolved into a kind of uneasy partnership of rivals. With the passing of the Ottoman dynasty and the caliphate, external organization of the hajj beyond the frontiers of the Hijaz and, later, the fledgling Kingdom of Saudi Arabia passed from Ottoman hands to the British Empire and Eurocentric international institutions.

Roughly a year before the Arab Revolt, the first shot in the battle for the hajj already had been fired. In 1915, British forces took decisive steps to colonize critical infrastructures of the steamship hajj. In June of that year, the British warship the *Empress of Russia* occupied the Ottoman-run quarantine on Kamaran Island. During the invasion a physician, a pharmacist, an engineer, and five other Ottoman civil officials were taken as prisoners of war. Given Kamaran's strategic importance to British India, it was fitting that these Ottoman prisoners of war would find themselves shipped into exile and confinement across the Indian Ocean. Two would wind up in Aden, where both died. The other six were sent to Hyderabad and eventually transferred to Thayetmyo in Burma.[22]

Britain's capture and detainment of Ottoman quarantine officials was a blatant violation of the revised 1906 Geneva Convention's protections for civilian and military health officials. As Ottoman officials bitterly complained, they believed that the British occupation of the island was meant to "disturb the pilgrims and obstruct their religious duty." In a telegram from Istanbul to Tehran, the Ottomans urged the Qajar state to spread the news that Britain was intent on preventing pilgrims from making the hajj. Given that the Ottoman state had no possibility of challenging the British Navy, this effort to seek support from other Muslim states and to propagandize against this act of British aggression is wholly understandable. And yet however justified the Ottomans' outrage, they fundamentally misread Britain's long-term intentions. Britain wanted to facilitate the hajj and continue to brandish it as proof of its benevolence.[23]

As early as October 1914, Lord Hardinge pointed out that if Kamaran Island were to be occupied in the course of hostilities with either the Ottomans or the Italians, it was very likely that Indian public opinion would see this as interference with the hajj. Hardinge rightly worried that Indian Muslims would interpret the occupation of Kamaran as something dangerously close to an attack on the Hijaz itself. Hardinge preferred Port Sudan as a naval base from which Ottoman movements in the southern Red Sea might be monitored. However, with Italy's entrance into the war, London feared that Italian forces might try to occupy the islands of the Red Sea. In light of this complicating factor, Hardinge acquiesced and even expressed his belief that the occupation could be repackaged as proof of Britain's desire to protect the pilgrimage.[24]

Due to the ongoing hostilities, almost no pilgrims traveled to Mecca in 1915, nor did the British forces occupying Kamaran open the quarantine. The Kamaran Island quarantine station would remain closed until 1917. After forging its alliance with Sharif Ḥusayn, in 1916, the port of Jeddah was opened to British and Allied shipping and a trickle of 6,800 pilgrims. Although oceangoing pilgrimage traffic would largely lay dormant throughout the war, in 1917 and 1918, the British, French, and Italians all managed to send small delegations of Muslim soldiers, carefully chosen for their exemplary service or degree of religious devotion.[25] In 1917, the Hashemite government in the Hijaz directed quarantine operations in Jeddah (see figure epi.1). However, this effort proved so disastrously "inefficient" that the British once again reopened the dormant Ottoman quarantine facilities on Kamaran Island. In 1918, this pattern was repeated.[26]

Although Ḥusayn initially acknowledged Britain's suzerainty over the sanitary administration of the postwar hajj, agreeing to its control over the

JEDDAH. „Office Sanitaire." „Quarantine office."

FIGURE EPI.1 Postcard of the Jeddah Quarantine Office. *Source:* Khalili Family Trust, Hajj and the Arts of Pilgrimage Collection, ARC.PC 294.

Jeddah quarantine in April 1920, by late May, Anglo-Hashemite relations reached new lows. Embittered by the recently published San Remo decisions on the creation of the Mandates, Britain's betrayal of its promises related to Palestine, and its refusal to renew his subsidies, Ḥusayn abruptly reversed his decision. Although the risk of hajj-related cholera outbreaks had declined precipitously over the preceding decade, from Britain's perspective, Hashemite maladministration threatened to undo the hard-fought progress that Ottoman and international measures had achieved. By 1922, only 11 patients were treated for cholera at Kamaran Island's hospital. Moreover, there had been no reported cases of cholera since 1920, and just 44 cases had been documented since 1911. The situation at al-Tur station at the northern end of the Red Sea was almost identical. However, Ḥusayn's intransigence threatened to undermine these gains. His administration continued to insist that pilgrims spend twenty-four hours at the Ottoman quarantine station at Ebu Saad near Jeddah. As a result, pilgrims were being forced to endure a "double quarantine" at either al-Tur or Kamaran and then again in Jeddah.[27] Thus, although Ḥusayn insisted that British interference with the Jeddah quarantine was an affront to his sovereignty, the imposition of redundant quarantine procedures led both British officials and pilgrims themselves to believe that the extra quarantine was simply a ploy to generate additional tax revenues in the wake of Britain's discontinuation of his subsidies.[28]

Quarantine fees were not the only new costs confronting pilgrims traveling during the Hashemite interregnum. Pilgrims were taxed for health certificates, baggage, empty containers, and even the clothes on their backs. The sharif's attempts to fill the void left by the absence of Ottoman or British subsidies also led him to exact an increased share of camel revenues, taking up to 50 percent of the fares charged by camel drivers and guides. Thus as had been the case in the Ottoman era, transport costs witnessed a corresponding rise. As Ḥusayn's subsidies dried up, his relations with the Bedouin also rapidly deteriorated. As a result, he began to lose control of the Mecca–Medina road. By 1923, the caravan routes to Medina had collapsed into chaos. However, the Hijaz's internal security problems were soon solved by the Saudi ouster of the Hashemites in 1924.[29]

With Ḥusayn's failure to provide adequate sanitary services, it became abundantly clear that Britain would have to continue offering quarantine services for Indian Ocean pilgrims at Kamaran. As the settlement of territorial claims to the former Ottoman Empire played out in Paris, British representatives argued that due to "the proximity of the Arabian Peninsular to parts of British Empire and of the maritime communications with India," Britain "had special political interests in the Peninsula and the in the Islands" of the Red Sea. Authorities from London, Egypt, Aden, and India put forward arguments in favor of the permanent British occupation of Kamaran. While the peace talks in Paris largely centered on more pressing problems than those related to the Red Sea islands, Britain quietly continued to occupy and operate the Kamaran quarantine station from Aden.[30]

In 1926, the British and Dutch, the two principal empires administering the Indian Ocean hajj, agreed to jointly staff and regulate the postwar hajj. By the terms of the 1926 Anglo-Dutch Agreement Regarding the Sanitary Control Over Mecca Pilgrims at Kamaran Island, the British civil administrator of Kamaran Island henceforth would act as director of the quarantine station, assisted by two medical officers, one appointed by the British government of India and the other by the Dutch East Indies.[31] The Anglo-Dutch agreement became the backbone of the "Pilgrimage Clauses" ratified in the 1926 Paris International Sanitary Convention. The 1926 convention would require medical observation both in the Hijaz and infected ports of embarkation and aboard ships. It detailed required vaccinations for cholera and smallpox. And as had been stipulated in previous sanitary conferences and conventions, ships arriving from the north were required to call at al-Tur while ships from the south were required to stop at Kamaran Island. Article 93 of the convention also required all pilgrims to have a round-trip ticket and prove that they possessed the financial means to complete the journey.[32] Between 1923 and 1926, revisions to the Indian Merchant Shipping Act finally took the steps that India's colonial authorities had long resisted. Together these new regulations made it obligatory for Indian or foreign pilgrims sailing from an Indian port to purchase a return ticket or make a minimum deposit with the government prior to embarkation.[33] Freed from its half-century rivalry with the Ottoman Caliphate, the sanitary administration of the oceangoing hajj became an almost wholly colonial affair. As a result, the British Empire did precisely what it had proclaimed so often that it would not do: it moved to directly legislate who could and could not make the hajj. The British Empire found itself operating an Ottoman-built quarantine station and enforcing many of the same passport and steamship regulations that it had spent decades obstructing and undermining.

Operating under the auspices of the League of Nations, the 1926 International Sanitary Convention called for the creation of the Office International d'Hygiène Publique in Paris. This new body featured a standing Pilgrimage Commission, which met annually to ensure that the health of the hajj remained under constant European supervision. Working alongside the colonial governments of the relevant European powers, the Paris office and the Egyptian Quarantine Board coordinated sanitary control over the Hijaz, the al-Tur quarantine, and the Suez Canal.[34] In essence the Paris office, an arm of the League of Nations, assumed the international oversight role that previously had been carried out through the Ottoman Board of Health under the terms of the Capitulations. Made an orphan by the death of its Ottoman parent, the steamship hajj had become a ward of the British Empire and the international regulation of the European colonial powers. Outside the Hijaz itself, the hajj had been colonized or—perhaps more accurately—fallen under something akin to the Mandatory control and imperial tutelage suffered by the rest of the Middle East during the interwar years.

This system remained in place until the creation of the World Health Organization in 1948. Though the Saudis had gained political and religious authority over the hajj's land-based elements in 1926, international-cum-colonial control of the hajj lingered on until 1956–57. Much like the slow unwinding of the British and French Mandate system in other parts of the Arab Middle East, the decolonization of the hajj would drag on for another three decades. Between 1935 and 1956, no steamship pilgrims landed on Kamaran Island. The quarantine evolved into a checking station to verify that pilgrimage vessels complied with all international regulations. Nevertheless, the British kept Kamaran at the ready in the event that cholera, plague, or some other infectious disease should threaten the hajj. Although its function as a quarantine station was waning, in 1945, Kamaran's airstrip welcomed its first pilgrims traveling to the Hijaz by plane. By this stage, however, the quarantine process amounted to little more than verification that pilgrims possessed the required medical certifications.[35]

In addition to the receding threat of epidemic cholera and plague, in 1947, India and Pakistan gained their independence amid Britain's ill-conceived partition plan and a spasm of communal violence. Although there were considerable continuities between the hajj policies of the Raj and the newly independent governments of India and Pakistan, the loss of the organizing focus of Britain's Muslim empire portended a dramatic diminution of Britain's role in the organization of the hajj. However, even this did not mark the end of Britain's interest in the administration of the hajj. Its hajj bureaucracies in colonies such as Nigeria, Malaya, and Singapore took on new importance.

As the drama of decolonization unfolded, Saudi Arabia also became more vocal in its calls for an end to colonial control over the hajj. In the wake of World War II, as the World Health Organization began to revisit the Pilgrim Clauses of the 1926 International Sanitary Convention, Saudi Arabia protested that colonial control over the hajj's external relations and sanitary regulation constituted a serious infringement on the kingdom's sovereignty.[36] With the independence of Indonesia in 1949, the logic of the colonial hajj unraveled further still. A year later Indonesia withdrew from the 1926 Anglo-Dutch agreement on Kamaran's status. India and Pakistan were similarly disinclined to support the continuation of this much-reviled symbol of colonial medical humiliation and surveillance. Despite Saudi Arabia's desire to take full control of the hajj, however, in 1950, when the kingdom sent a medical mission to Kamaran to prepare for the final decolonization of the pilgrimage's public health, the Saudis concluded that it would be ill-advised to dismantle Kamaran's battle-tested facilities and staff until comparable facilities could be provided at Jeddah.[37]

After considerable protest from Saudi Arabia and a coalition of Muslim states, in 1951–52 the World Health Organization agreed to phase out the now outdated Pilgrim Clauses of the 1926 International Sanitary Conference. It was agreed that Britain would continue to operate the Kamaran Island quarantine station until Saudi Arabia was prepared to assume full responsibility for the administration of hajj-related quarantines and medical inspections. After five years of planning and construction, in 1956, the Kingdom of Saudi Arabia presented its new Jeddah quarantine facilities to a delegation of World Health Organization inspectors. Satisfied with the quality of Saudi Arabia's new facilities, on May 23, 1956, the Ninth World Health Assembly officially revoked all international controls over the sanitary administration of the hajj. The new regulations came into effect on the first of January 1957.[38]

In 1956–57, the Kamaran Island quarantine station was retired (see figure epi.2). During its 75-year tenure, oversight of the Indian Ocean steamship hajj had passed from the Ottoman sultan-caliph to British and Dutch

FIGURE EPI.2 Remnants of the Kamaran Island Quarantine Station. Photographs by the author.

hands and been regulated by the internationalized membership of the Ottoman Board of Health, the League of Nations, and the World Health Organization. For nearly a century, between 1866 and 1957, the pilgrimage to Mecca, the most spectacular physical and communal embodiment of the Muslim spiritual experience, had been subject to some level of European colonial intervention and interference.

Although Britain continued to maintain a substantial imperial presence across Africa, the Middle East, and the Indian Ocean in 1957, its Victorian-era dreams of leadership and dominion over the Muslim world—dreams that had seemed so tantalizingly attainable in the wake of World War I—had evaporated like a mirage during the interwar years. By the 1950s, the new realities of Britain's greatly diminished global status were slowly sinking in. In 1933, Saudi Arabia signed a concessionary agreement with the Standard Oil Company of California, which led to the creation of the oil giant known as the Arabian American Oil Company (Aramco). In 1938, the first commercially viable oil was discovered in Jabal Dhahran. In 1945, Ibn Saʿūd and President Franklin D. Roosevelt met aboard the USS *Quincy* at Great Bitter Lake in the Suez Canal Zone. Their meeting was emblematic of the emerging post–World War II partnership between Saudi Arabia and the United States. In the decades to come, the two nations' shared commercial interests would lead to increasingly intimate diplomatic and strategic relations. From oil refineries to desalination plants, aqueducts to electricity, and radio stations to munitions, the American government and U.S. corporations would assist Saudi Arabia's dramatic transformation from a fledgling tribal kingdom and British client state to a fabulously wealthy petro-state.[39]

In turn, Britain gradually found itself eclipsed in the peninsula that it had long considered an appendage of its Indian empire. Only a few years prior, Saudi Arabia had been deeply dependent on Britain. During World War II, Saudi Arabia had relied on Britain to keep the hajj open to Egyptian and Indian Ocean pilgrims and to deliver food aid. British and American subsidies to Saudi Arabia topped four million pounds sterling. By 1945, however, as the postwar wreckage at home became clearer, Britain was forced to slash its financial aid to the kingdom by 50 percent.[40] In the 1930s and 1940s, the Saudi state had remained dependent on tax revenues from the hajj. By the late 1940s, these taxes provided as much as four million pounds in a good year. By 1949, however, oil revenues of $90 million dwarfed hajj receipts.[41] This massive infusion of capital underscored

Aramco's and the United States' growing importance to the Saudi economy. By 1952, the influx of postwar petrodollars enabled Ibn Saʿūd to abolish all pilgrimage taxes.[42]

The repeal of these taxes marked a sharp break with the Ottoman and colonial pilgrimage experience of previous decades. In 1926, the fledging Saudi administration in the Hijaz immediately promulgated a comprehensive series of regulations aimed at eliminating the coercive and monopolistic practices of the previous Ottoman-Hashemite eras. At the heart of this new hajj services regime was an effort to bring the *muṭawwifīn* and their guild system under strict licensing and regulation. By doing so, the Saudi state set out to end the "shakedown system" enforced by the Hashemites. Saudi reforms transformed the old Ottoman-Hashemite pilgrimage services complex of official corruption and "unbridled laissez faire capitalism" into something more like a benign "public utility."[43]

Coupled with the colonial powers' belated post–World War I implementation of mandatory round-trip tickets, stronger passport regulations, and new vaccination requirements, the pre–World War I controversies surrounding pauper pilgrims and pathogens lost their urgency. The 1952 abolition of pilgrimage taxes represented the final step in this transformation. The influx of new oil revenues meant that the hajj no longer would serve as a financial lifeline for the Saudi kingdom. Reliance on subsidies and foodstuffs from an imperial power or the extraction of excessive profits from ordinary pilgrims no longer would be necessary.

As a result, by the early 1950s, the imperial logic that once had necessitated the erection of the British Empire's pilgrimage bureaucracy, a virtual protectorate of the hajj, had been all but relegated to the past. Britain's misguided rivalry with the Ottoman Caliphate and fancifully racist and paternalistic attempts to style itself as the world's "great Muhammadan power" came to naught. Cholera was no longer an omnipresent threat to the hajj. India and Pakistan were independent. Even the iconic steamship companies of the colonial era halted their pilgrimage services in 1950s. And, perhaps unsurprisingly, the rapid decline of the pauper pilgrim controversies coincided neatly with the decolonization of Muslim lands and the hajj itself. By 1956, decolonization had made it clear that Britain was no longer in a position to shoulder the burdens that it had once been so eager to take from the Ottoman state, nor did Saudi Arabia or other Muslim nations need or want the British to continue trying.

In addition to the shuttering of the Kamaran Island quarantine station, 1956 also witnessed Britain's humiliation on the global stage. The diminished empire's shameful role in the Suez Crisis drew intense pressure from both the United States and the Soviet Union. Egyptian sovereignty and ownership over the Suez Canal were upheld by the United States and the United Nations. The crisis was a humbling public demonstration that Britain and France were no longer the global superpowers they had once been, nor were they free to act with impunity in a Middle East increasingly shaped by America's Cold War strategic interests.[44]

The Suez Crisis brought an ignominious end to Britain's stewardship of the colonial hajj. In retaliation, Saudi Arabia led an oil embargo against Britain and France and cut diplomatic relations. As Britain's remaining pilgrim subjects arrived in 1957, for the first time in roughly a century, there would be no British diplomatic presence to greet them in Jeddah. Between 1957 and 1971, all of Britain's remaining Muslim territories across Africa, the Persian Gulf, and Southeast Asia gained their independence. Nearly half a century after the demise of the Ottoman Empire and the caliphate, administration of the hajj finally passed back into independent Muslim hands, where it had always rightfully belonged.[45]

Conclusion

This book has described the tangled global crises of Muslim mobility, pandemic cholera, and the interimperial legitimacy struggles that forged the modern hajj. In the wake of India's Great Revolt of 1857–58, British colonial administrators increasingly singled out Muslims as a racialized minority that was uniquely predisposed to jihad and anticolonial rebellion. In 1858, by sheer coincidence, an almost wholly unrelated set of circumstances led to the massacre of Jeddah's Christian population. For British officials, however, these two events blurred into a single narrative of anticolonial conspiracy. Thus even before cholera's arrival on the global stage in 1865–66 marked Mecca as a perennial epidemic threat, the Hijaz already had emerged in the colonial imagination as a haven for fanatical Indian exiles and revolutionaries.

From 1858 on, colonial administrators repeatedly struggled to see the Hijaz or the hajj through any lens other than the perceived threat posed by this supposedly radicalized transimperial Indian Muslim diaspora or as an outlet for Ottoman propaganda and conspiracy. In the decades that followed, colonial officials came to imagine the Hijaz and the Indian Ocean's steamship hajj as dangerous spaces of colonial disorder, vehicles for both medical and political contagion. And although British and European involvement and familiarity with the hajj evolved and deepened dramatically between 1850 and 1950, colonial pilgrimage administration remained tainted by these foundational assumptions.

As British officials became increasingly reliant on ethnographic knowledge to understand and control their Muslim subjects, they thoroughly conflated Islam and its institutions with the roots of anticolonial subversion. However, Islam also became central to the colonial state's efforts to represent and legitimate its mission to its Muslim subjects in India and elsewhere. As a result, although European colonial engagement with the hajj never fully outgrew its impulse to spy on and monitor the pilgrimage to Mecca, over time surveillance did yield new understandings of the day-to-day mechanics of pilgrimage. From the 1880s on, efforts that initially had been driven exclusively by a thirst for medical and political intelligence gradually morphed into a more nuanced effort to position the colonial state as a facilitator, promoter, and even protector of Muslim rights to safe, clean, affordable, and efficient access to the hajj. It was always a deeply flawed strategy born out of an acute legitimacy deficit. As a Christian colonial power, Britain was often paralyzed by the fear that overt efforts to regulate or restrict the hajj—even in the face of dire epidemic threats—would be interpreted as attacks on Muslim religious liberty, which British officials believed would be met with political agitation or even violence.

By contrast, traditionally scholars have understood stewardship over the hajj as the ultimate symbolic asset of Ottoman religious and political legitimacy. In theory, the Ottoman sultan-caliph's status as the Servant of the Two Holy Places, underscored by some four centuries of sovereignty over the Hijaz, stood in sharp contrast to the British Empire's flimsy and often deeply hypocritical appeals to Muslim loyalty. And yet in practice, the advent of the steamship, mass pilgrimage, and the arrival of sustained European extraterritorial interests in the Hijaz all placed new burdens on the Ottoman state. Traditional modes of Ottoman sovereignty and semiautonomous rule over the Hijaz and the Sharifate of Mecca and stewardship of the caravan-based hajj no longer would be adequate to meet the rapidly changing demands of the modernizing hajj. As pilgrims experienced colonial modernity in the ports and rail hubs of the colonial world, Mecca's comparatively underdeveloped sanitary and infrastructural arrangements drew sharp criticism from both colonial officials and their Muslim subjects. By touting their sponsorship and protection of the steamship hajj, British colonial administrators found that they could shift the terms of the debate from the symbolic to the material. British officials found that even as they struggled to compete with the inherent spiritual authority of the Ottoman Caliphate, they could undermine that prestige by pointing to the sultan-caliph's failures to rapidly modernize and effectively manage the hajj.

As this book has demonstrated, from international law to bacteriology and quarantines to telegraph lines and railways, the Ottoman state struggled valiantly to keep up with the rapidly evolving challenges presented by the steamship hajj and European extraterritoriality. Ottoman officials confronted empire-wide fiscal constraints and frontier-specific logistical limitations. In the face of horrific cholera outbreaks, they struggled to provide for pilgrims and to protect the rest of the empire in the face of Britain's repeated failures to acknowledge and forcefully address the public health and humanitarian crises that it had unleashed in India and globally. By World War I, the Ottoman state's battle against epidemic cholera had begun to pay real dividends. And even after the passing of Ottoman rule in the Hijaz, the aqueducts, desalination machines, and quarantine infrastructures that they built and operated, often in the face of British opposition, continued to play critical roles in preventing further suffering.

As it turned out, the much-maligned late Ottoman state, that famous "Sick Man of Europe," was still more than capable of executing tremendously ambitious technological feats. But technical fixes such as the extension of telegraph and rail services could not overcome the underlying weaknesses inherent in the Hijaz's semiautonomous relationships with the Sharifate of Mecca and the region's Bedouin inhabitants. As a result, the Ottoman state's calculated reticence and military incapacity to dramatically alter the constitutional terms of these relationships would continue to undermine the modernizing dreams of Istanbul's experts and technocrats.

Thus despite the remarkable speed and scale of Ottoman adoption of new technologies of modern imperial rule, they could not always govern the spaces that these projects traversed. Every new technopolitical development project emerged as a new point of vulnerability, a new tool of political protest against centralization in the hands of the sharif and his Bedouin and urban allies. The Ottoman state was never able to fully leverage its modernizing expertise to produce the intensity of territoriality or the thickness of biopolitical control over the Hijaz's population that was necessary to eliminate autonomous forms of frontier political life. In the end, neither Pan-Islamic legitimacy nor modernizing technology could mask or overcome the symbiotic threats posed by the durability of local autonomy, Bedouin resistance, and colonial extraterritoriality and intervention.

Not unlike the Ottoman Empire's simplistic representation as the Sick Man of Europe, one of the enduring myths reproduced in most studies of the Saudi state that ultimately inherited much of Ottoman Arabia has been that the kingdom's rulers and its society "are essentially 'traditional' and that each has historically been and continues to be culturally and socially determined by a timeless Islam." This misleading stereotype tends to "look uncritically at the importance of religion, and even adopt the official state narrative that the Saudis are the guardians of the faith and Saudi society is essentially 'conservative' as an article of faith." As Toby Jones argues, Wahhabi interpretations of Islam have played a key role in legitimizing the Saudi regime since its inception. However, he cautions, "religion was not the only instrument of power," and often "it was not even the most important" or effective tool. Saudi Arabia was forged through a series of bloody campaigns to conquer, unite, and centralize the kingdom. Violence compelled submission but resulted in "the establishment of a weak polity vulnerable to various pressures, including from a mutinous army, a contentious clergy, and legions of imperial subjects who bristled at Saudi rule." The situation was made more precarious by unyielding demands of conformity to the state's strict Wahhabi vision of Islam and Najdi cultural traditions. Wahhabism was a legitimizing force among some communities, but for the cosmopolitan Hijaz and the kingdom's Shiʿi subjects in the Eastern Province, it remains an alienating symbol of subjugation. Despite official claims to the contrary, Wahhabism generally has remained more of a sectarian obstacle than an asset in Saudi Arabia's quest for national unity and legitimacy in the eyes of the rest of the Muslim world.[46]

In much the same way that the late Ottoman Hijaz has been framed almost exclusively by the historiography of Pan-Islam, the study of Saudi Arabia has a parallel issue. By attributing too much power to the relationship between the Saudi monarchy and its claims to Islamic legitimacy, scholars generally have paid too little attention to the other ways in which Saudi leaders sought to consolidate power and build a modern state, most notably efforts to control the Arabian Peninsula's natural resources. In this sense Saudi Arabia's twentieth century echoes, and in several areas built directly on, the infrastructures left behind by its Ottoman predecessors. During the fledgling monarchy's first decades, water and oil emerged as the twin pillars of the Saudi state's geological conquest of most of the peninsula. In this respect the state's evolution has been far from exceptional. As was the case with other postcolonial and developing states of the twentieth century, Saudi officials "jumped aboard the development bandwagon." Saudi rulers came to believe that mastery over science, technology, and the environment held the key to the monarchy's power and legitimacy both at home and abroad. Gradually the Saudis were able to use their access to foreign expertise and oil revenues to break down tribal autonomy and achieve a level of symbiotic mastery over the peninsula's natural resources, territory, and population that had remained beyond the more distant grasp of their Ottoman predecessors.[47]

On the face of it, one might assume that the Anglo-Ottoman dilemmas of legitimacy, governmentality, territoriality, and modernization bear little relationship to today's postcolonial hajj. And although it is tempting to assume that the decolonization of the hajj represented a sharp break with the past, in reality Saudi Arabia continues to face echoes of the same challenges. And though it is certainly true that Saudi Arabia's power at home and abroad rests on its vast oil wealth, the monarchy, not unlike its Ottoman and British predecessors, also has understood that the safe and efficient conduct and constant modernization of the hajj remain its greatest sources of legitimacy, offering it a measure of protection from a variety of domestic and foreign threats.

Each year, the kingdom spends hundreds of millions of dollars to deploy a small army of medical professionals, security personnel, and traffic engineers to manage the hajj. Over the decades, Saudi public health authorities have grappled successfully with potential threats from cholera, meningitis, yellow fever, and polio. More recently, however, emerging pathogens that include swine flu (H1N1 influenza), Ebola, and Middle East Respiratory Syndrome (MERS) have renewed global fears of the hajj's epidemic potential. Indeed, even as I have attended to this book's final revisions, an especially deadly novel coronavirus (COVID-19) pandemic has engulfed the globe, forcing the Saudi government to effectively cancel the 2020 hajj for millions of prospective pilgrims, and restricting this year's proceedings to a symbolic gathering of roughly a thousand pilgrims of various nationalities currently in residence in the kingdom. During each of these public health scares, we find the rearticulation of colonial narratives in the Western media, marking the hajj as a uniquely dangerous mode of travel and a standing threat to global health and security.[48] In reality, in recent decades the most deadly threat to pilgrims has come not from epidemic disease but from human stampedes and failures to effectively manage the hajj's size and complexity.[49] Due to both the lingering perception of the hajj's pandemic potential and the very real risks caused by overcrowding, the hajj remains one of the world's most tightly regulated forms of travel. Intending pilgrims must endure a dizzying, almost Kafkaesque bureaucratic maze of national quotas and passport, visa, and vaccination regulations to secure their place in the pilgrimage.[50]

However, as the Anglo-Ottoman legitimacy struggles featured in this book illustrate, the biopolitical surveillance of the modern hajj involved more than just the medicalization of the pilgrimage. Yes, passports and other mobility regulations screened for the sick and the poor. However, these measures also grew out of the desire to identify and track exiled or politically subversive subjects or those whose country of origin marked them as a potential legal or political threat to state authority. In other words, the regulation and surveillance of the hajj never was only a question of public health. It was always a struggle to manage the presumed threats that Muslim mobility posed to state security and sovereignty.

Although much has changed since the late nineteenth century, in some respects the stakes remain the same. Whether it was the Ottomans, the British Raj, or today's Saudi monarchy, the governments tasked with managing the hajj derive legitimacy, religious authority, and international power and status from it. In the past, colonial governments racialized and pathologized Muslim mobility. The hajj was feared as a potential vehicle for the spread of both contagious diseases and subversive ideas. Today those Islamophobic fears have shifted from the specter of imperial rivalry and anticolonial violence to sectarian and ideological opposition to the Saudi monarchy and the Wahhabi moral order that it claims to enforce.[51]

In 1979, the Saudi kingdom was shaken by both internal and external challenges to the monarchy's legitimacy. In November and December of that year, Juhaymān al-ʿUtaybī and a group of Salafi dissidents seized the *Masjid al-Ḥarām*. At the core of al-ʿUtaybī's brazen attack was his belief that the oil-rich Saudi state had become too enamored with Western-style modernization and had lost its devotion to the religious principles on which a truly Islamic state was supposed to rest. To his mind, oil and the wealth that it rapidly generated had sapped the monarchy and the Wahhabi religious establishment's ability to resist the temptations of materialism.[52] In addition to internal Sunni opposition, 1979 also saw the birth of Saudi Arabia's greatest rival, the Islamic Republic of Iran. Ayatollah Khomeini's revolutionary Islamism reimagined Muslim solidarity as a Cold War struggle against Western hegemony.[53] For Iran's revolutionary ayatollahs, the hajj was recast as a "movement of militants," providing an ideal venue to consolidate the revolution and export it abroad. Throughout the 1980s, Iranian demonstrators turned the hajj into a standing protest highlighting Saudi oppression of its Shiʿi subjects and foreign pilgrims as well as the hypocrisy of the kingdom's pro-Western alliances.[54]

In order to undermine the potential appeal of these twin assaults, King Fahd (r. 1982–2005) undertook a massive effort to rebrand and reinvent the Saudi dynasty's religious credentials at home and abroad. In service of this effort to reappropriate the power of Islam from the kingdom's critics, in 1986, Fahd formally took up the title of Khādim al-Ḥaramayn al-Sharīfayn.[55] Since then the political capital accumulated through the Saudi state's custodianship of Mecca and Medina has been deployed to support the monarchy's claims to de facto leadership of the Sunni world, inching ever closer to a national-cum-sectarian reformulation of Abdülhamid II's transimperial Muslim internationalism. By doing so, the Saudi monarchy repeatedly has signaled its willingness to use its custodianship over the holy places as a tool of counterinsurgency and an ideological weapon against both its critics and sectarian enemies at home and abroad. In the four decades since 1979, this Saudi-Iranian clash of competing sectarian Islamisms has helped to plunge the Middle East into a quagmire of Western interventions, terrorism, overlapping civil wars, and proxy conflicts across Iraq, Syria, Yemen, and beyond.[56] It also has helped to fuel the reanimation of older scripts of Western Islamophobia, reawakening racialized fears of transnational Muslim solidarities, mobilities, and immigration as inherently violent threats to Western civilization.[57]

As this study has sought to illustrate, service to the holy places and the hajj can confer tremendous political advantages and even harness genuine expressions of Muslim solidarity. However, as the checkered fortunes of the Ottoman, British, Hashemite, and Saudi rulers who have attempted to wield it suggest, ownership of this title and its responsibilities has never been a political panacea. The burdens and profound risks of instrumentalizing Islam in the service of imperial rivalry, state security, counterterrorism, or sectarian struggle—as opposed to earnest solicitude for the welfare of ordinary pilgrims—have always outweighed the illusory powers that its claimants have sought, but repeatedly failed, to fully grasp.

Notes

Abbreviations

Archives

Başbakanlık Osmanlı Arşivi (BOA), Istanbul, Turkey

A.DVN.MKL: Sadaret Divan-ı Hümayun Kalemi Mukavele Kısmı Belgeleri
A.MKT.MHM: Sedaret Mektubi Kalemi Mühimme Kalemi (Odası) Belgeleri
A.MKT.NZD: Sadaret Mektubi Kalemi Nezaret ve Devair Yazmışmalarına Belgeler
A.MKT.UM: Sadaret Mektubi Kalemi Umum Vilayet Yazmışmalarına Ait Belgeler
BEO: Bab-ı Ali Evrak Odası
DH.EUM.5.Şb: Dahiliye Nezareti Emniyet-i Umumiye Beşinci Şübe
DH.İD: Dahiliye Nezareti İdare Evrakı
DH.MKT: Dahiliye Nezareti Mektubi
DH.MUİ: Dahiliye Muhaberat-ı Umumiye İdaresi Evrakı
DH.SAİD.d: Dahiliye Nezareti Sicill-i Ahval Komisyonu Defterleri
HAT: Hatt-ı Hümayun Tasnifi
HR.HMŞ.İŞO: Hariciye Nezareti Hukuk Müşavirliği İstişare Odası Evrakı
HR.SFR.3: Hariciye Nezareti Sefaretler Evrakı (Londra)
HRT.h: Haritalar
İ.DH: İrade, Dahiliye
İ.HR: İrade, Hariciye
İ.HUS: İrade, Hususi
İ.MMS: İrade, Meclis-i Mahsus
İ.MVL: İrade, Meclis-i Vala
İ.PT: İrade, Telgraf ve Posta

İ.ŞD: İrade, Şura-yı Devlet
MV: Meclis-i Vükela Mazbataları
PLK.p: Plan-Proje-Kroki
ŞD: Şura-yı Devlet
Y.A.HUS: Yıldız Sadaret Hususi Maruzat Evrakı
Y.A.RES: Yıldız Sadaret Resmi Maruzat Evrakı
Y.EE: Yıldız Esas Evrakı
Y.MTV: Yıldız Mütenevvi Maruzat Evrakı
Y.PRK.ASK: Yıldız Perakende Evrakı, Askeri Maruzat
Y.PRK.AZJ: Yıldız Perakende Evrakı, Arzuhaller ve Jurnaller
Y.PRK.AZN: Yıldız Perakende Evrakı, Adliye ve Mezahib Nezareti Maruzatı
Y.PRK.BŞK: Yıldız Perakende Evrakı, Mabeyn Başkitabeti
Y.PRK.EŞA: Yıldız Perakende Evrakı, Elçilik ve Şehbenderlikler Tahriratı
Y.PRK.HR: Yıldız Perakende Evrakı, Hariciye Nezareti Maruzatı
Y.PRK.KOM: Yıldız Perakende Evrakı, Komisyonlar Maruzatı
Y.PRK.MK: Yıldız Perakende Evrakı, Müfettişlik ve Komiserlikler Tahriratı
Y.PRK.SH: Yıldız Perakende Evrakı, Sıhhiye Nezareti Maruzatı
Y.PRK.ŞD: Yıldız Perakende Evrakı, Şura-yı Devlet Maruzatı
Y.PRK.TKM: Yıldız Tasnifi Perakende Evrakı, Tahrirat-ı Ecnebiye ve Mabeyn Mütercimliği
Y.PRK.UM: Yıldız Tasnifi Perakende Evrakı, Umum Vilayetler Tahriratı
ZB: Zabtiye Nezareti Evrakı

The British Library (BL), London, United Kingdom

Asia, Pacific, and Africa Collections
IOR: India Office Records and Private Papers
Qatar Digital Library

Khalili Family Trust, London, United Kingdom

Hajj and the Arts of Pilgrimage Collection

Thomas Cook Group Archives (TC), Peterborough, United Kingdom

Guardbook no. 27

The National Archives (TNA), Kew, United Kingdom

CO: Colonial Office
FO: Foreign Office

Introduction: Between Two Worlds:
An Ottoman Island Adrift on a Colonial Ocean

The chapter epigraph is from the Başbakanlık Osmanlı Arşivi (hereafter BOA), Y.PRK.EŞA, 31/156 (25 N 1316/6 February 1899). See also BOA, Y.PRK.BŞK, 58/63 (25 N 1316/6 February 1899).

1. Gökhan Çetinsaya, "The Ottoman View of British Presence in Iraq and the Gulf: The Era of Abdulhamid II," *Middle Eastern Studies* 39, no. 2 (2003): 199–200.
2. BOA, Y.PRK.TKM, 53/4 (29 Z 1327/11 January 1910).
3. Juan R. I. Cole, "Of Crowds and Empires: Afro-Asian Riots and European Expansion, 1857–1882," *Comparative Studies in Society and History* 31, no. 1 (1989): 113–14.
4. The National Archives of the United Kingdom (hereafter TNA): FO 685/1 (March 24, 1879.
5. John Slight, *The British Empire and the Hajj, 1865-1956* (Cambridge, MA: Harvard University Press, 2015), 66–67.
6. Selim Deringil, *The Well-Protected Domains: Ideology and Legitimation of Power in the Ottoman Empire, 1876-1909* (London: I. B. Tauris, 1999), 56.
7. On the conceptualization of the Arabian Peninsula's Indian Ocean orientations, see Michael Christopher Low, "The Indian Ocean and Other Middle Easts," *Comparative Studies of South Asia, Africa and the Middle East* 34, no. 3 (2014): 549–55. See also Nile Green, "Rethinking the 'Middle East' after the Oceanic Turn," 556–64, featured in the same special section.
8. James Gelvin and Nile Green, eds., *Global Muslims in the Age of Steam and Print* (Berkeley: University of California Press, 2014), 1–14; Nile Green, "The *Hajj* as Its Own Undoing: Infrastructure and Integration on the Muslim Journey to Mecca," *Past and Present* 226, no. 1 (2015): 193–226; and Green, "Spacetime and the Industrial Journey West: Industrial Communications and the Making of the 'Muslim World'," *American Historical Review* 118, no. 2 (2013): 401–29.
9. Valeska Huber, *Channelling Mobilities: Migration and Globalisation in the Suez Canal Region and Beyond, 1869-1914* (Cambridge: Cambridge University Press, 2013).
10. William Roff, "Sanitation and Security: The Imperial Powers and the Nineteenth Century Hajj," *Arabian Studies* VI (1982): 145.
11. Alan de L. Rush, ed., *Records of the Hajj: A Documentary History of the Pilgrimage to Mecca*, vol. 3 (London: Archive Editions, 1993), 733.
12. Roff, "Sanitation and Security," 150.
13. In Ottoman documents the term *Jawi* was a capacious category. It included Southeast Asian pilgrims from British Malaya and the Straits Settlements (Singapore) as well as Dutch subjects of Java and Sumatra. It could even include other groups traveling via Singapore, such as Chinese and Filipinos.
14. Gülden Sarıyıldız and Ayşe Kavak, eds., *Halife II. Abdülhamid'in Hac Siyaseti: Dr. M. Şakir Bey'in Hatıraları* (İstanbul: Timaş, 2009), 60.
15. David Edwin Long, *The Hajj Today: A Survey of the Contemporary Makkah Pilgrimage* (Albany: State University of New York Press, 1979), 127–32.

16. BOA, İ.DH, 537/37312 (10 M 1282/5 June 1865).
17. F. E. Peters, *The Hajj: The Muslim Pilgrimage to Mecca and the Holy Places* (Princeton, NJ: Princeton University Press, 1994), 301–2.
18. From 1851 to 1926, thirteen international sanitary conferences were convened to address the threat of pandemic cholera. Peter Baldwin, *Contagion and the State in Europe, 1830–1930* (Cambridge: Cambridge University Press, 1999), 228–31; Valeska Huber, "The Unification of the Globe by Disease? The International Sanitary Conferences on Cholera, 1851–1894," *Historical Journal* 49, no. 2 (2006): 453–76; and Norman Howard-Jones, *The Scientific Background of the International Sanitary Conferences, 1851–1938* (Geneva: World Health Organization, 1975).
19. Slight, *The British Empire and the Hajj*, 84–105; and Kasım İzzeddin, *Hicaz'da Teşkilat ve Islahat-ı Sıhhiye ve 1330 Senesi Hacc-ı Şerifi: Hicaz Sıhhiye İdaresi Senevi Rapor* (İstanbul: Matbaa-ı Amire, 1330/1914–15), 52–66.
20. Eric Tagliacozzo, *The Longest Journey: Southeast Asians and the Pilgrimage to Mecca* (Oxford: Oxford University Press, 2013), 134.
21. Mark Harrison, "Quarantine, Pilgrimage, and Colonial Trade: India 1866–1900," *Indian Economic and Social Review* 29, no. 2 (1992): 127–44; and Saurabh Mishra, *Pilgrimage, Politics, and Pestilence: The Haj from the Indian Subcontinent, 1860–1920* (New Delhi: Oxford University Press, 2011).
22. Slight, *The British Empire and the Hajj*, 13–14.
23. Gülden Sarıyıldız, *Hicaz Karantina Teşkilatı, 1865–1914* (Ankara: Türk Tarih Kurumu Basımevi, 1996), 5–11.
24. Here I take inspiration from Cemil Aydın's work on European Islamophobia and the homogenization of the "Muslim world" as a colonial racial category in *The Idea of the Muslim World: A Global Intellectual History* (Cambridge, MA: Harvard University Press, 2017).
25. Roff, "Sanitation and Security," 143.
26. Slight, *The British Empire and the Hajj*, 16, 316–21; and Eileen Kane, *Russian Hajj: Empire and the Pilgrimage to Mecca* (Ithaca, NY: Cornell University Press, 2015), 9–10.
27. Slight, *The British Empire and the Hajj*, 16, 62–123.
28. Lâle Can, *Spiritual Subjects: Central Asians and the Ottoman Hajj at the End of Empire* (Stanford, CA: Stanford University Press, 2020), 24–26.
29. On Ottoman patronage in Jerusalem, see especially Amy Singer, *Constructing Ottoman Beneficence: An Imperial Soup Kitchen in Jerusalem* (Albany: State University of New York Press, 2002).
30. Akif Erdoğru, "Konya Mevlevî Dergâhı'nın Malî Kaynakları ve İdaresi Üzerine Düşünceler ve Belgeler," *Türk Tarih Kurumu Belgeler* 27, no. 21 (1996): 41–71; and İsmail Yaşayanlar, "Hac Yolunda Bir Durak: Şâm-ı Şerîf Süleymaniye Külliyesi," in *Kanunî Sultan Süleyman Dönemi ve Bursa*, ed. Burcu Kurt (Bursa, Turkey: Gaye Kitabevi, 2019), 536–46.
31. Jane Hathaway, *The Chief Eunuch of the Ottoman Harem: From African Slave to Power-Broker* (Cambridge: Cambridge University Press, 2018), 219.
32. Bruce Masters, *The Arabs of the Ottoman Empire, 1516–1918* (Cambridge: Cambridge University Press, 2013), 31.

33. Gökhan Çetinsaya, *Ottoman Administration of Iraq, 1890-1908* (London: Routledge, 2006), 102–5; and Stephanie Mulder, "Abdülhamid and the ʿAlids: Ottoman Patronage of "Shi'i" Shrines in the Cemetery of Bāb al-Ṣaghīr," *Studia Islamica* 108 (2013): 16–47.

34. Timur Hammond, "Mediums of Belief: Muslim Place Making in 20th Century Turkey" (PhD diss., University of California, Los Angeles, 2016).

35. Lâle Can, "Connecting People: A Central Asian Sufi Network in Turn-of-the-Century Istanbul," *Modern Asian Studies* 46, no. 2 (2012): 373–401; and Rishad Choudhury, "The Hajj and the Hindi: The Ascent of an Indian Sufi Lodge in the Ottoman Empire," *Modern Asian Studies* 50, no. 6 (2016): 1888–1931.

36. Stanford Shaw and Ezra Kural Shaw, *History of the Ottoman Empire and Modern Turkey*, vol. 2 (Cambridge: Cambridge University Press, 1977), 136–38; and Alexander Schölch, "Britain in Palestine, 1838–1882: The Roots of the Balfour Policy," *Journal of Palestine Studies* 22, no. 1 (1992): 39–56.

37. Kane, *Russian Hajj*, 24–27. For a more Balkan-Ottoman–centric view of Orthodox Christian pilgrimage to Jerusalem, see also Valentina Izmirlieva, "Christian Hajjis—The Other Orthodox Pilgrims to Jerusalem," *Slavic Review* 73, no. 2 (2014): 322–46.

38. Birsen Bulmuş, *Plague, Quarantines and Geopolitics in the Ottoman Empire* (Edinburgh: Edinburgh University Press, 2012), 154.

39. Aydın, *The Idea of the Muslim World*, 97–98.

40. Gelvin and Green, *Global Muslims in the Age of Steam and Print*, 1–14.

41. Can, *Spiritual Subjects*, 17.

42. Deringil, *The Well-Protected Domains*; Kemal H. Karpat, *The Politicization of Islam: Reconstructing Identity, State, Faith, and Community in the Late Ottoman State* (Oxford: Oxford University Press, 2001). See also Azmi Özcan, *Pan-Islamism: Indian Muslims, the Ottomans and Britain, 1877-1924* (Leiden: Brill, 1997); and Adeeb Khalid, "Pan-Islamism in Practice: The Rhetoric of Muslim Unity and Its Uses," in Elisabeth Özdalga, ed., *Late Ottoman Society: The Intellectual Legacy* (London: Routledge-Curzon, 2005), 201–24.

43. On the Hijaz Railway, see William Ochsenwald, *The Hijaz Railroad* (Charlottesville: University Press of Virginia, 1980); Jacob Landau, *The Hejaz Railway and the Muslim Pilgrimage: A Case of Ottoman Political Propaganda* (Detroit, MI: Wayne State University Press, 1971); Ufuk Gülsoy, *Hicaz Demiryolu* (İstanbul: Eren, 1994); and Murat Özyüksel, *The Hejaz Railway and the Ottoman Empire: Modernity, Industrialisation and Ottoman Decline* (London: I. B. Tauris, 2014).

44. For the nineteenth century, see William Ochsenwald's encyclopedic classic, *Religion, Society, and the State in Arabia: The Hijaz Under Ottoman Control, 1840-1908* (Columbus: Ohio State University Press, 1984), which remains the only English-language study of Ottoman rule in the Hijaz based on Ottoman archival sources. Although published too late in this book's production to be given careful consideration here, see also Ulrike Freitag's more Arab-centric account of the region, *A History of Jeddah: The Gate to Mecca in the Nineteenth and Twentieth Centuries* (Cambridge: Cambridge University Press, 2020). Likewise, for the early modern period, Suraiya Faroqhi's *Pilgrims and Sultans: The Hajj Under the Ottomans,*

1517-1683 (London: I. B. Tauris, 1994) is the only English-language study dedicated to Ottoman pilgrimage administration.

45. Faroqhi, *Pilgrims and Sultans*, 7–10, 33, 176–87.

46. Faroqhi, *Pilgrims and Sultans*, 54–91.

47. Faroqhi, *Pilgrims and Sultans*, 156–58. See also Cengiz Orhonlu, *Osmanlı İmparatorluğu'nun Güney Siyaseti: Habeş Eyaleti* (İstanbul: Edebiyat Fakültesi Yayınları, 1974), 129–40.

48. Khaled Fahmy, *All the Pasha's Men: Mehmed Ali, His Army, and the Making of Modern Egypt* (New York: Cambridge University Press, 1997).

49. Ochsenwald, *Religion, Society, and the State in Arabia*, 131–37.

50. Mostafa Minawi, *The Ottoman Scramble for Africa: Empire and Diplomacy in the Sahara and the Hijaz* (Stanford, CA: Stanford University Press, 2016), 101.

51. Ochsenwald, *Religion, Society, and the State in Arabia*, 167–69.

52. Faroqhi, *Pilgrims and Sultans*, 176.

53. Aimee M. Genell, "Ottoman Autonomous Provinces and the Problem of Semi-Sovereignty," *Balkan and Near Eastern Studies* 18, no. 6 (2016): 533–49.

54. Ayhan Ceylan, *Osmanlı Taşra İdarî Tarzı Olarak Eyâlet-i Mümtâze ve Mısır Uygulaması* (İstanbul: Kitabevi, 2014).

55. Sinan Kuneralp, *Son Dönem Osmanlı Erkân ve Ricali, 1839-1922: Prosopografik Rehber* (İstanbul: İsis Press, 1999), 43.

56. Aimee M. Genell, "Empire by Law: Ottoman Sovereignty and the British Occupation of Egypt, 1882–1923" (PhD diss., Columbia University, 2013), 7–12.

57. Thomas Kuehn, *Empire, Islam, and Politics of Difference: Ottoman Rule in Yemen, 1849-1919* (Leiden: Brill, 2011), 36–37.

58. Ochsenwald, *Religion, Society, and the State in Arabia*, 131–52.

59. Selim Deringil, " 'They Live in a State of Nomadism and Savagery': The Late Ottoman Empire and the Post-Colonial Debate," *Comparative Studies in Society and History* 45, no. 2 (2003): 312–17.

60. Minawi, *The Ottoman Scramble for Africa*, 2–6, 12–16.

61. Ussama Makdisi, "Ottoman Orientalism," *American Historical Review* 107, no. 3 (2002): 768–72.

62. Deringil, " 'They Live in a State of Nomadism and Savagery,' " 317–18.

63. Tahsin Pasha, *Sultan Abdülhamid: Tahsin Paşa'nın Yıldız Hatıraları* (İstanbul: Boğaziçi Yayınları, 1999), 205, 341–42.

64. On indirect rule and native princely states in Arabia, see John M. Willis, *Unmaking North and South: Cartographies of the Yemeni Past* (New York: Columbia University Press, 2012), 10, 19–24. On native princely states and minor sovereignty in India, see also Eric Lewis Beverley, *Hyderabad, British India, and the World: Muslim Networks and Minor Sovereignty, c. 1850-1950* (Cambridge: Cambridge University Press, 2015), 19–53.

65. Kuehn, *Empire, Islam, and Politics of Difference*, 91–145, 207–26, 213–14, 251. On Ottoman practices of autonomy on the empire's Arab, Kurdish, and Balkan tribal frontiers, see also Sabri Ateş, *The Ottoman-Iranian Borderlands: Making a Boundary, 1843-1914* (Cambridge: Cambridge University Press, 2013); Isa Blumi, *Rethinking the Late Ottoman Empire: A Comparative Social and Political History of Albania and Yemen, 1878-1918* (Istanbul: Isis Press, 2003); Janet Klein, *The Margins*

of Empire: Kurdish Militias in the Ottoman Tribal Zone (Stanford, CA: Stanford University Press, 2011); and Eugene Rogan, *Frontiers of the State in the Late Ottoman Empire: Transjordan, 1850-1921* (Cambridge: Cambridge University Press, 1999).

66. Kuehn, *Empire, Islam, and Politics of Difference*, 10–14, 135.

67. Minawi, *The Ottoman Scramble for Africa*, 15.

68. On governmentality, see especially Michel Foucault, "Governmentality," in *The Essential Foucault: Selections from the Essential Works of Foucault, 1945-1984*, ed. Paul Rabinow and Nikolas Rose (New York: New Press, 2003), 229–45. For useful discussions of governmentality in Ottoman settings, see Emine Ö Evered, *Empire and Education Under the Ottomans: Politics, Reform and Resistance from the Tanzimat to the Young Turks* (London: I. B. Tauris, 2012), 9–15; M. Safa Saraçoğlu, *Nineteenth-Century Local Governance in Ottoman Bulgaria* (Edinburgh: Edinburgh University Press, 2018); Kent F. Schull, *Prisons in the Ottoman Empire: Microcosms of Modernity* (Edinburgh: Edinburgh University Press, 2014); and Brian Silverstein, "Sufism and Governmentality in the Late Ottoman Empire," *Comparative Studies of South Asia, Africa and the Middle East* 29, no. 2 (2009): 171–85.

69. Beverley, *Hyderabad, British India, and the World*, 26–27, 43–44. On "lumpy" frontier sovereignties, see also Lauren Benton, *A Search for Sovereignty: Law and Geography in European Empires, 1400-1900* (Cambridge: Cambridge University Press, 2010).

70. For useful definitions of *technopolitics* and *technostates*, see Gabrielle Hecht, *The Radiance of France: Nuclear Power and National Identity After World War II* (Cambridge, MA: MIT Press, 1998), 15–17; and Timothy Mitchell, *Rule of Experts: Egypt, Techno-politics, Modernity* (Berkeley: University of California Press, 2002), 12, 15. On the notion of an Ottoman "technocratic gaze," see also Chris Gratien, "The Ottoman Quagmire: Malaria, Swamps, and Settlement in the Late Ottoman Mediterranean," *International Journal of Middle East Studies* 49, no. 4 (2017): 583–604. Here I also draw on Arun Agrawal's idea of "environmentality," marrying notions of environmental management with Foucauldian "biopolitical governmentality" in *Environmentality: Technologies of Government and the Making of Subjects* (Durham, NC: Duke University Press, 2005), 8.

1. Blurred Vision: The Hijaz and the Hajj in the Colonial Imagination

1. John M. Willis, "Making Yemen Indian: Rewriting the Boundaries of Imperial Arabia," *International Journal of Middle East Studies* 41, no. 1 (2009): 24, 35.

2. James Onley, *The Arabian Frontier of the British Raj: Merchants, Rulers, and the British in the Nineteenth-Century Gulf* (Oxford: Oxford University Press, 2007), 30–32, 216–17; Sugata Bose, *A Hundred Horizons: The Indian Ocean in the Age of Global Empire* (Cambridge, MA: Harvard University Press, 2006), 36–71; John Darwin, "An Undeclared Empire: The British in the Middle East, 1918-1939," *Journal of Imperial and Commonwealth History* 27, no. 2 (1999): 159–76; and Peter Sluglett, "Formal and Informal Empire in the Middle East," in *Oxford History of the British Empire*, vol. 5, ed. Robin W. Winks (Oxford: Oxford University Press, 1999), 416–36.

3. Robert Blyth, *Empire of the Raj: India, Eastern Africa and the Middle East, 1858-1947* (New York: Palgrave MacMillan, 2003), 1–11.

4. William Roff, "Sanitation and Security: The Imperial Powers and the Nineteenth Century Hajj," *Arabian Studies* VI (1982): 144.

5. M. Abir, "The 'Arab Rebellion' of Amir Ghālib of Mecca (1788–1813)," *Middle Eastern Studies* 7, no. 2 (1971): 189–91. On Mughal subsidies in support of the Hijaz and the hajj, see Naimur Rahman Farooqi, *Mughal-Ottoman Relations: A Study of the Political and Diplomatic Relations Between Mughal India and the Ottoman Empire, 1556-1748* (Delhi: Idarah-i Adabiyat-i Delli, 1989), 113–16; Suraiya Faroqhi, *Pilgrims and Sultans: The Hajj Under the Ottomans, 1517-1683* (London: I. B. Tauris, 1994), 131–34; and Michael N. Pearson, *Pilgrimage to Mecca: The Indian Experience, 1500-1800* (Princeton, NJ: Markus Wiener Publishers, 1996), 107–21.

6. Edward Ingram, "A Preview of the Great Game in Asia—1: The British Occupation of Perim and Aden in 1799," *Middle Eastern Studies* 9, no. 1 (1973): 3–18.

7. John Slight, *The British Empire and the Hajj, 1865-1956* (Cambridge, MA: Harvard University Press, 2015), 65–66.

8. Slight, *The British Empire and the Hajj*, 65–66.

9. Ulrike Freitag, "Helpless Representative of the Great Powers? Western Consuls in Jeddah, 1830s to 1914," *Journal of Imperial and Commonwealth History* 40, no. 3 (2012): 359–60.

10. Roff, "Sanitation and Security," 144; Caesar E. Farah, *The Sultan's Yemen: Nineteenth-Century Challenges to Ottoman Rule* (London: I. B. Tauris, 2002), 1–13.

11. Daniel Headrick, *The Tools of Empire: Technology and European Imperialism in the Nineteenth Century* (Oxford: Oxford University Press, 1981), 129–56; Valeska Huber, *Channelling Mobilities: Migration and Globalisation in the Suez Canal Region and Beyond, 1869-1914* (Cambridge: Cambridge University Press, 2013), 22; and On Barak, *On Time: Technology and Temporality in Modern Egypt* (Berkeley: University of California Press, 2013), 21–53.

12. Slight, *The British Empire and the Hajj*, 66–67.

13. Farah, *The Sultan's Yemen*, 14–29; David Killingray, Margarette Lincoln, and Nigel Rigby, eds., *Maritime Empires: British Imperial Maritime Trade in the Nineteenth Century* (Rochester, NY: Boydell Press, 2004), 68–83; and Sayyid Muṣṭafā Sālim, *al-Baḥr al-Aḥmar wa-l-Juzur al-Yamaniyya: Tārīkh wa Qaḍiyya* (Ṣanʿāʾ, Yemen: Dār al-Mithāq li-l-Nashr wa-l-Tawzīʿ, 2006), 43–58.

14. Giancarlo Casale, *The Ottoman Age of Exploration* (Oxford: Oxford University Press, 2010), 42–47, 63–66, 199.

15. Thomas Kuehn, *Empire, Islam, and Politics of Difference: Ottoman Rule in Yemen, 1849-1919* (Leiden: Brill, 2011), 1–51.

16. Freitag, "Helpless Representatives of the Great Powers?," 359–60; Eileen Kane, *Russian Hajj: Empire and the Pilgrimage to Mecca* (Ithaca, NY: Cornell University Press, 2015), 69; Slight, *The British Empire and the Hajj*, 66; and Eric Tagliacozzo, *The Longest Journey: Southeast Asians and the Pilgrimage to Mecca* (Oxford: Oxford University Press, 2013), 54–55.

17. Quoted in David Kimche, "The Opening of the Red Sea to European Ships in the Late Eighteenth Century," *Middle Eastern Studies* 8, no. 1 (1972): 71.

18. Alexis Wick, *The Red Sea: In Search of Lost Space* (Berkeley: University of California Press, 2016), 147–54.
19. Yeniçeşmeli Hâfız Fâik Efendi, *İstanbul'dan Bombay'a Bir Osmanlı Fırkateyni'nin Keşif Seyahati*, A. Ergun Çınar, ed. (İstanbul: Kitabevi, 2014), 23, 30–32.
20. Johann Ludwig (John Lewis) Burckhardt, *Travels in Arabia* (London: Henry Colburn, 1829), 16, 191, 259.
21. Roff, "Sanitation and Security," 146.
22. Richard Burton, *Personal Narrative of a Pilgrimage to al-Medinah and Meccah*, vol. 2 (London, 1855; reprint of the 1893 ed., New York: Dover, 1964), 184–86.
23. Ayesha Jalal, *Partisans of Allah: Jihad in South Asia* (Cambridge: Harvard University Press, 2008), 58–175; William Dalrymple, *The Last Mughal: The Fall of a Dynasty: Delhi, 1857* (New York: Vintage, 2008); Ilyse R. Morgenstein Fuerst, *Indian Muslim Minorities and the 1857 Rebellion: Religion, Rebels, and Jihad* (London: I. B. Tauris, 2017); and Salahuddin Ahmad, *Mutiny, Revolution or Muslim Rebellion? British Public Reaction to the Indian Crisis of 1857* (Oxford: Oxford University Press, 2008).
24. Jalal, *Partisans of Allah*, 65, 70–71; and Kemal H. Karpat, *The Politicization of Islam: Reconstructing Identity, State, Faith, and Community in the Late Ottoman State* (Oxford: Oxford University Press, 2001), 28–33.
25. W. W. Hunter, *The Indian Musalmans* (London: Williams and Norgate, 1871), 1, 11, 36; and Hunter, *A Brief History of the Indian Peoples* (Oxford: Clarendon Press, 1895), 222–29.
26. Francis Robinson, *Islam and Muslim History in South Asia* (New Delhi: Oxford University Press, 2000), 188–89; and William Roff, "Islamic Movements: One or Many?," in *Islam and the Political Economy of Meaning*, ed. William Roff (London: Croom and Helm, 1987), 31–52.
27. Cemil Aydın, *The Idea of the Muslim World: A Global Intellectual History* (Cambridge, MA: Harvard University Press, 2017), 5–6.
28. Nicholas Dirks, *Castes of Mind: Colonialism and the Making of Modern India* (Princeton, NJ: Princeton University Press, 2001), 43–45, 148–72.
29. Ussama Makdisi, *The Culture of Sectarianism: Community, History, and Violence in Nineteenth-Century Lebanon* (Berkeley: University of California Press, 2000), 1–14.
30. Dirks, *Castes of Mind*, 149–72.
31. Julia Stephens, "The Phantom Wahhabi: Liberalism and the Muslim Fanatic in Mid-Victorian India," *Modern Asian Studies* 47, no. 1 (2013): 22–52.
32. Jalal, *Partisans of Allah*, 114–16, 136–39, 176–77.
33. Seema Alavi, " 'Fugitive Mullahs and Outlawed Fanatics': Indian Muslims in Nineteenth-Century Trans-Asiatic Imperial Rivalries," *Modern Asian Studies* 45, no. 6 (2011): 1337–82.
34. Juan R. I. Cole, "Of Crowds and Empires: Afro-Asian Riots and European Expansion, 1857–1882," *Comparative Studies in Society and History* 31, no. 1 (1989): 106–33.
35. For full accounts of the British investigations into these events, see TNA: FO 881/848, "Papers Relating to the Outbreak at Jeddah in June 1858" (July 1858 to December 1859). For the Ottoman investigations, see BOA, İ.MMS, 14/597-1 (13 B 1275/16 February 1859); and BOA, İ.HR, 160/8566 (25 S 1275/4 October 1858).
36. Cemil Aydın, *The Politics of Anti-Westernism in Asia: Visions of World Order in Pan-Islamic and Pan-Asian Thought* (New York: Columbia University Press, 2007), 24, 32.

37. William Ochsenwald, *Religion, Society, and the State in Arabia: The Hijaz Under Ottoman Control, 1840–1908* (Columbus: Ohio State University Press, 1984), 137.

38. Ehud Toledano, *The Ottoman Slave Trade and Its Suppression: 1840–1890* (Princeton, NJ: Princeton University Press, 1983), 130–38.

39. Cevdet Pasha, *Tezâkir*, 1–12, ed. Cavid Baysun (Ankara: Türk Tarih Kurumu Basımevi, 1986), 102–3.

40. Cevdet Pasha, *Tezâkir*,103, 111–13.

41. BOA, İ.DH, 1289/101423 (7 Z 1272/9 August 1856).

42. Toledano, *The Ottoman Slave Trade and Its Suppression*, 135–38.

43. TNA: FO 881/848 (19 June 1858), 72–73.

44. BOA, İ.MMS, 14/597-1 (13 B 1275/16 February 1859).

45. TNA: FO 881/848 (22 February 1859), 266–67.

46. BOA, İ.MVL, 316/13320 (22 M 1271/15 October1854); BOA, İ.HR, 310/19768 (7 S 1271/30 October 1854); BOA, İ.MVL, 319/13514 (27 S 1271/19 November 1854); and BOA, İ.MVL, 370/16223 (16 Ş 1273/11 April 1857).

47. William Ochsenwald, "The Jeddah Massacre of 1858," *Middle Eastern Studies* 13, no. 3 (1977): 314–26.

48. TNA: FO 881/848 (14 January 1859), 241–43.

49. TNA: FO 881/848 (19 June 1858), 72–73; and BOA, İ.MMS, 14/597-1 (13 B 1275/16 February 1859).

50. TNA: FO 881/848 (19 June 1858), 72–73; and BOA, İ.MMS, 14/597-1 (13 B 1275/16 February 1859).

51. Emphasis mine. TNA: FO, 881/848 (19 and 25 June 1858); and TNA: FO 195/579 (15 June 1858).

52. Aḥmad ibn Zaynī Daḥlān, *Tarīkh Ashrāf al-Ḥijāz, 1840–1882: Khulāṣat al-Kalām fī Bayān Umarāʾ al-Balad al-Ḥarām*, ed. with introduction by Muḥammad Amīn Tawfīq (Cairo, 1887; repr., Beirut: Dār al-Sāqī, 1993), 48.

53. BOA, İ.MMS, 532/13 (5 Z 1274/17 July 1858).

54. BOA, İ.HR, 160/8566 (25 S 1275/4 October 1858); and TNA: FO 881/848 (8 August 1858), 93–98.

55. BOA, İ.HR, 160/8566 (25 S 1275/4 October 1858); and TNA: FO 881/848 (12 August 1858), 109.

56. Ulrike Freitag, "Symbolic Politics and Urban Violence in Late Ottoman Jeddah," in *Urban Violence in the Middle East: Changing Cityscapes in the Transition from Empire to Nation*, ed. Ulrike Freitag, Nelida Fuccaro, Claudia Ghrawi, and Nora Lafi (Oxford: Berghahn, 2015), 124–29.

57. TNA: FO 424/159, "Correspondence Respecting the Interpretation of Article 42 of the English Capitulations of 1675" (May 1889), 2, 16–17, 19–20, 22–23.

58. TNA: FO 881/848 (November 1858), 187–88.

59. BOA, İ.MMS, 14/597-1 (13 B 1275/16 February 1859).

60. Ulrike Freitag, *Indian Ocean Migrants and State Formation in Hadhramaut: Reforming the Homeland* (Leiden: Brill, 2003), 52–53, 199–208; Ochsenwald, *Religion, Society, and the State in Arabia*, 138–43; and Ochsenwald, "Muslim-European Conflict in the Hijaz: The Slave Trade Controversy, 1840–1895," *Middle Eastern Studies* 16 (1980): 115–26.

61. BOA, İ.MMS, 14/597-1 (13 B 1275/16 February 1859); and BOA, İ.HR, 172/9399 (11 Ca 1276/6 December 1859).
62. TNA: FO 881/848 (25 June 1858; 5 July 1858).
63. Quoted in Roff, "Sanitation and Security," 147.
64. On Sayyid Faḍl, see especially Wilson Chacko Jacob, *For God or Empire: Sayyid Fadl and the Indian Ocean World* (Stanford, CA: Stanford University Press, 2019); and Seema Alavi, *Muslim Cosmopolitanism in the Age of Empire* (Cambridge, MA: Harvard University Press, 2015). On the Hadrami diaspora in the Indian Ocean, see also Engseng Ho, *The Graves of Tarim: Genealogy and Mobility Across the Indian Ocean* (Berkeley: University of California Press, 2006).
65. Stephen Dale, *Islamic Society on the South Asian Frontier: The Mappilas of Malabar, 1498-1922* (Oxford: Clarendon Press 1980), 127-37, 164-69.
66. *Correspondence on Moplah Outrages in Malabar for the Years, 1853-59*, vol. 2 (Madras: United Scottish Press, 1863), 390-92.
67. Ş. Tufan Buzpınar, "Abdülhamid II and Sayyid Fadl Pasha of Hadramawt: An Arab Dignitary's Ambitions, 1876-1900," *Osmanlı Araştırmaları* 13 (1993): 227-39.
68. TNA: FO 881/848 (31 December 1859), 174-75.
69. TNA: FO 881/848 (31 December 1859), 174-75.
70. TNA: FO 881/848 (25 November 1958), 188.
71. TNA: FO 881/848 (31 January 1859), 267. See also Jacob, *For God or Empire*, 102-104.
72. Alavi, *Muslim Cosmopolitanism in the Age of Empire*, 93-168.
73. Jalal, *Partisans of Allah*, 66-68.
74. Azmi Özcan, *Pan-Islamism: Indian Muslims, the Ottomans and Britain, 1877-1924* (Leiden: Brill, 1997), 19-20.
75. M. Naeem Qureshi, *Pan-Islam in British India: The Politics of the Khilafat Movement, 1918-1924* (Oxford: Oxford University Press, 2009), 8-9.
76. Qureshi, *Pan-Islam in British India*, 5.
77. Eric Hobsbawm and Terence Ranger, *The Invention of Tradition* (Cambridge: Cambridge University Press, 1983), 5; and Selim Deringil, "The Invention of Tradition as Public Image in the Late Ottoman Empire," *Comparative Studies in Society and History* 35, no. 1 (1993): 3-29.
78. Aydın, *The Idea of the Muslim World*, 69-70; and Özcan, *Pan-Islamism*, 115-26.
79. Karpat, *The Politicization of Islam*, 148-50; Benjamin Fortna, "The Reign of Abdülhamid II," in *Cambridge History of Turkey*, vol. 4, ed. Reşat Kasaba (Cambridge: Cambridge University Press, 2008), 47-53.
80. Selim Deringil, *The Well-Protected Domains: Ideology and Legitimation of Power in the Ottoman Empire, 1876-1909* (London: I. B. Tauris, 1999), 44-134.
81. Erdem Çıpa, *The Making of Selim: Succession, Legitimacy, and Memory in the Early Modern Ottoman World* (Bloomington: Indiana University Press, 2017), 233-38. On Ottoman uses of the title dating from the reign of Süleyman I, see Hüseyin Yılmaz, *Caliphate Redefined: The Mystical Turn in Ottoman Political Thought* (Princeton, NJ: Princeton University Press, 2018).
82. Richard Bulliet, "The History of the Muslim South," *Al-ʿUsur al-Wusta: The Bulletin of Middle East Medievalists* 20, no. 2 (2008): 59-64; Farooqi, *Mughal-Ottoman Relations*, 109; and Faroqhi, *Pilgrims and Sultans*, 7-10, 184-86.

83. For a survey of Eyüp Sabri Pasha's writings on the Ottoman Caliphate, see Mehmet Akif Fidan, *Eyüp Sabri Paşa ve Tarihçiliği* (Ankara: Türk Tarih Kurumu Basımevi, 2011), 143–54. See also Eyüp Sabri Pasha, *Mirat-ı Mekke* (İstanbul: Bahriye Matbaası, 1301/1883), 1167–72. For other examples of Hamidian-era works on the caliphate, see also İsmail Kara, ed., *Hilafet Risâleleri*, vols. 1–2 (İstanbul: Klasik, 2002).

84. Eyüp Sabri Pasha, *Mirat ül-Haremeyn: Mirat-ı Medine*, vol. 2 (İstanbul: Bahriye Matbaası, 1304), 505–22; Fidan, *Eyüp Sabri Paşa ve Tarihçiliği*, 143–47, 158.

85. Cevdet Pasha, *Tarih-i Cevdet* (Dersaadet [İstanbul]: Matbaa-ı Osmaniye, 1309/1891), I: 208, II, 122; Mona Hassan, *Longing for the Lost Caliphate: A Transregional History* (Princeton, NJ: Princeton University Press, 2016), 145–49; Özcan, *Pan-Islamism*, 29–30; and Farooqi, *Mughal-Ottoman Relations*, 181–83.

86. Aydın, *The Idea of the Muslim World*, 97.

87. Lâle Can and Michael Christopher Low, "The 'Subjects' of Ottoman International Law," *Journal of the Ottoman and Turkish Studies Association* 3, no. 2 (2016): 227–28.

88. Aydın, *The Idea of the Muslim World*, 97.

89. Faiz Ahmed, *Afghanistan Rising: Islamic Law and Statecraft Between the Ottoman and British Empires* (Cambridge, MA: Harvard University Press, 2017), 13–17, 32–33.

90. Aydın, *The Idea of the Muslim World*, 97–98.

91. Özcan, *Pan-Islamism*, 15–18.

92. Quoted in Qureshi, *Pan-Islam in British India*, 14–15, 23–24.

93. Karpat, *The Politicization of Islam*, 140–55.

94. M. S. Anderson, *The Eastern Question, 1774-1923: A Study in International Relations* (London: Macmillan, 1966), 178–260.

95. Qureshi, *Pan-Islam in British India*, 12–24.

96. Özcan, *Pan-Islamism*, 115–26; and Qureshi, *Pan-Islam in British India*, 21–22, 25.

97. Özcan, *Pan-Islamism*, 68–70.

98. Faiz Ahmed, "Contested Subjects: Ottoman and British Jurisdictional Quarrels in re Afghans and Indian Muslims," *Journal of the Ottoman and Turkish Studies Association* 3, no. 2 (2016): 328–34; and Eric Lewis Beverley, *Hyderabad, British India, and the World: Muslim Networks and Minor Sovereignty, c. 1850-1950* (Cambridge: Cambridge University Press, 2015), 45–49, 122–24.

99. Jeffery Dyer, "Pan-Islamic Propagandists or Professional Diplomats?: The Ottoman Consular Establishment in the Colonial Indian Ocean," in *The Subjects of Ottoman International Law*, ed. Lâle Can, Michael Christopher Low, Kent F. Schull, and Robert Zens (Bloomington: Indiana University Press, 2020).

100. Özcan, *Pan-Islamism*, 74–75.

101. Özcan, *Pan-Islamism*, 90–93.

102. John F. Keane, *My Journey to Medinah: Describing a Pilgrimage to Medinah* (London: Tinsley Brothers, 1881), 190–91.

103. TNA: FO 685/1 (September 1879); and F. E. Peters, *Mecca: A Literary History of the Holy Land* (Princeton, NJ: Princeton University Press, 1994), 340.

104. Slight, *The British Empire and the Hajj*, 96–98.

105. This quote comes from Zohrab's successor, Lynedoch Moncrieff. TNA: FO 539/21 (10 May 1882).

106. Karpat, *The Politicization of Islam*, 245–48.

107. Ş. Tufan Buzpınar, "Opposition to the Ottoman Caliphate in the Early Years of Abdülhamid II: 1877–1882," *Die Welt des Islams* 36, no. 1 (1996): 65–69. For an opposing British view, see James W. Redhouse's defense of the Ottoman Caliphate, *A Vindication of the Ottoman Sultan's Title of "Caliph"; Shewing Its Antiquity, Validity, and Universal Acceptance* (London: Effingham Wilson, Royal Exchange, 1877).
108. George Birdwood, *The Times*, 12 June 1877.
109. Slight, *The British Empire and the Hajj*, 96–98.
110. Wilfrid Scawen Blunt, *The Future of Islam* (London: Kegan Paul, Trench & Co., 1882), 194–95.
111. Blunt, *The Future of Islam*, 208–209.
112. Blunt, *The Future of Islam*, 209–11.
113. TNA: FO 685/1 (3 July 1879); and Özcan, *Pan-Islamism*, 93–94.
114. Slight, *The British Empire and the Hajj*, 16.
115. Christiaan Snouck Hurgronje, *Mekka in the Latter Part of the 19th Century* (Leiden: Brill, 1931), 290–91; and Tagliacozzo, *The Longest Journey*, 167–76.

2. Legal Imperialism: Foreign Muslims and Muslim Consuls

1. Turan Kayaoğlu, *Legal Imperialism: Sovereignty and Extraterritoriality in Japan, the Ottoman Empire, and China* (Cambridge: Cambridge University Press, 2010), 6.
2. Lâle Can and Michael Christopher Low, "The 'Subjects' of Ottoman International Law," *Journal of the Ottoman and Turkish Studies Association* 3, no. 2 (2016): 227–28.
3. BOA, Y.PRK.AZJ, 16/13 (13 Ra 1307/8 November 1889).
4. BOA, Y.PRK.TKM, 28/68 (29 Z 1310/14 July 1893); BOA, Y.PRK.AZN, 11/52 (10 L 1312/6 April 1895); Nurtaç Numan, "The Emirs of Mecca and the Ottoman Government of Hijaz, 1840–1908" (master's thesis, Boğaziçi University, 2005), 144–47, 158–60; and Rifat Uçarol, *Gazi Ahmet Muhtar Paşa (1839–1919): Askeri ve Siyasi Hayatı* (İstanbul: Derin Yayınları, 2015), 238–42.
5. Thomas Kuehn, *Empire, Islam, and Politics of Difference: Ottoman Rule in Yemen, 1849–1919* (Leiden: Brill, 2011), 1–90.
6. BOA, Y.PRK.MK, 4/42 (23 Ra 1306/27 November 1888).
7. BOA, Y.EE, 118/10 (3 C 1315/30 October 1897).
8. Butrus Abu-Manneh, "Sultan Abdülhamid and the Sharifs of Mecca, 1880–1890," *Asian and African Studies* 9, no. 1 (1973): 5.
9. Murat Özyüksel, *The Hejaz Railway and the Ottoman Empire: Modernity, Industrialisation and Ottoman Decline* (London: I. B. Tauris, 2014), 161–62.
10. Emphasis mine. BOA, Y.EE, 5/59 (9 R 1323/13 June 1905). Note that this 1905 file documents Cevdet's earlier opinions on the matter, which were recorded before his death in 1895. On Cevdet's participation in this debate, see also Numan, "The Emirs of Mecca and the Ottoman Government of Hijaz," 159–60.
11. F. A. K. Yasamee, *Ottoman Diplomacy: Abdülhamid II and the Great Powers, 1878–1888* (Istanbul: Isis Press, 1996), 90.

12. BOA, Y.EE, 4/59, undated *muhtıra-ı seniye* from Ahmed Midhat Efendi to Abdül-hamid, reproduced in Sultan İkinci Abdülhamid Han, *Devlet ve Memleket Görüşlerim*, ed. A. Atilla Çetin (İstanbul: Çamlıca, 2011), 2:241.

13. Undated *layiha*, BOA, Y.EE, 101/95 (6 R 1327/27 April 1909).

14. Undated *layiha*, BOA, Y.EE, 101/95 (6 R 1327/27 April 1909).

15. On the Capitulations, see Umut Özsu, "Ottoman Empire," in *The Oxford Handbook of the History of International Law*, ed. Bardo Fassbender and Anne Peters (Oxford: Oxford University Press, 2012), 429–48; Feroz Ahmad, "Ottoman Perceptions of the Capitulations, 1800–1914," *Journal of Islamic Studies* 11, no. 1 (2000): 1–20; and Maurits Van der Boogert, *The Capitulations and the Ottoman Legal System: Qadis, Consuls, and Bertalıs in the 18th Century* (Leiden: Brill, 2005). On the politics of pro-tégés and protected persons, see Lâle Can, "The Protection Question: Central Asians and Extraterritoriality in the Late Ottoman Empire," *International Journal of Middle East Studies* 48 (2016): 679–99; Will Hanley, *Identifying with Nationality: Europeans, Ottomans, and Egyptians in Alexandria* (New York: Columbia University Press, 2017); and Mary Dewhurst Lewis, *Divided Rule: Sovereignty and Empire in French Tunisia, 1881–1938* (Berkeley: University of California Press, 2014).

16. Umut Özsu, "The Ottoman Empire, the Origins of Extraterritoriality, and International Legal Theory," in *The Oxford Handbook of the Theory of International Law*, ed. Florian Hoffman and Anne Orford (Oxford: Oxford University Press, 2016), 129.

17. Nasim Sousa, *The Capitulatory Régime of Turkey: Its History, Origin, and Nature* (Baltimore: Johns Hopkins University Press, 1933), 71, 81–82, 321.

18. Ehud Toledano, *The Ottoman Slave Trade and Its Suppression: 1840–1890* (Princeton, NJ: Princeton University Press, 1983), 1, 129–35.

19. The law, *Tebaa-yı Ecnebiyenin Emlake Mutasarrıf Olmaları Hakkında Kanun*, was promulgated on 10 June 1867 (7 S 1284). Article 1 specifies that foreigners are eligible to own real estate anywhere but the Hijaz. See H. Nedjib Chiha, "Osmanlı Devletinde Gayrimenkul Mülkiyeti Bakımından Yabancıların Hukuki Durumu," trans. Halil Cin, *Ankara Üniversitesi Hukuk Fakültesi Dergisi* 24 (1967): 246–74.

20. Selim Deringil, *The Well-Protected Domains: Ideology and Legitimation of Power in the Ottoman Empire, 1876–1909* (London: I. B. Tauris, 1999), 60.

21. Davide Rodogno, *Against Massacre: Humanitarian Interventions in the Ottoman Empire, 1815–1914* (Princeton, NJ: Princeton University Press, 2012), 29–35, 38–41, 43–47.

22. Selim Deringil, *Conversion and Apostasy in the Late Ottoman Empire* (Cambridge: Cambridge University Press, 2012), 181–82.

23. Will Hanley, "What Ottoman Nationality Was and Was Not," *Journal of the Ottoman and Turkish Studies Association* 3, no. 2 (2016): 277–98.

24. On *mücavirin* and their theoretically distinct status from Muslim refugees and migrants (*muhacirin* or *mülteciler*), see Lâle Can, *Spiritual Subjects: Central Asian Pilgrims and the Ottoman Hajj at the End of Empire* (Stanford, CA: Stanford University Press, 2020), 161–74. As Can points out, while *mücavirin* were technically not supposed to be permanent migrants or would-be Ottoman subjects, in reality, many did settle in Mecca and Medina, forming semi-permanent diaspora populations.

25. Deringil, *Conversion and Apostasy in the Late Ottoman Empire*, 181–82.

26. TNA: FO 195/1451 (17 April 1883; 13 May 1883); and BOA, A.DVN.MKL, 25/25 (15 R 1301/14 January 1884).
27. Can, "The Protection Question," 683.
28. On the requirement to produce proof of foreign nationality, see Article 9 of the Ottoman nationality law in *Sâlnâme-i Nezâret-i Umûr-ı Hâriciyye: Osmanlı Dışişleri Bakanlığı Yıllığı, 1320/1902* (İstanbul: İşaret Yayınları, 2003), 166–67.
29. Ziad Fahmy, "Jurisdictional Borderlands: Extraterritoriality and 'Legal Chameleons' in Precolonial Alexandria, 1840–1870," *Comparative Studies in Society and History* 55, no. 2 (2013): 305–29.
30. James Meyer, *Turks Across Empires. Marketing Muslim Identity in the Russian-Ottoman Borderlands, 1856–1914* (Oxford: Oxford University Press, 2014), 1–47.
31. Can, "The Protection Question," 681; and Julia Stephens, "An Uncertain Inheritance: The Imperial Travels of Legal Migrants, from British India to Ottoman Iraq," *Law and History Review* 32, no. 4 (2014): 749–72.
32. John Slight, *The British Empire and the Hajj, 1865–1956* (Cambridge, MA: Harvard University Press, 2015), 96–97.
33. Slight, *The British Empire and the Hajj*, 96–97.
34. Ulrike Freitag, "Helpless Representative of the Great Powers? Western Consuls in Jeddah, 1830s to 1914," *The Journal of Imperial and Commonwealth History* 40, no. 3 (2012): 357–81.
35. Slight, *The British Empire and the Hajj*, 105–14.
36. TNA: FO 685/1 (3 July 1879); and F. E. Peters, *Mecca: A Literary History of the Holy Land* (Princeton, NJ: Princeton University Press, 1994), 340–42.
37. Azmi Özcan, *Pan-Islamism: Indian Muslims, the Ottomans and Britain, 1877–1924* (Leiden: Brill, 1997), 93–95.
38. William Roff, "Sanitation and Security: The Imperial Powers and the Nineteenth Century Hajj," *Arabian Studies* VI (1982): 147–48.
39. British Library (hereafter BL): Asia, Pacific, and Africa Collections, W 4087 (24 June 1879), 46.
40. Roff, "Sanitation and Security," 147–48, 156.
41. BOA, Y.PRK.UM, 4/72 (5 Za 1298/29 September 1881).
42. Slight, *The British Empire and the Hajj*, 120.
43. Slight, *The British Empire and the Hajj*, 104–14, 112, 120–21.
44. Michael Christopher Low, "Empire and the Hajj: Pilgrims, Plagues, and Pan-Islam Under British Surveillance, 1865–1908," *International Journal of Middle East Studies* 40, no. 2 (2008): 280–85.
45. Slight, *The British Empire and the Hajj*, 17.
46. Slight, *The British Empire and the Hajj*, 17, 105–22, 319.
47. BOA, Y.PRK.UM, 4/37 (13 Ra 1298/13 February 1881).
48. Emphasis mine. TNA: FO 195/375 (17 February 1881).
49. TNA: FO 195/375, English translation of ʿAbd al-Muṭṭalib's reply, undated.
50. TNA: FO 195/1415 (9 November 1882).
51. BOA, Y. PRK.UM, 5/80 (25 R 1300/5 Mach. 1883).
52. TNA: FO 195/1415 (9 November 1882). On parallel Russian efforts to open a consulate in Mecca, see also Eileen Kane, *Russian Hajj: Empire and the Pilgrimage to Mecca* (Ithaca, NY: Cornell University Press, 2015), 42–46.

53. TNA: FO 424/159 (May 1889), 2, 16–17, 19–20, 22–23.
54. Emphasis mine. BOA, A.MKT.UM, 511/80 (25 R 1278/30 September 1861).
55. TNA: FO 195/1610 (14 December 1888); and TNA: FO 539/18 (20 September 1880).
56. TNA: FO 424/159 (May 1889), 16, 19–20.
57. TNA: FO 195/1482 (4 November 1884); and TNA: FO 195/1514 (20 March 1885).
58. TNA: FO 195/1514 (22 October 1884).
59. TNA: FO 195/1514 (20 March 1885).
60. TNA: FO 195/1482 (4 November 1884).
61. TNA: FO 195/1482, "Deposition of Amna, Widow of the Late Hadji Ibrahim Abdus Sattar" (9 November 1884).
62. TNA: FO 195/1482, "Deposition of Amna, Widow of the Late Hadji Ibrahim Abdus Sattar" (9 November 1884).
63. TNA: FO 195/1514 (20 March 1885).
64. Stanford Shaw and Ezra Kural Shaw, History of the Ottoman Empire and Modern Turkey, vol. 2 (Cambridge: Cambridge University Press, 1977), 114–15.
65. Thomas Kuehn, Empire, Islam, and Politics of Difference: Ottoman Rule in Yemen, 1849-1919 (Leiden: Brill, 2011), 91–92; Gökhan Çetinsaya, Ottoman Administration of Iraq, 1890-1908 (London: Routledge, 2006), 8–9, 20, 74; and Stanford Shaw, "The Nineteenth Century Ottoman Tax Reforms and Revenue System," International Journal of Middle East Studies 6, no. 4 (1975): 427.
66. Belkıs Konan, "Osmanlı Devletinde Yabancıların Kapitülasyonlar Kapsamında Hukuki Durumu" (PhD diss., Ankara University, 2006), 98–111.
67. TNA: FO 685/1 (24 March 1879).
68. Roff, "Sanitation and Security," 148, 158.
69. William Ochsenwald, Religion, Society, and the State in Arabia: The Hijaz Under Ottoman Control, 1840-1908 (Columbus: Ohio State University Press, 1984), 17.
70. BOA, İ.DH, 1295-2/102011 (2 R 1299/21 February 1882).
71. Selçuk Akşin Somel, "Osman Nuri Paşa'nın 17 Temmuz 1885 Tarihli Hicaz Raporu," Tarih Araştırmaları Dergisi 18/29 (1996): 13–14.
72. BOA, Y.PRK.UM, 5/57 (21 S 1300/1 January 1883).
73. BOA, Y.A.RES, 15/38 (17 Ca 1299/6 April 1882), quoted in Deringil, The Well-Protected Domains, 56.
74. BOA, Y.EE, 88/67 (11 M 1298/14 December 1880); and BOA, Y.PRK.UM, 5/57 (21 S 1300/1 January 1883).
75. Can, "The Protection Question," 689.
76. TNA: FO 539/21 (7 May 1882), 110.
77. Can, "The Protection Question," 688.
78. BOA, İ.DH, 1295-2/102011 (2 R 1299/21 February 1882).
79. BOA, Y.EE, 88/67 (11 M 1298/14 December 1880); and BOA, İ.DH, 1295-2/102011 (2 R 1299/21 February 1882).
80. BOA, Y.A.RES, 15/38 (17 Ca 1299/6 Apil. 1882).
81. Can, "The Protection Question," 688–89.

82. Hanley, *Identifying with Nationality*, 61, 256–79.
83. Can, "The Protection Question," 688–89.
84. Somel, "Osman Nuri," 13–14.
85. BOA, İ.MMS, 104/4442 (24 Ş 1306/25 April 1889).
86. Hanley, *Identifying with Nationality*, 137–52.
87. Karen M. Kern, *Imperial Citizens, Marriage and Citizenship in the Ottoman Frontier Provinces of Iraq* (Syracuse, NY: Syracuse University Press, 2011), 89–137; and Can, *Spiritual Subjects*, 154–61.
88. Kern, *Imperial Citizens*, 97–102, 159; Yitzhak Nakash, *The Shi'is of Iraq* (Princeton, NJ: Princeton University Press, 1994), 17; and Çetinsaya, *Ottoman Administration of Iraq*, 99–126.
89. On the Awadh Bequest and British consular influence in Iraq, see Çetinsaya, *Ottoman Administration of Iraq*, 100, 106, 127–46; Gökhan Çetinsaya, "The Caliph and Mujtahids: Ottoman Policy Towards the Shiite Community of Iraq in the Late Nineteenth Century," *Middle Eastern Studies* 41, no. 4 (2005): 561–74; and Meir Litvak, "Money, Religion, and Politics: The Oudh Bequest in Najaf and Karbala', 1850–1903," *International Journal of Middle East Studies* 33 (2001): 1–21.
90. Kern, *Imperial Citizen*, 60–88.
91. Can, *Spiritual Subjects*, 157–61.
92. Arzu Terzi, *Hazine-i Hassa Nezareti* (Ankara: Tarih Kurumu Basımevi, 2000); and Arzu Terzi, *Bağdat-Musul'da Abdülhamid'in Mirası: Petrol ve Arazi* (İstanbul: Timaş, 2009).
93. Roy S. Fischel and Ruth Kark, "Sultan Abdülhamid II and Palestine: Private Lands and Imperial Policy," *New Perspectives on Turkey* 39 (2008): 129–66; and Johann Büssow, *Hamidian Palestine: Politics and Society in the District of Jerusalem, 1872–1908* (Leiden: Brill, 2011).
94. On the origins and function of the *Hukuk Müşavirliği İstişare Odası*, see Aimee M. Genell, "The Well-Defended Domains: Eurocentric International Law and the Making of the Ottoman Office of Legal Counsel," *Journal of Ottoman and Turkish Studies Association* 3, no. 2 (2016): 255–75.
95. BOA, ŞD, 2256/23 (8 Ca 1306/10 January 1889), quoted in Can, *Spiritual Subjects*, 159–60.
96. Slight, *The British Empire and the Hajj*, 121.
97. BOA, Y.PRK.ŞD, 3/34 (29 Z 1320/29 March 1903).
98. BOA, HR.HMŞ.İŞO, 200/7 (28 Z 1328/31 December 1910).
99. BOA, HR.HMŞ.İŞO, 200/8 (8 C 1329/6 June 1911); and BOA, HR.HMŞ.İŞO, 200/11 (27 M 1330/17 January 1912).
100. BOA, HR.HMŞ.İŞO, 200/7 (28 Z 1328/31 December 1910).
101. BOA, HR.HMŞ.İŞO, 200/10 (28 L 1329/22 October 1911).
102. BOA, HR.HMŞ.İŞO, 200/5 (2 N 1332/25 July 1915).
103. BOA, HR.HMŞ.İŞO, 200/10 (28 L 1329/22 October 1911); and BOA, HR.HMŞ.İŞO, 201/47 (27 Ca 1329/26 May 1911).
104. BOA, HR.HMŞ.İŞO, 200/10 (28 L 1329/22 October 1911).
105. Emphasis mine. TNA: FO 424/159 (May 1889), 22.

3. Microbial Mecca and the Global Crisis of Cholera

1. Murat Gül, *The Emergence of Modern Istanbul: Transformation and Modernisation of a City* (London: I. B. Tauris, 2009), 42.
2. BOA, İ.DH, 1242/97329 (16 S 1309/21 September 1891); and BOA, Y.A.HUS, 251/138 (20 S 1309/25 September 1891).
3. BOA, İ.DH, 1242/97329 (16 S 1309/21 September 1891); and BOA, Y.A.HUS, 251/138 (20 S 1309/25 September 1891).
4. Gülden Sarıyıldız, *Hicaz Karantina Teşkilatı, 1865-1914* (Ankara: Türk Tarih Kurumu Basımevi, 1996), 14.
5. Mesut Ayar, *Osmanlı Devletinde Kolera: İstanbul Örneği (1892-1895)* (İstanbul: Kitabevi, 2007), 28-29.
6. Sadri Sema, *Eski İstanbul Hatıraları*, ed. Ali Şükrü Çoruk (İstanbul: Kitabevi, 2002), 31.
7. Michel Foucault, *Discipline and Punish: The Birth of the Prison* (New York: Vintage Books, 1995) 189-91. See also Foucault, *Security, Territory, Population: Lectures at the Collège de France, 1977-1978* (New York: Picador, 2007); and Alison Bashford, "Global Biopolitics and the History of World Health," *History of the Human Sciences* 19, no. 1 (2006): 67-88.
8. William H. McNeill, *Plagues and Peoples* (New York: Anchor Books, 1976), 269.
9. Ayar, *Osmanlı Devletinde Kolera*, 17-33.
10. İzzeddin, *Mekke-i Mükerreme'de Kolera ve Hıfzısıhha* (İstanbul: Mahmud Bey Matbaası, 1327/1911), 77-80; and Sarıyıldız, *Hicaz Karantina Teşkilatı*, 67.
11. Ayar, *Osmanlı Devletinde Kolera*, 457.
12. Alan Mikhail, *Under Osman's Tree: The Ottoman Empire, Egypt & Environmental History* (Chicago: University of Chicago Press, 2017), 199-203; Nükhet Varlık, *Plague and Empire in the Early Modern Mediterranean World: The Ottoman Experience, 1347-1600* (Cambridge: Cambridge University Press, 2015), 8; and Sam White, *The Climate of Rebellion in the Early Modern Ottoman Empire* (Cambridge: Cambridge University Press, 2011), 17.
13. David Arnold, "The Indian Ocean as a Disease Zone, 1500–1950," *South Asia: Journal of South Asian Studies* 14, no. 2 (1991): 1–21.
14. On the symptoms, causative agent, etiology, and prevention of cholera, see the World Health Organization's Cholera Fact Sheet, http://www.who.int/news-room/fact-sheets/detail/cholera; Mayo Clinic, "Cholera," https://www.mayoclinic.org/diseases-conditions/cholera/symptoms-causes/syc-20355287; and Jason B. Harris, Regina C. LaRocque, Firdausi Qadri, Edward T. Ryan, Stephen B. Calderwood, "Cholera," *Lancet* 379, no. 9835 (2012): 2466–76.
15. Elizabeth Zachariadou, "Natural Disasters: Moments of Opportunity," in *Natural Disasters in the Ottoman Empire: Halcyon Days in Crete III: A Symposium Held in Rethymnon 10-12 January 1997*, ed. Elizabeth Zachariadou (Rethymnon, Greece: Crete University Press, 1999), 7-11.
16. Yaron Ayalon, *Natural Disasters in the Ottoman Empire: Plague, Famine, and Other Misfortunes* (Cambridge: Cambridge University Press, 2015), 171-207.
17. On the evolution of Ottoman conceptions of epidemic diseases, their etiology, and prevention, from the realms of Islamic-legal, theological, and mystical

discourses to those of modern medicine and state institutions, see Varlık, *Plague and Empire in the Early Modern Mediterranean World*, 207–47; and Birsen Bulmuş, *Plague, Quarantines and Geopolitics in the Ottoman Empire* (Edinburgh: Edinburgh University Press, 2012).

18. Ira Klein, "Death in India, 1871–1921," *Journal of Asian Studies* 32, no. 4 (1973): 639–59.

19. David Arnold, "Cholera and Colonialism in British India," *Past and Present* 113 (1986): 118–51.

20. Sunil Amrith, *Unruly Waters: How Rains, Rivers, Coasts, and Seas Have Shaped South Asia's History* (New York: Basic Books, 2018); Rohan D'Souza, "Water in British India: The Making of a 'Colonial Hydrology,' " *History Compass* 4, no. 4 (2006): 621–28; David Gilmartin, "Scientific Empire and Imperial Science: Colonialism and Irrigation Technology in the Indus Basin," *Journal of Asian Studies* 53, no. 4 (1994): 1127–49; and Michael M. Mann, "Ecological Change in North India: Deforestation and Agrarian Distress in the Ganga-Jamna Doab, 1800–1850," *Environment and History* 1, no. 2 (1995): 201–20.

21. Klein, "Death in India," 646.

22. Mike Davis, *Late Victorian Holocausts: El Niño and the Making of the Third World* (New York: Verso, 2001), 10, 26–27; Daniel R. Headrick, *The Tentacles of Progress: Technology Transfer in the Age of Imperialism, 1850–1940* (New York: Oxford University Press, 1998), 18–208; and Sheldon Watts, *Epidemics and History: Disease, Power and Imperialism* (New Haven, CT: Yale University Press, 1997), 202.

23. Davis, *Late Victorian Holocausts*, 1–59.

24. David Arnold, *Colonizing the Body: State Medicine and Epidemic Disease in Nineteenth-Century India* (Berkeley: University of California Press, 1993), 161, 200.

25. Davis, *Late Victorian Holocausts*, 7, 33–47; David Arnold, "Social Crisis and Epidemic Disease in the Famines of Nineteenth-Century India," *Social History of Medicine* 6, no. 3 (1993): 385–404; and Tim Dyson, "On the Demography of South Asian Famines: Part I," *Population Studies* 45, no. 1 (1991): 5–25.

26. Myron Echenberg, *Africa in the Time of Cholera, 1817 to the Present* (Cambridge: Cambridge University Press, 2011), 15–18; and McNeill, *Plagues and Peoples*, 266–76.

27. Christopher Hamlin, *Cholera: The Biography* (Oxford: Oxford University Press, 2009), 4.

28. Ayar, *Osmanlı Devletinde Kolera*, 10, 23–25; and Mark Harrison, *Contagion: How Commerce Has Spread Disease* (New Haven, CT: Yale University Press, 2012), 139–42.

29. Peter Baldwin, *Contagion and the State in Europe, 1830–1930* (Cambridge: Cambridge University Press, 1999), 211–43.

30. Charles Issawi, *The Fertile Crescent, 1800–1914* (New York: Oxford University Press, 1988), 51–53.

31. Baldwin, *Contagion and the State in Europe*, 227.

32. Ayar, *Osmanlı Devletinde Kolera*, 15–16.

33. Arnold, *Colonizing the Body*, 186.

34. Ḥamdī bin ʿAzīz, *Kolera* (İstanbul: Mekteb-i Tıbbiye-i Şahane Matbaası, 1311/1893–94), 10, 12.

35. Bulmuş, *Plague, Quarantines and Geopolitics in the Ottoman Empire*, 145–74.

36. BOA, İ.MMS, 37/1555 (25 Ca 1286/2 September 1869).
37. Gülden Sarıyıldız, "Karantina Meclisi'nin Kuruluşu ve Faaliyetleri," *Belleten* 222 (1994): 329–76.
38. Ayalon, *Natural Disasters in the Ottoman Empire*, 190–91.
39. Bulmuş, *Plague, Quarantines and Geopolitics in the Ottoman Empire*, 108–13.
40. Ayar, *Osmanlı Devletinde Kolera*, 383–88.
41. M. Cemil Bilsel, *Lozan*, vol. 2 (İstanbul: Ahmet Ihsan Matbaası, 1933), 156–58; and Osman Şevki Uludağ, "Son Kapitülasyonlardan Biri Karantina," *Belleten* 2, no. 7/8 (1938): 445–67.
42. Turan Kayaoğlu, *Legal Imperialism: Sovereignty and Extraterritoriality in Japan, the Ottoman Empire, and China* (Cambridge: Cambridge University Press, 2010), 108–10.
43. Valeska Huber, "The Unification of the Globe by Disease? The International Sanitary Conferences on Cholera, 1851–1894," *Historical Journal* 49, no. 2 (2006): 463–64.
44. Ahmed Midhat, "Devlet-i Aliye-i Osmaniye'de Karantina Yani Usul-ı Tahaffuzun Tarihçesi," in *Salname-i Nezaret-i Hariciye, 1318* (İstanbul: Matbaa-ı Osmaniye 1318/1900-1901), 468–69.
45. Thomas Kuehn, *Empire, Islam, and Politics of Difference: Ottoman Rule in Yemen, 1849-1919* (Leiden: Brill, 2011), 32–52.
46. BOA, İ.MMS, 31/1286 (3 Ş 1282/22 December 1865); BOA, İ.MMS, 34/1387 (16 L 1283/21 February 1867).
47. BOA, İ.MVL, 562/25242 (8 C 1283/18 October 1866); BOA, İ.MMS, 35/1448 (12 N 1284/7 January 1868).
48. Ayalon, *Natural Disasters in the Ottoman Empire*, 205.
49. BOA, İ.MMS, 34/1387 (16 L 1283/21 February 1867).
50. Sarıyıldız, *Hicaz Karantina Teşkilatı*, 19–22.
51. LaVerne Kuhnke, *Lives at Risk: Public Health in Nineteenth-Century Egypt* (Berkeley: University of California Press, 1990), 92–111.
52. BOA, İ.MMS, 34/1387 (16 L 1283/21 February 1867).
53. Ehud Toledano, *The Ottoman Slave Trade and Its Suppression: 1840-1890* (Princeton, NJ: Princeton University Press, 1983), 206–12.
54. Valeska Huber, *Channelling Mobilities: Migration and Globalisation in the Suez Canal Region and Beyond, 1869-1914* (Cambridge: Cambridge University Press, 2013), 82–89, 241–71.
55. *Murāsalāt al-Bāb al-ʿAlī ilá Wilāyat al-Ḥijāz (Makkah al-Mukarrama-al-Madinah al-Munawwara), 1283-1291 H.*, ed. and trans. Suhail Şābān (London: al-Furqan Islamic Heritage Foundation, Encyclopedia of Makkah and Medina Branch, 2004), 122, 143; and William Ochsenwald, *Religion, Society, and the State in Arabia: The Hijaz Under Ottoman Control, 1840-1908* (Columbus: Ohio State University Press, 1984), 100–101.
56. BOA, İ.DH, 583/40599 (25 B 1285/11 November 1868); BOA, A.MKT.MHM, 390/46 (5 Ca 1284/24 August 1868); BOA, A.MKT.MHM, 427/6 (4 Ş 1285/20 November 1868); BOA, A.MKT.MHM, 436/58 (13 Za 1285/25 February 1869); and Sarıyıldız, *Hicaz Karantina Teşkilatı*, 27–29.
57. Şābān, *Murāsalāt al-Bāb al-ʿAlī ilá Wilāyat al-Ḥijāz*, 141–42.

58. Sarıyıldız, *Hicaz Karantina Teşkilatı*, 29–32; and Ayar, *Osmanlı Devletinde Kolera*, 388.
59. Norman Howard-Jones, *The Scientific Background of the International Sanitary Conferences, 1851-1938* (Geneva: World Health Organization, 1975), 35–41.
60. TNA: FO 7/982, "International Sanitary Convention, Commission of Enquiry, Permanent Council, vol. 1, Proposals for Preventing the Spread of Cholera" (December 1874–December 1876; and FO 881/5155X (April 1885), 3–4.
61. TNA: FO 7/982, "International Sanitary Convention, Commission of Enquiry, Permanent Council, vol. 1" (December 1874–December 1876; and FO 881/5155X (April 1885), 3–4.
62. TNA: FO 7/982, "International Sanitary Convention, Commission of Enquiry, Permanent Council, vol. 1" (December 1874–December 1876; FO 881/5155X (April 1885), 3–4.
63. TNA: FO 881/5011, W. Maycock, "Memorandum Respecting the Quarantine Restrictions Adopted by Foreign Countries in Consequence of the Outbreak of Cholera in Europe" (30 September 1884), 2, 42.
64. William Coleman, "Koch's Comma Bacillus: The First Year," *Bulletin of the History of Medicine* 61 (1987): 315–42.
65. Sheldon Watts, "From Rapid Change to Stasis: Official Responses to Cholera in British-Ruled India and Egypt, 1860 to c. 1921," *Journal of World History* 12, no. 2 (2001): 347–56; and Jeremy D. Issacs, "D. D. Cunningham and the Aetiology of Cholera in British India, 1869-1897," *Medical History* 42 (1998): 281–83.
66. Hamlin, *Cholera*, 158–159; and Margaret Pelling, *Cholera, Fever and English Medicine, 1825-1865* (Oxford: Oxford University Press, 1978), 1–80.
67. TNA: FO 881/5155X (April 1885), 5; and Watts, *Epidemics and History*, 205.
68. J. M. Cunningham, *Cholera: What Can the State Do to Prevent It?* (Calcutta: Superintendent of Government Printing, India, 1884), 24.
69. Watts, "From Rapid Change to Stasis," 354.
70. Arnold, *Colonizing the Body*, 194.
71. Mariko Ogawa, "Uneasy Bedfellows: Science and Politics in the Refutation of Koch's Bacterial Theory of Cholera," *Bulletin of the History of Medicine* 74, no. 4 (2000): 687, 694–99. See also TNA: FO 881/5155X (April 1885), 34–39; and FO 881/5172X, Drs. H. Gibbes and E. Klein, "An Enquiry Into the Etiology of Asiatic Cholera" (1885).
72. Howard-Jones, *The Scientific Background of the International Sanitary Conferences*, 46–57.
73. Mark Harrison, "Quarantine, Pilgrimage, and Colonial Trade: India 1866–1900," *Indian Economic and Social Review* 29, no. 2 (1992): 127–31.
74. Ḥamdī bin ʿAzīz, *Kolera*, 82–97.
75. Huber, "The Unification of the Globe by Disease?," 466.
76. Watts, *Epidemics and History*, 192.
77. "Cholera in Egypt," *Lancet* 122, no. 3133 (15 September 1883): 482.
78. Ochsenwald, *Religion, Society, and the State in Arabia*, 67.
79. John F. Keane, *Six Months in Mecca: An Account of the Muhammedan Pilgrimage to Mecca* (London: Tinsley Brothers, 1881), 176–86.
80. Ḥamdī bin ʿAzīz, *Kolera*, 11–12.
81. Gülden Sarıyıldız and Ayşe Kavak, eds., *Halife II. Abdülhamid'in Hac Siyaseti: Dr. M. Şakir Bey'in Hatıraları* (İstanbul: Timaş, 2009), 60–62, 150, 248, 297–300.

82. BOA, Y.A.HUS, 168/98 (25 Za 1298/19 October 1881).
83. Gülden Sarıyıldız, "XIX Yüzyılında Osmanlı İmparatorluğu'nda Kolera Salgını," in *Tarih Boyunca Anadolu'da Doğal Afetler ve Deprem Semineri* (İstanbul: Globus Dünya Basımevi, 2000), 317.
84. TNA: FO 195/1415 (25 January 1882).
85. Ayar, *Osmanlı Devletinde Kolera*, 22–38, 80–82.
86. BOA, İ.DH, 840/67562 (5 M 1299/27 November 1881); and BOA, İ.DH, 841/67635 (11 M 1299/3 December 1881).
87. BOA, Y.EE, 143/46 (28 Za 1298/22 October 1881); BOA, Y.A.RES, 7/29 (25 N 1297/31 August 1880); BOA, Y.A.RES 21/4 (9 N 1300/14 July 1883); and BOA, Y.A.RES, 23/30 (1 B 1301/27 April 1884).
88. BOA, İ.DH, 892/70972 (27 L 1300/31 August 1883); and BOA, İ.ŞD, 69/4058 (7 N 1301/1 July 1884).
89. "Kamarān," in *Mawsuʿat al-Yamaniyya*, 2nd ed., vol. 4, ed. Aḥmad Jābir ʿAfīf (Ṣanʿāʾ, Yemen: Muʾassasat al-ʿAfīf al-Thaqāfiyya, 2003), 2456–57; and Great Britain, Naval Intelligence Division, *Western Arabia and the Red Sea* (Oxford: Naval Intelligence Sub-Centre, 1946), 464–72.
90. BOA, İ.ŞD, 72/4233 (10 Ra 1302/28 December 1884).
91. Sarıyıldız, *Hicaz Karantina Teşkilatı*, 54–60.
92. TNA: FO 195/1415 (17 November 1882).
93. BOA, İ.ŞD, 69/4058 (7 N 1301/1 July 1884); and Sarıyıldız, *Hicaz Karantina Teşkilatı*, 54–60.
94. BOA, İ.ŞD, 72/4233 (10 Ra 1302/28 December 1884).
95. BOA, MV, 65/30 (7 Za 1308/13 June 1891); and BOA, ŞD, 2618/34 (6 M 1311/20 July 1893).
96. BOA, İ.DH, 1137/88673 (1 N 1306/1 May 1889); and BOA, MV 64/25 (6 N 1308/15 April 1891).
97. John Baldry, "The Ottoman Quarantine Station on Kamaran Island, 1882–1914," *Studies in the History of Medicine* 2 (1978): 32–45.
98. TNA: FO 195/1415 (17 November 1882).
99. Sarıyıldız, *Hicaz Karantina Teşkilatı*, 54–60.
100. Gülden Sarıyıldız and Oya Dağlar Macar, "Cholera, Pilgrimage, and International Politics of Sanitation: The Quarantine Station on the Island of Kamaran," in *Plague and Contagion in the Islamic Mediterranean*, ed. Nükhet Varlık (Kalamazoo, MI: Arc Humanities Press, 2017), 253–54.
101. TNA: FO 195/1415 (17 November 1882 and 24 November 1882).
102. TNA: FO 881/4942X (1883).
103. Alan de L. Rush, ed., *Records of the Hajj: A Documentary History of the Pilgrimage to Mecca* (London: Archive Editions, 1993), vol. 9, 217.
104. Yeniçeşmeli Hâfız Fâik Efendi, *İstanbul'dan Bombay'a Bir Osmanlı Fırkateyni'nin Keşif Seyahati*, A. Ergun Çınar, ed. (İstanbul: Kitabevi, 2014), 27.
105. TNA: FO 195/1415 (17 November 1882).
106. Baldry, "The Ottoman Quarantine Station on Kamaran Island," 33–34.
107. TNA: FO 195/1451 (2 January 1883).
108. Sarıyıldız and Kavak, *Halife II. Abdülhamid'in Hac Siyaseti*, 60–64, 150, 297–98.
109. Sarıyıldız and Kavak, *Halife II. Abdülhamid'in Hac Siyaseti*, 172.

110. BOA, İ.DH, 1229/96213 (8 L 1308/17 May 1891).
111. İzzeddin, *Mekke-i Mükerreme'de Kolera ve Hıfzısıhha*, 39.
112. Sarıyıldız, *Hicaz Karantina Teşkilatı*, 87.
113. Sarıyıldız, *Hicaz Karantina Teşkilatı*, 65–67.
114. BOA, Y.PRK.SH, 6/55 (7 Ra 1310/29 September 1892).
115. İzzeddin, *Mekke-i Mükerreme'de Kolera ve Hıfzısıhha*, 80.
116. BOA, Y.PRK.SH, 6/55 (7 Ra 1310/29 September 1892).
117. Ayar, *Osmanlı Devletinde Kolera*, 61–75.
118. Christopher Hamlin, "Cholera Forcing: The Myth of the Good Epidemic and the Coming of Good Water," *American Journal of Public Health* 99, no. 11 (2009): 1946–54; and Richard J. Evans, *Death in Hamburg: Society and Politics in the Cholera Years, 1830–1910* (Oxford: Oxford University Press, 1987).
119. Howard-Jones, *The Scientific Background of the International Sanitary Conferences*, 58–77.
120. TNA: FO 412/58 (29 January 1894).
121. F. E. Peters, *The Hajj: The Muslim Pilgrimage to Mecca and the Holy Places* (Princeton, NJ: Princeton University Press, 1994), 304.
122. Harrison, "Quarantine, Pilgrimage, and Colonial Trade," 135.
123. Huber, "The Unification of the Globe by Disease?," 474–75.
124. Mehmed Şakir's report, *Hicaz'in Ahval-i Umumiye-i Sıhhiye ve Islahat-ı Esasiye-i Hazırasına Dair Bazı Müşahedat ve Mülahazat-i Bendeganemi Havi Layiha-i Tıbbiye*, was originally prepared in 1890. See BOA, Y.A.HUS, 58/8 (17 Ş 1309/17 March 1892).
125. See also Dr. Kasım İzzeddin's proposals in BOA, DH.MKT, 57/34 (19 Ra 1313/9 September 1895).
126. Sarıyıldız, *Hicaz Karantina Teşkilatı*, 94–98.
127. Feza Günergun, "XIX. Yüzyılın İkinci Yarısında Osmanlı Kimyager-Eczacı Bonkowski Paşa, 1841–1905," *I. Türk Tıp Tarihi Kongresi* (Ankara: Türk Tarih Kurumu Basımevi, 1992), 229–48.
128. As this comparison implies, I have taken inspiration from Bruno Latour, *The Pasteurization of France* (Cambridge, MA: Harvard University Press, 1988).
129. Ayar, *Osmanlı Devletinde Kolera*, 295–319, 347–66; and İlhami Yurdakul, *Aziz Şehre Leziz Su: Dersaadet (İstanbul) Su Şirketi (1873–1933)* (İstanbul: Kitabevi, 2010), 29.
130. BOA, İ.DH, 1238/96943 (26 Z 1308/2 August 1891); and BOA, Y.A.RES, 56/10 (11 M 1309/17 August 1891).
131. Ayar, *Osmanlı Devletinde Kolera*, 399–400; and Sarıyıldız, *Hicaz Karantina Teşkilatı*, 88–89.
132. BOA, BEO 185/13815 (30 N 1310/7 April 1893); BOA, DH.MKT, 368/60 (3 Za 1312/28 April 1895); BOA, MV, 84/84 (22 R 1312/17 October 1894); BOA, Y.MTV, 92/56 (16 N 1311/23 March 1894); and Nuran Yıldırım, "Tersane-i Âmire Fabrikaları'nda Tebhir Makinesi/Etüv Üretimi ve Kullanımı," in *14. Yüzyıldan Cumhuriyet'e Hastalıklar Hastaneler Kurumlar: Sağlık Tarihi Yazıları-I* (İstanbul: Tarih Vakfı Yurt Yayınları, 2014), 437–46.
133. BOA, Y.A.HUS, 281/84 (27 Ra 1311/8 October 1893); BOA, Y.A.HUS, 282/24 (4 R 1311/15 October 1893); and BOA, Y.A.HUS, 283/73 (26 R 1311/6 November 1893).
134. Ayar, *Osmanlı Devletinde Kolera*, 308–23.

135. BOA, İ.MMS, 127/5443 (22 C 1309/23 January 1892); BOA, İ.MMS, 129/5506 (14 B 1309/13 February 1892); and BOA, Y.A.HUS, 291/15 (18 Ş 1311/24 February 1894). Dr. Cozzonis, an Ottoman physician of Italian origin, served as inspector of the İzmir quarantine station from 1885 to 1887 and then as inspector general of Ottoman quarantines from 1888 to 1902. See BOA, Y.PRK.SH, 3/23 (29 Z 1307/16 August 1890); BOA, Y.PRK.SH, 3/35 (1 Z 1308/8 July 1891); and Ayar, *Osmanlı Devletinde Kolera*, 94–95, 325, 399.

136. Sarıyıldız, *Hicaz Karantina Teşkilatı*, 87–94, 102–11.

137. Sarıyıldız and Macar, "Cholera, Pilgrimage, and International Politics of Sanitation," 256–57.

138. Sarıyıldız, *Hicaz Karantina Teşkilatı*, 55, 87–94, 102–11.

139. BOA, ŞD, 586/21 (8 L 1313/23 March 1896).

140. Sarıyıldız and Macar, "Cholera, Pilgrimage, and International Politics of Sanitation," 256–58.

141. Baldry, "The Ottoman Quarantine Station on Kamaran Island," 52–54, 62.

142. BOA, Y.A.HUS, 290/8 (2 Ş 1311/8 February 1894); BOA, Y.A.HUS, 291/31 (20 Ş 1311/26 February 1894); BOA, Y.A.HUS, 291/53 (23 Ş 1311/1 March 1894); and BOA, Y.A.HUS, 292/83 (19 N 1311/ 26 March 1894). See also Cassim Izzeddine (Kasım İzzeddin), *La défense sanitaire dans le Golfe Persique* (Paris: A. Maloine, 1912), 33–43; Bulmuş, *Plague, Quarantines and Geopolitics in the Ottoman Empire*, 155–59; and Isacar A. Bolaños, The Ottomans During the Global Crisis of Cholera and Plague: A View from Iraq and the Gulf," *International Journal of Middle East Studies* 51, no. 4 (2019): 603–620.

143. Sabri Ateş, "Bones of Contention: Corpse Traffic and Ottoman-Iranian Rivalry in Nineteenth-Century Iraq," *Comparative Studies of South Asia, Africa and the Middle East* 30, no. 3 (2010): 512–32.

144. Myron Echenberg, *Plague Ports: The Global Urban Impact of Bubonic Plague, 1894–1901* (New York: New York University Press, 2007), 47–78.

145. Baldry, "The Ottoman Quarantine Station on Kamaran Island," 65.

146. Howard-Jones, *The Scientific Background of the International Sanitary Conferences*, 79.

147. Baldry, "The Ottoman Quarantine Station on Kamaran Island," 65.

148. TNA: FO 195/1987 (11 June 1897).

149. TNA: FO 78/4981 (19 January 1898).

150. Baldry, "The Ottoman Quarantine Station on Kamaran Island," 66.

151. Echenberg, *Plague Ports*, 80–81.

152. Howard-Jones, *The Scientific Background of the International Sanitary Conferences*, 79.

153. Nuran Yıldırım, *A History of Health in Istanbul* (İstanbul: Düzey Matbaacılık, 2000), 30.

154. Sarıyıldız, *Hicaz Karantina Teşkilatı*, 120.

155. Jules Gervais-Courtellemont, *Mon voyage à la Mecque* (Paris: Hachette, 1896), 120–21.

156. TNA: FO 78/4788 (17 June 1895).

157. Ochsenwald, *Religion, Society, and the State in Arabia*, 196–97.

158. BOA, BEO, 633/47468 (8 Z 1312/2 June 1895); BOA, BEO 638/47787 (15 Z 1312/9 June 1895); BOA, İ.HUS, 38/4 (16 Z 1312/10 June 1895); BOA, Y.A.HUS, 329/98

(8 Z 1312/2 June 1895); BOA, Y.A.HUS, 330/19 (16 Z 1312/10 June 1895); BOA, Y.PRK.UM, 32/27 (16 Z 1312/10 June 1895); and TNA: FO 78/4788.

159. Sarıyıldız, *Hicaz Karantina Teşkilatı*, 119–20.
160. Ochsenwald, *Religion, Society, and the State in Arabia*, 198–200.
161. TNA: FO 78/4788.
162. BL: Asia, Pacific, and Africa Collections, W 4087, 46.

4. Bedouins and Broken Pipes

1. Edward Frankland, "The Cholera and Hagar's Well at Mecca," *Lancet* (August 11, 1883), 256–57. For similar debates surrounding water analysis in Cairo, see Shehab Ismail, "Epicures and Experts: The Drinking Water Controversy in British Colonial Cairo," *Arab Studies Journal* 26, no. 2 (2018): 8–42.
2. Gülden Sarıyıldız, *Hicaz Karantina Teşkilatı, 1865–1914* (Ankara: Türk Tarih Kurumu Basımevi, 1996), 77–79.
3. Mehmed Şakir Bey, *Hicaz Hacılığı Hakkında Şireli Doktor Stekoulis Cehl ve Hatası* (1308/1888), 106–12, cited in Sarıyıldız, *Hicaz Karantina Teşkilatı*, 77–79.
4. Frankland, "The Cholera and Hagar's Well at Mecca," 256.
5. TNA: FO 78/4335 (March 1887).
6. Sarıyıldız, *Hicaz Karantina Teşkilatı*, 77–79, 121. Similar suspicions applied to Dr. Abdur Razzack, whose official self-representation as a Muslim was referred to in Ottoman documents as a "great sham" (*fesad-ı azime*). See BOA, İ.HUS, 30/60 (19 R 1312/20 October 1894); and BOA, BEO, 499/37373 (21 R 1312/22 October1894).
7. Peter Baldwin, *Contagion and the State in Europe, 1830–1930* (Cambridge: Cambridge University Press, 1999), 228–31.
8. TNA: FO 881/5155X (April 1885).
9. Sheldon Watts, "From Rapid Change to Stasis: Official Responses to Cholera in British-Ruled India and Egypt, 1860 to c. 1921," *Journal of World History* 12, no. 2 (2001): 321–74.
10. Michael Worboys, *Spreading Germs: Disease Theories and Medical Practice in Britain, 1865–1900* (Cambridge: Cambridge University Press, 2000), 38–39.
11. William Coleman, "Koch's Comma Bacillus: The First Year," *Bulletin of the History of Medicine* 61 (1987): 315–42.
12. For more examples of attacks on Zamzam water, see C. W. Heaton, "Hagar's Well at Mecca: Analysis of the Water" and Stanley Lane Poole, "Traditional History of the Well," in *Lancet*, 5 (January 1884); and Dr. John Wortabet, "The Holy Places of Arabia: Their Water-Supply and General Sanitary Conditions," *Lancet* (May 14, 1892); "Dr. Hart in Hyderabad: Failure of Dr. Harte's Mission," *Moslem Chronicle* (March 1895), in BOA, Y.A.HUS, 323/84 (9 L 1312/5 April 1895).
13. William Ochsenwald, *Religion, Society, and the State in Arabia: The Hijaz Under Ottoman Control, 1840–1908* (Columbus: Ohio State University Press, 1984), 196.
14. Kasım İzzeddin, *Hicaz'da Teşkilat ve Islahat-ı Sıhhiye ve 1330 Senesi Hacc-ı Şerifi: Hicaz Sıhhiye İdaresi Senevi Rapor* (İstanbul: Matbaa-ı Amire, 1330/1914–15), 39–51.

15. Butrus Abu-Manneh, "Sultan Abdülhamid and the Sharifs of Mecca, 1880–1890," *Asian and African Studies* 9, no. 1 (1973): 5.

16. BOA, DH.SAİD.d, 18, 277; and M. Metin Hülagü, "Topal Osman Nuri Paşa Hayatı ve Faaliyetleri, 1840–1898," *Ankara Üniversitesi Osmanlı Tarihi Araştırma ve Uygulama Merkezi Dergisi* no. 5 (1994): 145–53.

17. Kemal H. Karpat, *The Politicization of Islam: Reconstructing Identity, State, Faith, and Community in the Late Ottoman State* (Oxford: Oxford University Press, 2001), 166, 246.

18. Gabriel Charmes, "La situation de la Turquie: La politique du califat et ses conséquences," *Revue des Deux Mondes* 47 (1881): 740–45; and BOA, Y.EE, 91/39 (29 Z 1299/11 November 1882).

19. TNA: FO 195/1415 (1 February 1882).

20. Karpat, *The Politicization of Islam*, 195–96, 245–47.

21. Ş. Tufan Buzpınar, "Abdulhamid II and Amir Hussein's Secret Dealings with the British, 1877–1880," *Middle Eastern Studies* 31 no. 1 (1995): 99–123.

22. TNA: FO 195/1415 (1 February 1882).

23. See also İsmail Hakkı Uzunçarşılı, *Mekke-i Mükerreme Emirleri* (Ankara: Türk Tarih Kurumu Basımevi, 1972), 34–36.

24. Yılmaz Öztuna, *II. Abdülhamid: Zamanı ve Şahsiyeti* (İstanbul: Kubbealtı, 2008), 191.

25. In 1884, Midhat Pasha was strangled, most likely at the behest of the sultan. Osman Nuri likely oversaw the extrajudicial execution and superficial investigation to conceal the cause of death. Ochsenwald, *Religion, Society, and the State in Arabia*, 188.

26. BOA, Y.EE, 6/3 (27 Za 1298/31 October 1880); and BOA, Y.EE, 6/7 (29 Za 1298/2 November 1880). See also İsmail Hakkı Uzunçarşılı, *Midhat Paşa ve Tâif Mahkûmları* (Ankara: Türk Tarih Kurumu Basımevi, 1992), 34–37.

27. BOA, Y.EE, 88/64 (3 R 1299/22 February 1882); and BOA, Y.EE, 88/61 (15 M 1299/7 December 1881).

28. Quoted in Abu-Manneh, "Sultan Abdülhamid and the Sharifs of Mecca," 10–11.

29. Ochsenwald, *Religion, Society, and the State in Arabia*, 182.

30. BOA, Y.EE, 88/47 (29 L 1299/13 September 1882); BOA, Y.EE, 88/49 (23 Za 1299/6 October 1882); and Uzunçarşılı, *Mekke-i Mükerreme Emirleri*, 133–34.

31. TNA: FO 195/1514 (5 March 1885).

32. BOA, Y.A.HUS, 196/32 (8 S 1304/6 November 1886); and BOA, Y.A.HUS 196/33 (8 S 1304/6 November 1886).

33. BOA, Y.A.HUS, 194-2/55 (6 Z 1303/5 September 1886).

34. BOA, Y.A.HUS, 194-2/55 (6 Z 1303/5 September 1886).

35. For the full text of the report, see Selçuk Akşin Somel, "Osman Nuri Paşa'nın 17 Temmuz 1885 Tarihli Hicaz Raporu," *Tarih Araştırmaları Dergisi* 18/29 (1996): 1–38.

36. Selim Deringil, " 'They Live in a State of Nomadism and Savagery': The Late Ottoman Empire and the Post-Colonial Debate," *Comparative Studies in Society and History* 45, no. 2 (2003): 327–29.

37. Eugene L. Rogan, "Abdulhamid II's School for Tribes (1892–1907)," *International Journal of Middle East Studies* 28, no. 1 (1996): 83–107.

38. Somel, "Osman Nuri," 11, 25–26.
39. Timothy Mitchell, *Rule of Experts: Egypt, Techno-politics, Modernity* (Berkeley: University of California Press, 2002), 12, 61.
40. Diana K. Davis, "Imperialism, Orientalism, and the Environment in the Middle East," in *Environmental Imaginaries of the Middle East and North Africa*, ed. Diana K. Davis and Edmund Burke III (Athens: Ohio University Press, 2011), 3–4.
41. Mitchell, *Rule of Experts*, 15, 210.
42. Deringil, " 'They Live in a State of Nomadism and Savagery,' " 327–29.
43. See especially his 1884 report, "İstikbal'de Ceziret ül-Arab," in BOA, Y.EE, 13/29 (2 R 1326/4 May 1908); and Ufuk Gülsoy, *Hicaz Demiryolu* (İstanbul: Eren, 1994), 33–35.
44. Somel, "Osman Nuri," 31.
45. Mitchell, *Rule of Experts*, 90.
46. Somel, "Osman Nuri," 21–22, 36–38; and Gülsoy, *Hicaz Demiryolu*, 33–35.
47. Somel, "Osman Nuri," 21–22, 36–38.
48. William Ochsenwald, *The Hijaz Railroad* (Charlottesville: University Press of Virginia, 1980), 23.
49. BOA, Y.EE, 118/10 (3 C 1315/30 October 1897).
50. Yakup Bektaş, "The Sultan's Messenger: Cultural Constructions of Ottoman Telegraphy, 1847–1880," *Technology and Culture* 41, no. 4 (2000): 669–96; Sean McMeekin, *The Berlin-Baghdad Express: The Ottoman Empire and Germany's Bid for World Power* (Cambridge, MA: Harvard University Press, 2010); and Soli Shahvar, "Tribes and Telegraphs in Lower Iraq: The Muntafiq and the Baghdad-Basrah Telegraph Line of 1863–65," *Middle Eastern Studies* 39, no. 1 (2003): 89–116.
51. Mostafa Minawi, *The Ottoman Scramble for Africa: Empire and Diplomacy in the Sahara and the Hijaz* (Stanford, CA: Stanford University Press, 2016), 46–49, 57, 78, 85, 95, 113, 131; and Minawi, "Telegraphs and Territoriality in Ottoman Africa during the Age of High Imperialism," *Journal of Balkan and Near Eastern Studies* 18, no. 6 (2016): 567–87.
52. Davis, "Imperialism, Orientalism, and the Environment in the Middle East," 3.
53. Eyüp Sabri Pasha, *Tercüman-ı Hakikat* (9 B1297/17 June 1880); (13 B 1297/21 June 1880); (14 B 1297/22 June 1880); (15 B 1297/23 June 1880); (16 B 1297/24 June 1880); and (17 B 1297/25 June 1880). For more on Eyüp Sabri, see Mehmet Akif Fidan, *Eyüp Sabri Paşa ve Tarihçiliği* (Ankara: Türk Tarih Kurumu Basımevi, 2011).
54. Eyüp Sabri Pasha, *Mirat ül-Haremeyn*, 3 vols. (İstanbul: Bahriye Matbaası, 1301–06/1883–88).
55. On Ottoman-Wahhabi relations, see Cevdet Pasha, *Tarih-i Cevdet*, vol. 7 (İstanbul: Matbaa-ı Osmaniye, 1309/1893), 182–207; Frederick F. Anscombe, *The Ottoman Gulf: The Creation of Kuwait, Saudi Arabia, and Qatar* (New York: Columbia University Press, 1997); Emine Ö. Evered, "Rereading Ottoman Accounts of Wahhabism as Alternative Narratives: Ahmed Cevdet Paşa's Historic Survey of the Movement," *Comparative Studies of South Asia, Africa and the Middle East* 32, no. 3 (2012): 622–32; and Zekeriya Kurşun, *Necid ve Ahsa'da Osmanlı Hakimiyet: Vehhabi Hareketi ve Suud Devleti'nin Ortaya Çıkışı* (Ankara: Türk Tarih Kurumu Basımevi, 1998).

56. Gerald DeGaury, *Rulers of Mecca* (New York: Dorset Press, 1991); F. E. Peters, *Mecca: A Literary History of the Holy Land* (Princeton, NJ: Princeton University Press, 1994), 135–37.

57. BOA, HRT.h, 541 (29 Z 1264/26 November 1848).

58. Eyüp Sabri Pasha, *Tercüman-ı Hakikat* (17 B 1297/25 June 1880), 3; and Eyüp Sabri, *Mirat ül-Haremeyn*, vol. 1, 748.

59. Eyüp Sabri Pasha, *Mirat ül-Haremeyn*, vol. 1, 748–50; and BOA, HAT, 344/19624 (29 Z 1232/9 November 1817).

60. Johann Ludwig (John Lewis) Burckhardt, *Travels in Arabia* (London: Henry Colburn, 1829), vol. 1, 194–95.

61. Eyüp Sabri Pasha, *Tarih-i Vehhabiyan* (İstanbul: Kırk Ambar Matbaası, 1296/1879; repr.), Süleyman Çelik, ed. (İstanbul: Bedir Yayınevi, 1992), 62.

62. BOA, HAT, 1359/53403 (29 Z 1220/20 March 1806).

63. Eyüp Sabri Pasha, *Mirat ül-Haremeyn*, vol. 1, 748. Here Eyüp Sabri somewhat exaggerated the level of neglect. For examples of Ottoman repair efforts from the 1840s to the 1860s, see Ömer Faruk Yılmaz, *Belgelerle Osmanlı Devrinde Hicaz*, vol. 1 (İstanbul: Çamlıca, 2008), 145, 172–73, 188–89; and ʿĀdil Muḥammad Nūr ʿAbd Allāh Ghubāshī, *al-Munshaʾāt al-māʾiyya li-khidmat Makka al-Mukarrama wa-al-mashāʿir al-muqaddasa fī al-ʿAṣr al-ʿUthmānī: Dirāsa ḥaḍāriyya* (Makkah: al-Mamlakat al-ʿArabiyya al-Saʿūdiyya, Wizārat al-Taʿlīm al-ʿĀlī, Jāmiʿat Umm al-Qurá, 2005), 227–32.

64. Sarıyıldız, *Hicaz Karantina Teşkilatı*, 73.

65. Eyüp Sabri Pasha, *Mirat ül-Haremeyn*, vol. 1, 748–50.

66. BOA, İ.DH, 486/32805 (19 Ş 1278/19 February 1862); BOA, A.MKT.UM, 548/17 (14 N 1278/15 March 1862); and BOA, A.MKT.NZD, 407/65 (17 N 1278/18 March 1862).

67. John F. Keane, *Six Months in Mecca: An Account of the Muhammedan Pilgrimage to Mecca* (London: Tinsley Brothers, 1881), 176–86.

68. Eyüp Sabri Pasha, *Mirat ül-Haremeyn*, vol. 1, 748–51.

69. BOA, Y. PRK. UM, 5/96 (30 Ca 1300/8 April 1883).

70. BOA, Y.A.RES 6/68 (19 Ra 1297/1 March 1880); BOA, Y.A. RES 9/91 (19 Ra 1298/19 February 1881); and TNA: FO 195/1514 (10 January 1885).

71. Sarıyıldız, *Hicaz Karantina Teşkilatı*, 73.

72. John Slight, *The British Empire and the Hajj, 1865–1956* (Cambridge, MA: Harvard University Press, 2015), 115.

73. Seema Alavi, *Muslim Cosmopolitanism in the Age of Empire* (Cambridge, MA: Harvard University Press, 2015), 146–48.

74. BOA, İ.DH 800/64862 (22 Ra 1297/4 March 1880); BOA, Y.PRK.UM, 5/96 (30 Ca 1300/8 April 1883); and BOA, İ.DH 901/71633 (4 M 1301/5 November 1883).

75. BOA, Y.PRK.UM, 5/96 (30 Ca 1300/8 April 1883). See also Muhammad el-Emin el-Mekki, *Osmanlı Padişahlarının Haremeyn Hizmetleri* (İstanbul: Çamlıca, 2008), 25–26.

76. el-Mekki, *Osmanlı Padişahlarının Haremeyn Hizmetleri*, 25–26; and Sarıyıldız, *Hicaz Karantina Teşkilatı*, 72–74.

77. Dr. Kasım İzzeddin, *Mekke-i Mükerreme'de Kolera ve Hıfzısıhha* (İstanbul: Mahmud Bey Matbaası, 1327/1911), 96–101.

78. On prebacteriological understandings of waste disposal and public space, see David S. Barnes, *The Great Stink of Paris and the Nineteenth-Century Struggle Against Filth and Germs* (Baltimore, MD: Johns Hopkins University Press, 2006), 78–82.

79. TNA: FO 195/1514 (10 January 1885).

80. Gülden Sarıyıldız and Ayşe Kavak, eds., *Halife II. Abdülhamid'in Hac Siyaseti: Dr. M. Şakir Bey'in Hatıraları* (İstanbul: Timaş, 2009), 130–31.

81. BL: Asia, Pacific, and Africa Collections, W 4087 (24 June 1879), 22–24.

82. TNA: FO 195/1514, Jeddah (10 January 1885).

83. TNA: FO 686/68, "Mecca Water Supply and Egyptian Ministry of Wakfs Grant" (1920).

84. Sarıyıldız and Kavak, *Halife II. Abdülhamid'in Hac Siyaseti*, 165–67.

85. Yeniçeşmeli Hâfız Fâik Efendi, *İstanbul'dan Bombay'a Bir Osmanlı Fırkateyni'nin Keşif Seyahati*, ed. A. Ergun Çınar (İstanbul: Kitabevi, 2014), 23.

86. Sarıyıldız and Kavak, *Halife II. Abdülhamid'in Hac Siyaseti*, 165–67, 243–72.

87. On the notion of milieu and the social mediation of nature, see Paul Rabinow, *French Modern: Norms and Forms of the Social Environment* (Chicago: University of Chicago Press, 1985), 31–34.

88. Bruno Latour, *The Pasteurization of France* (Cambridge, MA: Harvard University Press, 1988), 23.

89. BL, Asia, Pacific, and Africa Collections, W 4087 (24 June 1879), 18, 40.

90. Eyüp Sabri Pasha, *Mirat ül-Haremeyn*, vol. 3, 194–95; and Yeniçeşmeli Hâfız Fâik Efendi, *İstanbul'dan Bombay'a Bir Osmanlı Fırkateyni'nin Keşif Seyahati*, 23–24.

91. Syed Mohsen Alsagoff, *The Alsagoff Family in Malaysia: A.H. 1240 (A.D. 1824) to A.H. 1382 (A.D. 1962)* (Singapore, 1963), 9–11; and Ulrike Freitag and William Clarence-Smith, eds., *Hadrami Traders, Scholars, and Statesmen in the Indian Ocean* (Leiden: Brill, 1997), 288, 298–300.

92. Eric Tagliacozzo, *The Longest Journey: Southeast Asians and the Pilgrimage to Mecca* (Oxford: Oxford University Press, 2013), 72–75.

93. Ochsenwald, *Religion, Society, and the State in Arabia*, 101–2, 109.

94. Sarıyıldız and Kavak, *Halife II. Abdülhamid'in Hac Siyaseti*, 62–64.

95. Selman Soydemir, Kemal Erkan, and Osman Doğan, eds., *Hicaz Vilayet Salnamesi, H. 1303/M. 1886* (İstanbul: Çamlıca, 2008), 120.

96. TNA: FO 78/4094 (27 February 1886).

97. BOA, MV, 21/65 (19 L 1304/11 July 1887); BOA, DH.MKT, 1456/90 (5 S 1305/23 October 1887); and BOA, Y.A.HUS, 207/103 (17 S 1305/4 November 1887).

98. el-Mekki, *Osmanlı Padişahlarının Haremeyn Hizmetleri*, 26.

99. BOA, MV, 21/65 (19 L 1304/11 July 1887); BOA, DH.MKT, 1456/90 (5 S 1305/23 October1887); and BOA, Y.A.HUS, 207/103 (17 S 1305/4 November 1887).

100. Sarıyıdız and Kavak, *Halife II. Abdülhamid'in Hac Siyaseti*, 62–64.

101. Dr. Frank G. Clemow, "Some Turkish Lazarets and Other Sanitary Institutions in the Near East," *Lancet* (29 June 1907), 1811–12; (6 July 1907), 51–52; and Dr. F. G. Clemow, *Le Eaux de Djeddah* (Constantinople: Imprimerie F. Loeffler, Lithographe de S.M.I. le Sultan, 1906), 3–7, cited in Birsen Bulmuş, *Plague, Quarantines and Geopolitics in the Ottoman Empire* (Edinburgh: Edinburgh University Press, 2012), 165.

102. El-Hac Hüseyin Vassaf, *Hicaz Hatırası*, ed. Mehmet Akkuş (İstanbul: Kubbealtı, 2011), 71–72.

103. On Barak, "Outsourcing: Energy and Empire in the Age of Coal, 1820–1911," *International Journal of Middle East Studies* 47, no. 3 (2015): 426.

104. On Barak, *Powering Empire: How Coal Made the Middle East and Sparked Carbonization* (Berkeley: University of California Press, 2020), 11, 42–52.

105. James D. Birkett and D. Radcliffe, "Normandy's Patent Marine Aërated Fresh Water Company: A Family Business for 60 Years, 1851–1910," *IDA Journal of Desalination and Water Reuse* 6, no. 1 (2014): 25–26.

106. James D. Birkett, "A Brief History of Desalination from the Bible to 1940," *Desalination* 50 (1984): 40–45.

107. Barak, *Powering Empire*, 42–44.

108. BOA, İ.HUS, 20/68 (26 R 1311/2 February 1894); BOA, Y.A.HUS, 294/41 (13 Ş 1311/19 April 1894); and Ömer Faruk Yılmaz, *Hicaz'da Deniz Suyu Arıtma Tesisleri Projesi* (İstanbul: Çamlıca, 2012).

109. Ḥamza ʿAlī Luqmān, *Tārīkh al-Juzur al-Yamaniyya* (Beirut: Maṭbaʿat Yūsuf wa Fīlīb al-Jumayyil, 1972), 10.

110. BOA, BEO, 577/42360 (29 Ş 1312/25 February 1895).

111. BOA, BEO, 571/42805 (21 Ş 1312/17 February 1895).

112. Sarıyıldız, *Hicaz Karantina Teşkilatı*, 127.

113. BOA, DH.MKT 582/97 (21 C 1320/25 September 1902); BOA, DH.MKT, 892/29 (15 B 1322/25 September 1904); BOA, Y.MTV, 291/32 (12 L 1324/29 November 1906); BOA, Y.MTV, 297/153 (30 Ra 1325/13 May 1907); and BOA, Y.MTV, 299/63 (8 Ca 1325/19 June 1907); Sarıyıldız, *Hicaz Karantina Teşkilatı*, 128.

114. Clemow, "Some Turkish Lazarets and Other Sanitary Institutions in the Near East," 52; and Bulmuş, *Plague, Quarantines and Geopolitics in the Ottoman Empire*, 166.

115. Barak, *Powering Empire*, 44.

116. Bulmuş, *Plague, Quarantines and Geopolitics in the Ottoman Empire*, 160–71.

117. İzzeddin, *Hicaz'da Teşkilat ve Islahat-ı Sıhhiye*, 39–43; and Sarıyıldız, *Hicaz Karantina Teşkilatı*, 128.

118. TNA: FO 195/2376 (6 October 1911); and BOA, BEO, 4004/30028 (29 S 1330/18 February 1912).

119. İzzeddin, *Hicaz'da Teşkilat ve Islahat-ı Sıhhiye*, 43, 51.

120. Bulmuş, *Plague, Quarantines and Geopolitics in the Ottoman Empire*, 164–71; and Sarıyıldız, *Hicaz Karantina Teşkilatı*, 134–43.

121. İzzeddin, *Hicaz'da Teşkilat ve Islahat-ı Sıhhiye*, 40–41.

122. İzzeddin, *Hicaz'da Teşkilat ve Islahat-ı Sıhhiye*, 51, translation (with my corrections to the Rumi calendar date conversion) quoted in Bulmuş, *Plague, Quarantines and Geopolitics in the Ottoman Empire*, 166.

123. Andrew Barry, "Technological Zones," *European Journal of Social Theory* 9, no. 2 (2006): 239, 241, 246.

124. Peters, *The Hajj*, 305–307; and Slight, *The British Empire and the Hajj*, 250.

125. Timothy Mitchell, "The Life of Infrastructure," *Comparative Studies of South Asia, Africa and the Middle East* 34, no. 3 (2014): 438.

126. Timothy Mitchell, *Carbon Democracy: Political Power in the Age of Oil* (London: Verso, 2011), 103; and Barak, *Powering Empire*, 47–48.

127. BOA, BEO, 4313/323430 (9 Za 1332/1 October 194); BOA, BEO, 4313/323453 (11 Za 1332/3 October 1914); and BOA, DH.EUM.5.Şb (27 S 1333/14 January 1915).

128. Bulmuş, *Plague, Quarantines and Geopolitics in the Ottoman Empire*, 166–67, 171.
129. Michael Christopher Low, "Ottoman Infrastructures of the Saudi Hydro-State: The Technopolitics of Pilgrimage and Potable Water in the Hijaz," *Comparative Studies in Society and History* 57, no. 4 (2015): 964–73.

5. Passports and Tickets

1. BOA, Y.PRK.AZJ, 22/41 (29 Z 1309/25 July 1892).
2. Nile Green, "The *Hajj* as Its Own Undoing: Infrastructure and Integration on the Muslim Journey to Mecca," *Past and Present* 226, no. 1 (2015): 193–226.
3. Green, "The *Hajj* as Its Own Undoing," 196; Radhika Singha, "Passport, Ticket, and India-Rubber Stamp: 'The Problem of the Pauper Pilgrim' in Colonial India c. 1882–1925," in *The Limits of British Colonial Control in South Asia: Spaces of Disorder in the Indian Ocean Region*, ed. Ashwini Tambe and Harald Fischer-Tiné (London: Routledge, 2009), 49–83.
4. Adam McKeown, *Melancholy Order: Asian Migration and the Globalization of Borders* (New York: Columbia University Press, 2008), 47, 111–12; and Adam McKeown, "Global Migration, 1846–1940," *Journal of World History* 15, no. 2 (2004): 155–89.
5. Peter Baldwin, *Contagion and the State in Europe, 1830–1930* (Cambridge: Cambridge University Press, 1999), 228–31; and Milton J. Lewis and Kerrie L. MacPherson, eds., *Public Health in Asia and the Pacific: Historical and Comparative Perspectives* (London: Routledge, 2008).
6. David Edwin Long, *The Hajj Today: A Survey of the Contemporary Makkah Pilgrimage* (Albany: State University of New York Press, 1979), 127–35.
7. Radhika Singha, "Passport, Ticket, and India-Rubber Stamp," 49–55; and Oishi Takashi, "Friction and Rivalry Over Pious Mobility: British Colonial Management of the Hajj and Reaction to It by Indian Muslims, 1870–1920," in *The Influence of Human Mobility in Muslim Societies*, ed. Kuroki Hidemitsu (London: Kegan Paul, 2003), 163–67.
8. Singha, "Passport, Ticket, and India-Rubber Stamp"; and Takashi, "Friction and Rivalry Over Pious Mobility."
9. On the legal conditions of *istitaat*, see Wael B. Hallaq, *Sharīʿa: Theory, Practice, Transformations* (Cambridge: Cambridge University Press, 2009), 238; BL: IOR, V/26/844/6, *Report of the Haj Inquiry Committee* (Calcutta: Government of India Central Publication Branch, 1930), 17. Despite the diversity of legal opinions on this issue, even within one particular school of Islamic law, in this case the interimperial conversation between Ottoman and British authorities primarily assumed that Hanafi law was the most widely practiced legal school in both the Ottoman Empire and India.
10. Kasım İzzeddin, *Hicaz'da Teşkilat ve Islahat-ı Sıhhiye ve 1330 Senesi Hacc-ı Şerifi: Hicaz Sıhhiye İdaresi Senevi Rapor* (İstanbul: Matbaa-ı Amire, 1330/1914–15), 56, 60–62.
11. John Slight, *The British Empire and the Hajj, 1865–1956* (Cambridge, MA: Harvard University Press, 2015), 107, 131–43.

12. TNA: FO 78/4882 (4 September 1896).

13. BOA, DH.MKT, 1349/101 (7 N 1303/9 June 1886).

14. Thomas Cook Group Archives, Guardbook no. 27 (hereafter referred to as TC), Appendix no. 2, extract from the *Times of India*, 9 November 1885 in John Mason Cook to H. Luson, Under Secretary to the Government of India (Home Department-Sanitary), 1894.

15. TC, John Mason Cook, "The Mecca Pilgrimage," *The Excursionist*, 26 March 1887.

16. Singha, "Passport, Ticket, and India-Rubber Stamp," 50, 63

17. Alan de L. Rush, ed., *Records of the Hajj: A Documentary History of the Pilgrimage to Mecca* (London: Archive Editions), vol. 3, 616.

18. *Records of the Hajj*, vol. 3, 616.

19. Gülden Sarıyıldız and Ayşe Kavak, eds., *Halife II: Abdülhamid'in Hac Siyaseti: Dr. M. Şakir Bey'in Hatıraları* (İstanbul: Timaş, 2009), 300–302.

20. Sarıyıldız and Kavak, *Halife II: Abdülhamid'in Hac Siyaseti*, 300–304.

21. Sarıyıldız and Kavak, *Halife II: Abdülhamid'in Hac Siyaseti*, 299.

22. Süleyman Şefik Söylemezoğlu, *Hicaz Seyahatnâmesi*, ed. Ahmet Çaycı and Bayram Ürekli (İstanbul: İz Yayıncılık, 2012), 151–52.

23. Singha, "Passport, Ticket, and India-Rubber Stamp," 53; Takashi, "Friction and Rivalry Over Pious Mobility," 164.

24. İzzeddin, *Hicaz'da Teşkilat ve Islahat-ı Sıhhiye*, 51–52; TNA: FO 78/4777, "Mouvement général du pèlerinage du Hedjaz par les ports de la Mer Rouge, Année de l'Hégire 1312/1894-95"; and TNA: FO 78/4882 (4 September 1896).

25. Sarıyıldız and Kavak, *Halife II: Abdülhamid'in Hac Siyaseti*, 304.

26. Singha, "Passport, Ticket, and India-Rubber Stamp," 51–55.

27. İzzeddin, *Hicaz'da Teşkilat ve Islahat-ı Sıhhiye*, 52–66.

28. İzzeddin, *Hicaz'da Teşkilat ve Islahat-ı Sıhhiye*, 52–59.

29. Anthony Reid, "Nineteenth Century Pan-Islam in Indonesia and Malaysia," *Journal of Asian Studies* 26, no. 2 (1967): 267–83; Daniel Brower, "Russian Roads to Mecca: Religious Tolerance and Muslim Pilgrimage in the Russian Empire," *Slavic Review* 55, no. 3 (1996): 567–84; and Eileen Kane, *Russian Hajj: Empire and the Pilgrimage to Mecca* (Ithaca, NY: Cornell University Press, 2015), 55–57, 64–65.

30. Singha, "Passport, Ticket, and India-Rubber Stamp," 50.

31. İzzeddin, *Hicaz'da Teşkilat ve Islahat-ı Sıhhiye*, 55–58, 64; and Gülden Sarıyıldız, "II. Abdülhamid'in Fakir Hacılar İçin Mekke'de İnşa Ettirdiği Misafirhane," *Tarih Enstitüsü Dergisi* 14 (1994): 121–45.

32. On the history of the international passport regime, see John Torpey, *The Invention of the Passport: Surveillance, Citizenship, and the State* (New York: Cambridge University Press, 2000).

33. On biopolitical surveillance and the ideals and norms of the global passport and visa documentation systems, see Mark B. Salter, "The Global Visa Regime and the Political Technologies of the International Self: Border, Bodies, Biopolitics," *Alternatives: Global, Local, Political* 31, no. 2 (2006): 167–89; and John Torpey, "Coming and Going: On the State Monopolization of the Legitimate Means of Movement," *Sociological Theory* 16, no. 3 (1998): 239–59.

34. Torpey, *Invention of the Passport*, 6–10.

35. John Torpey, "The Great War and the Birth of the Modern Passport System," in *Documenting Individual Identity: The Development of State Practices in the Modern World*, ed. Jane Caplan and John Torpey (Princeton, NJ: Princeton University Press, 2001), 256–70.

36. TNA: FO 194/1451 (17 April 1883).

37. Musa Çadırcı, "Tanzimat Döneminde Çıkarılan Men'-i Mürur ve Pasaport Nizamnameleri," *Belgeler* 25, no. 19 (1993): 169–81; Hamiyet Sezer, "Osmanlı İmparatorluğu'nda Seyahat İzinleri (18–19. Yüzyıl)," *Tarih Araştırma Dergisi* 21, no. 33 (2003): 105–24; and Nalan Turna, *19. Yüzyıldan 20. Yüzyıla Osmanlı Topraklarında Seyahat, Göç ve Asayış Belgeleri: Mürûr Tezkereleri* (İstanbul: Kaknüs Yayınları, 2013).

38. David Gutman, "Armenian Migration to North America, State Power, and Local Politics in the Late Ottoman Empire," *Comparative Studies of South Asia, Africa and the Middle East* 34, no. 1 (2014): 177; and Gutman, "Travel Documents, Mobility Control, and the Ottoman State in an Age of Global Migration, 1880–1915," *Journal of the Ottoman and Turkish Studies Association* 3, no. 2 (2016): 347–68.

39. Gutman, "Travel Documents," 351. Here we find interesting parallels with British surveillance of internal Indian mobilities. For example, see Radhika Singha, "Providential Circumstance: The Thugee Campaign of the 1830s and Legal Innovation," *Modern Asian Studies* 27, no. 1 (1993): 83–146.

40. On the relationships among citizenship, nationality laws, and the actual paper documents of identification that underpinned them, see especially Will Hanley, *Identifying with Nationality: Europeans, Ottomans, and Egyptians in Alexandria* (New York: Columbia University Press, 2017), 70–97.

41. TNA: FO 195/1451 (13 May 1883; 17 April 1883).

42. TNA: FO 195/1482 (15 July 1884).

43. TNA: FO 195/1451 (Apr. 1883).

44. TNA: FO 195/1451 (13 May 1883); Çoksun Çakır, *Tanzimat Dönemi Osmanlı Maliyesi* (İstanbul: Küre Yayınları, 2001), 53; and Turna, *Seyahat, Göç ve Asayış Belgeleri*, 210–15.

45. BOA, A.DVN.MKL, 25/25 (15 R 1301/14 January 1884).

46. BOA, Y.A.RES, 33/19 (2 B 1303/6 April 1886).

47. In 1895, there was a renewed effort to impose the visa fees and penalties described in the *Pasaport Nizamnamesi*, but Britain secured an exemption for Indian pilgrims. Similarly, when the Ottoman state attempted to raise visa fees from 6 to 12 or even 20 *kuruş*, the British Embassy intervened. BOA, HR.HMŞ. İŞO, 179/17 (23 Ca 1311/2 December 1893); BOA, İ.DH, 1319/26 (29 B 1312/26 January 1895); BOA, HR.HMŞ.İŞO, 235/37 (16 Za 1312/11 May 1895); and BOA, ŞD, 2675/18 (4 L 1314/8 March 1897).

48. Even as late as 1910, the CUP government attempted to implement the *Pasaport Nizamnamesi*'s call for visas to be secured from an Ottoman consulate prior to departure. There was also an attempt to raise the visa fee to twenty *kuruş*. BOA, BEO, 3820/286466 (5 Za 1328/8 November 1910); BOA, MV, 151/10 (4 R 1329/4 April 1911).

49. TNA: FO 195/1482 (15 July 1884).

50. TNA: FO 195/1451 (17 April 1883). On the parallel problem of poor Indian and Afghan pilgrims and sojourners traveling to Jerusalem without an appropriate passport or Ottoman *mürur tezkeresi*, see also BOA, DH.MKT, 1499/30 (24 B 1305/6 April 1888).

51. TNA: FO 195/1451 (13 May 1883).

52. Singha, "Passport, Ticket, and India-Rubber Stamp," 56.

53. Selim Deringil, "Legitimacy Structures in the Ottoman State: The Reign of Abdülhamid II (1876–1909)," *International Journal of Middle East Studies* 23, no. 3 August 1991),351–52.

54. Takashi, "Friction and Rivalry Over Pious Mobility," 169–71.

55. TC, Cook, *The Mecca Pilgrimage*, 6–7.

56. BOA, İ.MMS, 65/3071 (19 S 1297/1 February 1880); and TNA: FO 881/3079, "Correspondence Respecting Turkish Regulations for Pilgrim Traffic, 1875–1877." For its amending act of 1883, see *Manual for the Guidance of Officers and Others Concerned in the Red Sea Pilgrimage Traffic* (Shimla, India: Government Central Branch Press, 1884) in TNA: FO 78/4093, "Pilgrimage Traffic, 1884–1885."

57. TNA: FO 78/4328, "Turkey, Pilgrim Traffic, 1890."

58. Gülden Sarıyıldız, *Hicaz Karantina Teşkilatı, 1865-1914* (Ankara: Türk Tarih Kurumu Basımevi, 1996), 40.

59. Singha, "Passport, Ticket, and India-Rubber Stamp," 51, 62–63; and Takashi, "Friction and Rivalry Over Pious Mobility," 171–72.

60. TC, Appendix no.2, extract from the *Times of India*, 9 November 1885 in Cook to Luson, 1894.

61. *Records of the Hajj*, vol. 3., 595.

62. TC, Appendix no. 1, in Cook to Luson, 1894.

63. FO 881/5155X (April 1885), 7–8; and William Roff, "Sanitation and Security: The Imperial Powers and the Nineteenth Century Hajj," *Arabian Studies* 6 (1982): 147–48.

64. Michael Gilsenan, "And You, What Are You Doing Here?," review of *A Season in Mecca: Narrative of Pilgrimage*, by Abdellah Hammoudi, trans. Pascale Ghazaleh, *London Review of Books* (19 October 2006), 3; and Roff, "Sanitation and Security," 151.

65. Joseph Conrad, *Lord Jim* (Edinburgh: Blackwood and Sons, 1900). See also Eric Tagliacozzo, *The Longest Journey: Southeast Asians and the Pilgrimage to Mecca* (Oxford: Oxford University Press, 2013), 109–32.

66. TC, Appendix no.2, extract from the *Times of India*, 9 November 1885, in Cook to Luson, 1894.

67. On government-backed shipping lines operating in the Indian Ocean, see Johan Mathew, *Margins of the Market: Trafficking and Capitalism Across the Arabian Sea* (Berkeley: University of California Press, 2016), 44–51.

68. TC, Cook, *The Mecca Pilgrimage*, 4–6; Cook to Luson, 1894, 3; Piers Brendon, *Thomas Cook: 150 Years of Popular Tourism* (London: Secker & Warburg, 1991), 205–6; and John Pudney, *The Thomas Cook Story* (London: Michael Joseph, 1953), 221–24.

69. TC, Cook to Luson, 1894, 5–6; and TC, *Bombay Gazette*, 16 January 1895.

70. Singha, "Passport, Ticket, and India-Rubber Stamp," 52–53.

71. TC, Extract from the Proceedings of the Government of India in the Home Department (Sanitary), Calcutta, 11 January 1895.

72. Mark Harrison, "Quarantine, Pilgrimage, and Colonial Trade: India 1866–1900," *Indian Economic and Social Review* 29, no. 2 (1992): 133.

73. Singha, "Passport, Ticket, and India-Rubber Stamp," 59.

74. Takashi, "Friction and Rivalry Over Pious Mobility," 167.

75. Sarıyıldız and Kavak, *Halife II: Abdülhamid'in Hac Siyaseti*, 60–64, 297–98.

76. TC, Extract from the Proceedings of the Government of India in the Home Department (Sanitary), Calcutta, 11 January 1895, 3–4.

77. TC, *The Pioneer*, 16 January 1895.

78. Singha, "Passport, Ticket, and India-Rubber Stamp," 59.

79. TC, Cook to Luson, 1894, 7–8.

80. TC, *Bombay Gazette*, 16 January 1895.

81. TC, Report of the Arrangements Carried Out by Thos. Cook and Son in Connection with the Movement of Pilgrims for the Hadj of 1887.

82. TC, Cook, "The Mecca Pilgrimage."

83. F. Robert Hunter, "The Thomas Cook Archive for the Study of Tourism in North Africa and the Middle East," *Middle East Studies Association Bulletin* 36, no. 2 (2003): 157–64.

84. TC, 15–23 October 1886.

85. On pilgrimage guides, see Fuʿad ʿAbd al-Ḥamīd ʿAnqāwī, *Makkah: al-Ḥajj wa-al-ṭawāfah* (Saudi Arabia, 1994), 273–82, 299–303; Süleyman Kâni İrtem, *Osmanlı Devleti'nin Mısır Yemen Hicaz Meselesi*, ed. Osman Selim Kocahanoğlu (İstanbul: Temel, 1999), 175–81; and Christiaan Snouck Hurgronje, *Mekka in the Latter Part of the 19th Century* (Leiden: Brill, 1931), 24. For a more sympathetic view of the critical services rendered by *muṭawwifīn*, see Shakīb Arslān, *al-Irtisamāt al-liṭāf fī khāṭir al-Ḥajj ilā aqdas maṭāf* (Cairo: Matbaʾat al-Minar, 1931), 71–80.

86. İrtem, *Osmanlı Devleti'nin Mısır Yemen Hicaz Meselesi*, 175.

87. İrtem, *Osmanlı Devleti'nin Mısır Yemen Hicaz Meselesi*, 188.

88. ʿAnqāwī, *Makkah: al-Ḥajj wa-al-ṭawāfah*, 280–85, 330–33; and Mary Byrne McDonnell, "The Conduct of Hajj from Malaysia and Its Socio-Economic Impact on Malay Society: A Descriptive and Analytical Study, 1860–1981," vol. 1 (Ph.D. diss., Columbia University, 1986), 58–60.

89. İrtem, *Osmanlı Devleti'nin Mısır Yemen Hicaz Meselesi*, 175.

90. William Ochsenwald, *Religion, Society, and the State in Arabia: The Hijaz Under Ottoman Control, 1840–1908* (Columbus: Ohio State University Press, 1984), 101–6, 193–95.

91. TC, October 1886.

92. Sarıyıldız and Kavak, *Halife II: Abdülhamid'in Hac Siyaseti*, 300.

93. Syed Mohsen Alsagoff, *The Alsagoff Family in Malaysia: A.H. 1240 (A.D. 1824) to A.H. 1382 (A.D. 1962)* (Singapore, 1963), 9–11; and Ulrike Freitag and William Clarence-Smith, eds., *Hadrami Traders, Scholars, and Statesmen in the Indian Ocean* (Leiden: Brill, 1997), 288, 298–300.

94. Jacob Vrendenbredgt, "The Haddj: Some of Its Features and Functions in Indonesia," *Bijdragen tot de Taal-, Land-en Volkenkunde* 118, no. 1 (1962): 127–29.

95. William Roff, *Studies on Islam and Society in Southeast Asia* (Singapore: National University of Singapore Press, 2009), 79–80.

96. Edwin Lee, *The British as Rulers: Governing Multiracial Singapore, 1867-1914* (Singapore: National University of Singapore, 1991), 165-67.

97. Lee, *The British as Rulers*, 166-67.

98. Vredenbredgt, "The Haddj," 128.

99. Vredenbredgt, "The Haddj," 127-30.

100. Tagliacozzo, *The Longest Journey*, 72-73.

101. Ochsenwald, *Religion, Society, and the State in Arabia*, 102-3.

102. TC, 8 February 1888.

103. *Records of the Hajj*, vol. 4, 27-110.

104. TNA: FO 78/4328 (11 August 1889). It would appear that the public notice was originally produced in February 1889. See BOA, Y.PRK.UM, 14/9 (12 C 1306/13 February 1889).

105. Ochsenwald, *Religion, Society, and the State in Arabia*, 102-103.

106. Ochsenwald, *Religion, Society, and the State in Arabia*, 102-103 109.

107. BOA, Y.PRK.ASK, 10/144 (21 S 1299/12 January 1882); BOA, İ.DH, 871/69603 (11 S 1300/22 December 1882).

108. For more on Ahmed Esad and his position within the wider coterie of Arab religious dignitaries surrounding Abdülhamid at Yıldız Palace, see Roger Allen, *Spies, Scandals, and Sultans: Istanbul in the Twilight of the Ottoman Empire: The First English Translation of Egyptian Ibrahim al-Muwaylihi's Ma Hunalik* (Lanham, MD: Rowman & Littlefield, 2008), 133-53.

109. Mahmud Nedim Bey, *Arabistan'da Bir Ömür: Son Yemen Valisinin Hatıraları veya Osmanlı İmparatorluğu Arabistan'da Nasıl Yıkıldı?*, ed. Ali Birinci (İstanbul: İsis Yayıncılık, 2001), 71-72.

110. TNA: FO 78/4533 (25 August 1893).

111. BOA, HR.SFR 3, 396/73 (24 March 1892); TNA: FO 195/1847 (1 July 1894). See also Thomas Kuehn, *Empire, Islam, and Politics of Difference: Ottoman Rule in Yemen, 1849-1919* (Leiden: Brill, 2011), 209.

112. Ochsenwald, *Religion, Society, and the State in Arabia*, 194.

113. İzzeddin, *Mekke-i Mükerreme'de Kolera ve Hıfzısıhha* (İstanbul: Mahmud Bey Matbaası, 1327/1911), 80-83; and Sarıyıldız, *Hicaz Karantina Teşkilatı*, 66-67.

114. TNA: FO 78/4532, Turkey, Pilgrim Traffic, 1892-1893; TNA: FO 78/4533, Turkey Pilgrim Traffic, September to December 1893; BOA, HR.SFR 3, 409/76 (3 August 1893); Michael Francis Laffan, *Islamic Nationhood and Colonial Indonesia: The Umma Below the Winds* (New York: RoutledgeCurzon, 2003), 103-6; and Mahmud Nedim Bey, *Arabistan'da Bir Ömür*, 73-77.

115. TNA: FO 195/1805 (25 August 1893).

116. TNA: FO 78/4600 (7 April1894).

117. Seema Alavi, *Muslim Cosmopolitanism in the Age of Empire* (Cambridge, MA: Harvard University Press, 2015), 137-38. See also BOA, İ.DH, 1318/21 (7 C 1312/6 December 1894); Y.A.HUS, 315/40 (13 December 1894); BOA, Y.A HUS, 340/132 (13 C 1313/1 December 1895); BOA, BEO, 795/59609 (5 M 1214/16 June 1896); and BOA, BEO 799/59852 (12 M 1314/23 June 1896).

118. TNA: FO 78/4777 (22 March 1896); and TNA: FO 78/4778 (30 April 1896; 4 May 1896; 30 May 1896; 28 September 1896).

119. BOA, Y.A.HUS, 292/150 (29 N 1311/5 April 1894); BOA, İ.DH, 1318/21 (7 C 1312/6 December 1894); BOA, İ.HUS, 32/9 (8 C 1312/7 December 1894); and Alavi, *Muslim Cosmopolitanism in the Age of Empire*, 138.
120. BOA, İ.DH, 1318/21 (7 C 1312/6 December 1894); BOA, İ.HUS, 32/9 (8 C 1312/7 December 1894); and Ochsenwald, *Religion, Society, and the State in Arabia*, 103, 194–95.
121. Mahmud Nedim Bey, *Arabistan'da Bir Ömür*, 72.
122. BOA, BEO, 107/8011 (27 R 1310/18 November 1892).
123. Ochsenwald, *Religion, Society, and the State in Arabia*, 214.
124. Ochsenwald, *Religion, Society, and the State in Arabia*, 103–4.
125. Ochsenwald, *Religion, Society, and the State in Arabia*, 213.
126. Murat Özyüksel, *The Hejaz Railway and the Ottoman Empire: Modernity, Industrialisation and Ottoman Decline* (London: I. B. Tauris, 2014), 164.
127. Butrus Abu-Manneh, "Sultan Abdülhamid and the Sharifs of Mecca, 1880–1890," *Asian and African Studies* 9, no. 1 (1973): 18–21.

6. The Camel and the Rail

1. Nile Green, "The *Hajj* as Its Own Undoing: Infrastructure and Integration on the Muslim Journey to Mecca," *Past and Present* 226, no. 1 (2015): 193–208.
2. Alan de L. Rush, ed., *Records of the Hajj: A Documentary History of the Pilgrimage to Mecca* (London: Archive Editions, 1993), vol. 4, 139–80; 569–612; 675–86.
3. Süleyman Kâni İrtem, *Osmanlı Devleti'nin Mısır Yemen Hicaz Meselesi*, ed. Osman Selim Kocahanoğlu (İstanbul: Temel, 1999), 175–76.
4. Valeska Huber, *Channelling Mobilities: Migration and Globalisation in the Suez Canal Region and Beyond, 1869–1914* (Cambridge: Cambridge University Press, 2013), 1–6, 164–66, 204.
5. On Barak, "Three Watersheds in the History of Energy," *Comparative Studies of South Asia, Africa and the Middle East* 34, no. 3 (2014): 440–53; and On Barak, *Powering Empire: How Coal Made the Middle East and Sparked Carbonization* (Berkeley: University of California Press, 2020), 33–35, 53–82.
6. On the decline of camel labor and transport caused by the adoption of fossil-fueled mobilities, see Richard Bulliet, *The Camel and the Wheel* (New York: Columbia University Press, 1990), 237–68; Dawn Chatty, *From Camel to Truck: The Bedouin in the Modern World* (Cambridge: White Horse Press, 2013), 17–27, 90–154; and Alan Mikhail, *The Animal in Ottoman Egypt* (Oxford: Oxford University Press, 2014), 59–63.
7. Barak, "Three Watersheds in the History of Energy," 445–48.
8. Huber, *Channelling Mobilities*, 155–58, 164–66.
9. On the Hijaz Railway as a Pan-Islamic foreign policy and fundraising tool, see William Ochsenwald, *The Hijaz Railroad* (Charlottesville: University Press of Virginia, 1980), 69–82; Ufuk Gülsoy, *Hicaz Demiryolu* (İstanbul: Eren, 1994), 74–85; Muhammad Inshallah, *The History of the Hamidia Hedjaz Railway Project* (Lahore,

India: Central Printing Works, 1908); and Syed Tanvir Wasti, "Muhammad Inshallah and the Hijaz Railway," *Middle Eastern Studies* 34, no. 2 (1998): 60–72.

10. On the limited capacity of "technological fixes" to solve complex economic, environmental, social, and political problems, see Thomas P. Hughes, *Human-Built World: How to Think About Technology and Culture* (Chicago: University of Chicago Press, 2004), 14–15, 154.

11. Murat Özyüksel, *The Hejaz Railway and the Ottoman Empire: Modernity, Industrialisation and Ottoman Decline* (London: I. B. Tauris, 2014), 63; and Gülsoy, *Hicaz Demiryolu*, 31.

12. Özyüksel, *The Hejaz Railway and the Ottoman Empire*, 63; Gülsoy, *Hicaz Demiryolu*, 31.

13. Gülsoy, *Hicaz Demiryolu*, 32.

14. Wilfrid Scawen Blunt, *The Future of Islam* (London: Kegan Paul, Trench & Co., 1882), 208–9.

15. BOA, Y.PRK.AZJ, 22/41 (29 Z 1309/25 July 1892); Süleyman Şefik Söylemezoğlu, *Hicaz Seyahatnâmesi*, ed. Ahmet Çaycı and Bayram Ürekli (İstanbul: İz Yayıncılık, 2012), 154; and Özyüksel, *The Hejaz Railway and the Ottoman Empire*, 150.

16. Gülden Sarıyıldız and Ayşe Kavak, eds., *Halife II: Abdülhamid'in Hac Siyaseti: Dr. M. Şakir Bey'in Hatıraları* (İstanbul: Timaş, 2009), 70–71, 333.

17. Gülsoy, *Hicaz Demiryolu*, 34.

18. Gülsoy, *Hicaz Demiryolu*, 34.

19. BOA, Y.MTV, 59/38 (18 B 1309/17 January 1892).

20. Tahsin Pasha, *Sultan Abdülhamid: Tahsin Paşa'nın Yıldız Hatıraları* (İstanbul: Boğaziçi Yayınları, 1999), 348

21. Gülsoy, *Hicaz Demiryolu*, 31–55; and Özyüksel, *The Hejaz Railway and the Ottoman Empire*, 63–68.

22. On the strategic logic of interior rail links to the Hijaz, see Süleyman Şefik Söylemezoğlu's 1892 report, *Hicaz Seyahatnamesi*, 199–200; İzzet Pasha's 1892 memo in BOA, Y.MTV, 59/64 (B 26 1309/25 February 1982); and Ahmed Muhtar Pasha's 1897 report on the subject, BOA, Y. EE, 118/10 (3 C1315/30 October 1897).

23. Mostafa Minawi, *The Ottoman Scramble for Africa: Empire and Diplomacy in the Sahara and the Hijaz* (Stanford, CA: Stanford University Press, 2016), 124.

24. Gülsoy, *Hicaz Demiryolu*, 36–37.

25. Minawi, *The Ottoman Scramble for Africa*, 129–31.

26. Özyüksel, *The Hejaz Railway and the Ottoman Empire*, 52–53.

27. Minawi, *The Ottoman Scramble for Africa*, 130–31.

28. Minawi, *The Ottoman Scramble for Africa*, 130–31.

29. Ochsenwald, *The Hijaz Railroad*, 23.

30. Minawi, *The Ottoman Scramble for Africa*, 132–33.

31. Mostafa Minawi, "Beyond Rhetoric: Reassessing Bedouin-Ottoman Relations Along the Route of the Hijaz Telegraph Line at the End of the Nineteenth Century," *Journal of the Economic and Social History of the Orient* 58, nos. 1–2 (2015): 87–90.

32. Gülsoy, *Hicaz Demiryolu*, 34.

33. Minawi, *The Ottoman Scramble for Africa*, 120–21.

34. Minawi, *The Ottoman Scramble for Africa*, 120–21, 135–39.
35. BOA, DH.MKT, 2103/2 (21 R 1316/8 September 1898); BOA, DH.MKT, 2103/18 (21 R 1316/8 September 1898); BOA, DH.MKT, 2125 (13 C 1316/29 October 1898).
36. Minawi, *The Ottoman Scramble for Africa*, 124.
37. Minawi, *The Ottoman Scramble for Africa*, 133.
38. BOA, İ.PT, 13/39 (6 C 1319/20 September 1901).
39. BOA, BEO 1858/139298 (24 S 1320/2 June 1902); and BOA, İ.PT, 15/6 (10 S 1320/19 May 1902).
40. Minawi, *The Ottoman Scramble for Africa*, 133–34. See also Hynek Burda, Sabin Begall, Jaroslav Červený, Julia Neef, and Pavel Němec, "Extremely Low Frequency Electromagnetic Fields Disrupt Magnetic Alignment of Ruminants," *Proceedings of the National Academy of Sciences of the United States* 106, no. 14 (2009): 5708–13. For parallel complaints surrounding the impact of rail and telegraph infrastructures on camels in Egypt, see also On Barak, *On Time: Technology and Temporality in Modern Egypt* (Berkeley: University of California Press, 2013), 37–40.
41. BOA, DH.MKT, 2490/58 (9 S 1319/28 May 1901); BOA, DH.MKT, 463/23 (21 Z 1319/31 March 1902); BOA, İ.HUS, 93/18 (9 L 1319/19 January 1902); and BOA, İ.HUS, 93/34 (12 L 1319/22 January 1902).
42. Minawi, *The Ottoman Scramble for Africa*, 135; and Ochsenwald, *The Hijaz Railroad*, 23, 130.
43. Minawi, *The Ottoman Scramble for Africa*, 135–36.
44. Minawi, *The Ottoman Scramble for Africa*, 136–39.
45. On the *maḥmal* and the *sürre*, see Yusuf Sarınay, *Osmanlı Belgelerinde Surre Alayları* (Ankara: T. C. Başbakanlık Devlet Arşivleri Genel Müdürlüğü, 2010); Arthur E. Robinson, "The Mahmal of the Moslem Pilgrimage," *Journal of the Royal Asiatic Society of Great Britain and Ireland* 1 (1931), 117–27; and İbrahim Rifat Pasha, *Mir'atü'l Harameyn: Bir Generalin Hac Notları*, trans. Lütfullah Yavuz (İstanbul: Yitik Hazine Yayınları, 2010), 587–94.
46. Suraiya Faroqhi, *Pilgrims and Sultans: The Hajj Under the Ottomans, 1517-1683* (London: I. B. Tauris, 1994), 46.
47. David Edwin Long, *The Hajj Today: A Survey of the Contemporary Makkah Pilgrimage* (Albany: State University of New York Press, 1979), 127.
48. Özyüksel, *The Hejaz Railway and the Ottoman Empire*, 164.
49. İrtem, *Osmanlı Devleti'nin Mısır Yemen Hicaz Meselesi*, 175–77, 188. One challenge in recording the fluctuations in camel pricing is that multiple Ottoman and European currencies were in wide circulation in the Hijaz during this period. For a rough sense of the exchange rates in the Hijaz at that time, see Hafez Farmayan and Elton Daniel, eds., *A Shi'ite Pilgrimage to Mecca, 1885-1886: The Safarnâmeh of Mirzâ Moḥammad Ḥosayn Farâhâni* (Austin: University of Texas Press, 1990), 126–27.
50. BOA, İ.HUS, 32/9 (9 C 1312/7 December 1894).
51. Rifat Pasha, *Mir'atü'l Harameyn*, 111–13, 473, 516. Similar complaints about camel pricing, Bedouin violence, and the abuses of the pilgrimage guides can be found in İbrahim Rifat Pasha's contemporaneous notes, Khalili Family Trust: Hajj and the Arts of Pilgrimage Collection (hereafter referred to as KFT), ARC.MX 17

(undated); KFT, ARC.MX 19 (25 March 1904); KFT, ARC.MX 21; KFT, ARC.MX 23 (24 February 1904); KFT, ARC.MX 34 (May 1904); and KFT, ARC.MX 37.4 (1905).

52. Özyüksel, *The Hejaz Railway and the Ottoman Empire*, 57.

53. Özyüksel, *The Hejaz Railway and the Ottoman Empire*, 111–13. For complaints to the central government from the *deveciler*, see also BOA, BEO, 3826/286907 (18 Za 1328/21 November 1910); and BOA, DH.İD, 58/6 (21 Z 1328/24 December 1910).

54. İrtem, *Osmanlı Devleti'nin Mısır Yemen Hicaz Meselesi*, 188.

55. Özyüksel, *The Hejaz Railway and the Ottoman Empire*, 163. Here Özyüksel, citing Karl Auler Pasha, claims that Ahmed Ratib received a 5-lira kickback per camel, which would have totaled roughly 500,000 lira per year. Given the lower prices for camels from Jeddah to Mecca, I presume that the 5-lira tax would have had to come primarily from rentals between Mecca and Medina. I am somewhat skeptical of these claims. Given the total prices charged per pilgrim, especially on the Jeddah-Mecca route, I believe that the more likely denomination for the governor's share of the camel revenues should be 5 *mecidiye* coins (worth approximately 20 *kuruş* each, for a total of one lira) per camel. This alternative number still would have yielded 100,000 lira per year. For support for this 5-*mecidiye* tax, see Jacob Landau, *The Hejaz Railway and the Muslim Pilgrimage: A Case of Ottoman Political Propaganda* (Detroit, MI: Wayne State University Press, 1971), 164.

56. Ochsenwald, *The Hijaz Railroad*, 18–19; and Ochsenwald, *Religion, Society, and the State in Arabia: The Hijaz Under Ottoman Control, 1840-1908* (Columbus: Ohio State University Press, 1984), 31–32.

57. İrtem, *Osmanlı Devleti'nin Mısır Yemen Hicaz Meselesi*, 189.

58. BOA, Y.PRK.BŞK, 25/13 (12 B 1309/11 February 1892).

59. İrtem, *Osmanlı Devleti'nin Mısır Yemen Hicaz Meselesi*, 189–92.

60. BOA, Y.PRK.UM, 32/99 (10 Ra 1313/31 August 1895).

61. İrtem, *Osmanlı Devleti'nin Mısır Yemen Hicaz Meselesi*, 189.

62. BOA, Y.PRK.UM, 70/105 (15 C 1322/27 August 1904); and İrtem, *Osmanlı Devleti'nin Mısır Yemen Hicaz Meselesi*, 189–90.

63. Ochsenwald, *Religion, Society, and the State in Arabia*, 204–209.

64. Ochsenwald, *Religion, Society, and the State in Arabia*, 204–209.

65. Minawi, *The Ottoman Scramble for Africa*, 138–39.

66. Aykut Kansu, *The Revolution of 1908 in Turkey* (Leiden: Brill, 1997), 145–46; and Diane Brillari and Ezio Godoli, *Istanbul 1900: Art-Nouveau Architecture and Interiors* (Rome: Rizoli International, 1996), 194–95.

67. TNA: FO 195/2286 (23 and 25 August 1908); TNA: FO 194/2277 (2 September 1908); and Hasan Kayalı, *Arabs and Young Turks: Ottomanism, Arabism, and Islamism in the Ottoman Empire, 1908-1918* (Berkeley: University of California Press, 1997), 146.

68. BOA, DH.MKT, 2618/62 (1 N 1326/27 September 1908).

69. BOA, ZB, 414/65 (27 Mayıs [May] 1325/27 May 1909).

70. BOA, Y.PRK.UM, 81/48 (21 L 1325/27 November 1907); Gülsoy, *Hicaz Demiryolu*, 214–17; and Özyüksel, *The Hejaz Railway and the Ottoman Empire*, 163–64.

71. Ochsenwald, *The Hijaz Railroad*, 130–31.

72. TNA: FO 195/2286 (15 March) 1908.

6. THE CAMEL AND THE RAIL

73. BOA, DH.MKT, 2618/62 (3 N 1326/29 September 1908).
74. BOA, DH.MKT, 2906/3 (3 Ş 1327/20 August 1909).
75. See also Minawi, *The Ottoman Scramble for Africa*, 137–38.
76. BOA, DH.MUİ, 43/9 (2 Za 1327/15 November 1909); and BOA, DH.MKT, 2901/84 (28 B 1327/15 August 1909).
77. Mustafa Selçuk, "Üsküdar'dan Darülfünun'a: Kız Öğrencilerin Eğitimi," *Tarih Dergisi* 48, no. 2 (2008): 68.
78. İbnülemin Mahmud Kemal İnal, *Osmanlı Devrinde Son Sadrazamlar* (İstanbul: Türkiye İş Bankası Kültür Yayınları, 2012), vols. 1–5, 85; vols. 6–10, 1518–19.
79. This cleverly alliterative play on words is an allusion to the notorious al-Ḥajjāj ibn Yūsuf (661–714). Al-Ḥajjāj was an Umayyad governor of Iraq, infamous for his bloodthirsty, tyrannical suppression of ʿAlid and Kharijite uprisings and rebellions against the Umayyad caliphate during the second *fitna* (680–92). Caliph ʿAbd al-Malik ibn Marwān entrusted him to dislodge ʿAbd Allāh ibn al-Zubayr's rebel forces from Mecca. Although successful in putting down the Zubayrid insurrection, al-Ḥajjāj besieged and bombarded Mecca in the midst of the hajj, destroying the Kaʿba in the process. As a result, al-Ḥajjāj is often remembered as *Haccac-ı Zalim* or Ḥajjāj the Oppressor. Cenap Çakmak, *Islam: A Worldwide Encyclopedia*, vol. 2 (Santa Barbara: ABC-CLIO, 2017), 553–55; Peters, *The Hajj*, 65–69.
80. Ochsenwald, *The Hijaz Railroad*, 23.
81. Özyüksel, *The Hejaz Railway and the Ottoman Empire*, 96–98; and Ochsenwald, *The Hijaz Railroad*, 25–32.
82. Özyüksel, *The Hejaz Railway and the Ottoman Empire*, 153–54. For subsequent discussions of purchasing armored cars and machine guns for protection against the Bedouin, see also BOA, DH.İD, 1/1 (28 N 1328/3 October 1910).
83. Ochsenwald, *The Hijaz Railroad*, 35–37.
84. KFT, ARC.PC 433.
85. Ochsenwald, *The Hijaz Railroad*, 43.
86. Özyüksel, *The Hejaz Railway and the Ottoman Empire*, 131.
87. BOA, Y.PRK.KOM, 15/5 (10 S 1324/5 April 1906).
88. BOA, Y.MTV, 262/46 (5 Ca 1322/18 July 1904); BOA, Y.MTV, 280/6 (3 N 1323/1 November 1905); and Özyüksel, *The Hejaz Railway and the Ottoman Empire*, 130–32.
89. Ochsenwald, *The Hijaz Railroad*, 44–45.
90. BOA, Y.PRK.BŞK, 62/60 (21 Ra 1318/19 July 1900).
91. Gülsoy, *Hicaz Demiryolu*, 134.
92. Ömer Faruk Yılmaz, *Belgelerle Osmanlı Devrinde Hicaz* (İstanbul: Çamlıca, 2008), vol. 2, 249–50.
93. Ochsenwald, *The Hijaz Railroad*, 129.
94. Özyüksel, *The Hejaz Railway and the Ottoman Empire*, 129–30.
95. Ochsenwald, *The Hijaz Railroad*, 128.
96. BOA, Y.MTV, 306/34 (8 M 1326/11 February 1908); TNA: FO 371/539 (3 February 1908); TNA: FO 195/2320 (27 March 1909); and Ochsenwald, *The Hijaz Railroad*, 124.
97. BOA, DH.MKT, 1226/70 (18 Z 1325/22 January 1908); and Özyüksel, *The Hejaz Railway and the Ottoman Empire*, 154.
98. Özyüksel, *The Hejaz Railway and the Ottoman Empire*, 154–55.

99. TNA: FO 195/2286 (18 November 1908).

100. Ochsenwald, *The Hijaz Railroad*, 125.

101. Arthur John Byng Wavell, *A Modern Pilgrim in Mecca and a Siege in Sanaa* (London: Constable & Co, 1912), 60–61.

102. Landau, *The Hejaz Railway*, 168–70.

103. Gülsoy, *Hicaz Demiryolu*, 141; Özyüksel, *The Hejaz Railway and the Ottoman Empire*, 159–60.

104. Hasan Kayalı, *Arabs and Young Turks*, 159–61.

105. King Abdullah, *Memoirs of King Abdullah of Transjordan* (London: Jonathan Cape, 1950), 89.

106. Özyüksel, *The Hejaz Railway and the Ottoman Empire*, 166–67; and Gülsoy, *Hicaz Demiryolu*, 212–23.

107. King Abdullah, *Memoirs of King Abdullah of Transjordan*, 109; and Ochsenwald, *The Hijaz Railroad*, 131.

108. King Abdullah, *Memoirs of King Abdullah of Transjordan*, 120–21; and Özyüksel, *The Hejaz Railway and the Ottoman Empire*, 170–73.

109. BOA, İ.DUİT, 1/28 (3 M 1333/22 November 1914).

110. On Ottoman decision making in the lead-up to World War I and the declaration of jihad, see Mustafa Aksakal, *The Ottoman Road to War in 1914: The Ottoman Empire and the First World War* (Cambridge: Cambridge University Press, 2008); Aksakal, "Holy War Made in Germany? Ottoman Origins of the 1914 Jihad," *War in History* 18, no. 2 (2011): 184–99; and Erik-Jan Zürcher, *Jihad and Islam in World War I: Studies on the Ottoman Jihad on the Centenary of Snouck Hurgronje's "Holy War Made in Germany"* (Leiden: Leiden University Press, 2016).

111. Cemil Aydın, *The Idea of the Muslim World: A Global Intellectual History* (Cambridge, MA: Harvard University Press, 2017), 99–141.

112. John Slight, *The British Empire and the Hajj, 1865-1956* (Cambridge, MA: Harvard University Press, 2015), 169–70.

113. Slight, *The British Empire and the Hajj*, 170–74.

114. TNA: FO 141/710 (27 May 1915).

115. Faiz Ahmed, *Afghanistan Rising: Islamic Law and Statecraft Between the Ottoman and British Empires* (Cambridge, MA: Harvard University Press, 2017), 135.

116. Timothy J. Paris, *Britain, the Hashemites and Arab Rule: The Sherifian Solution* (London: Routledge, 2003), 29, 321.

117. On Fahreddin Pasha's defense of Medina, see Naci Kaşif Kıcıman, *Medine Müdafaası Hicaz Bizden Nasıl Ayrıldı?* (İstanbul: Sebil Yayınları, 1971); Feridun Kandemir, *Fahreddin Paşa'nın Medine Müdafaası: Peygamberimizin Gölgesinde Son Türkler* (İstanbul: Yağmur Yayınevi, 2012); and Alia El Bakri, " 'Memories of the Beloved': Oral Histories from the 1916–1919 Siege of Medina," *International Journal of Middle East Studies* 46, no. 4 (2014): 703–17.

118. Eugene Rogan, *The Fall of the Ottomans: The Great War in the Middle East* (New York: Basic Books, 2015), 297–98, 301–309.

119. Ochsenwald, *The Hijaz Railroad*, 144–47.

120. Ahmed, *Afghanistan Rising*, 354; and Kandemir, *Fahreddin Paşa'nın Medine Müdafaası*, 17, 469–70.

Epilogue: Legacies and Afterlives

1. TNA: FO 141/786/5 (9 July 1918).
2. John Buchan, *Greenmantle* (London: Hodder & Stoughton, 1916).
3. M. Emin Elmacı, "Osmanlı Hukuk Reformunda Bir Öncü: Kont Leon Ostrorog," *Osmanlı Tarihi Araştırma ve Uygulama Merkezi Dergisi* 29 (2011): 1–30.
4. TNA: FO 141/786/5 (9 July 1918).
5. TNA: FO 141/786/5 (9 July 1918).
6. On the Khilafat movement, see Gail Minault, *The Khilafat Movement: Religious Symbolism and Political Mobilization in India* (New York: Columbia University Press, 1982); M. Naeem Qureshi, *Pan-Islam in British India: The Politics of the Khilafat Movement, 1918–1924* (Oxford: Oxford University Press, 2009); and Faiz Ahmed, *Afghanistan Rising: Islamic Law and Statecraft Between the Ottoman and British Empires* (Cambridge, MA: Harvard University Press, 2017), 186, 190–206.
7. Cemil Aydın, *The Idea of the Muslim World: A Global Intellectual History* (Cambridge, MA: Harvard University Press, 2017), 125–26.
8. Lâle Can and Michael Christopher Low, "The 'Subjects' of Ottoman International Law," *Journal of the Ottoman and Turkish Studies Association* 3, no. 2 (2016): 227–28.
9. Aydın, *The Idea of the Muslim World*, 126–27.
10. Aydın, *The Idea of the Muslim World*, 124–30.
11. On the Turkish and wider global debates surrounding the abolition of the caliphate, see Mona Hassan, *Longing for the Lost Caliphate: A Transregional History* (Princeton, NJ: Princeton University Press, 2016), 142–217; and M. Şükrü Hanioğlu, *Atatürk: An Intellectual Biography* (Princeton: Princeton University Press, 2011), 135–52.
12. Cemil Aydın, *The Politics of Anti-Westernism in Asia: Visions of World Order in Pan-Islamic and Pan-Asian Thought* (New York: Columbia University Press, 2007), 137–39.
13. Joshua Teitelbaum, "Sharif Husayn ibn Ali and the Hashemite Vision of the Post-Ottoman Order: From Chieftaincy to Suzerainty," *Middle Eastern Studies* 34, no. 1 (1998): 103–22.
14. Timothy J. Paris, *Britain, the Hashemites and Arab Rule: The Sherifian Solution* (London: Routledge, 2003), 348–57.
15. Sugata Bose, *A Hundred Horizons: The Indian Ocean in the Age of Global Empire* (Cambridge, MA: Harvard University Press, 2006), 64; and Minault, *The Khilafat Movement*, 65–110.
16. Aydın, *The Idea of the Muslim World*, 121–22.
17. Aydın, *The Idea of the Muslim World*, 137–38.
18. Bose, *A Hundred Horizons*, 211–28; and John M. Willis, "Governing the Living and the Dead: Mecca and the Emergence of the Saudi Biopolitical State," *American Historical Review* 122, no. 2 (2017): 346–70.
19. TNA: FO 371/102813 (6 July 1925).
20. Susan Pedersen, *The Guardians: The League of Nations and the Crisis of Empire* (Oxford: Oxford University Press, 2015), 25.

21. TNA: FO 686/86 (26 April 1921).
22. BOA, DH.EUM.4.Şb, 4/19 (28 M 1334/6 December 1915); BOA, DH.EUM.5.Şb, 24/32 (18 B 1334/21 May 1916); BOA, HR.SYS, 2187/4 (6 December 1915); BOA, HR.SYS, 2187/5 (7 February 1916); BOA, HR.SYS, 2187/6 (1 October 1917); and BOA, HR.SYS, 2411/27 (17 July 1915).
23. Gülden Sarıyıldız and Oya Dağlar Macar, "Cholera, Pilgrimage, and International Politics of Sanitation: The Quarantine Station on the Island of Kamaran," in *Plague and Contagion in the Islamic Mediterranean*, ed. Nükhet Varlık (Kalamazoo, MI: Arc Humanities Press, 2017), 270–71.
24. John Baldry, "The Ottoman Quarantine Station on Kamaran Island, 1882–1914," *Studies in the History of Medicine* 2 (1978): 111–12.
25. Bose, *A Hundred Horizons*, 209; and F. E. Peters, *The Hajj: The Muslim Pilgrimage to Mecca and the Holy Places* (Princeton, NJ: Princeton University Press, 1994), 326–29.
26. Baldry, "The Ottoman Quarantine Station on Kamaran Island," 113.
27. Paris, *Britain, the Hashemites and Arab Rule*, 299–300, 311, 355–57.
28. Paris, *Britain, the Hashemites and Arab Rule*, 300–301.
29. Paris, *Britain, the Hashemites and Arab Rule*, 300–301.
30. Baldry, "The Ottoman Quarantine Station on Kamaran Island," 113. See also TNA: CO 725/92/1, "The Future of Kamaran Island" (1947). This file traces the legal status of Kamaran Island back to the 1923 Lausanne Treaty and includes the 1926 Anglo-Dutch agreement on the island's administration after World War I.
31. Baldry, "The Ottoman Quarantine Station on Kamaran Island," 114–15.
32. David Edwin Long, *The Hajj Today: A Survey of the Contemporary Makkah Pilgrimage* (Albany: State University of New York Press, 1979), 74–75.
33. John Slight, *The British Empire and the Hajj, 1865-1956* (Cambridge, MA: Harvard University Press, 2015), 214.
34. Norman Howard-Jones, *The Scientific Background of the International Sanitary Conferences, 1851-1938* (Geneva: World Health Organization, 1975), 93–100; and Valeska Huber, "International Bodies: The Pilgrimage to Mecca and International Health Regulations," in *The Hajj: Pilgrimage in Islam*, ed. Eric Tagliacozzo and Shawkat M. Toorawa (Cambridge: Cambridge University Press, 2016), 184–90.
35. Baldry, "The Ottoman Quarantine Station on Kamaran Island," 115–16.
36. Long, *The Hajj Today*, 75–77.
37. Baldry, "The Ottoman Quarantine Station on Kamaran Island," 116–18.
38. Long, *The Hajj Today*, 78.
39. Daniel Yergin, *The Prize: The Epic Quest for Oil, Money & Power* (New York: Free Press, 2009), 266–75, 283–85, 385–87; and Robert Vitalis, *America's Kingdom: Mythmaking on the Saudi Oil Frontier* (New York: Verso, 2009).
40. Slight, *The British Empire and the Hajj*, 305–306.
41. Vitalis, *America's Kingdom*, 131.
42. Slight, *The British Empire and the Hajj*, 313.
43. Long, *The Hajj Today*, 27–38.
44. Yergin, *The Prize*, 461–80.

45. Slight, *The British Empire and the Hajj*, 314–15.
46. Toby Craig Jones, *Desert Kingdom: How Oil and Water Forged Modern Saudi Arabia* (Cambridge, MA: Harvard University Press, 2010), 7–8, 15–16, 250–51.
47. Jones, *Desert Kingdom*, 13–15.
48. Michael Christopher Low, "Global Public Health and the Ghosts of Pilgrimages Past," *Jadaliyya*, 22 October 2012, http://www.jadaliyya.com/Details/27263 /Global-Public-Health-and-the-Ghosts-of-Pilgrimages-Past.
49. Robert Bianchi, *Guests of God: Pilgrimage and Politics in the Islamic World* (Oxford: Oxford University Press, 2004), 11, 22, 52, 117.
50. Abdellah Hammoudi, *A Season in Mecca: Narrative of a Pilgrimage*, trans. Pascale Ghazaleh (New York: Hill and Wang, 2005), 20–27.
51. Willis, "Governing the Living and the Dead," 346–50.
52. Jones, *Desert Kingdom*, 218–21; Yaroslav Trofimov, *The Siege of Mecca: The 1979 Uprising at Islam's Holiest Shrine* (New York: Random House, 2007).
53. Aydın, *The Idea of the Muslim World*, 177–78.
54. Bianchi, *Guests of God*, 52, 61; Martin Kramer, *Arab Awakening and Islamic Revival: The Politics of Ideas in the Middle East* (New Brunswick, NJ: Transaction, 1996), 161–87.
55. Toby Matthiesen, *The Other Saudis: Shiism, Dissent and Sectarianism* (Cambridge: Cambridge University Press, 2015), 126–29.
56. Willis, "Governing the Living and the Dead," 369–70; Rosie Bsheer, "A Counter-Revolutionary State: Popular Movements and the Making of Saudi Arabia," *Past and Present* 238, no. 1 (2018): 233–77.
57. Aydın, *The Idea of the Muslim World*, 178.

Index

Page numbers in *italics* refer to figures.